Historical Perspectives
on Business Enterprise Series

❖ ❖ ❖

American Public Finance and Financial Services 1700–1815

❖ ❖ ❖

Edwin J. Perkins

Ohio State University Press

Columbus

336.73
P44a

Library of Congress Cataloging-in-Publication Data
Perkins, Edwin J.
    American public finance and financial services, 1700–1815 / Edwin J.
Perkins.
        p.   cm. — (Historical perspectives on business enterprise series)
    Includes bibliographical references.
    ISBN 0–8142–0619–0 (cloth). — ISBN 0–8142–0620–4 (pbk.)
    1. Finance, Public—United States—History—18th century.   2. Financial
services industry—United States—History—18th century.   I. Title.
II. Series.
    HJ241.P47   1994
    336.73′09′033—dc20   93-28736
                                                                                          CIP

Text and jacket design by Bruce Gore, Gore Studio.
Type set in Baskerville by Tseng Information Systems, Durham, NC.
Printed by Thomson-Shore, Inc., Dexter, MI.

9 8 7 6 5 4 3 2 1

For
my mentors
at Johns Hopkins
Alfred D. Chandler, Jr.
and
Louis Galambos

Contents

Tables

ix

Preface

At my doctoral dissertation defense two decades ago, Paul Uselding, then an assistant professor in the economics department at Johns Hopkins, asked a perplexing question. I had just completed a thesis on the House of Brown, a firm that emerged as a leader in the foreign exchange and letter of credit markets in the United States over the course of the nineteenth century. The thrust of his inquiry, as I vividly recall, ran as follows: how important was the development of the American financial system in the economic growth of the new nation? Was its early development an absolute prerequisite; was it something important but not essential; or was it merely coincidental to growth in other sectors? Unprepared for such a sweeping question in pressure-packed surroundings, I struggled for a sensible response. I'm fairly sure that I fudged and took a position somewhere between the two extremes—critical for success and merely coincidental. Of course, I had only the vaguest idea about how to respond appropriately because my knowledge of the history of American finance still had many huge gaps. To cite one obvious shortcoming, I knew next to nothing about events before 1790. Over the past two decades, my store of knowledge on that earlier period has increased markedly.

Now, Paul, it's time to reconvene the examination committee, a trio which included Al Chandler for certain and Lou Galambos as a distinct possibility. Given the additional time to ponder the question, I have moved much closer to a more definitive answer. Be prepared for a long meeting, however—days and perhaps even weeks—because what I have to report encompasses several hundred pages, single-spaced, with accompanying endnotes, tables, appendix, and bibliography. The short answer is that the institutional infrastructure associated with the financial sector was largely in place and functioning exceptionally well by 1815; financial services moved forward in advance of the new technologies applied to manufacturing and transportation. The financial system that developed during the

xi

nation's first quarter century was instrumental in the success of the U.S. economy in the decades that followed, and its roots can be traced back to the first three quarters of the eighteenth century.

Long books require short prefaces, and with that axiom in mind, I will try to keep it short and sweet. The acknowledgments are arranged for the most part in chronological order. My initial interest in banking and finance was sparked during my student days in the M.B.A. program at the University of Virginia in the early 1960s. I worked for several years for the Chase Manhattan Bank in New York and Seaboard Citizens Bank in Norfolk, Virginia. Later, I taught introductory courses in accounting, finance, and statistics at Virginia Polytechnic Institute in Blacksburg, Virginia. Relying on the sound advice of my colleague Gus Williamson, I left to pursue a doctoral degree in economic and business history. Al Chandler and Lou Galambos were my mentors at Johns Hopkins, and they encouraged me to pursue my interest in financial history. Chandler always expressed much admiration for the work of financial historian Fritz Redlich, his friend and former colleague at Harvard.

After I had left Johns Hopkins and taken a position at the University of Southern California, my interest in colonial financial history was stimulated when I was asked in the mid-1970s to review Joe Ernst's book on money and politics during the two decades before independence. I wrote a book on the colonial economy soon thereafter. Once I had started on this current project in the late 1980s, several scholars with similar interests offered encouragement. Ron Michener and Bruce Smith, two economic historians with conflicting views about colonial fiat currency, shared their thoughts, and both read drafts of chapters. At one point or another, Naomi Lamoreaux reviewed all my chapters and offered many helpful comments. Members of the economic seminar at UCLA discussed some of my work, particularly Mary Yeager, Ken Sokoloff, and Jean-Laurent Rosenthal. I got useful feedback from students as well—especially Robert Jackman, an undergraduate at USC who enrolled at Kentucky in 1990 to work with Lance Banning, and from Hans Eicholz, a graduate student working with Joyce Appleby at UCLA. Others who contributed in one way or another to this project include Don Swanson, Elmus Wicker, Geoff Jones, Jacob Price, Mira Wilkins, Peter Temin, Lawrence Officer, Eugene White, Dennis Flynn, Gary Walton, Charles Myers, Joyce Appleby, John Brewer, Robert Becker, Bruce Stark, Larry Schweikart, and Mary Schweitzer. I wrote Don Swanson in September

1992 asking him to review the entire manuscript before it went to press, but I received a return note from his dean informing me sadly about Don's recent death.

I conducted most of the research for this book at my desk in the Henry Huntington Library in San Marino, luckily just a few blocks away from my home. Known primarily for its rare literary manuscripts, the library's holdings are surprisingly strong in economic history, including banking and finance. A good many of its turn-of-the-century volumes were gifts from the personal library of Frederick Jackson Turner, who signed them all, listed the purchase price, and wrote frequently in the margins—often in bright red pencil. The Huntington staff was exceedingly helpful, and it graciously allowed me to maintain a permanent desk in the stacks next to the bookcases filled with the volumes that I regularly needed. During my visits to that marvelous library, I learned much about history, and current events as well, from informal lunchtime conversations and during leisurely walks around the beautiful grounds with resident and visiting scholars. I want to mention especially John Reid, Gordon Bakken, Paul Zall, Tom Purvis, Bill Deverell, Michael Engh, Margaret Newell, Lige Gould, Wilbur Jacobs, Jim McPherson, and the library's director of research, Martin Ridge.

At USC I received steady encouragement from colleagues Jack Wills and Steve Ross, and from my best friend and regular tennis partner for more than a decade, Lloyd Moote. I also want to thank the university administration for a generous sabbatical leave in the late 1980s that enabled me to dive quickly and deeply into the research for this book.

The staff associated with Ohio State University Press and members of the OSU history department were uniformly helpful and supportive. Editor Alex Holzman solicited the manuscript and carried it through to acceptance. The corps of business historians at Ohio State—Mansel Blackford, Austin Kerr, and Bill Childs—are owed a tremendous debt of gratitude by all active members of our profession for creating and sustaining this thriving series and for developing an outstanding program at both the undergraduate and graduate levels in economic and business history.

I also want to thank Judy Gladstone for all her love and support and to acknowledge her contributions to this book.

Introduction

THIS BOOK focuses on the evolution of financial services from the colonial period through the early national era, emphasizing their importance in laying the foundation for the future development of the American economic and political systems. During the seventeenth and eighteenth centuries, the British colonies in North America made substantial progress in shaping a financial environment that generally provided a fair degree of stability and, secondly, fostered steady economic advancement. Partially as a result of improved financial services, the rate of economic growth in the British colonies, on both an aggregate and per capita basis, was among the highest in the world from 1650 to 1775.

After the achievement of political independence, the expansion of financial services continued unabated. Experimentation was evident in virtually every financial market, and improvements became more pronounced as the decades passed. A diverse and responsive financial sector was one of the great strengths of the American economy in the preindustrial era—and thereafter as well. By 1815 the most institutionally advanced sector of the U.S. economy was the broad-based financial infrastructure. A quarter century after the formation of the new federal government, incorporated commercial banks and insurance companies were numerous and typically well managed; in combination, they attracted millions of dollars in private investment in their common stock. By comparison, most contemporary transportation and manufacturing firms were relatively small enterprises, with the majority in manufacturing still operating as partnerships or proprietorships.

1

From the mid-eighteenth century forward, a more sophisticated capital market was in the process of emerging, and was progressing at accelerating rates. By the early nineteenth century, the market accommodated the placement and subsequent trading of the common stock of many financial services firms and, equally importantly, the long-term bonds of the federal government. Meanwhile, the monetary system, based on the circulation of specie coins and bank notes continuously convertible into specie, was generally sound and secure—the only exception being the temporary suspension of conversion privileges caused by the economic dislocations surrounding the War of 1812. The solid base established in the financial sector laid the groundwork for growth and development in other complementary sectors of the economy after 1815.

This study concentrates largely on the institutional development of the American financial services sector from the last decade of the seventeenth century through the first fifteen years of the nineteenth century. New technologies made no significant impact during that time; the innovations were exclusively institutional arrangements. Most of the services discussed here originated in European financial markets and migrated to Great Britain; thereafter, they crossed the ocean to the North American colonies. The study identifies the continuities that persisted throughout the colonial, confederation, and early national eras, and, when appropriate, it highlights a series of innovative departures from financial traditions.

One of the book's main claims to originality rests on its broad chronological sweep. Most previous examinations of American financial history have concentrated strictly on the colonial period or, alternatively, started with Alexander Hamilton's bold initiatives in the early 1790s and moved forward in time. E. James Ferguson's *Power of the Purse* remains one of the few accounts of financial activities during the intervening confederation years. Within the fields of political, social, and intellectual history, overlapping studies of the colonial and early national periods have become more common in scholarly circles during the last quarter century, and this book adds more fuel to that historiographical trend.

To convey the scope, I chose the term "financial services sector" to describe the breadth of the analysis. That descriptive phrase entered the language of business journalists in the late twentieth century and was completely unfamiliar to contemporaries two hundred years ago. Nonetheless, I was attracted by its comprehensive character; financial services sector is an umbrella term designed to unite under its shadow a host of related but varying functions. In this book, that umbrella encompasses all of the following: the money stock, governmental loan facilities (land banks), commercial banking, and capital markets plus, in a secondary role, the occupations of investment banker, stock and bond broker, foreign exchange, dealer, lottery organizer, and insurance underwriter.

Three overriding themes dominate these pages: continuity, innovation, and maturation. Governments in North America consistently sought to establish financial systems responsive to the needs of the population. Most legislatures enacted laws designed to permit the wide-scale participation by diverse groups of citizens—both as the providers and the consumers of financial services. That legacy eventually became a pillar of the Jeffersonian-Jacksonian political tradition.

When economic and political conditions changed, American society possessed the flexibility to alter institutional arrangements within the financial sector. Almost immediately after independence, the general movement was from public to private control of money and banking. In the colonial era, provincial legislatures were directly involved in the provision of financial services; but in the 1790s state governments retreated, in part because of constitutional restrictions. Private enterprises were granted greater leeway, and entrepreneurs took advantage of the opportunities to create new institutions.

The revolution in financial services moved ahead at a faster pace than corresponding revolutions in transport, energy, and manufacturing. Even before independence, colonial legislatures were innovators in the use of fiat currency—a form of government-issue paper money unconvertible into coin at fixed exchange rates. A healthy share of those monies entered the economy through government-owned mortgage loan offices, which made long-term loans in moderate amounts (the maximum sum was restricted by law) to private citizens secured by real estate. Most borrowers used the funds to increase productive assets, including more land, new barns, fences, tools, livestock, and the contracts of bonded workers —both indentured servants and slaves.

The use of fiat currency was a departure from monetary traditions in the mother country. Fiat paper had an unsavory reputation in Europe and was not a component of the money stock in Great Britain. Its issuance in the colonies was regularly challenged by imperial officials, who nevertheless reluctantly approved most emissions after warning of the dangers of depreciation and the potential for financial catastrophe. In several colonies, primarily in New England, fiat monies did in fact lose most of their purchasing power; they were steadily withdrawn from circulation under parliamentary directive after 1751. But in the middle colonies and every southern colony except North and South Carolina, fiat currency never succumbed to spiraling depreciation. Instead, it continued to play a positive role in facilitating everyday trade and served as a fairly reliable store of liquid wealth.

Fiat currency also provided the mechanism to finance approximately two-thirds of the cost of the War for Independence. The solid reputation fiat currency had established during the third quarter of the century allowed it to provide sufficient purchasing power to carry the American military forces through the first five years of the war—a notable achievement critical to the final victory. Although fiat currency, both the congressional and state varieties, depreciated irreversibly from 1778 to 1780 and finally fell to less than 1 percent of face value in relation to hard monies, in the postwar decade seven state legislatures voted for its reissuance. Only the constitutional prohibition on direct state emissions of currency after 1789 eliminated it as a component of the money stock.

Other innovative features of the colonial economy were the birth of a market for short-term government debt and expanded marine and fire insurance. After the parliamentary ban on their fiat currency issues, the New England colonies financed periodic budget deficits through the direct sale of treasury bills, with maturities ranging from one to five years, to private investors. Prior to 1750 investors seeking a safe harbor for their capital had little choice but to invest their savings in real estate, make well-secured mortgage loans to neighbors, or hoard specie—a sterile, unremunerative asset. Treasury bills, which typically paid interest at the legal limit, were a new investment vehicle. They provided the seed bed for the broader capital market that emerged in the last decade of the century.

The insurance market also witnessed substantial development during the eighteenth century. Initially, American shippers arranged marine coverage through their London agents. Syndicates of underwriters operating from waterfront coffeehouses, of which Lloyd's was the most famous, accepted the risks associated with overseas trade. Beginning in the second quarter of the eighteenth century, independent American underwriters began to cover the risks on shipments to the Caribbean and southern Europe, plus intercoastal routes. A decade or so later, Benjamin Franklin spearheaded the movement to establish the first successful American fire insurance company in Philadelphia. That firm was organized as a nonprofit, mutual enterprise—another American first.

As a result of advances and refinements dating back centuries, but more pronounced after 1650, the fundamental techniques of insuring ships and buildings, plus their contents, against various hazards were generally well understood by the last quarter of the eighteenth century. In the colonies the indigenous institutional framework was woefully deficient, although a few American underwriters entered the market beginning in the 1720s. This arrested financial sector was transformed after independence; the U.S. insurance market literally exploded. Numerous state-chartered companies, with millions of dollars in equity capital, began operations between 1790 and 1815, and with the blessings of political leaders of every stripe. Generally speaking, those firms engaged in marine and fire insurance (but not life insurance) had already traveled far down the road to maturation on the eve of the War of 1812.

The adaptive and innovative character of the American financial system was likewise evident in the movement toward the privatization of currency issuance in the postwar era. Firms issuing monies convertible into coin at the holder's option were commonplace in Great Britain by the mid-eighteenth century, but similar enterprises had never been sustained in the colonies. In the 1780s state-chartered commercial banks with transferable shares opened their doors in three states—Pennsylvania, New York, and Massachusetts. The chartered banks endured some controversy during their first decade of operations, especially in Philadelphia, but all carried out faithfully their responsibility to provide a sound currency, and they operated profitably. Based partially on the success of that experiment, chartered financial institutions assumed total responsibility for providing the American public with paper monies in the 1790s. Although state legislatures were required to abstain from the issuance of fiat currency after ratification of the Constitution, they often joined private citizens in acquiring shares in the commercial banks operating within their borders. The federal government made the greatest public investment in commercial banking when it took 20 percent of the equity in the Bank of the United States. Mixed enterprises, partially private and partially public, were commonplace in the early national era.

Continuing their bias in favor of wide-scale citizen participation and access to financial services, a legacy from colonial times, Americans opted for a decentralized, atomistic system of commercial banks linked closely to their communities. Many of the initial objections to the creation of a well-capitalized, centrally administered, and federally chartered national bank dissipated in the first year after the board of directors voted to spread the benefits geographically throughout the nation by opening a chain of branch offices. The branches received capital allocations from the Philadelphia office; branch capital grew over time and eventually exceeded the amount retained at headquarters. Meanwhile, the branches functioned largely independently of central control. Each branch's local board of directors made loans strictly to local customers.

In the state systems, intrastate branch banking sprang up in some areas, but even the most ambitious institutions rarely operated more than three or four satellite offices. The most common organizational form was the single-unit banking enterprise. Federalists and Republicans alike agreed on this basic concept—namely, the importance of local control over commercial banking services. The scattered institutional pattern persisted in the United States well into the twentieth century. Interestingly, no other nation around the world chose to imitate the fragmentation of the U.S. banking system—another fact lending support to historians who argue the uniqueness of the American experience.

The American capital market that sprang forth in the 1790s was composed of government bonds and the equities of private banks and insurance companies. The bonds, which totaled approximately $70 million face value, were remnants of the leftover debts incurred in fighting the War for Independence. The long delay in repaying the principal ran counter to the policies implemented by most colonial legislatures following the largest previous military confrontation in North America—the Seven Years' War. In the 1760s the thirteen colonies had increased taxes, and aided by reimbursements from Parliament, the majority set out to retire the bulk of their outstanding debts within a decade or so. Most colonies actually accomplished their goals or at least made substantial progress in reducing their outstanding obligations.

In the 1780s most states hoped to duplicate the success of their efforts a generation earlier. Legislative factions that felt a heightened sense of urgency passed joint taxation and debt retirement acts designed to put a huge dent in their respective indebtedness by the end of the decade. Many states tentatively adopted optimistic plans to eliminate their entire public debt by the mid-1790s at the very latest. Generally ignoring the pleas of the Continental Congress for financial contributions to help service the federal debt, the several states decided instead to draw on local resources to make inroads on local obligations.

The urgency factions in state capitals justified programs of high taxes, huge budget surpluses, and systematic debt retirement on several grounds. They argued that accelerated principal repayment would save taxpayers money in the long run by reducing the aggregate revenues spent on interest. Other anticipated societal benefits included fewer opportunities for speculation in the public debt. By retiring the public debt promptly, citizens would also discourage the emergence of a permanent monied class—a group of allegedly unproductive parasites who owned a disproportionate share of the public debt and lived off the interest income, generation after generation. Those classes were prominent in allegedly corrupt European states but were unwelcome in the new United States. At the national level, Jeffersonian Republicans adopted most of the principles of the urgency factions in debates about how to service properly the nation's wartime debts.

Urgency factions took the lead in most states, but after the mid-1780s they backed off and gave way to the gradualist position—everywhere, that is, except in Massachusetts. The size of the public debt after the War for Independence was many times greater than what had accumulated during the Seven Years' War, and the taxes necessary to extinguish it were burdensome. Even raising enough revenues to maintain interest payments was difficult; retiring the principal with dispatch required too much sacrifice over too long a time. Some states, like Virginia, made progress for one or two years but then decided to maintain the status quo.

Gradualists, like Alexander Hamilton in New York, argued that the emphasis should be placed on generating only sufficient tax revenues to meet recurring interest obligations. The retirement of principal should proceed slowly, extending over a quarter century or more. Federalists rejected Jefferson's axiom that each generation should assume the entire financial burden for the military expenditures it had incurred. Correspondingly, Hamilton hoped a perpetual national debt would provide the core for an American capital market that might eventually rival London. The financial strain on citizens in the late 1780s allowed Hamiltonian strategies to come to the fore at both the federal and state levels in the 1790s.

Massachusetts was the exception in that context. The urgency faction adopted a plan to retire the state's public debt over a five-year period starting in 1785. When citizens protested the accelerating taxes and threatened revolt, the state government refused to budge. Shays' Rebellion was the result. The outcome was a consequence of political miscalculation and gross fiscal mismanagement, pure and simple. Given the unprecedented magnitude of the public debt, patience and good common sense were seriously lacking within the legislative leadership. The irony remains that if Massachusetts had waited until the congressional committee charged with settling wartime debts among the thirteen states had finished its work, which finally occurred in 1793, the legislature would have learned that its creditor position was sufficiently large to cover all the state's wartime obligations. In truth, heavy local taxation was not required—not in Massachusetts, a state that had done more than its share on a per capita basis to aid the cause. The intervening federal assumption of the states' outstanding debts was not a necessary condition for that result. Federal assumption represented a preemptive advance payment, so to speak; Massachusetts would have received overwhelming financial relief from the national government three to five years later in any event. The preceding nutshell analysis provides only a preview. How the complex events, with all the elements of a comic-tragic opera, transpired in Massachusetts during the 1780s consumes an entire chapter of this volume.

Once the state and federal debts were consolidated in the early 1790s, the American capital market blossomed. The prices of the new federal bonds rose as the confidence of investors in the government's ability to sustain interest payments strengthened. Shares in the Bank of the United States came on the market soon thereafter and were gobbled up by eager investors. State-chartered commercial banks and insurance companies floated stock issues as well; the new firms were generally profitable and paid regular dividends, which supported the value of their securities. Once Jefferson assumed the presidency and actually began to retire the federal debt in earnest, the reputation of American securities received an added boost.

What emerged in the first decade of the nineteenth century was essentially a Jeffersonian-Hamiltonian hybrid. The nation possessed a maturing capital market, fulfilling Hamilton's dream, but its core steadily shifted away from public bond issues, which drew on tax revenues, toward the securities of a multitude of private firms, most of which were concentrated in the financial services sector. They operated under charters issued by state governments that periodically expired and thus became subject to renegotiation, thereby making the enterprises accountable to the general public. No highly visible monied class—no easily identifiable group of rentiers living in perpetual luxury off the proceeds of government interest payments—arose in American society.

Meanwhile, the maturation of the financial services sector was a mutually supportive and reinforcing phenomenon. The successes of the U.S. Treasury's debt retirement program as well as the operations of a host of private financial enterprises—not generally manufacturing and transportation firms—invigorated the institutional structure of financial markets, broadly speaking, and lubricated the wheels of commerce. Financial firms and corresponding financial markets—in the latter case, for example, securities trading and foreign exchange transactions—progressed in parallel during the nation's first quarter century. Improved and expanded financial services became the first pillar in the underlying infrastructure of the American economy.

Although this volume was not written with the intention of testing the applicability of broader theories about the links between republican and capitalist ideology in the early national era, especially the hypotheses advanced by Joyce Appleby about the market orientation of Jeffersonian Republicans, the compatibility of many of those revisionist concepts and the conclusions of this study are undeniable. Regarding the shape and character of the emerging financial services sector, many leaders of the two major political factions shared similar values and attitudes. They agreed by and large on the following: the importance of establishing a sound monetary system—(convertible bank notes were not controversial after 1790); the importance of local control over local financial institutions; the importance of widespread access to financial services; and the importance of meeting the government's legitimate debt obligations, with only the timing of principal repayment a matter of debate.

After 1795, Republicans were as entrepreneurial as Federalists in seeking state charters for commercial banks and insurance companies. Once they realized that commercial banking would evolve as a decentralized system, most Jeffersonians modified their complaints about the dangers of privatization. Once they could see that the national debt was not destined to climb to new heights and attract thereby a swarm of speculators and stockjobbers, most Jeffersonians welcomed the emergence of a functioning capital market that financed new enterprises and provided liquidity for persons seeking to adjust their investment portfolios. Reservations about the constitutionality of the First Bank of the United States admittedly lingered, but the congressional refusal to renew the federal charter in 1811 should not be interpreted as anything more than a Republican repudiation of Hamilton's centralizing principles. The financial services sector that developed in the early national era was compatible with the ideological outlook of the vast majority of Americans. After the turn of the century, its development reflected the expressed goals of Jeffersonians and Hamiltonians alike.

Part I

The Colonial Era

1

The Coinage System

Pᴿɪᴍᴀʀɪʟʏ ᴛʜʀᴏᴜɢʜ its supervision of the coinage system for the British Empire, Parliament exercised control over the monetary systems of its North American colonies from their founding in the seventeenth century. Great Britain's policies in the western hemisphere were highly arbitrary, but consistent with policies in other parts of the empire. Parliament forbade the private export of English coin overseas,[1] yet it simultaneously refused to allow the permanent establishment of an overseas branch of the royal mint to meet the monetary needs of the local population.[2] As a result, the colonists were forced to resort to the use of foreign monies, in particular silver coins minted in Mexico and other parts of Spanish America.

By exercising control over the coinage, Parliament was operating in traditional governmental fashion. Regulating the composition of the money stock had been a function of strong governments around the globe for centuries. At least three major reasons for establishing a stable monetary system were evident: to create a uniform measure of value for the maintenance of accounts such as tax revenues and governmental expenses; to provide a convenient store of value (purchasing power) for governments and persons wishing to hold liquid wealth; and to provide a convenient medium of exchange for routine transactions in goods and services. An economy with a functioning monetary system was able to avoid many of the uncertainties and inconveniences associated with barter and payment-in-kind of all varieties.

For the purposes of storing liquid wealth and accommodating very large financial transactions, governments usually created a series of high-value coins that were never expected to circulate widely within the economy. For the purpose of facilitating routine daily transactions, on the other hand, governments authorized the minting of coins with intermediate and low values. The physical volume of the lesser coinage was typically very great, yet even when considered together, their total value still comprised only a small percentage of the overall monetary stock. (Comparable units in the modern era might include $1 to $20 bills in the intermediate range; and quarters, dimes, nickels, and pennies in the very low range.)

Money was normally defined in terms of metallic units. Governments authorized the manufacture of coins at officially sanctioned mints from several metals—ranging from gold, the scarcest and thus the most valuable by weight, to silver, the next most valuable, and, at the bottom of the scale, to lower valued coins minted from metals such as copper, tin, and lead. Even high-value coins were not pure gold or silver but alloyed with less valuable metals in order to harden their texture and increase their durability.

To determine the proper relationship among its coins, every government established a fixed ratio for the value of one metal vis-à-vis every other metal in its monetary system. It then authorized the establishment of a mint, or several mints, to produce coins that were recognized as the legal medium of exchange for monetary transactions within its territories. The value of a coin authorized for manufacture from a specified weight of a given metal was called the mint ratio. It represented the value of the coins that holders received in payment upon presenting a specified amount of the metal to the mint; the coinage rate became that metal's mint price in the domestic economy.

In addition to its mint price within a given country, every metal always had an alternative valuation—its value on the open market, first, for nonmonetary uses and, second, and more importantly, for export out of the country as bullion to competing coinage systems in other countries. The second valuation was the metal's *market* price—a figure that fluctuated over time and that was rarely precisely in unison with the fixed price paid at the mint. The existence of differentials in the mint price, or the official internal price, and the market price, or the export price, for precious metals is a factor that complicates greatly all discussions of monetary systems and frequently leads to much confusion in historical accounts. The confusion is compounded by the fact that, beyond its own borders, one government's mint price was merely one of many components influencing the market price for a specific precious metal on world markets. Mint prices were singular prices determined by government decree and operational only within its jurisdiction, whereas market prices overseas were the outcome of hundreds of competing economic forces and subject to wide fluctuation.

Although governments exercised the power to establish the mint ratios for their respective coinages, they were unable to control precisely the aggregate size of the money stock circulating within their economies. Monetary developments beyond their borders had a significant impact. The amount of money in circulation in a given economy reflected, in part, the volume of designated metals brought to the mint from all sources for conversion into coin. Normally, there were no upward limits placed on the size of the coinage since everyone assumed that increasing the monetary stock was generally a positive factor contributing to economic growth.

The sources of specie were varied. Some metal arriving at the mint had been recently mined, but in other instances it represented amounts extracted from coins—domestic and foreign—already in circulation either by clipping their edges or melting them down. (Clipping generally declined with the introduction of milled edges, which occurred in England in the 1660s.) In many coinage systems, little precious metal was mined in the home market, thus most specie entered the money stock from overseas. England is a prime example of such a country since it contained few easily accessible deposits of gold and silver.

The maintenance of an enduring monetary standard, with fixed values among coins, proved difficult for all governments. No single country was able to manage its coinage in isolation from the influences of immediate neighbors and all other countries with which its citizens regularly conducted commerce, including countries thousands of miles across the seas. Precious metals were easily stored and transported, and gold and silver gravitated over time out of those regions where their respective coinage values were relatively low and into areas where one or the other was valued more highly for monetary purposes. Because the international flow of metals was impossible to control in the long run, alterations in the mint prices in one country affected the supply of metals available for conversion into coin elsewhere, and thereby the size of money stocks in other territories. In other words, how one country managed its coinage system influenced the volume and price of metals available for inclusion in the monetary systems of others. The larger the size of a given monetary system, the greater its influence overseas. In short, governments participating in the development of organized monetary systems functioned and responded like participants in oligopolistic markets generally.

The volume of coins in all the world's monetary systems combined also varied considerably from century to century, both in terms of aggregate supplies and specific metals. The discovery of metallic ores was sporadic and unpredictable, but new sources were frequently located in various parts of the globe. As the centuries passed, the metal extracted from ores increased because of technological improvements leading to higher yields per ton. While new discoveries and higher yields acted to increase the supply of metal available for coinage, on the opposite side of the equation other factors were at work shrinking the available supply. The demand for metals for nonmonetary purposes, such as the use of silver in crafting tableware and art objects, was one factor—albeit a minor one—in decreasing supplies available for minting. The mundane forces of excessive wear and tear, plus the outright loss of bullion and coins on land or at sea, had a greater role in depleting supplies.

In establishing a coinage system, governments aimed at setting a somewhat higher price at the mint for a given metal than its prevailing market price. The pricing policy was necessary because whenever the market price of a given metal exceeded its value at the mint, not only was little forthcoming for conversion into coin but the existing coinage was steadily melted down by individuals and sold overseas as bullion if the differential was great enough. In establishing and maintaining a sound monetary system, government officials engaged in something of a balancing act. They tried to set a mint price high enough to guarantee the maintenance of the country's coinage but not a price so high that it gave local miners and bullion importers the opportunity to reap windfall gains.

Over time, however, difficulties invariably arose for coinage systems because of fluctuations in the market prices for silver and gold. When those fluctuations were great enough and persisted long enough, a country's coinage was threatened, and to meet that danger, its rulers had to consider readjustments in the structure of prices at the mint. Otherwise, they faced several undesired consequences. If the mint price for either gold or silver, or both, remained far *above* the market price, then constant inflows of specie created inflationary pressures. If, on the other hand, the mint price was far *below* the market price, continual outflows caused a serious depletion of the coinage. In some countries the depletion problem was so great that the coins of foreign nations became an important component of the domestic money stock. Foreign coins were sometimes even officially recognized as a legitimate and even *unrefusable* form of domestic payment. (An unrefusable form of money is defined as legal tender, meaning that it must be accepted by recipients in the payment for goods and services as well as in the settlement of debts.)

Rarely did any two countries establish identical schedules of mint prices for the two most valuable metals, gold and silver. Meanwhile, any country that maintained a mint price for either metal sufficiently below the prevailing market price, meaning low enough to cover the cost of overseas transport, experienced a steady loss of that metal—called a drain in monetary circles—to other coinage systems. As a rule, most nations ended up with mint prices that overvalued one of the two most precious metals and undervalued the other in relation to prevailing market prices.

The net result was that most European monetary systems in the early modern period had a tendency to become centered on either gold or silver. Bimetallism, or the continual minting and widespread circulation of both gold and silver coins, was functional only if a country was willing to make frequent adjustments in mint prices. The French were among the most devoted to the concept of bimetallism. By making a series of adjustments in the mint price of silver, the government was reasonably successful in keeping in circulation coins produced from both metals during the eighteenth century. Elsewhere, as a result of uncontrollable changes in relative market prices for gold and silver or because of deliberate readjustments in their mint ratios, countries shifted back and forth numerous times between gold and silver as the primary component of their monetary systems. England will emerge as a prime example in that category.

By the same token the general price level throughout Europe, and later the western hemisphere, was likewise governed by outside forces, which no single government could control. Price movements reflected changes in the size of the total money stock over time *relative* to changes in the overall output of goods and services. Price stability existed when the money stock and the size of the European economy moved forward, or backward, in unison. During some eras both moved ahead at a slow, steady pace, producing steady prices, whereas in others the money stock accelerated at a faster pace than the expansion of the European economy, resulting in constant inflation. Because gold and silver were easily transferred across borders and because no government was prepared to renounce those two metals as the base of its monetary system, every country with an active market economy was affected by general trends in the regional price level.

Even when a country's mint prices were well managed to promote long-term monetary stability, periodic fluctuations in the size of the domestic stock of money could still occur because of a temporary disequilibrium in the overall balance of trade. A persistent trade deficit, for example, could lead to an outflow of specie as importers attempted to settle their accounts with overseas creditors.

The normal mechanism for balancing a country's overseas debits and credits came about through the transfer of bills of exchange drawn in various currencies—not the transport of specie. Bills of exchange were financial instruments very similar to postdated checks. Merchants and their customers typically used bills of exchange to settle accounts associated with shipments taking weeks or even months to reach their destination. So long as the value of imports and exports was reasonably balanced over a period of years, the relative prices of bills of exchange drawn in the leading world currencies in the seventeenth and eighteenth centuries remained fairly stable.

If, however, a given country accumulated too many overseas debts and foreign creditors suddenly demanded repayment, then the prices of bills of exchange drawn in currencies of creditor nations typically rose. At some point, determined largely by the cost of transporting precious metals, debtors would refuse to purchase additional bills of exchange at the prevailing high prices. They began to shift instead to the shipment of gold or silver, either in bullion or in coin, which was always an alternative means of international payment. When large numbers of debtors substituted precious metals for bills of exchange in the settlement of international accounts, their country (or colony in the American context) experienced a steady drain of specie that depleted the domestic stock of money.

As a rule, however, an adjustment mechanism soon came into play that would reverse the direction of the flow. The prices of foreign goods climbed so high that imports were sharply curtailed; meanwhile, domestic prices fell sufficiently low to generate an expansion of exports. Correspondingly, the demand for foreign monies to purchase new goods and to settle existing debts dropped off, and the prices of foreign bills of exchange, in turn, declined. The outflow of specie halted. As foreign bill prices continued to fall, gold and silver began to flow back into the country, thus replenishing the domestic stock of money. Within months or several years at most, the cycle had come full circle. All the movements of goods and financial instruments across state borders—the ongoing adjustments and readjustments—were possible without the necessity of altering the mint prices for gold and silver so long as the market prices for those precious metals did not undergo a lasting realignment.

This complicated, self-correcting mechanism—involving the relative prices of bills of exchange in several currencies and linked to specie flows in and out of a given economy—occurred at fairly regular intervals in Europe and in the colonies maintained by the European powers in the western hemisphere.

English Coinage

During most of the seventeenth century, silver was at the base of the monetary system in Great Britain. As a result of the implementation of recoinage legislation in the 1690s, however, the nation shifted abruptly to gold. Because the market price for silver was consistently higher than its mint price after 1697, very little silver arrived at the English mint for conversion into new coins. Meanwhile, the existing silver coins, many in deteriorating condition, were steadily removed from circulation. Silver was exported to India and the Far East where it had more purchasing power than in the British market and in most locations in Europe. In much of Asia from eight to ten ounces of silver equaled one ounce of gold, whereas in Europe the exchange ratio was in the range of thirteen or fifteen ounces of silver to one ounce of gold. The price differential resulted in a continuous outflow of silver to the Far East.

The outflow could have been halted, or even reversed, if Parliament had decided to change the mint ratio and devalue its silver coinage. But following a lengthy debate in the 1690s, in which John Locke was an important participant, it rejected that option. Locke was instrumental in convincing political leaders of the logic of the "bullionist" argument, which was based on abstract principles. It is an argument often encountered in the American setting as well, but

more often in the nineteenth century than the eighteenth. Locke
claimed that gold and silver had traditionally fixed values, at home
and abroad, and that any governmental policy that tried to alter
those values was destined to be ineffective and self-defeating.

Equating the value of coins strictly with their metallic content,
Locke asserted that the English government possessed insufficient
power to exert control over the composition of its coinage in the
long run. Locke was so persuasive that a majority in Parliament
voted to insist upon a recoinage of the existing silver coins at the
former mint price: sixteen ounces of silver was equal to one ounce
of gold. For our purposes here it is not critically important whether
Locke's assertions about absolutes in determining coinage values
were valid or specious. What did matter is that the value Locke insisted upon in 1695 was substantially below the prevailing market
price for silver outside the British Empire. Thus, the implementation of his master plan to restore silver to its proper role in the
English financial system had very much the reverse outcome. The
net effect was to halt the minting of silver coins in England and
reduce by approximately one-half the number in circulation by the
end of the eighteenth century.[3]

Nonetheless, the policy's overall effect on the English economy
and the functioning of the monetary system was not highly detrimental because the de facto abandonment of silver stimulated, in
turn, the production of gold coins in amounts totaling in the millions of pounds. Supplemented by bank notes issued by the Bank
of England after 1694, the total money stock of England changed
hardly at all during the 1690s. The money stock for 1693 is estimated at £21.5 million, with silver accounting for 61 percent of the
total; five years later the money stock had actually risen to £22.8
million, with gold coins already surpassing silver in total value.[4] The
rapid and relatively smooth shift from silver to gold as the primary
metal in the coinage system illustrates again the flexibility and responsiveness of the European monetary markets to shifts in relative
prices for gold and silver at domestic mints.

The gold coins minted in Great Britain were, as elsewhere, so
high in value that few actually circulated widely among the general
public. The most commonly minted gold coin was called a guinea;
it was worth twenty-one shillings and six pence until 1717, when on
the advice of Isaac Newton, the new rate became twenty-one shillings alone. A guinea represented more than a week's income for
the typical English worker. The coins concentrated in the hands of

wealthy landowners and merchants or rested behind the doors of government vaults. By modern standards, therefore, the operation of the monetary system in the seventeenth century was highly unusual because the nation's basic monetary stock, which determined the general level of domestic prices, was centered on a metal so valuable that common people had little personal contact with it. Yet, no matter how low their station in life, everyone knew gold coins existed and, moreover, that they were the supreme monetary unit in England. Still, most of the population never actually possessed a guinea throughout their lifetimes.

The everyday mediums of exchange for the general English population in the eighteenth century were the dwindling supplies of silver coins from the major recoinage of the 1690s plus the coinage minted regularly from less valuable metals such as copper, tin, and lead. Although more numerous in quantity than coins minted from precious metals, the low-value coins, called as a matter of convenience "token" coins, comprised only a small fraction of the aggregate money stock. Issued in amounts ranging from one shilling (twenty shillings = one pound) to pence (twelve pennies = one shilling), and even as low as halfpennies and farthings (one-fourth of a penny), the coins were the closest equivalent to our modern nickels, dimes, and quarters. By rough estimate—to provide some idea of the magnitude of the amounts involved—a silver coin valued at one shilling was worth from $3.00 to $3.50 in 1990 U.S. dollars, while an English halfpenny would have been worth from $.10 to $.15.

Throughout the eighteenth century, the English economy apparently had an insufficient quantity of low- and intermediate-denomination coins to facilitate everyday, routine transactions. Complaints about the unavailability of monies were frequent among the middling and lower classes. The most serious shortage occurred in coins of intermediate values, ranging from around six pence up to five shillings or thereabout. In England, and throughout Europe, silver was universally the favored metal for the production of coins of intermediate values. The reason for the scarcity of silver coins was, to repeat, the consequence of the recoinage laws passed in the 1690s.

Meanwhile, thousands of very low-valued token coins were issued not only by the national government but also by municipal and private mints. Since the face values of token coins invariably exceeded the market prices of their respective metals, counterfeiting was a persistent problem in England and elsewhere. Indeed, monetary historians have estimated that, in the middle of the eighteenth century, more counterfeit token coins were probably in general circulation in England than their legal counterparts issued by authorized government mints.

Beginning in the 1670s, Parliament sponsored various issues of copper coins, and they soon became the most common form of money held by the general population. Counterfeiting became so pervasive, however, that copper coinage was suspended at the government mint in 1754. By the late eighteenth century, the existing copper coinage was deteriorating rapidly and the government had authorized nothing to take its place. Some contemporary observers, among them Adam Smith in 1776, suggested that silver be reintroduced into the English monetary system on a large scale by grossly overvaluing it at the mint and alloying it with lesser metals to produce a series of medium- to low-value coins. But nothing was done at the time because, according to the late British monetary historian Sir Alfred Feavearyear, "there was still a sacredness attaching to the metal which had been for so long standard . . . and no willingness as yet to see the silver coins degraded to mere tokens."[5] In other words, the power of the bullionist argument, advanced so forcefully by John Locke three quarters of a century earlier, still had tremendous influence over public officials.

Colonial Coinage

How does the preceding discussion of the status of the coinage system in Great Britain relate to the situation in the colonies? It is necessary to dispel the commonly held view, prevailing at the time and for decades thereafter, that American complaints about the absence of monies in the domestic economy represented a unique situation and a burden imposed maliciously upon the colonists by a tyrannical Parliament. In truth, the situation in the mother country was just as bad—and perhaps even worse. Throughout the period, English farmers and small merchants constantly complained about the paucity of convenient mediums of exchange for everyday transactions. But they received little relief from British political leaders who remained faithful to abstract principles about the role certain metals *ought* to play in the coinage system above all other practical considerations. (Until the United States officially renounced the linkage between the dollar and gold in 1971, similar attitudes about the intrinsic value of that precious metal and its proper role in the monetary system was a part of the American economic and intellectual heritage as well.)

Meanwhile, the colonists repeatedly claimed that the existing supply of silver coins purposely was being drained away to the mother country. That allegation was partly true since much of it did eventually cross the Atlantic to settle colonial debts. But most of the silver did not remain in England to bolster the local monetary stock as alleged; rather it was reexported to the Far East to pay, in turn, for British imports. Likewise, the complaint that Parliament maintained an inferior coinage system in its North American colonies was valid, but the government performed equally poorly at home. Its monetary policy should not be judged, therefore, as an instance of parliamentary discrimination against the colonies but rather as one more example of its indifference to complaints arising throughout the empire about the inadequacy of the coinage.

Parliament expected its American colonies to rely on foreign coins for a local medium of exchange, particularly Spanish coins minted in the western hemisphere. Given the ample supplies of new monies generated in the New World, that policy was reasonable and sensible. Millions of dollars (a Spanish monetary unit) in silver coins poured out of mints in Mexico and other Latin American locations throughout the seventeenth and eighteenth centuries and circulated widely in the North Atlantic economies, including the colonies of British America. The trade with the West Indies was extensive, and Spanish coins steadily flowed northward into the colonies as a result of that commerce.

Mints in Mexico, and in other Latin American locations, produced coins in several denominations. The basic unit of account in most of the western hemisphere was the dollar. The Spanish dollar was subdivided by eighths into smaller units called reales, and coins valued at ½, 1, 2, 4, and 8 reales were regularly minted. The highest valued coin in the series, known as "pieces of eight," was by all accounts one of the most commonly recognized monetary units by colonists resident from Georgia to Maine. Based on the standard weight of its silver content, an uncirculated Spanish dollar, if melted down and delivered to the government mint in England, would have yielded monies worth 4 shillings, 6 pence. The exchange rate between Spanish and British monies in silver units was thus $1.00 equaled £0.225 or, alternatively, $4.44 equaled £1. The smallest Spanish silver coin valued at only ½ real was roughly the equivalent of 3.5 pence (an amount equal to about $1 in U.S. currency in 1990).

In a practice that seems peculiar and somewhat perplexing to modern readers, governments in the colonies decided to *overvalue* the Spanish coins circulating in their domestic economies. As a result, the colonies maintained a monetary system containing coins valued partially by their metallic weight and partially by fiat— meaning in the latter instance that the coins were worth what government had mandated. (All currency and coin in the present U.S. monetary system represents strictly fiat money, although specially authorized full-weighted silver and gold commemorative coins, not intended for circulation, are periodically produced both by private and government mints and sold to collectors at prices directly related to their metallic content.)

What was the rationale for the colonial overvaluation of Spanish coins? First, overvaluation was a simple device for expanding the aggregate size of the monetary stock by up to one-third without introducing any more specie into the economy. But the most important reason was that the policy encouraged the importation and then the retention of foreign coins in the colonies since those monies were worth more to holders negotiating transactions in the domestic economy than in making payments overseas. The coins in greatest demand were in the small to intermediate range in terms of nominal value. By overvaluing foreign coins, the colonies could accumulate relatively easily a stock of money sufficient to accommodate domestic transactions without requiring either the importation of numerous English coins or the establishment of a branch of the English mint within the colonies—both of which, with one notable exception cited below, were prohibited by Parliament.

Colonial governments began rating foreign coins at higher values than warranted by their metallic content as early as the 1640s. The Massachusetts General Court in September 1642 stipulated that pieces of eight were to pass locally at five shillings, while Virginia in 1645 and later New York in 1672 put the official value at six shillings. During the seventeenth century various colonial governments devised their own diverse rating systems for coins issued by several European countries, including Spain, Holland, Portugal, and France. The English government finally became seriously concerned about the absence of uniformity in colonial monetary systems early in the eighteenth century. In 1704 Queen Anne issued a proclamation setting maximum limits of 133 percent for the overvaluation of specific foreign coins in all British colonies in the western hemisphere. The document made official the general practice of rating Spanish coins at higher values in the colonies than their comparable values (mint prices) in England.

It is worth recalling that several somewhat analogous plans for modest silver debasement in England had been rejected during the great monetary debates in Parliament late in the seventeenth century. No less than Sir Isaac Newton had been among the frustrated sponsors. In this instance, monetary principles assumed to be unsound for the mother country were judged acceptable, or at least justifiable exceptions, for operation in the distant colonies. Unintentionally and obliviously, England had, in truth, created a superior coinage system for its overseas empire than for the home market. Financial history is both blessed or burdened, depending upon one's outlook and sense of humor, with hundreds of such anomalies and absurdities.

The colonies used the proclamation ratio of 133:100 as a guideline in establishing par rates for paper currencies and foreign coins in their respective economies but, in acts of minor rebellion, some exceeded the limits. The official local rates of overvaluation relative to sterling varied from 125:100 in Virginia, to 177:100 in New York, and 700:100 in South Carolina. Contemporaries spoke of the local units as *colonial pence, colonial shillings,* and *colonial pounds.* Often they used the issuing colony's name as a prefix—for example, Maryland pence, Pennsylvania shillings, or Virginia pounds. Those monetary units were the medium of exchange in the local economy and the main units for measuring values within the borders of a given colony.

What emerged in North America during the eighteenth century was a highly confusing three-tiered valuation system. First, the standard English system of pence, shillings, and pounds reflected accurately the value of those monies in the mother country. That monetary system was used in North America mostly as an abstract unit of measurement. Since it was uniform throughout the British Empire, the "sterling" values permitted meaningful comparisons among various political units near and far. Coins actually denominated in sterling rarely circulated in the colonies, however, with the exception of some low-value token coins such as farthings. Second, after 1704, the British crown recognized proclamation units at values ranging up to one-third above the normal mint price in England. Third, locally legislated rating systems for foreign coins and paper monies (discussed in the next chapter) varied from colony to colony and sometimes exceeded the sanctioned 133 percent limit. To cite two examples: Virginia with a local overvaluation rate of 125 percent was within proclamation limits; New York at 177 percent was beyond the so-called lawful limit.

Needless to say, the simultaneous existence of three valuation systems using almost identical nomenclature—English pounds, proclamation pounds, and colonial pounds—led to much confusion in this earlier era, which has understandably persisted ever since. Without a clear understanding of the context within which a document was drafted, it is difficult for modern readers to know for certain whether the writer was quoting monetary sums in sterling, proclamation monies, or colonial pounds, although in most cases the colonial variety is the safest initial assumption.

Despite the problem of potential confusion because of the overlapping nomenclature, the general policy of overrating foreign coins in order to attract them to the colonies was prudent and reasonably successful. The best evidence for this favorable conclusion is that the colonial economy prospered over the long run. The monetary system functioned sufficiently well to promote aggregate and per capita income growth. Spanish coins minted in the western hemisphere were respected for their consistently high quality and prized by the general population for their availability.

The broad generalization about the absence of English coin in British America had at least two minor exceptions. Before colonization in the seventeenth century, the English government had already adopted the policy of prohibiting the private export of English coins to any point overseas—including its own colonies. But Parliament reserved the right to make overseas payments for its own account in English coin when necessary and convenient. Most overseas disbursements involved the payment of wages and salaries to military personnel and a few civil servants. Precise figures for the whole era are elusive, but in the last decade of colonial rule, the treasury estimated the shipment of about £100,000 specie annually to North America to pay British troops. Most of the monies were Spanish and Portuguese coins, but some sterling probably entered the colonies through that mechanism.[6]

Another infusion of English coins into the colonial economy came around midcentury. In 1748, when Parliament voted to reimburse the New England colonies for military expenses incurred in the course of defending and expanding the British empire, Massachusetts was allotted £183,649. After deductions for transportation expenses and other costs, the colony received about £174,000.

Most of that sum was paid in Spanish silver, but also included in the shipment were 726,800 halfpence and 573,184 farthings. The copper coins were largely fiat monies since the intrinsic value of the metal was only a small fraction of the assigned face value. Farthings and halfpennies were the lowest denominated coins in circulation in the colonies (equivalent to roughly 7 to 15 cents, respectively, in 1990 U.S. monies).[7] Their availability made more convenient the negotiation of small transactions among the general population. According to one numismatic scholar, the copper coins from this Parliamentary disbursement were the most actively circulated monies in the colonies, particularly New England, from 1750 until independence. Indeed, many remained in circulation and were accorded legal status in the new nation until well into the nineteenth century.[8]

Conclusion

The coinage system functioning in the colonies during the eighteenth century met the requirements of the era. The criterion here is not a modern standard of monetary adequacy but a relative one based on conditions prevailing in contemporary Europe. The coinage was mainly Spanish—with some English coins, mostly in the token category, also in circulation. The volume of high-value coins available for use as a reliable store of value was apparently more than sufficient since few wealthy colonials registered complaints about persistent shortages. Records of probated estates indicate that few colonists, including the very wealthy, held much of their wealth in monetary assets in any event, since specie produced no income. Meanwhile, intermediate- and low-value coins, supplemented by paper monies issued by the colonial legislatures in some regions at certain times, were normally present in sufficient amounts to serve as a medium of exchange for the general population. Few mutually beneficial transactions in goods or services were thwarted because of the lack of monies to settle accounts.

On balance, the colonists maintained as large a money supply, in the aggregate, as required to finance an unusually high output of goods and services per capita in comparison with other contemporaneous societies.[9] If more hard monies had, in fact, been necessary to support the economy, the population had other tangible goods in abundance; and a portion of those commodities could have been exchanged overseas to build up the size of the domestic coinage. In their portfolio of assets, both financial and nonfinancial, the colonists decided to hold only a certain amount of coins (and other forms of monies). The flow of goods and monies with other countries was free enough to ensure that they were able to exercise their preferences. Indeed, it is largely because of the existence of such wide freedom of action that modern monetary historians have concluded that the stock of money, with coins as one component, was almost certainly adequate to satisfy aggregate colonial demand.[10]

On the basis of these sweeping generalizations, readers should not infer that there were never periods when coins were not, in fact, temporarily in short supply. Coin shortages for periods ranging from six months to two years did occur intermittently in the colonies, as did shortages of other economic goods. During periods of credit stringency, almost always triggered by crises in the English money market, the outflow of silver coins from the colonies to meet creditor demands for the settlement of overseas debts was often excessive. But the shortages were neither chronic nor the consequence of severe institutional limitations imposed by Parliament or any other governmental unit.[11] Meanwhile, the fact that the primary source of coinage was Spanish America was a distinct advantage since fresh supplies were nearby and large quantities were minted regularly. The normal flow of trade and commerce usually brought the monetary system back into equilibrium. Unfortunately, the adjustment mechanism often took several years to accomplish that goal. During the interim, many colonists grew impatient, and they turned to their provincial governments to introduce a more convenient and more permanent medium of exchange to expedite local transactions. One solution chosen by every colony in varying degrees was the issuance of paper monies to supplement the fluctuating supplies of coin.

2

Fiat Currency

THE VARIOUS colonial governments were also directly involved in shaping the financial environment in North America. Their legislatures played a highly innovative role by emitting numerous issues of fiat currency—thereby making an extremely controversial addition to the money stock in the eyes of the British and other Europeans. In the eighteenth century, paper money itself was not universally condemned, just the fiat variety issued by governments. Paper money issued by chartered banks and other private firms that was adequately supported by specie reserves was considered perfectly legitimate, and it circulated as a component of the money stock in Great Britain.

Across the Atlantic Ocean, however, the colonial governments maintained no specie reserves whatsoever to support the value of their respective currencies. Unlike the holders of privately issued paper money in Britain, colonists in possession of governmental fiat currency were unable to convert their holdings into coin at predetermined, predictable values. Fiat money had no fixed value in relation to coin or other financial assets; in exchanges among private parties, its value was subject to fluctuations based on forces in the marketplace. Only in tax payments to the provincial treasury or transactions with other governmental agencies did fiat currency universally pass by law at face value. Critics of fiat currency focused on its unreliability as a store of wealth since theory and practice suggested that it was an unsafe form of money vulnerable to steady and possibly irreversible depreciation.

Because of its unsavory reputation in Europe, the issuance of unconvertible fiat monies in the colonies was not an idea encouraged by Parliament. On the contrary, British imperial officials strongly disapproved of the practice, and they articulated their profound reservations in the course of providing paternalistic guidance about monetary affairs in overseas territories. Despite misgivings, members of the Board of Trade reluctantly approved a series of American emissions, invariably after the fact. Representatives of the colonial legislatures and their respective governors constantly pleaded with board members sitting in London for their indulgence. The board had the power to disallow colonial legislation that contradicted British policies, but it typically let stand the unorthodox monetary experiments.

Frustrated with colonial indiscretions, parliamentary leaders mounted a campaign, launched in two phases in 1751 and 1764, to suppress fiat currency. They succeeded in curtailing issuance in New England, but failed in the subsequent attempt to extend the ban to the other nine colonies. Outside of New England, the conflict over the composition of the money stock was the second most divisive surface issue between the colonial assemblies and crown ministers in the 1760s and early 1770s, ranking just after the heated confrontations over parliamentary attempts to impose a greater burden of imperial taxation.

The thirteen colonies were not the first governmental units to issue fiat currency, but they were among the first organized political entities to embrace that form of money and to persist in its use.[1] In fact, some form of paper money, either the fiat currencies of governmental bodies or the bank notes of financial institutions, has been a feature of the American monetary system for nearly three centuries. During much of the nineteenth century, the composition of the U.S. money stock was an exceedingly controversial domestic issue, pitting the advocates of hard money (coin) versus the proponents of so-called soft money (paper). In this later era, the conflict was generally viewed as a clash between special interest groups or social classes: a battle between commercial interests favoring price stability, mainly creditors, and those wanting to promote gradual, or even rampant, inflation—primarily indebted farmers living on mortgaged lands.

In their interpretations of colonial monetary history, many scholars writing in the late nineteenth and early twentieth centuries extended the model of class conflict as far back as the eighteenth century. More recent research has revealed that the analogy is inappropriate, or at least requires substantial modification. The debtor versus creditor model does not apply in the colonial era. All social classes and occupational groupings in the colonies were generally in agreement about the merits of a monetary system that included fiat currency as a supplement to coinage. Occasionally, heated legislative debates arose over the terms of issuance, but the desirability of some type of fiat currency was rarely questioned. The major battles over the composition of the money stock in colonial times were with external, not internal, opponents. The opposition sprang from London merchants active in the colonial trade, who were almost exclusively creditors overseas, and their political allies on the Board of Trade.

The British Background

The British background relating to the issuance of paper monies and as a corollary to banking generally is critically important in any discussion of U.S. financial history. Not only did British finance affect events in the colonies but its heritage had a powerful influence on the principles and procedures that Americans followed in the decades after political independence. To cite one prime example: Alexander Hamilton drew up his plan for the First Bank of the United States based on the inspiration provided by the Bank of England. More than a century later, the same bank, which had expanded its duties during the nineteenth century, was again held up as an institutional model for the creation of the Federal Reserve System. Over the years American finance followed many peculiar paths and frequently deviated from the British example, but its roots can nonetheless be traced to the traditional practices and attitudes developed in eighteenth-century England and, as will later be shown, in Scotland as well.

By the middle of the eighteenth century, England and virtually every other European state had strong reservations about the issuance of fiat currency by governmental bodies because of serious doubts about its soundness and practicality. The fears were manifold and expressed on many levels. Critics appealed both to theory and, after 1675, to experience. Fiat currencies tended to depreciate, the argument went, because of ineffective and unreliable mechanisms for sustaining their relative value. Unless a government possessed the resolve to impose the high taxes necessary to retire a portion of the amount outstanding at regular intervals, public confidence waned and the currency soon passed at declining exchange rates. Few European governments had even tried to introduce a system of fiat currency, and those isolated attempts were all mismanaged. In particular, detractors pointed to events in England during the reign of Charles II in the seventeenth century and to one spectacularly disastrous monetary experiment in France in the first quarter of the eighteenth century. Indeed, no one was able to cite an instance when inconvertible monies had been successfully introduced on a large scale in a broad range of denominations into an economy in Europe or elsewhere.

The critics of fiat currency were, in contrast, much more tolerant of the paper money emitted by private issuers. Banks with corporate charters, proprietorships, and every partnership with fewer than seven members were permitted by law to issue paper money in Britain. Most unincorporated issuers were organized as private banks, but some predominantly mercantile firms also engaged in financial services, including currency emission, as a sideline. The term *merchant banker* was sometimes applied to firms with a dual focus—both merchandising and financial services. In every case, the public assumed that the private issuers, whether chartered banks or unincorporated firms, would shoulder the responsibility for maintaining the relative value of their respective currencies by holding reserves and honoring requests for conversion into coinage at equivalent values.

A clear distinction exists between historical developments associated with the issuance of currencies by governments, on the one hand, and by banks and private issuers, on the other hand. Their origins were quite dissimilar, and public attitudes about the merits and defects of those two monetary forms differed enormously as well. The origins of private monies in England are generally traced to goldsmiths, persons who accepted for safekeeping deposits of specie, either bullion or coin. Initially, goldsmiths issued warehouse receipts to depositors, and over the decades the receipts evolved into easily transferable financial instruments.

Beginning in the seventeenth century, goldsmiths began printing currency on their own initiative and loaning it out to third parties at interest. Printed on every bill was a bold statement informing the current holder that it was exchangeable for specie of equal value, either immediately upon presentation or after a short waiting period—usually just a few days. At first goldsmiths maintained 100 percent reserves—that is, they printed exactly one hundred pounds in notes for each one hundred pounds of specie in their vaults, either their own capital or sums on deposit from customers. Over the years other firms and individuals, including many merchants, began to perform similarly sophisticated banking functions.

An important distinction must be drawn between the institutional development of banking in England and its subsequent evolution in the United States. Prior to the mid-1820s, most English firms performing banking functions were proprietorships or partnerships that held no charter and were generally free from any governmental oversight. The linkage between commercial banking and government charters, which has prevailed throughout the history of the U.S. financial system (with a few little-known exceptions), was not the tradition in early modern Britain. Firms could freely enter the financial markets on their own initiative, and they operated with little or no supervision. Their success as issuers of paper money depended in large part on their reputation in the marketplace—meaning whether the public was willing to accept and hold their obligations. Paper money was not legal tender in either public or private transactions.

The American image of English finance, which prevailed throughout the nineteenth century and much of the early twentieth century and which pictured English banking as prudently organized and conservatively managed, was distorted. In truth, banking in England was an institutional hodgepodge from the outset and remained so for decades. Moreover, for most of its early history, English banking operations were no safer than in the United States despite widespread American belief to the contrary—a view that persisted well into the twentieth century.

Eventually, most English goldsmiths and other competing firms, hereafter lumped together and referred to as banks simply as a matter of convenience, began to hold less than 100 percent specie reserves against their outstanding circulation. Let us assume that a given firm decided to maintain 50 percent reserves. For every one hundred pounds of specie in its vault, the firm printed two hundred pounds worth of bank notes and loaned them out at interest. The rationale for holding only fractional reserves was a reflection of mathematical probabilities: how often would the holders of bank notes likely request conversion into specie and in what aggregate amounts. Experience revealed that, when normal business conditions prevailed, holders rarely exercised the privilege of conversion, preferring instead to hold their monetary assets in currency rather than coin.

Bankers eventually realized that their outstanding currency issues could be safely supported by fractional reserves. Holding reserves of 50 percent, as illustrated above, was considered a conservative business strategy in Great Britain. However, the reserve levels that contemporaries acknowledged as conservative or, alternatively, as dangerously speculative varied greatly from country to country. In France, for example, the prudent figure eventually was determined to be no less than 100 percent reserves. In Scotland specie reserves of only 3 percent to 10 percent were the rule. England fell somewhere between those two extremes, with specie reserves of 20 to 30 percent commonly held by banks.

The profitability of lending against fractional reserves led banks to begin the payment of interest to customers to attract more specie deposits. In this stage of development, banks emerged as intermediaries between individuals seeking a modest return on their surplus funds, plus a fair degree of safety, and borrowers seeking loans for a multitude of purposes. Without exception, banks paid lower interest rates to depositors—sometimes nothing at all—than they charged borrowers. The margin between the bank's cost of acquiring money and the rates paid by loan customers was a source of profits.

By printing paper money in amounts exceeding the value of reserves, bankers were, quite literally, creating new money. And it was a source of new money that did not need to be discovered in some distant location and subsequently mined, transported, and minted. What led banks to so eagerly create new monies? The incentive was the prospect of increased interest revenues from a larger volume of loans. More loans, in turn, led to a greater volume of bank notes in circulation vis-à-vis existing reserves. Leaving aside safety considerations, holding lower reserves increased interest revenues and produced a higher rate of profit on a given amount of capital.

But where there was heightened profit, there was also greater risk. The dangers associated with having too many loans outstanding and consequently a huge volume of bank notes in circulation were twofold. First, the accommodation of too many borrowers increased the probability that some loans might turn out badly and never be repaid. Second, and more important for the discussion here, the increased volume of paper money in circulation vis-à-vis reserves raised the probability that, at some given date in the future, the bank might not have sufficient specie on hand to satisfy all requests for conversion. Any loss of convertibility would lead the public to question the soundness of the bank and undermine confidence in the value of all its outstanding notes. Any bank unable to maintain convertibility of currency into coin, especially under normal business conditions, was threatened with a run on its remaining reserves and the possibility of failure. (During a panic or recession, when all banks simultaneously refused conversion—often called suspending payment—as a tactic to stave off runs, the danger to individual banks was usually less serious.)

Banking in Great Britain in the first half of the eighteenth century was viewed as a business enterprise similar to other private ventures in regard to the possibilities of success and failure. No special charter or license was necessary to enter the field. Firms issuing currency in the process of making loans did so at their own risk. Likewise, those members of the general public who were willing to accept private monies in business transactions and to hold them in lieu of specie did so at their own risk. Paper money was never legal tender—not even the bank notes issued by the esteemed Bank of England. No citizen was ever forced by law to accept a bank note in payment for goods and services, the settlement of outstanding debts, or the payment of taxes.

No governmental agencies in Britain intervened to set standards for firms engaged in banking activities. No minimum reserves were required against outstanding note issues. Banks that elected to stress the potential for profit over considerations of safety by making a large volume of loans and maintaining low fractional reserves were completely free to chose that course of action. If such high-risk banking operations subsequently led to difficulties because of too many bad loans or because anxious note holders drained away all the specie through conversion, the potential for sustaining losses fell on all investors in the banking enterprise plus any unfortunate customers who had not withdrawn their specie deposits in time.

Since most banking houses were either proprietorships or partnerships without the protection of limited liability, individuals with claims against a failed banking enterprise, including note holders and depositors, were free to proceed through the courts against all the assets of the owners, personal as well as business. The *unlimited* liability of private issuers for the redemption of all their paper in specie was thus one element expected to encourage prudent and safe operations. Most public figures who were unalterably opposed to the issuance of legal-tender fiat currency by the government or any of its agencies were perfectly willing, on the other hand, to allow private firms to emit bank notes, which were not legal tender, in the course of making loans to customers.

In addition to unincorporated private issuers, a few banks held corporate charters granted by Parliament. The first two chartered banks in Great Britain were the Bank of England and the Bank of Scotland. The former was chartered in 1694, the latter in 1695. The English bank was created explicitly to assist Parliament in financing the growing national debt, although it later accepted deposits from individuals and made a limited number of loans to large mercantile firms in the private sector. The Bank of England issued notes, but only in very large denominations—nothing less than twenty pounds initially, and ten pounds after 1759. By comparison, the lowest denominated gold coin, a half-guinea, was valued at just over half a pound. Even its smallest bank note represented several months' wages for the typical worker. As a consequence, Bank of England notes did not circulate widely among the general public but were held instead by governmental units and business enterprises.

Although Scotland was an integral part of the political unit of the United Kingdom after 1707, its banking sector evolved in a distinct manner. The Bank of Scotland, originally chartered in 1695, differed substantially from the Bank of England in several respects. From the outset, it was expected not only to aid the government but also to assist in financing trade and industry. The Bank of Scotland was unique too because it initiated the practice of routinely issuing a large volume of small notes in denominations as low as one pound. Indeed, prior to 1767, some notes were issued in shillings and pence. Like the Americans, the Scottish public in the eighteenth century became accustomed to making routine financial transactions in currency as well as coin. In Scotland token coins containing no gold or silver, in amounts ranging from pence to shillings, represented most of the coinage in circulation by the late eighteenth century. In that respect, the region had a very modern monetary system more than two hundred years before its emergence elsewhere.

During the eighteenth century, Parliament issued charters for several additional banking institutions in Scotland. After 1760, those chartered banks were innovators in the creation of systems of branch offices throughout the region. As a result, Scottish banking took on the characteristics of an oligopolistic market by the end of the eighteenth century. Perhaps the most striking feature of banking in Scotland was the maintenance of very low specie reserves against note issues. Few banks held reserves of higher than 10 percent, and many reportedly kept a mere 1 to 5 percent.[2]

Whereas the expanding system of privatized banking was recognized as contributing to the strength of the overall economy at the start of the eighteenth century in Great Britain, there were ample reservations about the propriety and practicality of unsecured fiat monies. Critics cited the dangers associated with schemes involving governmental emissions. What, they questioned, would be the mechanism to control the volume issued? The supply of specie was reasonably finite over the short to intermediate run. Since precious metals had to be discovered and mined, the value of the coinage and the specie reserves of banks had natural limitations. On the other hand, fiat currency in huge volumes and large denominations could be printed almost overnight without limit. Once a government started to issue currency, where would the process stop? Without tangible backing in the form of specie reserves, critics asserted that paper money issued arbitrarily by government would not be able to maintain its value relative to coin and bullion. Once the anticipated depreciation became a reality, the public would begin to hoard coins, especially the high-value coins. Eventually, the only monies still circulating would be the depreciating and debased fiat paper.

Proponents of fiat currency had argued that an augmentation of the money stock would stimulate economic activity and produce positive effects overall. But critics steadfastly maintained that the outcome would be just the opposite. Any increases in economic output would be transitory. At some point the injection of fiat currency would prove excessive and coins would cease to circulate, thereby reducing the overall stock of money in a given economy. The economist Thomas Gresham encapsulated the argument by formulating the axiom known quite universally as Gresham's Law: bad money drives good money out of circulation. Questions about the ability of government to manage a monetary stock with fiat currency as one component remained unresolved, and it led European political leaders to conclude that its issuance had the potential of undermining the entire economic system.

Experience supported what the theorists alleged. The only sustained governmental effort to issue unsecured paper money in England had occurred in the third quarter of the seventeenth century, and the experiment had ended on a decidedly sour note. In 1667, during the reign of Charles II, various government departments began issuing negotiable exchequer orders. Goldsmiths and other persons willing to loan specie to the crown received exchequer orders drawn in high denominations, but some were drawn in intermediate amounts as well. For the purchase of military goods, the government issued exchequer orders to suppliers in amounts as small as one pound to five pounds. Technically speaking, the instruments fell into the category of tax anticipation notes. When the crown collected taxes in specie at some later date, the revenues generated were pledged to redeem the outstanding exchequer orders in the exact sequence as originally issued. The debt instruments carried an interest rate component and thus increased in value over time because of compounding. Since they were transferable through endorsement, holders and recipients began treating the exchequer orders as a form of money, and they began to circulate.

As the years passed, the crown, pressed for increased financing in the face of war, demurred about making the scheduled reimbursements. Once the public began to worry about their prompt redemption, exchequer orders began to pass at discounted prices. In 1672, only five years after inaugurating the system, the government suddenly stopped payment on exchequer orders; estimates place the sum outstanding at £1.3 to £2.25 million.[3] Most of the orders in default were held by people of substantial wealth, with two goldsmiths alone accounting for more than half of the total. Eventually, the debt holders received compensation but the negotiations dragged on for more than three decades.

The lessons learned in the 1660s and 1670s provided confirmation of the dangers associated with any governmental issue of fiat currency—or any financial instruments closely related to fiat currency. Without any legal means of converting the exchequer orders into specie at face value, holders were totally dependent on the resolve of the crown to collect the future taxes required for reimbursement and, second, its willingness to use the sums available for actual redemption. Detractors concluded, and rightly so, that the orders had not been genuine money at all but simply another instrument used to promote government borrowing. The market value of exchequer orders steadily declined from 1667 to 1672; and after the stoppage of payments, none could accurately predict whether any of the outstanding sums would ever be redeemed at face value—

and the accrued interest was even more doubtful. That sad outcome was proof enough for the majority in Parliament who thereafter became adamantly opposed to the revival of any program designed to permit future governments to issue easily transferable financial instruments that might start to circulate as a component of the money stock.

One spectacular financial scandal on the European continent subsequently served to reinforce the views of skeptics about paper monies issued by governments or their appointed agencies. The infamous attempt to introduce paper money into a national economy on a grand scale was the work of the Scotsman John Law, who migrated to France in 1716. After gaining the ear of the regent for seven-year-old Louis XV, Law opened a private bank under a special governmental charter. The bank loaned millions to the king in the form of paper money. Although the money was not routinely convertible into specie, Law claimed it was adequately backed by reserves. In fact, the bank's vaults contained little more than thin air. The financial instruments were not genuine bank notes at all but just another example of a fiat currency. The bubble burst four years later in 1720, and it disrupted significantly, but not fatally, the French financial system and the economy.[4]

The objections in England were so formidable that Parliament never gave serious consideration to any plan for the emission of fiat currency in the home economy or any of its overseas dominions after 1675. Convertible bank notes backed by specie reserves represented the only form of paper money that British officials viewed as legitimate supplements to the supply of minted coins.

Colonial Fiat Currency

Public attitudes toward fiat currency were radically different in the thirteen colonies than in England. In North America pragmatism won out over theoretical abstractions and moralistic pronouncements. Based on their own experience, the colonists concluded that fiat paper provided a useful addition to the money stock. Every colony experimented with some form of fiat currency. Nine colonial legislatures persisted in its issuance despite parliamentary objections through the 1770s. After independence, seven states decided to reissue fiat currency in the 1780s until the Constitution forbade the practice.

The most serious political conflicts over the money stock were between the colonial legislatures and the Board of Trade in London, which claimed the authority to disallow any colonial acts that violated its interpretation of English law or the will of Parliament. After 1672 the board's membership reflected the strong reservations of English political leaders about the propriety of government-issue paper monies. Board members believed that any monetary idea deemed imprudent at home was equally dubious in other parts of the empire. They aimed at providing sensible guidance, hoping to rescue less experienced officials overseas from pursuing unsound policies. But colonial leaders viewed the currency issue differently and soon came to resent the interference of English officials in their domestic affairs.

The colonial effort to supplement the coinage with other forms of money predated the controversies over fiat currency. Beginning in the seventeenth century, several legislatures authorized the use of other types of near-money substitutes that eventually circulated as a convenient medium of exchange. These transferable documents are generally classified as commodity monies. They were receipts issued against the deposit of nonperishable agricultural products, most commonly tobacco but also sugar and sometimes grain, in a public warehouse. In the Chesapeake region, tobacco receipts were accepted for decades by local and provincial governments in the payment of taxes and fees. Two major problems were linked to that alternative form of money, however. First, the receipts fluctuated in value, moving in unison with the market price of the stored commodity; second, the volume in circulation was limited by the physical quantities of goods on deposit in warehouses.

While hard monies, fiat monies, and commodity monies circulated in the colonial economy, one type was notably absent—namely, private convertible monies issued by individuals such as colonial goldsmiths and silversmiths or by urban merchants seeking additional profits through diversification into financial services. English law presented no obstacles to the issuance of private monies backed by specie reserves as the first line of defense, plus, in the event of possible bankruptcy, a claim on all of an issuer's business and personal assets in legal proceedings. The number of private London bankers has been estimated at about twenty-five in the 1720s and more than fifty by the 1780s, while the number of country bankers located outside of London in England and Wales was somewhere in the neighborhood of one hundred by the 1770s.[5] But where were their counterparts in Philadelphia, New York, and Boston, to name three likely locations?

In the colonies, surviving records point to no private bankers who issued even modest amounts of currency over a sustained period of time. Some merchants may have signed IOUs that passed from hand to hand in limited geographical areas, but no American firm called itself a private bank and proceeded to solicit deposits and issue bank notes against fractional specie reserves. The absence of private bankers in port cities is surprising since the colonies were perennially short of capital, and a strong demand for financing, both short-term commercial credit and longer term mortgages, seems clearly evident.

On several occasions in the 1730s and 1740s, groups of colonists in Massachusetts and Connecticut organized, or attempted to organize, so-called land banks that issued currency against real estate mortgages. Those ventures were all ruled illegal, however, either because their activities exceeded the terms of their provincial charters or because they ran afoul of British law.[6] In 1708, when the Bank of England was renegotiating its charter with parliamentary leaders, the new terms outlawed the issuance of currency by any firm organized in England that included more than six partners irrespective of its primary line of business—whether goldsmith, mercantile, or whatever. The Bubble Act of 1720 prevented the formation of any new unincorporated joint-stock company— actually large partnerships with transferable shares—without first obtaining a charter from the crown. Since few corporate charters were granted throughout the empire, groups of individuals faced a severe restraint on their ability to pool large sums of capital for any type of business enterprise, including banking. Two private banks in Massachusetts were forced to suspend operations in the early 1740s, for example, because they were organized in violation of laws applicable in the mother country.[7]

Although monetary historians have usually cited legal restrictions as the prime reason for the stunted institutional development of American finance, closer analysis suggests that that fact alone could not explain the absence of private banks in the colonies. True, large groups of investors sponsoring private land bank schemes were stymied on several occasions by the Board of Trade's extension of English corporate law across the Atlantic; but no obstacle appears to have prevented a single individual or a partnership with six members or less from engaging in a full range of banking activities, including the issuance of currency supported by specie reserves as a first line of defense and then more fully by the issuers' entire net worth in the event of default or failure. Why more extensive financial services never materialized in the domestic market remains a profound mystery, especially in light of the general entrepreneurial instincts of numerous merchants in thriving port cities such as Philadelphia, New York, Boston, and Charleston.

Fiat Currency

In the colonial economy, the main supplement to coinage in the money stock was the fiat currency emitted under the auspices of the elected legislatures. The dates for initiating currency emissions varied considerably—the first colony being Massachusetts in the 1690s and the last being Virginia in the 1750s. The fiat currencies were legal tender in the payment of provincial taxes and other public obligations and sometimes in private transactions as well, depending on the specific issue in question and the colony of origin. Colonial treasuries issued currency in denominations ranging from large bills such as twenty pounds down to amounts as low as one shilling in four colonies. More than half of the bills were less than ten shillings, which made them widely accessible and convenient for negotiating routine transactions. The currency issued in one colony frequently spilled over the borders into neighboring colonies, where it was accepted on a voluntary basis and valued according to prevailing exchange rates. An active merchant in Philadelphia, for example, in addition to holding quantities of Spanish, Portuguese, Dutch, and English coins, might also have included among his financial assets the currencies of Pennsylvania, New Jersey, New York, and Maryland—and after 1755, maybe Virginia as well.

The provincial governments issued currency with two different backing, or support, mechanisms. In the first category were tax anticipation bills. Legislatures voted to emit a specific amount of currency to pay current obligations and simultaneously pledged to retire those monies from circulation with the proceeds of future taxes. The main stimulus for a fresh emission of paper money was an escalation in military expenses associated with a campaign against Native American tribes or rival European powers, usually the French. In Pennsylvania and Maryland, the legislatures emitted fiat currency in an effort to stimulate economic activity, and historians Richard Lester and Mary Schweitzer have suggested that those policies were generally successful.[8]

Legislatures fixed a final expiration date ranging from two to twenty years for each currency series. Occasionally outstanding issues overlapped. Some issues were retired in phases, while others were sunk in one lump sum in the expiration year. How the relative values of tax anticipation bills fared in the marketplace was closely related to public perceptions about the resolve of a given legislature to follow through on its pledge to collect the taxes required for retirement. When legislatures acted responsibly in regard to the imposition of taxes, the value of their tax anticipation bills remained fairly stable for decades with only minor, periodic fluctuations.

The methods of taxation to raise the funds for currency retirement varied considerably from colony to colony. In some instances a special tax assessment on persons or property was made in the last years before the scheduled expiration date. In Maryland treasury officials regularly collected an export tax on tobacco and accumulated it in a sinking fund, which was then drawn upon to redeem the outstanding currency. Other colonies showed less enthusiasm about raising tax revenues to fund the retirement of outstanding issues. At times, previous emissions were simply rolled over and kept in circulation because citizens did not wish to vote, and then pay, the required taxes. In some cases legislatures added new transfusions of currency into the money stock without retiring the old.

In colonies that lacked the discipline either to impose the requisite taxes or hold the rein on fresh emissions, the market value of their respective currencies steadily depreciated. Many previous accounts of colonial monetary history were written by authors determined to expose the failures of paper money, and they understandably concentrated on the atypical episodes of spiraling depreciation. The worst offenders were the New England colonies before 1750, South Carolina from 1710 to 1725, and North Carolina from 1712—the year it split off politically from South Carolina—to 1740.

In a circuitous manner, those fiat monies that depreciated steeply and were never fully redeemed functioned as an indirect means of public taxation. When currency was issued to pay for government expenditures and the direct taxes necessary for its retirement were never collected, the losses fell on those persons who had periodically held that form of money over the years. Since depreciating currency tended to lose purchasing power gradually over a period of years, a singular holder usually lost, at most, only a few percentage points in value before passing the currency to some other person. The overall effect was roughly similar to a modern excise tax; in perhaps hundreds of transactions over many years, each party suffering some degree of depreciation had unintentionally, but very effectively, assumed a portion of the provincial tax burden. An analogous situation arose during the War for Independence, when holders of depreciating continental dollars unwittingly bore about two-thirds of the tax burden imposed to finance the military effort.

This general issue is important because historians writing in the late nineteenth and early twentieth centuries tended to portray in very unflattering terms those colonial legislatures that failed to halt the unabated depreciation of their fiat monies. Those monetary purists saw all monetary depreciation—anytime, anyplace—not merely as bad public policy but as clear evidence of a lack of personal and political morality. Our understanding of monetary systems has progressed enormously in the last fifty years. Modern scholars recognize that the intolerant views of previous generations of economic and monetary historians were overstated and lacked analytical vigor. All the paper monies in the colonial era served useful economic purposes in varying degrees. Depreciating currencies continued to circulate and thereby provided a useful medium of exchange; a by-product was a mild form of equitable taxation. On the other hand, fiat currencies that resisted depreciation, and they were in the majority, provided both a medium of exchange and a safe store of value for persons seeking to hold wealth in the form of monetary assets.

In the second paper money category were fiat currencies issued by government loan offices, which functioned as agencies of the colonial legislatures. The loan offices were frequently called land banks in the eighteenth century, but the name was a misnomer because the agencies failed to accept deposits or perform a sufficient number of financial services to meet the modern criteria for financial institutions. Loans were granted to residents of the colony with real estate to offer as collateral.[9] Borrowers normally received currency worth up to half the value of the property mortgaged, and they were free to spend the loan proceeds in any manner without advance approval. Most customers presumably used the borrowed funds to make additions to their productive capacities, including land, livestock, and bonded workers.

To guarantee wide access to the government's credit facilities, legislatures placed limits on how much currency one person could borrow from the loan office. In New York the minimum figure was £25 ($2,250) and the maximum £100 ($9,000). The repayment schedules extended over relatively long periods, ranging up to a dozen years, with annual installments of interest and principal. (Interestingly, similar long-term loans against real estate with such prudent amortization plans were not widely available to American borrowers until the 1930s.) As currency flowed into the loan office to reduce the principal on outstanding loans, officials either retired it from circulation or made new loans to borrowers with adequate collateral.

This method of issuance was generally conducive to preventing depreciation, since in the absence of a prolonged collapse in real estate values in settled regions, which never occurred in North America, the currency was amply secured by mortgage assets. The periodic collection of principal and interest meant that the currency was continually in demand. By curtailing new loans in later periods, public officials had the option of reducing the circulation allotted to the loan office by roughly 5 to 10 percent in any given year.

The ultimate responsibility for the repayment of loans, and thereby the retirement of the outstanding currency, rested with individual borrowers, not the will of voters or their elected representatives. If a borrower was unable to repay, the loan office foreclosed the mortgage and sold the property at auction; it used the proceeds to settle the debt and retire the outstanding currency. The backing mechanism virtually assured that fiat currency issued by government loan offices would eventually be returned to the treasury for retirement or reissuance.[10]

The currency issued at colonial loan offices falls into the category of paper monies supported by physical or financial assets other than specie reserves—what economists usually call an "asset-backed" currency. The principle was similar to the concept later adopted by the states in establishing systems of so-called free banking and then by the federal government under the National Banking Act of 1863. In the latter instance, U.S. government bonds of equal or slightly greater value provided secure backing for every bank note issued by every financial institution holding a federal charter. In the colonial era, mortgages worth roughly twice the amount of currency in circulation likewise offered an adequate margin of safety.

In addition to injecting a reliable currency into the money stock, property loans generated a steady stream of interest income for colonial legislatures. Interest rates varied according to the colony in question, ranging as high as 12.5 percent in the Carolinas in the 1710s. In the middle colonies, government loans carried interest charges of 5 to 6 percent—incredibly low rates for a society

chronically short of loanable funds for long-term investments. Indeed, competitive loans extending over periods longer than two or
three years were generally difficult to obtain at any price from private sources. The low rates on publicly funded loans were probably
influenced by religious concerns about the problem of usury; in
most colonies the maximum legal rate on private transactions was
restricted to 6 to 8 percent. While the restriction could be circum-
vented by discounting the proceeds of debt instruments, the policy
of pegging government rates to legal rates normally prevailed at
government loan offices.

   Low interest rates clearly represented a public subsidy to borrowers but it was not an egregious diversion of taxpayers' resources.
First, the loans were widely distributed, which meant that many
property holders—who were simultaneously taxpayers—received
funds on equally generous terms. Second, defaults were low and
losses rare. Loan offices processed and serviced a large number of
customers, thus benefiting from the scale economies inherent in
volume operations. In terms of the number of borrowers and the
geographical spread of properties held as collateral, few financial
institutions in the nineteenth century were able to achieve a similar
degree of diversification in their loan portfolios. A possible exception was the federally chartered Bank of the United States which,
on two separate occasions before 1840, operated branch offices in
several states.

   The legislatures used the interest revenues generated from their
loan offices to meet government expenses. The sums were frequently large relative to the parsimonious budgets at local and provincial levels. In several colonies—New Jersey, Pennsylvania, and
New York—interest revenues were large enough to make a substantial contribution toward annual budgets. In some colonies interest
revenues covered all provincial expenditures in peacetime. As a result, the tax burden imposed on the general population was mild or
nonexistent for years and even decades.

Confrontation with the Board of Trade

The main bone of contention between the colonial legislatures and
the Board of Trade was over provisions that made certain currency
issues legal tender in the payment of private debts. Colonial proponents typically argued that such provisions were necessary to assist
in maintaining purchasing power. Members of the Board of Trade

were invariably skeptical about allowing the printing of fresh issues of fiat monies. For the most part, however, they willingly approved, invariably after the fact, legislation that gave the currency status as legal tender in the payment of taxes to colonial treasuries plus interest and principal at government loan offices. But the board expressed more serious reservations about provisions making the currency legal tender in the settlement of private debts.

The board had in mind the protection of English exporters who were major creditors in the colonies. Difficulties arose when the colonists attempted to pay debts long overdue with depreciated colonial monies that creditors could not legally refuse in the settlement of accounts. In more technical terms, English creditors were reluctant to assume an exchange risk related to colonial currency; they preferred payment in specie or in bills of exchange drawn in *English* pounds. When a colony's currency depreciated, English exporters understandably complained about being forced to accept the currency at face value rather than at its lower market value. They feared that the losses incurred in converting colonial currencies into other monetary units at unfavorable exchange rates could easily wipe out the profits on mercantile transactions.

The problem was hard to resolve because different colonies had different experiences in regard to currency depreciation. The fluctuations in exchange rates led to swings in the business and political outlook of English exporters, and those movements were, in turn, reflected in the attitudes of members of the Board of Trade. Uncertainties and inconsistencies were the rule, and those conditions ultimately led to a series of breakdowns in communication between the board and various legislative bodies. The board hoped to formulate policies with universal applicability, but differing financial realities in individual colonies made the achievement of that goal impossible. Imperial officials followed a piecemeal approach in negotiating with the colonial legislatures over currency matters. The British were never able to develop a comprehensive or consistent policy. In the 1760s, several promising solutions were rejected because of the fear that greater economic integration might foster too much political unity among the thirteen colonies.[11]

On several occasions, the board formulated restrictive policies to restrain colonial initiatives. South Carolina was among the first colonies to experience uncontrollable depreciation. From 1713 to 1726 the exchange ratio between local pounds and British sterling steadily rose from 1.5:1 to 7:1 and then stabilized. In an effort to maintain price stability, the board ordered the legislature in 1731 to limit the volume of currency in circulation during peacetime. The overall impact was not overly disruptive since the colony was not forced to abandon its existing monetary system. Old currency issues were renewable on their expiration dates, but no new fiat paper could be added to the stock of money. The prohibition achieved its goal by halting the currency's downward spiral, and exchange rates were generally stable thereafter.

On two occasions the Board of Trade induced Parliament to enact new laws specifically related to fiat currency. In the 1730s and 1740s, the rate of depreciation in the four New England colonies accelerated because of excessive emissions and lax taxation. British creditors complained about the deteriorating situation and lobbied the board to take stronger regulatory action. To deal with the problem once and for all, board members persuaded Parliament to pass the Currency Act of 1751. The law affected Rhode Island, Massachusetts, New Hampshire, and Connecticut. It forced them back to a strictly specie standard—back to the monetary system that had prevailed before the emission of fiat monies in the late seventeenth century. All outstanding currency issues were allowed to remain in circulation until their assigned expiration dates, which meant that some paper circulated in New England through the 1760s, but unlike the rules applied in South Carolina, no renewals or rollovers were permitted. Most of the unexpired fiat currency that continued to circulate had originally been issued to borrowers through loan offices and was backed by mortgage assets.

Although imperial officials forced New England to forego the convenience of issuing tax anticipation bills after midcentury, the mildly punitive realignment of financial policy had at least one positive long-term benefit. The Currency Act of 1751 indirectly nurtured the growth of a regional capital market. The new law granted the four legislatures the right to finance deficit budgets through the sale of interest-bearing treasury notes with two-year maturities in peacetime and five-year maturities when at war. The treasury notes, which can be viewed as reasonably analogous to modern U.S. Treasury notes, proved sound investment vehicles and a reliable store of wealth for prosperous citizens willing to finance government debt.

Coinciding with the enactment of the Currency Act of 1751, Parliament agreed to reimburse the four New England colonies for expenses incurred in the recent military campaigns against French Canada. The transfer of funds to the colonies eased the transition to a new monetary regime. Payment arrived mainly in Spanish coin. Massachusetts received the largest share of the reimbursement pot, and the legislature used the £183,000 to retire all of its outstanding tax anticipation bills. After midcentury the New England colonies moved rapidly to a monetary system that emphasized the use of coins as the sole medium of exchange. With fiat currency curtailed, the region was once again in general conformity with British monetary principles.

When the Currency Act of 1751 was under consideration by the Board of Trade, members gave some thought to extending its terms to the other nine colonies as well. English exporters serving the colonial trade were divided, however, and nothing was done in regard to the middle and southern colonies. Virginia was still four years away from emitting its first round of fiat currency so the whole issue was moot in that context. After the volume of currency had been limited in South Carolina in the early 1730s, the situation had stabilized. Depreciation rates in Pennsylvania, New York, New Jersey, Delaware, and Maryland were negligible or quite modest. The appointed overseas agents of those legislatures lobbied hard for an exemption from the harsh restraints. When a sufficient number of London merchants involved in the American trade had concluded that the exchange risk beyond New England was slight, or at least tolerable, members of the Board of Trade acceded to colonial pressures.

Within a decade, however, merchants in London had hardened their views about the propriety of allowing the nine remaining colonies to issue fiat currency with private as well as public legal tender status. In 1755 Virginia emitted its initial series with full legal tender provisions. Since Virginia had the largest bilateral trade with Great Britain, creditors grew increasingly uneasy about their exposure to currency risks. Their fears were accentuated by reports about alleged iniquities in court judgments involving the use of colonial currencies in the settlement of overdue debts owed to foreign merchants. The degree of iniquity was exaggerated, but the situation still compared unfavorably with conditions in New England where all private transactions were recorded strictly on a specie basis and the exchange risk was nonexistent.[12]

In the 1750s and early 1760s the attitude of the London mercantile community about the remaining colonial paper money waxed and waned. Joseph Ernst has argued that fluctuations in mercantile opinion coincided with fluctuations in the colonial balance of trade and market prices for sterling bills of exchange. During years when a given colony's outstanding trade debt became weighty and exchange rates climbed, London merchants feared that colonial courts were likely to settle debts in depreciated paper. At that point the merchants contemplated asking Parliament for a comprehensive ban on all further currency issues. Yet, when economic conditions improved, their views softened. When colonial sales were slack and exchange rates had declined, those same merchants were apt to welcome the news of a new emission of currency because they anticipated economic recovery and a corresponding increase in their exports. According to Ernst, the vacillating opinions of London merchants led to indecision on the part of the Board of Trade about formulating policy on currency emissions outside of New England.

When board members finally decided to take action, they did so in a very heavy-handed manner. The board convinced Parliament to pass the Currency Act of 1764, which forbade the issuance of any new paper that included any legal tender provisions whatsoever, private or public, in the colonies not covered by the 1751 legislation. For all practical purposes, the act threatened to eliminate all fiat currency from North America.

The colonies in question were outraged. First, they objected because their currency issues had been managed responsibly for decades and had experienced no steady depreciation. Second, they saw no logical reason for denying legal tender status in strictly public transactions since English creditors were not affected. The leadership of the colonial legislatures interpreted the Currency Act of 1764 as nothing less than a slap in the face and a challenge to colonial liberties.

During the next several years, elected officials continued to enact legislation authorizing the issuance of new currency with legal tender provisions irrespective of Parliament's stated will. They coerced their respective governors into submitting laws to the Board of Trade for approval by threatening to refuse the appropriation of funds to pay the governors' salaries. The board disallowed some of those acts, but after listening to special pleadings, it agreed to let others stand. Two South Carolina acts and one in New York were overturned because of unacceptable legal tender provisions. Yet in 1770 the board permitted Pennsylvania and New York to emit currency that was legal tender at the government loan office in the first instance and for all public purposes in the latter instance.

This perennially divisive issue was finally settled in 1773, when

Parliament enacted new regulations allowing the continued issuance of paper money with legal tender provisions in all public payments but not in private transactions. British creditors were now protected since they could insist on settlement in specie funds. A similar law in regard to private obligations now applied in the northern, middle, and southern colonies. In the last years before the rebellion, the Board of Trade had finally achieved a limited degree of uniformity. But it took decades of squabbling to achieve that goal, and the deliberations left political leaders on both sides of the Atlantic suspicious about the motivations of their adversaries. The atmosphere of festering distrust and indignation regarding monetary policy carried over into the final political battles leading to American independence.

The issues at stake in the Anglo-American conflict over fiat currency are difficult to assess because the debate raged at two levels. On one hand was the question of formulating sound economic policies; the other issue was the dispute about which political units had the right to exercise sovereign power over monetary policy—Parliament or the colonial legislatures. Members of the Board of Trade were genuinely concerned about the propriety and wisdom of issuing fiat currency, and English creditors had legitimate fears about legal tender provisions and exchange risks. Within the political realm, the two currency acts were clearly part and parcel of a general effort to tighten parliamentary control over colonial affairs. The law applied to New England was not highly controversial because the colonists acknowledged that depreciation had gotten out of hand in the 1740s, and the imposition of greater monetary discipline was justified. But the law enacted in 1764 was much more arbitrary and without just cause. The colonies affected had long records of monetary stability, and they were determined to resist unwarranted parliamentary interference in their domestic affairs.

The net result was that both sides overemphasized the importance of fiat currency as a political and economic issue. The British objections to currency emissions were overdrawn. Fiat paper was, in most instances, a valuable supplement to the stock of foreign coins. Its innovative role was especially justified given the fact that imperial officials had refused to authorize the establishment of an overseas mint to create an indigenous coinage. Occasionally, depreciation rates affected English creditors negatively but the losses incurred were not extensive since, as a rule, colonial courts usually took into account changes in the market value of currencies when adjudicating cases. The potential for losses was greater than the reality. The fears were genuine, however, and pressure from the London mercantile community led members of the Board of Trade and Parliament to attempt to create ironclad protection for creditors involved in overseas trade.

British merchants were not alone in condemning the consequences of currency depreciation. A century later most professional scholars tended to view colonial monetary practices with an even more jaundiced eye. Advocates of the maintenance of the gold standard in their own era—the late nineteenth and early twentieth centuries—the conservatives sought out "lessons" from the past to educate their contemporaries about the dangers of depreciating paper monies. They gleefully foisted their hard-money biases upon their colonial ancestors, recoiling in horror at the course of exchange rates in Carolina and New England before 1750. Those old-fashioned views have been largely repudiated, although they are still reflected in some out-of-date accounts.

Most modern experts have a more positive assessment of the role of fiat currency in the colonial economy, and they no longer decry the consequences of depreciation. Moreover, in the last quarter century before independence, depreciation rates were very low or nonexistent in every colony where new emissions were still permitted. This analysis suggests that political rather than economic considerations reigned supreme in Parliament's confrontation with the colonies in the 1760s and 1770s.

The claim of certain legislatures that private legal tender provisions were necessary to sustain the value of their currencies was a questionable argument not to be taken seriously today. Numerous fiat issues granted legal tender status in public but not in private transactions maintained their purchasing power. The key factor in supporting currency values was the willingness of legislatures to impose the requisite taxes for periodic retirements and the record of loan office customers in amortizing their mortgage debts. The legal tender issue was irrelevant in this context; it was another case of participants in an ongoing economic debate sticking to abstract principles rather than deferring to practical realities and the evidence right before their eyes. Opinion makers on both sides of the Atlantic Ocean engaged in rhetorical excesses.

For years scholars had assumed a linkage between the volume of paper money in circulation and the general level of colonial prices. The research efforts of Robert Craig West and Elmus Wicker have cast doubt on that assumption. Regression analysis of the volume of currency in circulation and the rate of price inflation in four major cities—Boston, Philadelphia, New York, and Charleston—revealed little correlation. Only in Boston between 1720 and 1749, when the volume of paper money in New England was exceedingly large, was there a clear relationship between the two factors. Although several colonies issued thousands of colonial pounds to cover war expenditures during the Seven Years' War (French and Indian), data for the period from 1755 to 1768 reveal generally stable exchange rates.

Fiat currency was not only fairly harmless, contrary to its alleged deficiencies, but its usage also had numerous beneficial effects. Although Spanish coins were often readily available in major port cities and along the Atlantic coast, hard monies flowed more slowly into regions farther inland that were less involved in international trade. As the frontier moved gradually westward during the eighteenth century, the residents of inland markets pressed their elected representatives to create a more convenient monetary system to facilitate routine transactions. Fiat paper was an ideal complement to the limited supply of coinage reaching areas distant from the coastline.

The evidence remains inconclusive, but some data suggest that the issuance of currency was one factor responsible for pulling some provincial economies out of prolonged business recessions. The injection of new monies into the Pennsylvania economy in the 1720s coincided with the revival of commerce at home and abroad. Contemporaries were convinced about the positive effects of the introduction of fiat currency, and virtually all classes and occupational groups unanimously supported its continued issuance. Similar degrees of class solidarity were evident in other colonies as well.[13]

While critics misjudged the alleged negative impact of fiat currency on the colonial economy, its supporters in the colonial assemblies likewise exaggerated its importance to the health of their economies. Paper money was not a necessary ingredient for growth and prosperity over the long haul, and that argument holds even if we concede its role as an economic stimulant in some colonies on certain occasions. Virginia, the most populous colony, functioned successfully without fiat currency for more than a century until emitting its first issue in 1755. The four New England colonies were on a specie standard after midcentury. No convincing evidence indicates that the presence or absence of fiat currency had any more than the slightest effect on per capita income growth in any province. In sum, fiat money was a convenient addition to the monetary stock, but it was by no means essential in promoting economic development.

Although the colonists frequently raised complaints about the lack of monies, there is little reason to believe that the population of British North America suffered much, if at all, from an inadequate monetary system. The colonial economy grew steadily, as measured on both an aggregate and per capita basis for more than roughly a century and a half. During that same era only two other countries were experiencing similarly steady increases in living standards—Holland and England, the mother country. Whatever its disadvantages and inadequacies, the colonial monetary system had the wherewithal to support the highest living standards the world had ever known for a free population totaling more than 1.5 million by the 1770s.

Certainly there were periodic business and agricultural recessions during which it appeared to contemporaries that the absence of monies in the aggregate was at the root of their economic distress. But the real problem almost always lay within another economic sector—either a slump in the demand for local output or a decline in production resulting from bad weather or from diseased or insect-infested crops. Over the decades the colonists held about as high a percentage of their total assets in financial instruments, including coins and currency, as they desired.

In fact, the colonists—just as citizens today—had, as a result of individual choices and preferences, more control over the total supply of monies in their asset portfolios than most probably realized. Few individuals perceived great benefits from holding large monetary balances because, given the absence of commercial banks, they had fewer opportunities to earn interest on accumulated savings. The colonists preferred instead to hold their wealth in land, livestock, inventories, slaves, personal items, and in other productive assets. They shipped coinage overseas to buy goods they could have gone without if building up the stock of money had been a high priority. Generous credit terms on purchases of merchandise were the rule, and the incentives for individuals to remain highly liquid to meet heavy short-term financial commitments were not that great. The colonists used monies, including paper and coinage, mainly as a mechanism to facilitate exchanges for other goods and services rather than as a store of wealth. In a detailed and comprehensive study of the distribution of assets in the estates of thousands of residents of Connecticut in the seventeenth and eighteenth centuries, Jackson T. Main discovered that even relatively wealthy men often died holding few monetary assets.[14]

Since no precise monetary records were kept in the colonial period with regard to coinage, we can only speculate about the size of the money stock. The tendency among economic historians has been to give a fair amount of credence to an estimate offered by Philadelphia merchant Pelatiah Webster in 1791. Webster guessed that the aggregate figure for coin and paper in circulation was $12 million in 1774, or approximately £1.5 sterling per capita for the free white population.[15] Alice Hanson Jones' more recent analysis of personal wealth from a sample of probated estates produced a cash estimate of £2,588,000 sterling for the thirteen colonies in 1774, or £1.40 per capita for free whites. Jones' numbers indicate that cash assets accounted for little more than 2 percent of aggregate physical wealth.[16]

The preceding analysis suggests that the money supply was completely adequate to serve the colonial economy, all contrary statements by contemporaries and subsequent historians notwithstanding. In fact, its adequacy becomes virtually a truism if we refer to the overall performance of the colonial economy. We can safely assert that the monetary system was, on balance, functioning very satisfactorily since the recent literature on comparative rates of economic growth reveals conclusively that the American colonies were advancing more rapidly on both an aggregate and per capita basis than any other economy in the world as early as the second half of the seventeenth century—and by a very wide margin.[17] Without a viable monetary system, the high growth rates experienced in the colonies would not only have been difficult but virtually impossible. The innovative policies of the colonial legislatures—including the issuance of tax anticipation bills and the establishment of government loan offices—helped to shape a financial system conducive to economic expansion.

3

The Credit System

THE EXTENSION of credit was a financial service commonly offered in the colonial era, and its availability and usage increased over the decades. Unfortunately, the absence of commercial banks and other financial institutions has tended to obscure the vital role of the broader credit system in supporting the flow of goods and services through the economy. Nonetheless, the existence of financial facilities to permit merchants to acquire larger and more varied inventories and later to assist their wholesale and retail customers in making purchases was no less critical in this earlier period than after independence. Beyond the mercantile sector, financial services were likewise frequently available to fund intermediate- and long-term investments in land, bonded workers, and an assortment of capital improvements.

In a sharp departure from the practice in Great Britain, where heavy expenditures on military operations led to the accumulation of a substantial national debt during the eighteenth century, provincial governments had no similarly organized capital market to draw on for debt financing. In peacetime the legislatures typically spent very little money—the governor's salary was often the single largest item in the budget. General tax rates at the provincial, county, and township levels were extremely low in comparison with prevailing rates in England—up to 75 percent lower in most years. User fees covered the cost of many government services at the local level. Interest revenues generated from the operations of governmental loan offices, which issued currency against mortgage assets, made substantial contributions to budgets in some colonies.

During military confrontations with Indian tribes and rival European states, colonial legislatures often ran substantial budget deficits. In most instances, provincial leaders decided to monetize their debts through the emission of tax anticipation bills—one of two categories of fiat currency common in this era. Special taxes were then collected to retire the monies. After Parliament banned the further emission of fiat currency in New England after 1751, regional legislatures issued interest-bearing, two-year treasury notes denominated in moderate to large amounts—most commonly one hundred pounds—to assist in financing annual budgets. The successful placement of the treasury notes was a key early event that contributed to the institutional maturation of credit markets in North America after independence. But the embryonic nature of capital markets in colonial urban centers precluded provincial governments from issuing public securities with extended due dates.

Private credit was more important than public credit in colonial America. Because of the seasonal nature of the largely agricultural economy, reliable financing between harvests was necessary to facilitate trade and stimulate economic activity. In the seventeenth century, when population was low and the region's economic performance still unproven, credit facilities were limited. As the economy expanded and savings accumulated during the next century, the availability of capital from private sources at home and abroad rose considerably. In addition, government loan offices periodically offered modest advances to citizens with equity in real property for periods as long as twelve years. Loans with similarly lengthy due dates were invariably unavailable from private sources given the risks involved and the restrictions on interest rates higher than the legal maximum—usually 6 to 8 percent.

The data on credit sources are scattered and incomplete, not only in the colonies but in mother England as well. Scholars have continued to unearth enlightening new information, but the general picture remains fuzzy and unfocused. What can be divulged here about the scope of the overall credit system must, as a consequence, retain a frustratingly unfinished and somewhat disjointed character. Despite reservations about the lack of comprehensiveness, a careful review of the facts is nevertheless worthwhile because the precedents established in the colonial years influenced greatly the development of the financial system in the ensuing national period.

The use of book credit was common in financing the exchange

of goods between producers and consumers through merchant intermediaries.[1] The sums needed to finance working capital, consisting mainly of inventories plus accounts receivable from customers, normally accounted for the bulk of the investment in a mercantile firm. Ambitious merchants generally invested profits in working capital, but they also expected to generate additional financing from outside suppliers of merchandise. Indeed, suppliers of inventories routinely offered financial services in conjunction with their merchandising functions since granting lenient credit terms was a critical factor in promoting sales. Because the pace of business was slow, payment terms frequently stretched over very long periods—measured not merely in months but sometimes in years. (In the modern economy, suppliers typically provide interest-free financing for only thirty to ninety days; firms planning to carry inventories over longer periods of time generally look to commercial banks for additional financing of their working capital requirements.)

The mercantile sector handled a substantial share of the goods produced and sold in the colonies. Estimates of the volume of transactions involving the exchange of goods among the colonists, compiled by historian Carole Shammas, indicate that the typical household in the mid-eighteenth century spent up to one-quarter of its annual income on items transported from beyond provincial borders.[2] Merchants also served as intermediaries in the exchange of local output, although there are no precise estimates of the probable volume of domestic trading activity based on an analysis of reliable statistical data.[3] A reasonable estimate of the overall extent of mercantile activity would place the total volume of goods entering the marketplace somewhere within the range of 30 to 40 percent of gross colonial output during the mid-eighteenth century.

Meanwhile, local exchanges of goods and services occurred regularly between citizens, bypassing completely the mercantile sector. Even in those cases credit services often remained an important factor in facilitating barter transactions since individual transactions between households did not always involve swaps of goods or services of equal monetary value. Many farmers, as a result, kept private account books that recorded exchange transactions in both physical and monetary units and kept running statements of the sums owed to them by neighbors as well as their own reciprocal debts.[4]

It is possible to generate a range of numbers suggesting the

TABLE 3.1
Financial Assets as Components of Net Worth in 1774
(in thousands of pounds sterling)

	Thirteen Colonies	New England	Middle Colonies	Southern Colonies
Net worth	105.7	19.0	29.7	57.0
Financial assets	17.6	3.9	9.4	4.3
Cash	2.7	.3	1.2	1.2
Receivables, good	14.0	3.6	8.1	2.3
Receivables, doubtful	1.0	—	.1	.9
Financial liabilities	21.4	7.1	6.5	7.8
Net financial assets	(3.8)	(3.2)	2.9	(3.5)

Source: Compiled from data in Alice Hanson Jones, *Wealth of a Nation To Be,* (New York: Columbia University Press, 1980), table 5.1, p. 128.

probable investment of funds required to finance colonial trading activities. The approach chosen here focuses on a few select years about which the most reliable quantitative data already exist. For the early 1770s scholars have gathered and analyzed information on several fronts. Alice Hanson Jones' study of wealth and its various components based on a broad sample of estates revealed that the colonists were liable for aggregate debts totaling £21.4 million in 1774.[5] They held financial assets amounting to £17.6 million, with £1 million listed as doubtful accounts. The missing £3.8 million presumably represented debts owed to foreigners, primarily the British.

Most households at every level of wealth had some financial assets and liabilities. Indeed, the higher the level of wealth, the greater the volume of debts a given household was likely to have incurred relative to its holding of financial assets (but not its total wealth). In the wealthiest category, persons with estates over £400 typically had financial liabilities of £112, a total one-quarter greater than their recorded financial assets. The reason for the disparity between purely financial assets and liabilities is readily apparent: the wealthy were considered the best credit risks because of large holdings of land and slaves; therefore, merchants were willing to grant them liberal amounts of credit.

At the lower end of the income scale, households with estates under £100 were typically liable for £14, a total only £1 greater than their financial assets. In addition to cash holdings, small estates frequently listed amounts receivable from transactions involving the exchange of goods with relatives and neighbors plus accrued wages for the performance of various types of labor services. In the latter instance, poorer families were often in the position of extending credit to the wealthier households, which demonstrates that the provision of credit services was a reciprocal arrangement encompassing in one way or another a majority of households. At some point during any given year, an adult male was normally in the position of debtor and creditor—often simultaneously with different parties.

Analyzed from a regional perspective, debt levels per capita in the northern, middle, and southern colonies showed little variation, averaging from £11 to £12 for the free population. On the other hand, the creditor position of households revealed sharp regional differences: amounts receivable ranged from a high of £14 per capita for the free population in the middle colonies, down to £6 in New England, and a low of £5 in the southern colonies. Indeed, inhabitants of the middle colonies were, on balance, net creditors, extending about £1.75 million in credit lines to purchasers of goods and services in the other mainland colonies, the Caribbean, and southern Europe.[6]

In another research project on Anglo-American capital and credit markets, Jacob Price estimated that British mercantile creditors were due approximately £6 million from the colonists on the eve of independence.[7] The data produced by Jones and Price are generally in harmony; together they indicate that British merchant capital provided sufficient funding to support about one-quarter of outstanding colonial debt in the early 1770s. The extension of foreign credit was regionally skewed, however, with up to 80 percent granted to residents of the southern colonies. British merchants loaned up to £7 per capita to the free population in the southern colonies versus only £1.5 to persons in the middle colonies and New England. Jones' numbers indicate that domestic sources funded 85 percent of regional debt in the eight northern colonies, whereas southern lenders financed only 40 percent of the outstanding loans in their region.

The regional differential in levels of foreign debt was a direct consequence of prevailing trading patterns. The southern colonies regularly shipped huge quantities of tobacco, rice, and indigo to British merchants, whereas exports from the northern colonies to Great Britain were limited. Southern customers had available a ready means of settling outstanding debts, namely, the shipment of marketable cash crops to British creditors. Southerners performing mercantile functions provided relatively safe havens for working capital, and they were the recipients of increasingly larger lines of credit. British merchants played a dual role in the southern market because they were involved in financing not only retail customers, an exceedingly large number of small to moderate accounts falling in the range of £20 to £100, but also in financing an increasing number of wholesale accounts with credit lines running as high as £5,000.

In the northern colonies, British merchants almost never transacted business directly with retail customers. Instead, they operated through mercantile intermediaries in the northern ports, extending credit strictly on a wholesale basis. For northern merchants to settle debts incurred in importing British goods, the payment mechanism was less direct. Shipping cargoes of goods directly to London was not a practical alternative since there was little English demand for northern output. As a consequence, merchants had to find markets for their exports in third countries, usually in the Caribbean or southern Europe; or, alternatively, they arranged to provide shipping services for foreign cargoes. To receive compensation, they drew bills of exchange against the funds that foreign buyers held in London and remitted those bills to their British creditors. The creditors, in turn, awaited the final collection of the bills of exchange, which usually came sixty to ninety days after the receipt of the bills and the establishment of a due date. Because of the greater uncertainties linked to multilateral trading patterns and the more convoluted payment mechanism associated with the settlement of northern debts, British merchants granted less credit in that region than in the southern colonies.

Economic historians have produced no breakdowns of how credit was distributed by various asset categories for all thirteen colonies, but Jones did generate data for three middle colonies— New Jersey, Pennsylvania, and Delaware.[8] In those colonies, book credit accounted for more than 70 percent of outstanding receivables; another 25 percent were notes and bonds at interest. Mary Schweitzer's work on Pennsylvania suggests that most formal notes with signatures added represented amounts originally owing on open account that had become past due according to prevailing standards within the local community, whereas bonds at interest usually represented direct cash advances.

Some portion of the more formal debt instruments can be traced back to trading activity. Assuming the following—that similar distributions of financial liabilities could be found in the other ten colonies; that at least one-third of colonial output actually entered the marketplace somewhere within the system, either locally, regionally, or abroad; and that in this era of slow transportation and equally slow communication, working capital turned over no faster than once every twelve to eighteen months—then the sum required to carry the credit associated with the sale of goods and labor services was somewhere around £16 million in the early 1770s. British credit was therefore sufficient to support about one-third of colonial trade debt in the early 1770s. The other two-thirds was financed from working capital investments generated largely from domestic sources—although Dutch, French, Spanish, and other European merchants may have made modest contributions to the American market.

The amount of credit that merchants at home and abroad offered in the colonial market fluctuated over time, with more funds advanced when economic conditions were favorable and credit grantors judged the debt-carrying capacity of borrowers to be relatively high. Despite the ongoing political confrontations between Parliament and the colonial assemblies in the 1760s and early 1770s, British merchants and manufacturers demonstrated enormous confidence in the tobacco economy of the Chesapeake colonies by expanding substantially the volume of credit granted both to retail customers and indigenous wholesalers. Thus, the last two decades of the colonial era might be viewed as unrepresentative of conditions in the credit markets in previous periods. Still, the long-term trend was toward increased allocations of British capital to the North American economy because the volume of Anglo-American trade was steadily growing.

Funds devoted to financing mercantile trade were the largest but not the sole component of the colonial credit structure. Also included were notes, bonds, and outstanding mortgages arising from the funds supplied by individuals with surplus funds for investment, by trustees holding assets supporting widows and orphans, and by governmental loan offices. Many colonists maintained high savings rates and accumulated substantial capital. For the first century after settlement, wealth holders tended to make direct investments in the expansion of physical assets, but over the decades financial instruments, primarily mortgages and bonds with multiple signatures, became popular investment vehicles.[9]

The capital invested in maintaining colonial credit facilities added up to a very tidy sum. In the Jones study of wealth holding, the volume of domestic credit was six times greater than the size of the monetary stock. The £21.4 million of financial liabilities listed in 1774 represented about 70 percent of the thirteen colonies' gross annual output; colonial debt supported about one-fifth of total physical wealth.[10] In comparison with the modern era, private debt was low. For example, private debt in the U.S. economy in the mid-1980s was 20 percent *greater* than the gross national product (GNP), while total debt, including all private and governmental obligations, reached a figure two-thirds higher than GNP and thus provided the financing for approximately half of the total national wealth.

By modern standards, outstanding per capita debt in the late colonial era was relatively modest. On the other hand, the North Atlantic economy that existed two centuries ago functioned without all the monetary and fiscal stabilizers that exist today, and its debt-carrying capacity was consequently much lower. In the eighteenth century, slow communications increased the risks associated with debt. A minor financial crisis in one part of the world could quickly escalate into a full-blown and widespread panic—as happened during the London credit crunch of 1772.

That financial crisis in the early 1770s caused British creditors as a group to reduce quite sharply—although only temporarily—their outstanding lines of credit at home and abroad. In the scramble for liquidity, they "protested" the nonpayment of many sterling bills of exchange drawn against previous shipments of colonial goods, particularly tobacco, and returned them to their overseas endorsers. Their efforts at self-preservation spread the financial pressure across the Atlantic. Some Americans, especially in the southern colonies, had been running large and steadily increasing debit balances for years, and they soon felt the pinch. Colonial debtors complained loudly about the bills returned unpaid as well as the unanticipated demands for quick settlements of outstanding debts since it created genuine hardship for many Americans and in some instances precipitated bankruptcies.

Historian Timothy Breen has argued that resentment ran deep among members of one elite economic class. Great planters in the Chesapeake felt completely betrayed by the allegedly unjustified demands emanating from their long-standing creditor "friends" in London who had willingly carried increasing volumes of debt

year after the year and who had never previously sought to curtail
outstanding accounts so sharply on such short notice. As a result
of their uncompromising demands, the British creditors were un-
masked and revealed to be no less than mercenary and ungrate-
ful merchants—not genuine friends at all. Inexplicably, they had
failed to follow the unwritten code of gentlemanly behavior related
to indebtedness that had arisen over the years within Chesapeake
society and that the planters blindly assumed prevailed throughout the whole North Atlantic economies. Breen concluded that the
lasting effects of the controversy over seemingly arbitrary British
demands for the settlement of colonial accounts is the key factor explaining why so many otherwise cautious southern political leaders
ultimately decided to follow the path of rebellion and independence
in the mid-1770s.[11]

Structure of Mercantile Debt

The entire mercantile community was tied together through chains
of credit that extended from domestic and foreign wholesalers and
manufacturers, who rested at the top of the ladder, down to part-
time storekeepers in remote areas. Individual merchants granted
each other credit facilities for the acquisition of inventories with the
goal of increasing their volume of sales. By modern standards, the
conditions offered were exceedingly generous in terms of due dates
and the interest rates nominally applied to outstanding accounts.
Because goods moved so slowly across water in ships and overland
in small carts along rutted roads, credit terms had to be extended
over long periods. If a large importer in one of the major port cities
sold goods to a smaller merchant in an outlying town, and if that
merchant subsequently resold the same inventory to a storekeeper
in a remote area, it usually took a year or more to settle accounts
under normal conditions.

The process of remitting funds to the original supplier did not
commence until the distant storekeeper had sold the goods to a local
farmer or artisan (probably also on credit), collected payment from
that customer (which might take six months or more), and then
acted to remit funds to the small-town merchant, who was himself
probably one of the lower links along the chain of credit financing. Several more remittances between merchants in progressively
larger trading centers might be necessary before the originating importer received final payment. American buyers generally received

interest-free credit for up to twelve months from British exporters. Since many credit sales to storekeepers in remote areas were strung out over eighteen to twenty-four months, American merchants were often required to invest some of their own capital in financing slow receivables. Some credit lines at home and abroad were rarely drawn down to a zero balance. Instead, debtors made payments in sufficient amounts to reveal an element of good faith and to demonstrate the capacity to service a portion of their outstanding debts and to cover any accrued interest. British merchants typically began adding interest charges to balances outstanding longer than twelve to eighteen months.

Pinpointing the sources of the credit extended by British firms in the colonial market has remained an elusive scholarly undertaking, but historian Jacob Price has identified the origins of a portion of the total investment of British mercantile firms in the American trade.[12] Of a total estimated investment of £4 million in 1774, Price calculated that £1.5 million arose from the equity accounts of owners. A small amount of capital, less than 5 percent, was raised through loans from British banks, which were cautious about making loans to mercantile firms heavily involved in the uncertainties of overseas trade. Perhaps £.5 was generated by "borrowing on bond" from individuals with surplus funds.

The mechanism linked to borrowing on bond is worth a brief description since it was employed in Great Britain and the colonies as one means of raising debt capital for longer periods of time. Bonds in England were notes signed by at least two persons, typically the borrower and an independent guarantor, which contained a heavy penalty for nonpayment—usually double the amount of the actual debt. The terms of repayment were negotiable and could vary with each contract. A bond agreement might specify the minimum length of time that the borrower would have use of the funds, such as three to twelve months, with the lender thereafter having the right to recall the funds at any time upon giving advance notice of a few days.

Many bonds remained outstanding for years, thereby providing borrowers with a reliable source of semipermanent debt capital. The interest rates offered were typically one to two percentage points higher than investors could earn on British government securities, which were considered the safest investment alternative. Transactions could be arranged in any amount, but typically ranged from ten pounds to several hundred pounds. Flexibility was a convenient feature of the call-bond market because borrowers and lenders alike could easily diversify their investments and obligations among numerous parties. The sources of funds were varied as well. They ranged from wealthy persons, who might be seeking a slightly higher return on liquid assets in comparison with yields on government bonds, to others with more modest savings, including numerous widows and the trustees of orphans who wanted a steady income combined with the likely preservation of capital. A plausible analogy can be made between the characteristics associated with the modern certificate of deposit and the English and colonial markets for private recallable bonds.

The British firms granting lines of credit in the colonies had to find some means of covering the cost of the capital employed in extending financial services. The most direct method of accomplishing that end would have been to apply interest charges at compensating rates against the debit accounts of their American customers. But that is not how business was customarily conducted. Instead, compensation for the cost of supplying funds to the Anglo-American credit market was hidden in the price of the goods bought and sold.

Interest rates applied to outstanding accounts were by custom and law usually low, typically zero for routine financing up to twelve months. Revenues to cover the cost of extending such lenient terms had to come from generous profit margins on the merchandise itself. Markups of 50 to 100 percent on every transaction occurring within the mercantile sector from original supplier to ultimate consumer were common. Profits on the merchandise sold had to cover the costs associated with the provision of these financial services: first, the use of the funds for several months while even the most reliable accounts remained outstanding and, second, the losses on accounts never paid because of bankruptcies resulting from fraud, mismanagement, or the sweeping financial panics that periodically engulfed the economy and threatened the solvency of every merchant. Cost accounting techniques were crude or nonexistent. Thus, firms simultaneously selling goods and granting credit were unable to analyze their operations and pinpoint the underlying sources of their profits and losses. Greater knowledge on that score probably would have made no difference in procedures in any event since, in the absence of the availability of commercial bank loans, the performance of merchandising and financing activities were inseparable functions with indivisible, joint costs.

Merchants everywhere were cautious about offering too much credit to new accounts. The fear of incurring losses because of unpaid accounts was the major factor that tended to restrict the extension of credit primarily to individuals personally known, or to third parties specifically recommended by trusted sources. No outside credit reporting agencies kept track of an applicant's credit-worthiness—current income, net worth, or previous credit history. Retail merchants tried to protect themselves by restricting credit to nearby residents and by limiting their exposure on each account to a fairly modest sum throughout most of the year. But the dual goals of restricting accounts receivable to prudent levels and maximizing profits on sales of merchandise often ran at cross-purposes. In heavily agricultural areas, potential buyers frequently ran short of monies, or marketable goods to barter, during the weeks immediately before the upcoming harvest. Merchants and storekeepers either stretched their financial resources to the limit in acquiring additional inventory and carrying a large volume of accounts receivable for an extra month or two, or they lost opportunities for sales at substantial markups.

The expectation of creditors was that their customers' accounts would be paid off annually, or at least drawn down significantly, with payments in monies or with the delivery of recently harvested grains, other cash crops, or marketable goods produced within the household. In most regions the prevailing custom was to convert amounts long past due on open accounts, other than trivial sums, into formal signature notes, with relatives as endorsers and guarantors. Interest accrued thereafter at the maximum legal rate—a rate that varied from 6 percent to as high as 12 percent, depending on the colony and the legislation in force at the time.

Other Credit Facilities

Beyond the mercantile sector, the credit available for financing other types of productive activity was strictly limited. Borrowers seeking mortgage money for the purchase of farmland had few sources of outside funding. Prior to marriage, most youths not only helped their parents at home but also worked as day laborers on neighboring farms for several years. Some of those earnings were saved and used to finance the items needed in their new households.[13] Adult children also expected to receive an inheritance from their fathers—or their widowed mothers—upon marriage. Every young couple hoped to receive free title to a farm, but the resources of parents did not always permit such generous gifts.

In cases where youthful buyers could not come up with the entire purchase price of farmland, they made a down payment and sought additional financing. The purchase of land was frequently financed by the seller, who took back a mortgage contract with a maturity date ranging in length from one to three years, and occasionally as long as five years. (Americans in the early 1980s labeled similar transactions "creative financing," not realizing that such arrangements had been the norm in many areas for centuries.) Many of the formal financial arrangements were among male relatives— fathers, sons, brothers, or in-laws. Even in the absence of a family connection, mortgage holders and mortgagees were typically residents of the same community or county. Owners preferred to negotiate sales to local acquaintances, very often the recently married sons and daughters of families in the local area. Given a reasonable down payment, however, they were sometimes willing to transact business with recent arrivals since the land securing the loan provided safe collateral.

The difficulties associated with financing prospective buyers ranked among the major problems that investors in vast tracts of raw land in frontier areas invariably faced. First, there was the difficulty of policing squatters and preventing them from acquiring legal rights by proclaiming privileges based on the continuous occupation of undisputed property over a period of years. Squatters were not universally unwelcome, of course, because they generally cleared fields and made other improvements, thereby increasing the value of the land for subsequent sale. Meanwhile, their presence in the area was a signal to prospective buyers that the region was desirable for immediate settlement. Moreover, threatened with legal action and the loss of access to the improvements resulting from their own labors, squatters often became legitimate buyers.

Second, land prices had to be set relatively low in order to attract a substantial volume of new settlers in a country where farmland, both developed and undeveloped, was not a particularly scarce commodity. Capital was scarce, however, and outside financing to carry the mortgage debts of farmers moving to untested frontier regions was simply unavailable. As a result, large-scale investors in western land companies, and other investors on a smaller scale, had to provide much of the financing for their own sales contracts. Since the collection of mortgage debts in remote locations was often an unpredictable enterprise, sellers aimed at collecting a substantial down payment up front—at least a third of the purchase price was a reasonable goal. If sellers stipulated the payment of too much money down, however, it discouraged too many legitimate buyers and simultaneously encouraged more squatters to take their chances with the legal system at some future date.

Sellers who provided the financing for purchasers, whether private sales of individual farms or numerous transactions involving hundreds of parcels, often assumed the entire financial burden by stipulating the accrual of no interest at all over the life of the original contract. Mortgages usually expired in less than five years and called for payment in full. A fairly typical payment schedule might call for equal installments over a three-year period. Interest-only mortgages with huge balloon payments due at the end of three to five years became common in rural areas in the nineteenth century. If the mortgagor was granted an extension of time, interest at the permissible legal rate was thereafter generally applied. By and large, however, the cost of financing real estate transactions fell on sellers rather than buyers. Profit margins on the sale of properties had to be high enough to cover the cost of financing sales. The opportunity cost of capital was probably somewhere in the range of 6 to 20 percent per annum, depending on dates and locations.

In other circumstances, a buyer could sometimes arrange to obtain mortgage financing from third parties. The sources of outside monies were generally very wealthy families in the local area. The motivations of lenders usually went beyond strictly a consideration of the financial gains accruing from interest revenues, which were limited by law to a moderate rate. Local elites were occasionally willing to advance surplus funds to a newly formed household purchasing its first farm in order to reinforce the lender's economic, social, and political power within the community. In other instances, the contract might include provisions for the borrower to provide vital labor services at market rates, often as high as three or four shillings per day, at certain critical times of the year, such as planting and harvesting, when labor markets were invariably tight. Sometimes local elites were willing to advance young households the down payment to acquire a farm, with the transaction financed by a note with family members and in-laws as endorsers and guarantors.

Elites with large estates frequently sought a means of guaranteeing a ready pool of day laborers near at hand, and among the strategies employed were the recruitment of reliable tenants on adjacent properties on favorable terms and the granting of modest loans to the new owners of farms in the local area. Paternalism was a strong social force in all regions, north and south, and one of the standard obligations of elites was the provision of limited financial services in their communities, and especially to newly married neighbors trying to become established as independent households since they would henceforth be beholden for favors granted.

Other sources of mortgage money during the eighteenth century were government loan offices, which existed in every colony except Virginia. Since they all issued paper currency in the process of making loans, their operations were discussed in some detail in the previous chapter. Jones' data on the distribution of various types of loans in three middle colonies reveal that mortgages were only about 1 percent of gross personal financial assets. One factor perhaps explaining the low percentage of mortgages in private portfolios was the heavy involvement of government in the mortgage market.

In the colonial era, the performance of mortgage services by governmental agencies had certain characteristics in common with modern markets for second and third mortgages. Loans rarely went to first-time buyers.[14] Instead, loans went to current owners who had already built up sufficient equity in the properties offered as collateral. The colonial legislatures tried to promote a wide geographical distribution of loans within their respective provinces by placing relatively modest limits on how much any citizen could borrow. Few were able to take out loans for much more than one hundred pounds, and the median in most locales was somewhere between thirty and seventy pounds.

Borrowers could use the loan proceeds for any purpose without prior approval. The only qualification to receive an advance was sufficient collateral, normally real estate with a market value at least twice the size of the loan. Most borrowers used the loan proceeds to acquire more land, make improvements on existing properties, or purchase the contract of an indentured servant or slave to provide additional labor services. Loans were amortized with regular payments of interest and principal over the remaining lifetime of a specific issue of fiat currency. Suppose, for example, the legislature authorized an issue of currency scheduled for retirement in ten years and allocated a portion to the loan office. Borrowers obtaining money in the first year after passage had use of the money for the entire period and likely repaid the loan in ten annual installments. If other applicants received funding three years later, however, their loans were outstanding for shorter terms. No matter when a loan was made, its maturity date coincided with the expiration date governing a specific issue of fiat currency.

The interest rates applied to government mortgage loans were typically very low in comparison to the rates for other long-term loans—when such loans could be found, which was almost never. The normal rate was the legal maximum, most commonly 6 to 8 percent per annum. The legislatures did not proscribe different legal rates for loans with differing terms; one maximum rate applied to every loan irrespective of how long it remained outstanding in a given colony. Because arranging loans at rates higher than the official maximum was illegal, private lenders could not be compensated adequately for the extra risks associated with loans having lengthy due dates. Therefore, lenders simply declined to supply funds to the long-term market. Occasionally, borrowers and lenders were able to circumvent the intent of the law by discounting the original proceeds of a loan, thereby raising the effective rate of interest upon repayment of the face amount, but no evidence suggests that the practice was especially widespread.

Since the loan offices conducted a volume business, the interest revenues made a major contribution to the budgets of colonial governments, especially at the provincial level. In some colonies, interest earnings on mortgage loans were the sole source of provincial revenue for decades; Pennsylvania and New Jersey are two prime examples. Since the loans were adequately secured and land prices never suffered a serious decline, but on the contrary rose steadily in settled areas, the losses associated with defaults were few. The judgment of modern financial historians is almost universally favorable about the benefits accruing to both the public and private sectors as an outcome of the credit services provided by government loan offices in the twelve colonies where they operated at various dates during the eighteenth century. The funds they loaned were instrumental in promoting more capital formation, which translated into greater output and higher incomes.

Economic historians have only recently begun to recognize that moderately active informal markets for direct cash loans between individual citizens were also in operation in some localities, and in rural as well as urban areas. What is known about the mechanism of borrowing on bond indicates that colonial practices were reasonably similar to techniques in London. Bonds were two-name paper callable by the lender and carrying interest rates at the colony's legal rate. In Pennsylvania, Schweitzer found that the suppliers of funds were typically older persons who had chosen to convert tangible property into interest-earning financial assets as well as persons entrusted with the investment of monies for the benefit of widows and orphans. Some loans remained outstanding for years, with recall occurring only in response to some specific family event such as the death of a lender, a widow's remarriage, or a youth's coming of age. Lenders tended to spread risks through diversification. The maximum loaned to any one borrower was normally no more than ten pounds, an amount no greater than one-fifth the annual income for the average adult male. Borrowers could be found in every occupational category—not only merchants seeking working capital but farmers and artisans as well.[15]

Conclusion

The credit system that served the colonial economy was somewhat peculiar in terms of its extremely decentralized structure. The system was institutionally immature, yet it managed to provide a reasonably adequate level of financial services. Indeed, despite the defects, its effectiveness was sufficient to support very high rates of aggregate growth for a premodern economy—an economy spurred on by a rapidly increasing population, plus income levels per capita for the free population which were the highest, or very near the highest, in the world during the eighteenth century.

Those achievements were realized despite the fact that financial intermediaries were almost completely absent in the colonies. No institutions existed to gather surplus funds from a diverse group of savers and to channel those monies to borrowers seeking additional capital for investment projects. Loans of all varieties were negotiated directly between savers and lenders, with the only exception being instances when trustees for orphans and widows managed small portfolios consisting primarily of two-name, recallable bonds in modest amounts plus a few short-term mortgages. Communities were still small enough and personal networks broad enough that search costs for lenders seeking fairly safe havens for their funds and for borrowers seeking credit facilities were not prohibitively high. Undoubtedly, some potentially profitable projects failed to get off the ground because of inaccessible financing, but the volume of thwarted ventures was less than might be anticipated given the institutional underdevelopment of financial markets.

Capital flows from Great Britain alleviated somewhat the short-age of loanable funds in the colonies. British capital was invested primarily in financing trade debt, with a disproportionate share of credit facilities allocated to the southern colonies because of the active bilateral trade between the tobacco and rice colonies and the mother country. Although the terms of repayment stipulated the settlement of individual accounts every twelve to eighteen months, in actuality the trade debts were constantly rolled over and thus became a semipermanent investment of British capital in sustaining the purchasing power of wholesale and retail customers in the colonies. When creditors called home the funds temporarily during the London credit crunch of 1772, their withdrawal from the colonial economy caused hardships for many borrowers who, lulled into ignoring the potentially volatile nature of mercantile credit, had become accustomed over the years to receiving generous and continuous financing for their purchases of foreign goods.

As a result of the inflow of British capital, the colonists were able to direct more of their own savings into developing the pro-ductivity of the abundant physical resources of North America and into the acquisition of more labor resources through purchasing the contracts of indentured servants and slaves. Alice Hanson Jones' data suggest that foreign capital financed up to perhaps 6 percent of the colonies' total physical wealth in the 1770s, a measurement that includes servants and slaves.

Meanwhile, domestic private sources of loanable funds were augmented in every colony but Virginia by the creation of gov-ernment loan offices that granted collateralized real estate loans against accumulated equity in existing properties. The loan offices served dual functions: providing a mechanism for the emission of paper currency to supplement the circulating coinage, while simul-taneously offering lending facilities to finance intermediate- and long-term investments for the expansion of productive capacity over fixed terms ranging up to a dozen years at moderate interest rates. Access to mortgage loans was generally widespread among property owners since fairly modest loan limits were placed on individual borrowers irrespective of accumulated wealth. In that way govern-ment offered services in one important financial market where the private sector had failed to respond because of the perceived risks associated with holding portfolios of financial assets with lengthy maturity dates. Private investors who sought interest income from financial assets over longer periods were more inclined to acquire a diversified portfolio of small personal bonds from numerous borrowers that were recallable upon demand and therefore served as highly liquid assets. The loan offices were notable too because they were formal institutions managed by a small bureaucracy of salaried workers and thus represented a departure from the prevailing pattern of highly personalized credit transactions.

The informality and personal character of the financial system belied its unusual degree of responsiveness to the requirements of the free population of North America during the colonial era. In the national period which lay ahead, citizens mobilized risk capital and in some cases passed new legislation that supported the creation of more formally organized, specialized institutions to complement the older system based mainly on personal negotiations among the suppliers and users of credit facilities. Despite a myriad of institutional innovations in the nineteenth century, Americans by and large sought to preserve much of the older heritage of communal interdependence and personal contact between savers and borrowers. As a consequence, they favored an atomized structure for the performance of financial services, a system subject to local control as much as possible. Such a system had served the colonies well for more than 150 years and had produced a general harmony of interests between debtors and creditors who viewed each other as playing vital and legitimate roles in the expansion of the general economy and the creation of personal wealth.

Competition in offering and receiving financial services was overwhelmingly among individuals acting alone or operating in unincorporated partnerships; institutions with specific charters and special privileges granted by governmental units did not exist. Law and legislation favored no group of debtors or creditors over other citizens in the financial marketplace. Government loan offices had a de facto monopoly over lending in the long-term market; but since no competitors from the private sector expressed any eagerness to enter that market, few critics rose to challenge the legitimacy of governmental involvement. In retrospect, it was probably among the least contentious periods in American financial history. The patterns of everyday life in North America were soon reshaped—first by the War for Independence and its aftermath, and second by new technology, new energy sources, and new transportation networks.

In combination, they transformed enormously and irrevocably the structure of farming, manufacturing, and commerce during the first half of the nineteenth century. The structure of the financial services sector was altered as well; indeed, the scale and sophistication of its operations underwent an equally dramatic revolution.

4

Colonial Financial Services

Before moving into the confederation and national periods, we should pause to make a broad assessment of the performance of the financial services sector during the colonial era. Much of what transpired in the eighteenth century had future repercussions. In many instances of historical analysis, insights into the workings of earlier societies are revealed by focusing not merely on the evidence at hand but also by identifying institutional patterns notably absent. For example, colonial political and economic elites never had cause to split into competing ideological factions regarding irreconcilable disputes about the structure of the financial system, as occurred soon after independence. For the most part, harmony reigned. Since provincial governments lacked the power to grant corporate charters to financial institutions, or any business enterprise for that matter, controversies surrounding the granting of special rights to a limited number of privileged citizens rarely arose as a potentially divisive political issue. The few documented efforts to create private land and specie banks in Massachusetts and Connecticut were quashed because of legal challenges based on British statutes. Some debates in the colonial legislatures generated a great deal of rhetorical heat, but the most serious conflicts over financial issues were with imperial officials.

All supplements to the money stock in the form of paper monies resulted from the direct intervention of legislative bodies. Private bankers played no significant role in the economy. Whereas virtually every other type of economic activity—whether on farms, in artisan shops, or in mercantile firms—was conducted solely within the parameters of private enterprise, the privatization of money and banking was a moot issue, an idea largely irrelevant and rarely confronted in colonial society. In that respect this period in American financial history differs substantially from events during the last two centuries.

One vital tenet of the colonial heritage was that every citizen with sufficient capital and an inclination toward the performance of financial services should always have a fair and equal chance of entering the market as a supplier of loanable funds. That factor goes far in explaining why the future United States ended up with an institutional hodgepodge within its commercial banking sector as exemplified by the establishment of not just thousands— but literally tens of thousands—of small, locally owned, and locally managed financial institutions. The absence of a feudal past had its impact on the realm of finance as well as on other elements of American society. A small group of extremely wealthy families never dominated the American financial services sector as happened so often in contemporary Europe. The colonial heritage was radically different because of the heavy involvement of provincial governments, and that factor encouraged the emerging nation to create and nourish an extremely atomized institutional structure. Colonial traditions led as well to the uncompromising desire of citizens for widespread participation in routine commercial banking services above and beyond all other considerations of soundness and prudence—and at all costs, including perennial threats to the underlying safety of the nation's currency and deposits from 1815 until regulatory reform in the mid-1930s and then again with the deregulation movement in the 1980s. Between 1780 and 1815—the last year covered in this volume—commercial banks numbered only in the hundreds, not the thousands. As a rule, they were exceptionally safe institutions.

Through their direct involvement in the market for mortgage loans, provincial governments demonstrated a strong commitment to the principle of equal opportunity for all current property holders. The acts authorizing the issuance of paper money by loan offices reflected prevailing attitudes about the justice of allowing a cross section of citizens to reap a share of the anticipated benefits. The mechanisms for making loans were not strictly egalitarian in any colony, but the rules and procedures did guarantee that a small group of very wealthy and influential families would be unable to exercise sufficient power to lay claim to most of the funds in the loan pool and exclude thereby voters with more modest property holdings.

In terms of maintaining the safety of financial assets, the overall record was much better than critics have alleged. Admittedly, persons desiring to store wealth in financial assets had few choices other than gold or silver—whether coins, bullion, or crafted jewelry and tableware—if their goal was absolute protection from the threat of lost purchasing power over extended periods of time. The holders of fiat currencies issued by Maryland, Pennsylvania, New Jersey, and New York were also safe from long-term depreciation. But the evidence arising from samples of probated estates in every region indicates that few individuals, including the very rich, chose to hold more than perhaps 2 to 3 percent of total wealth in any combination of coin and currency. All monies were sterile assets, which generated no current income, and coins and currencies therefore were not widely held by members of any occupational group.[1] Wealth holders seeking a safe haven for capital plus a return on their investment put their funds in real estate properties, such as developed farmland or urban rental housing, and assumed the role of landlord. Another investment alternative for savers was the personal bond, a debt instrument affixed with the signatures of several endorsers residing in the local area. The degree of safety was linked to the soundness and integrity of creditors and endorsers, the diversity of names in the loan portfolio, and the efficiency of the legal system as a collection agency for loans past due. Since most bonds were drawn for modest amounts, usually less than twenty pounds, they were normally safe vehicles for wealth holders who gave the preservation of capital a high priority.

All allegations about the absence of safety in colonial finance are related to the poor record of certain issues of fiat currency in specific colonies. In South and North Carolina before 1726 and in New England before 1750, numerous issues suffered heavy depreciation. Those monies were extremely unsafe as a store of value over the long run. Rapid depreciation overnight was not a threat; rather, the decline was steady and predictable over a period of months or even years in most cases. It remains doubtful whether citizens ever held large sums of depreciating currencies for any more than short periods of time.

Households concerned about safety normally had the option of swapping currency for specie or other tangible property. Reasonably active markets for depreciating currencies usually remained in operation at varying rates of exchange. While some currency issues were clearly unsafe as long-term stores of value, the risk was fairly remote that a given household that managed its finances sensibly would suffer an inordinately huge loss of purchasing power and an appreciable decline in net worth from holding monetary assets. Meanwhile, all currency issues, including those undergoing steady depreciation, made a valuable contribution to the economy by serving as a medium of exchange for the general population.

One group that can be identified as potential sufferers from the effects of depreciating monies were creditors in colonies where the currency had been designated as legal tender in the payment of private as well as public debts. Merchants who had extended trade credit to customers were the most vulnerable economic group; and the longer accounts remained outstanding, the more their vulnerability increased. If merchants were forced to accept devalued monies in the settlement of long overdue accounts, currency losses could override their initial profit margins. Under those conditions, it is reasonable to assume that members of the mercantile class would have unanimously opposed the issuance of paper monies with strong legal tender provisions in debates within the colonial assemblies. Yet, surprisingly, that was not their usual outlook. Some merchants were in opposition, of course, but the majority supported currency legislation designed to stimulate the local economy. Presumably, they thought mainly about the likelihood of higher sales generated from an expanded volume of trade, and they were reasonably confident that most judges and juries would take into account the shifting market values of currencies in any disputed claim related to the repayment of outstanding debts. Some merchants, realizing that their debt and credit balances were roughly offsetting during the course of a year, may have concluded that they had about as much to gain as lose from any volatility in currency values and that the net impact of depreciation would not be detrimental to their interests.

British merchants were most vulnerable to losses linked to depreciating currencies. For them, the safety factor was a more crucial issue since debt settlement often extended over several years, by which time major changes in currency values might have taken place. During the eighteenth century, they were progressively disinclined to assume the currency risks associated with conducting business in certain colonies. On the basis of exaggerated stories circulating in London in the early 1760s regarding some allegedly unfair settlements of long-standing debts, they eventually lost confidence in the willingness of colonial courts to take into account the market value of local currencies vis-à-vis specie and sterling bills of exchange. Moreover, by the late colonial era, British merchants had witnessed an increase in their exposure to currency risks because of the expanded volume of colonial trade and their collective decision to liberalize credit lines.

The irony is that, despite British fears, the safety record of every currency issue emitted in the colonies after midcentury was extremely good. Although exchange rates fluctuated over the years, none of the fiat paper emitted in the middle and southern colonies ever fell into an irreversible tailspin. The issues retained most of their purchasing power over the long run, and they served as a viable store of value. This positive assessment of the safety factor contradicts earlier historical depictions of the colonies as territories where monetary management was highly irresponsible. Uncontrollable depreciation was the exception, not the rule, in most regions. The older myth was fueled by monetary historians who were predisposed to believe the worst and who repeatedly cited atypical events and exaggerated their significance. The drama of financial failure has always had more power to draw the attention of historians and their reading public than the more mundane success stories.

Earlier accounts were also undoubtedly colored by subsequent events during the War for Independence, when the national Congress issued millions of dollars in paper monies that steadily depreciated and eventually lost all value. On the basis of monetary developments during wartime, some historians may have unjustifiably made retroactive judgments about the universal quality of the paper money issued during the previous three quarters of the eighteenth century. Ideological biases and the failure to pursue more thorough research on monetary systems are two factors that go far in explaining why colonial financial history has been so poorly understood until recently.

The bad reputation of Continental currency clearly made a powerfully negative impact on contemporaries as well. After ratification of the Constitution, state governments halted completely the issuance of fiat currency.[2] One legacy of the colonial past was summarily rejected—a curious outcome given the drawn-out battles that the assemblies had waged with Parliament over the right to provide that vital financial service under the terms and conditions of their choosing. In the newly organized state governments, the legislatures authorized chartered commercial banks to assume this quasi-public function. Ironically, the issuance of currency by private firms was one mechanism for supplementing the metallic money stock that had been recognized as legitimate for decades by British theorists and public officials.

Measured by the criterion of the availability of a full range of financial services, the colonial economy was deficient by modern standards. Without organized financial institutions, citizens had no convenient mechanism for the steady accumulation of monetary assets at compounded interest over long periods of time. The availability of personal loans for a myriad of purposes was more limited than today. The potential purchasers of virtually every item up for sale—including consumer goods, farm equipment and supplies, bonded workers, and real estate—had to rely primarily on the willingness and ability of sellers to provide a goodly portion of the required financing. The services available to borrowers seeking large sums of monies for permanent financing over longer periods were severely limited. Capital markets to generate equity investments did not exist. Provincial governments had no access to long-term debt financing, although the New England legislatures made some headway by successfully placing treasury notes with two-year maturities and even five years in some instances.

In terms of facilitating the daily exchange of routine goods and services among its citizenry, the colonial monetary system was by no means exemplary; but its shortcomings were probably less severe than, for example, in mother England. Where hard money was the normal medium of exchange, Spanish coins were most common. Surviving coinage records from mints in Mexico and other Latin American locations suggest that silver coins in a wide range of low to intermediate denominations were steadily produced and regularly flowed into the English colonies in North America. By comparison, the English masses suffered throughout the eighteenth century from a grossly inadequate volume of silver coins, which arose as a result of Parliament's ill-advised decision to adopt an unrealistic coinage ratio at the national mint. The colonists were also better served because of the introduction of supplemental paper monies into their economies. Those fiat currencies not only increased the aggregate volume of monies in circulation but their denominational structure included numerous bills at the lower end of the scale. The latter feature enhanced their usefulness as a medium of exchange and thus enhanced the overall quality of transactions services in the colonial economy.

The effort to assess the degree of efficiency displayed in the operation of colonial financial markets produces a somewhat paradoxical conclusion, especially in light of the general tone of the previous discussion. Given the absence of an organized institutional framework, the colonial financial system appears to have functioned surprisingly well. Population was sufficiently low and market activity sufficiently great so that many opportunities arose for personal interaction between savers and borrowers even without the participation of active intermediaries. Adequate sources of funding existed for personal consumption and for investments in inventories and other productive assets for periods up to one or two years.

The colonies experienced steady expansion in terms of both extensive and per capita income growth, which suggests that financial constraints were not serious enough to retard material progress. Persons genuinely in need of the financing to expand their productive bases were, for the most part, able to gain access to those funds on reasonable terms. Given the low level of agricultural skills and artisan technology as well as the crudeness of the inland transportation system, the colonial financial system merits high marks. Characterized by a high degree of decentralization and informal market activity, the system had the ability to marshall the financial resources at its disposal and to channel them into the hands of individuals, households, and business enterprises with the ambition and ability to make good use of them.

Part II

War and Confederation

❖ ❖ ❖

5

Wartime Finance

THE WAR FOR Independence, hard fought during the years from 1775 to 1781, with some military expenditures continuing until the signing of the Treaty of Paris with Great Britain in 1783, was among the most costly in American history. Historian E. James Ferguson estimated the total costs borne by American citizens at roughly $165 million specie.[1] Viewed in the context of one critical statistical measurement, namely total military expenditures as a percentage of GNP, the costs incurred during the War for Independence were roughly on a par with those incurred by the American population in fighting the Civil War and World War I. In all three major engagements, U.S. citizens diverted from 15 to 20 percent of their total output of goods and services to support military operations.[2] While those earlier wars were extremely costly, none came close to matching the staggering diversion of resources devoted to fighting World War II, a global battle on two fronts that absorbed more than two-fifths of national output during the early 1940s. With that lone exception, the War for Independence ranks as the equal of any other military conflict in terms of the economic and financial demands placed upon citizens. An analysis of the financing of the War for Independence and the management of the overhanging debt is crucial to understanding the development of the American financial system. The choices made during the turbulent period from 1775 through the early years of the rejuvenated national government under the new Constitution had a lasting impact on virtually every segment of the financial services markets.

One of the main alterations came in the mechanism for the

issuance of currency. After the war, the legislative branch of government at both the federal and state levels relinquished most of its previously exclusive jurisdiction over the size and composition of the money stock; those powers passed into the hands of chartered financial institutions. During the colonial era, those functions had fallen entirely within the domain of government; but starting in the 1780s and accelerating in the 1790s, monetary responsibilities were rapidly being transferred to commercial banks operating mainly within the private sector. Governments frequently supplied a share of the capital to chartered institutions, but management was firmly in the hands of private citizens rather than public officials. The federal government retained exclusive power over the mint, but its output of high-value specie coins was limited. U.S. coinage was not an important factor in bolstering the size of the money stock until the discovery of large gold and silver deposits in the western states after 1849.[3]

In examining the evolution of the organizational structure of the American economic system, the shift toward private control and responsibility within the realm of monetary affairs represents perhaps the foremost instance of the privatization of a formerly public function in American history. Not until the creation of the Federal Reserve System in 1913 did governmental representatives again play a prominent role in shaping the nation's monetary policy.

The War for Independence was not only costly in terms of aggregate expenditures relative to existing economic resources, but, in addition, its financing placed a heavy tax burden on the population. Most historical accounts of the war years leave the impression that the military effort was poorly financed because of the repeated failure of the states to meet congressional requests for voluntary contributions and, secondly, because at the end of the war both the federal government and individual states were left with millions of dollars in outstanding debts. In several states, and most prominently at the national level, governments generated insufficient revenues in the 1780s to pay the interest on their outstanding obligations. As a result, the interest accrued, thereby increasing the aggregate debt outstanding and compounding the overall financial difficulties. Most professional historians are familiar, at least in a general sense, with the financial complications facing the revolutionary generation, if for no other reason than because Charles Beard and his subsequent critics placed debt ownership at the center of their analysis of the ratification process.

Traditional beliefs about the lack of ongoing financial support for military operations require radical revision. In truth, the public supported the troops fighting for American independence to an extraordinary degree. Why then does the opposite assessment persist? The main difficulties leading to false perceptions have been twofold. First, historians failed to take into account fully the precedents established in earlier colonial wars, particularly financial policies during the Seven Years' War. Second, scholars neglected to establish the proper comparative framework before making evaluations of financial performance during the military crisis. Most modern governments finance wartime expenditures through long-term borrowing in capital markets rather than through current taxes.

Calculating the percentage of wartime financing generated from current taxes versus the percentage generated through governmental borrowing reveals some telling facts. During the course of the two world wars fought in the twentieth century, current taxes paid for less than one-quarter of all military expenditures; the U.S. government raised most of the necessary funds through the sale of bonds to individuals and financial institutions. During the Civil War, Union forces received approximately one-third of their financial support from current tax revenues and the other two-thirds from the sale of bonds.

The financial situation during the War for Independence was the obverse of circumstances prevailing in the 1860s. The American public in the late 1770s and early 1780s provided current funding for at least two-thirds of the costs incurred in the campaign against British forces; only one-third, and perhaps as little as one-quarter, of the monies expended arose from debts contracted at home and abroad. Breaking down the debt figures even further, little more than 10 percent came from the sale of bonds in capital markets, and at least half of those placements were overseas.

The main reason that the critical statistic revealing the preponderant role of taxation in financing the war has remained obscure, or has been downplayed generally, lies in the historiography of the independence era. For years financial scholars were unwilling to recognize the legitimacy of certain techniques of taxation and funding employed widely during colonial times, and especially in military crises. From the perspective of the nineteenth and early twentieth centuries, those techniques appeared unorthodox and financially irresponsible to economic and financial historians who had been trained to revere the maintenance of unfluctuating currency values tied to gold and to abhor the printing of fiat monies regardless of circumstances. Because the newly independent states and the newly formed Congress typically resorted to the printing of uncollateralized fiat monies to cover escalating military expenses, orthodox financial historians decried their lack of fiscal and monetary responsibility.

In the colonial era, legislators had not considered their financial policies to be deficient in practice or in principle. The monies issued by provincial governments were retired through special tax assessments or, in some colonies before 1750, currencies were simply allowed to depreciate steadily and irreversibly. In either case, the economic effect was virtually the same: the tax burden fell on citizens who used paper money to meet tax obligations to the provincial government, or it fell on persons who held paper money for short periods of time between transactions while its value progressively declined vis-à-vis other mediums of exchange. The War for Independence was financed mainly through the latter alternative—the taxation of the whole population via the depreciation of federal and state currencies, which were placed into circulation in vast sums during the war years to meet pressing military demands.

Seven Years' War

Examining the financial history of the Seven Years' War—the only other previous military campaign that had engaged the resources of all the mainland colonies—leads to a fuller comprehension of events in the 1770s and 1780s. The American phase of the conflict, called the French and Indian War by contemporaries in North America, lasted from 1755 to 1760. The war resulted in the capture and British acquisition of Canada and generally quashed the French dream of a vast colonial empire in the western hemisphere.

The costs of various military campaigns in the 1750s were borne partially by the colonial assemblies and partially by Parliament, which justified the expenditure of monies collected from British taxpayers as the unavoidable cost of expanding its rapidly growing global empire. The British sent thousands of troops, plus an accompanying corps of officers, across the Atlantic Ocean; and Parliament continued to meet, in specie coins no less, their regular salaries. The colonies were asked to bear a healthy share of the material and human burdens as well. They raised local military companies to complement the British regulars and commissioned some officers below the rank of general as well. George Washington began his military career as a major in the colonial militia and soon received promotion to colonel, the highest American rank beneath British generals.

The assemblies were induced to provide substantial manpower and financing for the war effort after Parliament promised to reimburse the colonies for a portion of the costs that each incurred in raising and equipping local troops. In the final accounting, colonial expenditures were placed at £2.5 million sterling, and Parliament made reimbursements of roughly £1 million, or just more than 40 percent of the combined total. The net burden assumed by the colonies amounted to £1.5 million, which translated into about £1.2 per capita for the free population in 1760. During the five years of the conflict, the net cost per citizen represented about 3 percent of annual income.

Some colonial governments bore a disproportionate share of the military costs. Massachusetts, for example, absorbed almost one-third of net colonial expenses. Neighbor Connecticut got off lightly, paying less than 2 percent of the colonial total after receiving reimbursements from Parliament that covered nearly 90 percent of the monies the colony had expended in the common military effort. In the six colonies where citizens bore the greatest burden—Massachusetts, South Carolina, New Jersey, Virginia, New York, and Pennsylvania—the impact on per capita incomes was about 5 percent per annum, a figure no more than one-third of the drain associated with the War for Independence.

The thirteen colonies were highly innovative and exceedingly successful in handling the financing of wartime expenditures. The methods adopted varied from location to location, and the precedents each colony established affected greatly the financial policies it followed in the more tumultuous 1770s and 1780s.

The New England colonies, which were banned from issuing fiat currency after midcentury, were the first American political units to develop local markets for public debt obligations. Their legislatures borrowed specie directly from individuals to cover periodic budget deficits. In the eighteenth century, those debt instruments were called treasury notes. They bore interest at the legal maximum, with maturity dates ranging up to two years during peacetime. (Today, government debts with intermediate maturities—more than six months and less than five years—are designated *notes,* a term used to distinguish them from shorter term *bills* and

TABLE 5.1
Colonial Contributions to the Seven Years' War
(columns 1 and 3 in thousands of pounds sterling)

	Amounts Expended	Percent of Total	Reimbursed by Parliament	Percent Reimbursed	Net Cost Per Capita[a]
Massachusetts	818	31.9	352	43	2.05
South Carolina	91	3.5	10	11	2.00
New Jersey	204	8.0	51	25	1.65
Virginia	385	15.0	99	26	1.35
New York	291	11.3	139	48	1.30
Pennsylvania	313	12.2	75	24	1.30
Rhode Island	81	3.2	51	63	.70
Maryland	39	1.5	—	—	.40
Georgia	2	.1	—	—	.35
Connecticut	259	10.1	232	90	.20
New Hampshire	53	2.1	47	89	.20
North Carolina	31	1.2	11	35	.15
Total	2,567	100.0	1,067	42	1.18

Source: Compiled from data in Elmus Wicker, "Colonial Monetary Standards Contrasted: Evidence from the Seven Years' War," *Journal of Economic History* (1985), table 3, p. 877. Per capita figures calculated by author.

[a] For free population in 1760. Pounds in last column are in decimal units, not shillings and pence.

longer term *bonds.*) The New England assemblies were punctual in redeeming their outstanding certificates, but they often rolled them over and thus maintained a modest level of public debt. Connecticut and Massachusetts had larger populations than New Hampshire and Rhode Island, and the two leading provinces incurred more than 85 percent of the region's military expenses. Massachusetts alone accounted for two-thirds of the expenditures in New England, and Boston emerged as the center of a small but active market for intermediate-term government loans. Massachusetts treasury certificates bore interest at 6 percent per annum, and the sum outstanding reached £700,000 colonial in 1760.[4]

The most remarkable aspect of Massachusetts financial policy during this period is that the assembly adopted a tax program designed to discharge a huge percentage of the public debt arising from the war within five years of its termination. The Currency Act of 1751 had stipulated that all legislation authorizing governmental issues of treasury notes include a rigid schedule of taxation designed to sink the outstanding debt within two years. Because of the military emergency, Parliament agreed to extend the allowable period for debt retirement by three additional years. To meet those stringent requirements, provincial tax rates, which had been low for decades, were raised to extraordinary heights during the late 1750s. Property and estate taxes in Boston, for example, were set at two-thirds of the assessed value—a levy several times higher than rates normally prevailing on real properties in England itself, where levies were normally the highest in Europe. Annual revenues climbed from under £10,000 in the 1740s to an average of £60,000 from 1756 to 1760 in Massachusetts. Excluding the reimbursement of £352,000 from Parliament, which was systematically applied to debt reduction, the colony had raised sufficient tax revenues by 1763 to cover about two-thirds of that portion of wartime expenses, £466,000 sterling, for which it was singularly responsible. Because of the strict terms of the 1751 currency act, which were harsh even after wartime liberalization, Massachusetts citizens carried an extremely heavy burden of taxation during the war and for several years thereafter.

Contemporary governments in Europe, including Great Britain, rarely generated sufficient tax revenues to cover even a portion of the expenses associated with any major war in less than twenty years. Typically, they paid only the interest due and never made any significant dent in the principal outstanding. The accomplishments of Massachusetts, therefore, were remarkable indeed. Rather than holding the line on current tax rates, allowing their public debt to skyrocket, and then reducing the principal gradually over time, which was the favored policy of most political units in the eighteenth century—and in almost every other era for that matter—the citizens of Massachusetts bore an uncharacteristically heavy tax burden during most of the decade from 1755 to 1765. After retiring about half of the outstanding principal in less than five years, citizens were happy to return as quickly as possible to the previous norm of low provincial taxation.

Although financial requirements under the rigid terms of the Currency Act of 1751 had been exceedingly demanding, political leaders in Massachusetts could look with great pride to their ability to extinguish so rapidly so much of the public debt arising during the French and Indian War. Their successes in overcoming those financial difficulties provided the model—however unrealistic—for the next generation of political leaders in the turbulent 1780s.

In colonies beyond New England, where the issuance of paper money was still permitted by Parliament, the assemblies met the demands for immediate funding in different ways. They emitted thousands of pounds of fiat currency to pay for pressing military expenses. Later the assemblies authorized special taxes to redeem portions of the newly issued paper. Meanwhile, Parliamentary reimbursements were routinely applied to currency retirement. Since all but South Carolina were exempt from parliamentary oversight, most felt little obligation to draft a comprehensive fiscal plan designed to collect sufficient tax revenues to cover their respective military expenditures within five to ten years.

South Carolina was a special case. The rules regulating its financial operations dated back to an earlier period when depreciation had been rampant. Like the New England colonies, it was required to toe the line and proceed deliberately with the retirement of all supplementary currencies issued above the tight monetary ceiling imposed in 1731. Every legislative act authorizing the issuance of new paper to finance the war had to include accompanying provisions laying out the specifics of a tax program aimed at complete retirement within five years. Because the reimbursement granted by Parliament covered only about 10 percent of the colony's military expenses, South Carolina's citizens had to endure high tax rates for several years in the late 1750s and early 1760s to meet the dictates of the law. By 1765 the colony had retired the whole amount outstanding; taxes had covered war expenditures totaling more than £80,000 sterling, or about £2 per capita for the free population.

Even without the mandate of English law, several colonies voluntarily enacted revenue programs calling for vigorous taxation during and immediately after the war. Virginia and Pennsylvania ranked second and third, respectively, behind Massachusetts in terms of aggregate defense spending, and each met its financial obligations diligently. By 1763 both colonies had collected sufficient revenues to retire about half of the fiat currency issued during the war years, and they had enacted tax programs that promised steady retirements of the outstanding paper during the next five to ten years. Neither Virginia nor Pennsylvania phased out its war-related paper liabilities as rapidly as South Carolina or Massachusetts, but they could nonetheless point to a record of fiscal responsibility that compared very favorably with contemporary governments in western Europe.

Two other colonies, New York and New Jersey, which in combination accounted for about one-fifth of colonial military expenditures, achieved respectable, but less spectacular, reductions in their domestic debt. In New York the financial burden was greatly eased after Parliament sent funds to cover almost half of the colony's military costs. By the mid-1760s New York had retired about one-quarter of the paper for which it was solely responsible. In 1766 the assembly implemented a tax program to reduce the sums outstanding during the next half decade. New Jersey was the most dilatory colony regarding the retirement of its wartime issues. The colony spent just over £200,000 sterling on defense, yet Parliament's reimbursements met only one-quarter of that figure. At the end of the war, New Jersey reported outstanding debts totaling £181,000, the highest level of war indebtedness on the mainland. Not only had New Jersey taxpayers failed to make inroads on the retirement of the paper issued during the wartime emergency, they had emitted another £25,000 or so in currency for other unspecified purposes. Nonetheless, by 1765 the assembly had adopted a revenue program that promised to redeem most of the outstanding paper slowly but steadily during the next fifteen years.

The fiscal programs pursued in New Jersey and New York were less stringent than in the other leading colonies with large populations. Still, measured by contemporary standards in Europe, their legislatures pursued generally sound policies in the management of their debt obligations. The ultimate proof that currency holders had confidence in the determination of both colonial assemblies to meet their retirement obligations on a regular schedule was the fact that their respective fiat monies held their value relative to specie and sterling bills of exchange. The exchange rates for their monies may have fluctuated over the years, but every currency issue was ultimately redeemed on its expiration date at face value.

The remaining colonies—Maryland, Rhode Island, New Hampshire, North Carolina, Georgia—accounted for a mere 8 percent of the colonial financial contribution to the war effort. Parliament sent the two New England colonies sufficient monies to cover more than two-thirds of their total expenses. North Carolina received reimbursement of about one-third of its outlays, while Maryland and Georgia got nothing at all. Although circumstances varied, the five colonies had no serious difficulties managing their wartime finances.

Within little more than five years after the signing of the peace treaty in 1763, the mainland colonies had raised the vast majority of the tax revenues required to meet their allotted share of British military expenses in North America. In some colonies, notably Massachusetts, South Carolina, Pennsylvania, and Virginia, citizens had to endure several years of escalated tax rates to make substantial contributions to ongoing military expenses and to make drastic retirements in their outstanding debts in the years immediately after the close of hostilities in North America. In those provinces and elsewhere, the colonial assemblies found the wherewithal to meet the formidable challenge of financing a series of fairly large-scale military campaigns that continued for more than half a decade.

The accomplishments during the late 1750s and early 1760s provided reassurance about the capacity of this group of politically distinct governments to finance military operations over vast territories and for lengthy periods of time. Revenues were generated entirely through direct taxation, as opposed to indirect taxation of money balances through currency depreciation. Moreover, a majority of the overhanging debts at the end of the war had been retired by 1765, and the remainder was on the path to extinction during the next five to ten years. The outstanding financial performance of the colonies was one factor in the calculated decision to break abruptly with Great Britain in 1776 and to risk the outbreak of renewed warfare on a grand scale.

On the contrary side, the financial triumphs in the thirteen diverse colonies created the false impression that future challenges could be met with equal dispatch by employing similar strategies and policies. The parallels failed to hold up particularly well two decades later, however, because circumstances were drastically altered. Military operations in the fight for independence cost citizens more than twenty times the tax burden associated with the Seven Years' War. What had proven a manageable task requiring a fairly moderate level of aggregate funding became a vastly more difficult challenge when the scale of operations multiplied many times over.

During the War for Independence and throughout the confederation period, the independent states in conjunction with the jointly sponsored congressional government tried to emulate the successful financial programs implemented during the 1750s and 1760s. Yet the outcomes almost everywhere were strikingly different. Variations in the financial performance of the individual thirteen states were also much greater two decades later, especially in regard to their respective programs of postwar debt management.

The greatest departure from the past was, of course, the prominent role played by the national Congress in wartime finance, both in terms of its policy of indirect taxation through currency depreciation during the war years and later the frustrations it encountered in trying to raise sufficient revenues to meet interest payments on its debt obligations during the 1780s. Moreover, Congress was unable to emulate the parliamentary model. It could provide no subsidies to help the states reduce their debts; quite the opposite, without an independent source of revenue, it continually requested additional funding to finance its own operations. In the previous era, the 1760s, Parliament had intermingled the unpaid obligations linked to military campaigns in North America with the overall national debt and forced British taxpayers to cover the annual interest on its borrowings. When the fighting ended in 1781, the American people could call upon no generous third parties for outside financial assistance. No matter how the responsibilities were finally apportioned, U.S. citizens would be forced to assume the debt obligations of their national government whether that goal was accomplished within the taxing systems of the respective states or as a result of a strengthened revenue system at the federal level.

War for Independence

When Congress and the thirteen newly independent states faced the problem of raising funds to support military operations in 1776, most of them decided to raise the bulk of their funds through the issuance of fiat currency. The general plan was to emit new monies to recruit and supply troops and then at some later date to consider adopting tax programs designed to generate inflows of currency back into governmental coffers. Currency collected in taxes during the conflict would be paid out again, lessening the need for fresh emissions. Most of the currency collected after the war would be retired, thereby reducing steadily the floating debt still outstanding.

Only the New England states had other options to ponder. Since they had been on a specie standard for the last quarter century, their legislatures might have attempted to rely primarily on public debt to finance the war effort. Foreseeably, the legislatures could have tried to raise substantial amounts of specie through the placement of securities in intermediate-term capital markets. They had successfully implemented that plan during the Seven Years' War. But suddenly freed from the strict requirements of British currency acts, the New England states took advantage of the opportunity to

shift back to fiat currency, bringing them temporarily into conformity with monetary practices in the other nine states.

Congress issued fiat currency beginning in 1775. It had no other
practical means of generating adequate funding for the Continental army. Raising substantial sums quickly through the negotiation
of intermediate- and long-term loans was impossible since an easily
accessible domestic capital market had not yet emerged. For political as well as financial considerations, foreign rivals of the British
Empire were initially hesitant to offer loans to a rebellious government that might soon collapse. No organized banks existed to provide short-term funding nor to assist in the placement of long-term
bonds with more permanent private investors. Congress eventually
opened its own domestic loan offices and borrowed monies from
citizens to fund somewhere around 4 to 7 percent of the cost of
the war, a respectable performance given the embryonic status of
American capital markets. Meanwhile, the issuance of paper money
was the mainstay of congressional fiscal policy.

The volume of continental currency emitted was small at first
but grew progressively larger after 1777, finally reaching the self-
imposed ceiling of $200 million sometime in 1780.[5] The broad
but unspecified financial plan called for the states to collect taxes
payable in continental currency and then to remit those funds to
the U.S. Treasury in response to congressional requisitions based
on wealth estimates—later translated into population estimates because of inadequacies in the techniques for measuring wealth. Congressional financial managers hoped that a continuous demand for
continental currency to pay current taxes plus the public's expectation of continued high taxes in the postwar period would act
together to maintain purchasing power. An ambitious program
based on similar principles had achieved good results in the former
colonies in 1755–65. As it happened, however, only a fraction of
the monies (less than 5 percent) issued by Congress were collected
in taxes and recycled through the federal government during the
first five years of the war.[6]

Continental paper was not viewed by the public as a strong currency after the British capture of New York in the fall of 1776. It
lost about two-thirds of its value in 1777, stabilized at about that
level during 1778 when it got a temporary boost from the announcement of the alliance with France, and then deteriorated badly in
1779 as the war dragged on. Because of the decline in market value,
Congress had to issue ever larger sums of continental currency to
purchase small volumes of goods and services.

TABLE 5.2
Estimated Value of Congressional Currency
(in millions)

	Face value	Specie value (Ferguson)
1775–1776	$ 25.0	$23.3
1777	13.0	4.5
1778	63.4	11.7
1779	124.8	6.0
Subtotal	$226.2[a]	$45.5
1780–1781	1.6[b]	1.5
Total	$227.8	$47.0

Source: E. James Ferguson, *The Power of the Purse: A History of American Public Finance, 1776–1790* (Chapel Hill: University of North Carolina Press, 1961), 30, 43.

[a] The actual sum in circulation may never be known. Congress officially voided $41.5 million and offered a swap program because of problems related to counterfeiting. As a result of escalating depreciation, the sums issued in 1779 and 1780 had only one-third of the purchasing power of the initial emissions in 1775 and 1776. By January 1780 it took more than $40 in paper to exchange for $1 in coin; a year later the exchange ratio had fallen to 100:1 or worse.

[b] The amounts issued in 1780 and 1781, called the new emissions, carried an interest rate of 5 percent and were more properly certificates of indebtedness rather than fiat currency. Congress funded them in 1790.

In 1781 Congress officially declared that its currency would be valued in tax remissions from the states at one-fortieth (0.025) of the printed face value. After official devaluation, the states made a greater effort to collect taxes in continental currency and remit the proceeds to the U.S. Treasury. They collected monies with a face value of $119 million ($3 million specie) in the early 1780s, approximately half the total volume issued by Congress. Upon receipt of the remitted funds, Congress authorized the issuance of two "new tenor" dollars for every forty "old tenor" dollars, keeping 40 percent of the new monies for itself and returning 60 percent to the states. The new bills were to accrue interest at 5 percent annually and were supposedly redeemable in specie in five years, but those terms were not met.

The swap program as a device for reestablishing the purchasing power of continental paper was doomed at birth. When issued, the new tenor bills were exchanged at the unrealistic ratio of 20:1, whereas the official devaluation ratio of 40:1 was much closer to prevailing market rates, and even that exchange rate represented an overvaluation. In other words, even under the most favorable market conditions, the new tenor bills were worth only half the value of identically denominated specie coins. Beginning with that handicap from the date of issuance, the new monies depreciated very rapidly. By the summer of 1781, the new tenor bills were worth only 15 to 20 percent of their face value, and the public soon viewed this second congressional emission in very much the same light as the older bills. The ambitious plan to restore confidence in the federal government's financial integrity was short-lived. But if viewed primarily as a stopgap measure, the program was moderately successful. The new tenor bills had generated about $2 million specie in purchasing power for Congress and up to $4 million for the several states in 1780 and 1781.

Congressional paper was not totally worthless, but was nearly so after 1781. In Hamilton's funding program in the early 1790s, the old tenor bills still extant, about $6 million, were funded at the ratio of 100:1, an exchange that translated into a mere $60,000. The surviving new tenor monies, which included an interest component and thus were considered debt instruments, were ultimately redeemed at par, totaling about $2 million.[7]

Through the mechanism of a depreciating national currency, citizens had assumed a federal tax burden, as applied to monetary balances, that provided ongoing financing to cover about one-quarter of the total cost of the war. The bulk of that support came during the first five years of the military conflict. An even greater burden of concurrent taxation was assumed at the state level.

The states largely ignored the requisitions for financial assistance routinely emanating from Congress in the 1770s. Most state legislatures never seriously contemplated a massive tax program to support the national government because they were too preoccupied in dealing with mounting fiscal and financial problems at their own level. Following the pattern established during the war emergency two decades earlier, the newly independent states contributed to the common defense by emitting their own fiat monies, which were used to recruit and equip local militias. And equally important to the war effort, individual states periodically authorized the spending of local currencies, or various substitutes such as requisition certificates, to purchase food and supplies for American soldiers encamped within their borders.

Some states did, in fact, impose higher taxes to drain off a portion of the surplus monies in circulation, but each typically used the larger share of tax revenues to shore up the purchasing power of

its own local currency. None was successful in preventing depreciation, however—not even Maryland, Pennsylvania, New Jersey, and
New York, which had managed their colonial currencies for decades
without any sustained loss of purchasing power. Once continental
paper had gone into a tailspin, the public lost confidence in state
monies as well, although some issues held up better than others.

The states in combination provided about two-fifths of the
monetary resources required to finance the War for Independence.
The currency emitted had a face value of about $210 million; its
specie value, determined after taking into account depreciation and
reduced purchasing power, was around $6 million.[8] In addition to
the emission of fiat paper, the states also generated funds by issuing interest-bearing certificates to suppliers. Each state developed
a different program of currency and debt financing.

Some states diligently collected taxes and indicated a firm resolve to redeem their fiat issues in due course, while others became
engulfed in a sea of paper and gave up all efforts to stave off depreciation. Massachusetts took firm steps to slow the depreciation
of the local currency in 1777 by halting its further issuance and
by converting the outstanding paper into interest-bearing debt certificates. In 1781 the Bay State returned to the specie standard to
which it had adhered from 1751 to 1774. Following the lead of the
federal government, most states periodically wrote down the value
of their paper to prevailing market rates and then instituted tax
programs designed to tax it out of existence.

State and federal governments differed in the timing of their
financial contributions to the war effort. Congress was the vital
factor from 1777 through 1780, but during the next three years,
state governments carried the heavier load. Soon after assuming the
office of superintendent of the Treasury in 1781, Robert Morris,
the Philadelphia merchant and financier, suspended indefinitely all
payments of wages to soldiers and officers in the Continental army
from congressional coffers. The suspension lasted until the armed
forces were disbanded two years later, when soldiers received payment in securities rather than specie or fiat currency.

After Yorktown, most states, following the precedents established in the Seven Years' War, enacted tax programs designed to
extinguish their devalued currency issues and to make substantial
inroads on the retirement of their public debts during the next decade or so. Several states made good progress on debt reduction
in the postwar era. After a sweeping devaluation of its outstanding

TABLE 5.3
Proceeds of Congressional Loans, 1775–1780
(in millions)

	Nominal Amounts	Real Value
Pennsylvania	$28.5	$ 3.95
Massachusetts	8.0	2.39
Connecticut	4.3	1.31
New York	3.5	.95
Rhode Island	1.9	.70
New Jersey	4.5	.66
Maryland	4.0	.41
New Hampshire	1.0	.36
Virginia	3.0	.31
South Carolina	3.8	.22
North Carolina	0.9	.11
Georgia	0.9	.10
Delaware	0.5	.10
Total	$64.8	$11.57

Source: Edward Forbes Robinson, "Continental Treasury Administration, 1775–1781: A Study in the Financial History of the American Revolution," Ph.D. diss., University of Wisconsin, 1969, table 9, p. 342.

Note: Real values reflect adjustments for currency depreciation according to the official government schedule. Some scholars believe that schedule was flawed and that the purchasing power of loan proceeds was closer to $5 or $6 million.

fiat paper, Virginia moved diligently to eradicate its debt burden. The state's aggregate debts were reduced systematically from about £4.2 million in 1784 to just over £1 million by 1790. Other states that reduced their debts substantially in the 1780s were Maryland, North Carolina, and Georgia. Two notable exceptions to the general pattern of debt reduction were Massachusetts and South Carolina; both states failed to make sustained progress in the 1780s.

By various means, the thirteen states had assumed ultimate responsibility for raising sufficient monies to cover about two-fifths of wartime expenditures. They did so mainly through taxation supplemented by proceeds from the sale of confiscated loyalist properties. Congressional fiat monies provided about one-quarter of the cost. Federal and state aggregate public revenues generated during the decade and a half from independence until ratification of the Constitution were sufficiently large to cover fully two-thirds of the military expenses incurred in winning the war.

In terms of retiring the overhanging public debt, the wartime generation did not match the record of its predecessor in retiring postwar indebtedness, but taxpayers made steady progress at the state level. Both the state and federal governments achieved a respectable record in managing the nation's financial affairs in the 1780s, and the rate of progress increased throughout the decade—notwithstanding historical accounts and scholarly judgments to the contrary. The evidence does not suggest that the formation of a stronger government under the Constitution was a necessary condition for the eventual settlement of all the debts incurred during the war years.

The debt obligations that remained unpaid in 1790 had provided the financing to support about one-third of the military operations. The loans outstanding fell into three distinct categories: federal domestic debt, $27 million; federal foreign debt, $10.5 million; assumed state debts, $18 million; and unassumed state debts, $8 million. Federal domestic debt broke down roughly as follows: $4 million arose from certificates issued by the quartermaster corps in lieu of monies to citizens who had supplied goods and services to the Continental army between 1780 and 1783; $12 million arose from certificates issued to military personnel, regular federal troops and their officers, in the early 1780s to cover unpaid wages during their last two years of service; and $11 million represented the specie value of loan certificates sold through government loan offices. The first two categories represented involuntary credit extensions by citizens and soldiers, who would have preferred cash payment if funds had been available. Loan office certificates, in contrast, arose from genuine monetary investments in the future of the new nation. Those debt instruments, issued through federal loan offices, generated somewhere between 4 to 7 percent of wartime funding. (The exact percentage is tentative because of our faulty understanding of the specie adjustment mechanism for certificates purchased with depreciated currency.) Overall, Congress probably generated slightly less purchasing power from the sale of securities to domestic investors than from the proceeds of its various foreign loans.

Despite the relatively small sums raised by Congress in the domestic public securities market, this sector merits closer inspection because its operations represent an important step toward the emergence of a more vigorous capital market in the United States. Congress announced its initial borrowing program in October 1776 aimed at raising $5 million in specie—a goal surpassed, incidentally,

only near the end of the war. The interest rate offered was 4 percent, payable in specie, or its equivalent in foreign bills of exchange,
on certificates with three-year maturity dates. The emphasis on the
market for intermediate-term funds was in harmony with previous
public debt programs in the New England colonies. Loan certificates were issued in large sums, two hundred dollars and above,
which virtually ensured that they would not be perceived as another
addition to the circulating money supply but held as a long-term
investment.

Congressional loan offices were set up in every state, but the
sale of certificates had a distinctly regional pattern. More than 90
percent of the purchases were in the northern states, with three
states—Pennsylvania, Connecticut, and Massachusetts—generating
two-thirds of the original subscriptions. In the two most populous
New England states, wealthy citizens had been accustomed to investing in government securities since midcentury. Historian Winifred
Rothenberg has discovered clear evidence of a nascent market in
private debt instruments in Massachusetts during the same period
as well. Thus the active participation of citizens of the Bay State
in the federal debt program represents a linear progression of increasing involvement in capital markets on several fronts. Pennsylvania likewise accounted for an inordinate volume of security sales
because Philadelphia had a large group of wealthy families with
surplus funds for investment and because it was the site of the new
national government. The placement of public securities in New
York City was presumably curbed because the port was occupied by
British troops for much of the war.

The terms of issuance and final redemption values were altered
several times in the late 1770s. Since the initial interest rate of 4 percent was not sufficiently attractive to investors, it was raised to 6 percent in February 1777 in an effort to stimulate demand. Due to increasing uncertainty about the probable length of the war, the new
securities had no fixed maturity dates. The three-year certificates
previously issued were not retired on schedule, since redemption
funds were nonexistent, but were converted into open-ended obligations as well. In March 1778 the offer to pay interest in specie was
withdrawn; security purchasers were promised interest payments
merely in currency, and later in the 1780s holders received payments in financial instruments called "indents," a glorified variation
of an IOU. By the late 1770s, mounting federal debts had taken on
the character, at least temporarily, of perpetual annuities, similar

TABLE 5.4
Estimated Funding Sources: War for Independence
(in millions of pounds sterling)

	Sterling £	Percentages
Fiat Currency		
Congressional monies	46	28
States' monies	64	39
Total fiat currency	110	67
Borrowed funds		
Congress—domestic bonds	6	3
Congress—debt certificates	16	10
Congress—foreign loans	10	6
States' indebtedness[a]	23	14
Total debts	54	33
Total cost of war	165	100

[a] No complete documentation for the states' combined indebtedness from 1775 to 1783 exists. The number used here is a plug inserted to bring the column into conformity with Ferguson's estimate of the total cost of the war. Substantial portions of the states' fiat issues were subsequently converted into debt instruments. In chapter 7, I estimated that the states' net indebtedness might have risen to a high point of $50 million sometime in the 1780s.

to the consols that Parliament had adopted as a permanent funding vehicle in the early eighteenth century. By the mid-1780s, no one knew when congressional debts would be repaid or when, and in what form, interest payments would be forthcoming.

A major stimulus to security sales in late 1777 was the depreciating market value of continental currency. For several months congressional loan offices accepted paper monies at face value, thereby granting buyers the opportunity to purchase government securities at heavily discounted *real* prices. Congress finally closed that loophole in March 1778; after that date the face value of all certificates was subject to final adjustment based on a sliding scale linked to the market value of currency when the transaction occurred. Securities were sold under those terms through 1781, when domestic borrowing ceased.

The face value of federal securities exceeded $67 million, but their adjusted specie value translated into a debt obligation of only $11 million in 1790. Historian E. James Ferguson estimated that Congress actually received only about $6 million in specie-equivalent funds from securities sales, meaning that the real cost of borrowed money to taxpayers was ultimately much higher, perhaps almost twice as high as the nominal interest rate of 6 percent paid on the face values of the certificates.

Given the risks associated with investing in a newly organized government under direct military attack by the British, real returns of 9 to 12 percent on U.S. government securities, if realized, would not have represented excessive compensation to investors in a country where long-term capital was scarce and financial markets were thin and local in character. Only governments in England and Holland were typically able to place their public debt at interest rates as low as 3 to 7 percent on long-term issues. Both nations had long histories of sound financial management and also contained within their respective borders London and Amsterdam, the only two capital-rich money centers in Europe. By comparison, the French government under the rule of Louis XVI routinely paid 10 to 12 percent to attract domestic savers to investments in lifetime annuities. Considering the difficult circumstances, congressional finance ministers performed commendably in raising at least a small portion of their funding requirements through domestic borrowing. They also took significant strides toward creating a broader and deeper market for long-term debt financing by governments and private parties.

Congress also received foreign assistance in financing the war. The French provided direct subsidies. They provided supplies for American forces, amounting to somewhere in the neighborhood of $2 million. French gifts accounted for only a small fraction of U.S. military expenditures, perhaps 1 to 2 percent of the total, but the assistance came at critical times. The announcement of the French alliance in 1777 temporarily reversed the depreciation of Continental currency and thereby provided Congress with more purchasing power through 1780 than it otherwise would have enjoyed. The sums spent independently by France on its own military operations in the American theater, including the movement of French land and naval forces to Yorktown in 1781, were estimated at between $50 and $60 million overall. They represented another significant financial contribution to the American cause, covering perhaps as much as one quarter of the joint costs of the Franco-American military alliance.

Other sources of foreign financial assistance were direct loans to

Congress from the French government and Dutch investors, with a token advance from the Spanish crown. France made two modest loans totaling $750,000 in 1778 and 1779; Dutch and Spanish loans during the same two years added $100,000. From 1780 to 1783, France offered four additional loans amounting to roughly $4 million. In an unusual and innovative transaction within the increasingly sophisticated realm of international high finance, France proposed, in 1781, to underwrite and to guarantee unconditionally an offering of roughly $1.8 million of U.S. securities in the Amsterdam market. As underwriters, the French government advanced the entire proceeds of the proposed Dutch issue to U.S. agents a few months before plans were finalized to offer the securities on the Amsterdam market, thus permitting the immediate purchase of military supplies for shipment across the Atlantic. The Amsterdam offering subsequently hit a snag when private investors showed disdain for the French guarantee, and the Dutch government had to be called in to act as a second, joint guarantor.

After the overwhelming victory at Yorktown, the United States made a breakthrough in Amsterdam on the strength of its own credit standing. John Adams was instrumental in forming a private syndicate to raise $2.8 million from Dutch investors, without the safety of a Dutch governmental guarantee, at the very favorable interest rate of 5 percent. The proceeds of the various foreign loans were used to purchase military supplies in Europe and to make current interest payments on prior overseas loans; some of the funds were converted into specie coins for shipment back to the United States. Foreign loans from 1777 to 1783 contributed almost $8 million to financing the war, or roughly 5 percent of total military expenditures.

Most of the Dutch funding came after the decisive battle at Yorktown. The monies raised in Amsterdam contributed little to victories on the battlefield, but the funds aided in keeping the Continental army intact, although reduced in numbers from twenty-nine thousand in 1781 to thirteen thousand in 1783—thus deterring any British thoughts about a resumption of hostilities. Some of the proceeds of the loan underwritten by France in 1781 were also used to provide the capital and specie reserves for the Bank of North America, the congressionally chartered financial institution that aided in placing the federal government on a specie footing in the early 1780s.

6

Robert Morris and the Bank of
North America

❖ ❖ ❖

Robert Morris was instrumental in arranging Dutch financing and in founding the Bank of North America, the nation's first chartered commercial bank, after his appointment to head the Treasury Department in 1781. Indeed, no discussion of financial developments in the 1780s would be complete without an assessment of the influence and impact that Morris had on events in the 1780s and on the long-term development of American financial markets. Like Alexander Hamilton, who rose to prominence a decade later, Morris ranks among the most important and powerful financial leaders in American history.

Morris' reputation rests first on his role as the forceful, and occasionally dictatorial, superintendent of finance from 1781 to 1784 and second on his contribution to the emergence and development of American commercial banking. His designation as the so-called financier of the revolution in older historical accounts is an example of nationalistic exaggeration (probably one result of an effort to identify and then deify a group of patriotic founding fathers). However, his impact on the banking sector was extraordinarily significant, both at the national level and within the state of Pennsylvania. Morris tried repeatedly, but failed, to obtain for Congress an independent system of taxation; he missed thereby his chance to buttress the power of the Confederation government vis-à-vis the states. His inability to convince members of Congress of the absolute necessity of securing an independent revenue, through a national tariff or some other means, was an important factor in Morris' resignation as superintendent in 1784. The lack of a reliable revenue system prompted the movement to reconsider the organization of the federal government under the Articles of Confederation. That reform movement, in turn, led to the drafting and ratification of the Constitution.

Born in Liverpool in 1734, Morris traveled to the colonies as a teenager and rejoined his father who had previously emigrated to Philadelphia. In 1754 he formed a successful mercantile partnership with Thomas Willing, who served as president of the Bank of North America and later the First Bank of the United States. The Philadelphia merchant was elected to the Continental Congress in 1775, where he initially expressed much hesitation about the idea of breaking irrevocably with Great Britain. Before his appointment as superintendent of finance, Morris served on several congressional committees, including the secret committee that handled the overseas procurement of military supplies. Morris pursued his public duties and private business affairs in tandem during the war years— a strategy which, if conducted in reasonable fairness and moderation, was considered perfectly legitimate and respectable for public officials in eighteenth-century society. The superintendent profited handsomely, but not excessively, from his close association with the federal government. After resigning his post in 1784, Morris remained active in Pennsylvania politics, serving in the state's unicameral legislature and then in the U.S. Senate from 1789 to 1795. Tragically, he became involved in massive, imprudent speculations in western lands in the mid-1790s and was forced to declare bankruptcy in 1797, owing creditors more than $3 million. In perhaps the ultimate public humiliation, Morris was confined to debtors' prison from 1798 to 1801; after his release, he lived quietly in Philadelphia until his death in 1806 at age 72.

During his tenure as superintendent of finance (1781–84), Morris employed uncompromising and spartan tactics in his effort to restore a measure of financial credibility to the federal government. When he assumed office in February 1781, Congress had exhausted most of its financial options in the domestic market. Its currency was virtually worthless and its borrowing power through the loan offices had evaporated. Given few other practical alternatives, the superintendent turned to the states and overseas capital markets for assistance. He extracted more than $2 million in specie, or its equivalent value, from the states in 1781 after the devaluation of Continental currency; and he used the revenue to meet at least a portion of his current expenses. In a daring move, which might have sparked a mutinous rebellion, he suspended the payment of wages to officers and soldiers in the Continental army. To placate the loyal troops who remained in the field, he promised a liberal final settlement of all back wages and salaries after the signing of a peace treaty with Great Britain, an event that, after the victory at Yorktown in October 1781, seemed only a matter of months away. When the armed forces were finally disbanded in the spring of 1783, Morris issued $11 million in interest-bearing debt certificates to members of the armed forces to cover accrued wages. It was a tidy sum, amounting to two-fifths of the federal government's outstanding obligations in 1790.

In another equally bold move, Morris forced upon state governments much of the responsibility for supplying and provisioning the troops encamped within their borders. He requisitioned few monetary assets after 1781 but challenged the states to find the wherewithal to provide the army with physical quantities of goods and services. His only inducement to gain local compliance was the continued promise to grant full credit to individual states for all monies expended on congressionally authorized military operations when federal auditors settled the accounts among the states at some future date—a settlement finally announced in 1793. In short, the superintendent curtailed drastically the outgo of monies and limited expenditures to the funds at his disposal; he even closed out his tenure with a small surplus in the treasury.

In terms of financing the military effort itself, Morris' role was limited since he took office less than nine months before the battle at Yorktown. Most of his tenure in office was during the three years after the last decisive battle in October 1781. His contribution to winning the war was not inconsequential since he had served on a number of vital congressional committees from 1775 to 1780, but his reputation as the financial genius who masterminded an American victory is overdrawn. Morris is most properly viewed as a transitional figure, a person who assumed power near the end of the War for Independence, at a very low point in the nation's financial history, and who adroitly proceeded to lay the groundwork for the adoption of Hamilton's comprehensive financial program in the 1790s.

The superintendent was notably successful in maintaining and strengthening the nation's credit reputation in continental capital markets. The decision to forego the domestic market and to concentrate on opportunities overseas was logical from several perspectives. France was a military and diplomatic ally, and the French crown was eager to consolidate and perpetuate the fruits of the decisive Franco-American victory over Great Britain. A thriving capital market was functioning in Amsterdam, and private Dutch investors were actively seeking sound investments in public securities. The Dutch were invulnerable to losses resulting from the depreciation of currencies since all transactions were in specie equivalents, and by 1782 many investors were eager to place their funds in American bonds at 5 to 6 percent. The higher returns appeared adequate compensation for the additional risks associated with investments in the securities of a new nation still struggling to put its financial house in order.

The Dutch were impressed by the economic potential of the United States based on its increasing strength throughout the eighteenth century, and they calculated that the national government would eventually iron out its financial problems and that, in due course, all foreign debts would be serviced properly. Indeed, the Dutch became so confident of Congress' willingness and ability to meet its obligations that, despite the financial disarray within the United States during much of the 1780s, investors in Amsterdam expressed their willingness to assume all the American debts still held in France in the event Louis XVI's financial ministers ever decided to liquidate that nation's holdings. The contemporary Dutch view of events in the United States was, in truth, more accurate in terms of its overall dimensions than the vast majority of crisis-oriented historical accounts of the 1780s that have appeared in print during most of the last two centuries.

Virtually all American political leaders, whatever their differences over other matters, were united on the wisdom of sustaining the credit reputation of the United States in European financial markets. The enhancement of the nation's standing as a political unit worthy of admiration and respect around the globe, an ideal expressed most forcefully in the Declaration of Independence, was considered an important goal. Many feared that, if overseas investors regarded the United States as a poor credit risk, that perception might tarnish the nation's political image. The maintenance of American credit was viewed, therefore, as sound policy from several standpoints. It publicized symbolically the political aspirations of the experimental American republic to a wide and influential audience, and it established the United States as a new nation that merited the confidence of investors in its debt obligations—and later in the securities issued by the congressionally chartered Bank of the United States.

Superintendent Morris, in conjunction with diplomat John Adams, arranged the first floatation of American bonds on the Amsterdam market in 1782 at the highly favorable interest rate of 5 percent. That offering netted about $2 million and opened the door to a series of U.S. loans taken up by Dutch private investors in the late 1780s and through the early 1790s. Three Amsterdam firms heavily involved in the placement of American bonds were Willink, Van Staphorst, and De la Lande and Fijnje. By 1795 Dutch loans totaled $12.5 million, about double the $6.5 million loaned by the French government between 1777 and 1781. The funds from France came during the military conflict itself and represented one facet of the crown's overall foreign policy. The Dutch loans, in contrast, came after the outcome of the war was already decided. They were strictly private, nonpolitical investments by wealthy individuals seeking a return on their monies commensurate with the presumed risks.

In the late 1780s interest rates on new American loans in Amsterdam climbed into the 7 to 9 percent range after investors had factored into their assessment of U.S. credit the difficulties that the federal government had encountered in securing a steady revenue during the immediate postwar era. Those difficulties had caused problems in servicing the outstanding debt. A healthy share of the proceeds of every loan floated in Amsterdam from 1784 through 1794 went to pay the annual interest due on the foreign principal already on the books. U.S. aggregate indebtedness, as a consequence, continued to compound.

Congress maintained regular interest payments to Dutch investors since they displayed a willingness to advance additional monies to cover the American shortfall. Congress raised fresh monies in Holland that went, in part, to pay the interest on debts already held by Dutch citizens. In other words, Dutch funds came out of one pocket and went into another—along, of course, with freshly drawn certificates of U.S. debt. Because the French government offered no further financing after 1781 and because the Paris capital market was undeveloped relative to London and Amsterdam and thus held no prospect for private funding, Congress suspended interest payments on that portion of its foreign debt from 1786 to 1790. The accrued French interest, about $1.6 million, was included in Hamilton's funding program.

Despite the delays and setbacks in reestablishing a viable system of congressional taxation and thereby reestablishing the international credit rating of the American public, lending patterns in the 1780s reveal most clearly that knowledgeable Amsterdam investors saw the newly formed United States as a promising locale in which to place their hard-earned savings in long-term portfolio investments. (Portfolio investments refer to financial instruments as opposed to direct investment in physical assets such as land and equipment.) A thriving capital market in Amsterdam quickly became accessible to the U.S. government. Private investors in London were likewise ready to lay out the red carpet once the political furor had passed. British merchants had rushed to extend short-term credit to U.S. customers as soon as the treaty was signed in 1783. With the nation's credit rating in Amsterdam and London reasonably well established, the next step toward financial maturity was the creation of a broader and more organized capital market in the domestic economy. Alexander Hamilton was determined to accomplish that outcome.

Despite his many achievements, Superintendent Morris failed in his campaign to generate an independent source of steady revenue for the Confederation government. Fearful of distant and centralized financial power and strapped for tax revenues to meet local expenditures, the states had not lived up to their mutual agreement to meet congressional requisitions for periodic monetary assistance, except in the most superficial manner. One of Morris' major goals was the passage through Congress, plus subsequent state ratification, of a bill granting the federal government the right to collect an impost, the eighteenth-century term for a tariff on goods imported into the United States. He was foiled primarily because of the structure and organization of the Confederation government, which placed strict limits on the power of the federal government to implement any system of national taxation. Congress had the power only to recommend a federal tariff to the states; to actually become law, their respective legislatures had to approve the granting of independent taxing power to the central government. According to the political rules in operation in the early 1780s, their approval had to be unanimous, which meant that a single state could exercise veto power. Rhode Island was the main naysayer in the early 1780s, but other states later climbed on the antitax wagon.

Even before Morris assumed office in the spring of 1781, nationalists in Congress had convinced their peers to make a formal request to the states for the right to impose a modest tariff of 5 percent ad valorem, with the amounts collected pledged to debt service. The main argument was that revenues were needed to maintain the payment of interest on the debt outstanding and thereby to reinforce the prestige and credibility of the Articles of Confederation as a viable form of government. Treasury officials estimated that the tariff would bring in $500,000 to $700,000 annually—enough to cover only about half the interest owed on foreign and domestic debts, but still a step toward greater fiscal responsibility.

Morris claimed that securing a steady revenue source was necessary to boost the nation's standing with creditors and thus enhance the ability of the Treasury Department to continue borrowing additional funds overseas, and possibly revive the confidence of investors at home. That rationale was seriously undermined when Morris negotiated the $2 million loan in Amsterdam in 1782, at a favorable 5 percent interest no less, even in the absence of positive action on the proposed federal tax plan by the states. During the next decade, Treasury officials used the proceeds of new Dutch loans to maintain interest payments on the existing debt in Amsterdam.

Meanwhile, every state except Rhode Island had agreed to the 5 percent tariff. A contentious majority in the state legislature was against granting such sweeping taxing powers to the central government on principle. Rhode Island legislators claimed that enactment of a modest tariff was just the opening wedge for increased federal taxation across the board at some later date, which was precisely what Morris had in mind. Many of the old arguments developed to protest Parliament's modest but precedent-setting stamp tax in 1765 were dusted off and used again to thwart the congressional will. Before a final appeal for reconsideration could be made to the Rhode Island legislature in the summer of 1782, word arrived that Virginia had rescinded its prior approval of the federal tariff—and the whole plan was temporarily suspended.

Morris and the nationalists made a second concerted effort to get approval for an independent taxing power in 1783 but it failed to get off the ground because of the opposition of three states—Rhode Island, Virginia, and Massachusetts. Without a steady income, Congress agreed to Morris' recommendation to halt the payment of interest on the domestic debt in 1782, which had been met for some time with drafts on Treasury balances in France. The cutoff was a tactical move. Morris hoped that an organized protest by investors in federal securities might be strong enough to revive his tariff proposal. But it floundered when several state legislatures volunteered to assume responsibility for making interest payments on federal debts to local citizens. In the winter of 1783, Congress again asked the states to approve the imposition of a 5 percent federal tariff, with the grant of federal taxing powers limited to 25 years, but some legislatures remained skeptical.

Under the Articles of Confederation, the national legislature came close on two occasions yet it never acquired the power to levy taxes. Thus it was unable to generate the revenues required to pay the interest on its debt obligations at home, much less to begin the process of extinguishing the principal. National fiscal policy remained in limbo for most of the decade. Morris resigned in frustration in late 1784 and became a spearhead of the movement to strengthen the powers of the central government in relation to the states.

The Bank of North America

Morris' most lasting contribution to the development of the American financial services sector relates to his instrumental role in promoting U.S. commercial banking, in particular the founding of the Bank of North America (BNA), the nation's first chartered bank, in 1781.[1] Morris gained congressional approval for this nationally chartered corporation in May 1781 only a few months after becoming superintendent of finance. The creation of a national bank was an idea advanced by American admirers of the functions routinely performed for the central government by the Bank of England, and prominent among them was Colonel Alexander Hamilton, who boldly laid out his views in correspondence with the superintendent. The request for corporate status was framed in language that stressed the bank's potential contribution to the general public welfare, a common characteristic of all ad hoc charter applications to legislatures prior to the enactment of general incorporation laws for commercial banks in the nineteenth century.

Some representatives questioned at the outset whether Congress possessed the authority to issue a corporate charter granting special monopoly status to a private banking organization. But supporters of the charter prevailed in early 1781, mainly because of their appeals for expediency in light of the nation's deteriorating finances. But the constitutional issue, which subsequently haunted two other nationally chartered banks over the next half century, reemerged when a newly elected Congress with many new faces convened for the fall session in 1781. Foreshadowing the attitudes of political leaders ranging from Thomas Jefferson to Andrew Jackson, congressional critics pointed out that the framers of the Articles of Confederation had not given the power to grant corporate charters to the federal government. Those objections were sustained in this first confrontation over federal incorporation powers, and the bank's proponents agreed to seek overlapping charters from the legislatures of the thirteen states. After the Bank of North America was granted charter privileges by several states in 1782—among them Pennsylvania, New York, and Massachusetts—its national charter was withdrawn.

Several state legislatures acted favorably because some believed bank directors might decide to establish branches within their borders, but no interstate branches were actually created. As a result, the bank operated in Philadelphia under the terms of its Pennsylvania state charter after 1783.[2] Thus, in the initial showdown between nationalists and states' rights advocates over the chartering and incorporation powers of the federal government, the strict constructionists, who envisioned a limited role for the national legislature, prevailed. Hamilton succeeded in reversing that outcome in the 1790s, but President Jackson got the last word regarding the continuance of a nationally chartered private bank in his veto message of 1832, bringing the whole issue full circle exactly a half century later.

The charter for the Bank of North America authorized an initial capitalization of only $400,000—a surprisingly moderate start for a bank that some hoped, and others feared, would develop into an influential national institution. A decade later, by way of comparison, the capitalization stipulated for the First Bank of the United States was twenty-five times greater. The BNA was a mere shadow of its counterpart, the Bank of England, and it never played a critical role in the management of the nation's finances. What it provided instead was strong proof that a prudently managed commercial bank could offer valuable financial services simultaneously to the private and governmental sectors. The BNA established a respectable record on a modest scale, and it demonstrated the potential benefits that might accrue to the federal government from chartering a vastly larger institution with the resources to make a substantial impact on the nation's financial markets.

Sponsors planned to raise capital through the sale of one thousand shares of stock with a par value of four hundred dollars. The high issue price guaranteed that all the owners would be persons of accumulated wealth. Because cautious investors were slow in subscribing to shares of the newly chartered bank, Morris used a portion of the proceeds of the French loan of 1781 as seed money, investing more than $250,000 of government specie in the bank and making Congress the majority stockholder at the outset of operations. A year later, when the bank had proven successful, the superintendent sold the government's shares to private investors at par, thereby converting the bank into a completely private corporation. Morris and three other Philadelphia merchants each acquired about one hundred shares for their personal accounts, giving them control of 40 percent of the shares by 1783. Morris strengthened the bank's position by naming it the American depository of government funds. The Treasury officially recognized BNA bank notes as legal tender in the payment of debts and taxes to the federal government.

While the bank was trying to establish a reputation for soundness and reliability during its first twelve months of operations, the superintendent was busy on a parallel front. Morris demonstrated his determination to revive the nation's credit at home by intermingling, temporarily, his official duties with his personal business affairs to mutual advantage. To supplement the bank notes issued by the Bank of North America, Morris placed into circulation a series of so-called post notes, monies convertible into specie thirty to sixty days after issue, to meet ongoing governmental expenses. Post notes were the banking community's variant of mercantile commercial paper, although the post notes were typically interest free.

Drawn in denominations ranging from twenty dollars to one hundred dollars on the Treasury, Morris provided a dual guarantee—first in his capacity as superintendent and second in his role as private citizen, which meant in the latter case that holders would have the legal right to proceed against his personal assets in the event of default. In a letter in January 1782, Morris explained: "My personal Credit has been substituted for that which the Country had lost."[3] The superintendent may have exaggerated his power and influence, but there was a strong element of truth in his braggadocio. By making himself contingently liable, he had contributed to reestablishing the power of Congress to emit paper monies that would gain public acceptance. The Treasury was careful to limit its emissions to amounts that could be unquestionably redeemed. The so-called Morris notes passed at face value in the mid-Atlantic states and at modest discounts in more distant regions.

During Morris' tenure, the BNA made a series of loans to the Treasury that helped smooth out the flow of funds. In the first year of operations, the federal government borrowed back its entire initial investment in the bank and more. The accumulated debt rose steadily to about $400,000. In late 1782, however, the government used the proceeds from the sale of its bank stock to private parties to reduce the balance by almost $300,000. While Morris was in office, aggregate government loans exceeded $1.2 million. That total seems impressive at first glance, but given the federal government's overwhelming financial obligations to creditors, bank loans did little more than help the Treasury tread water while it remained adrift in a sea of mounting debt. Most notably, the BNA never purchased any of the nation's long-term debt for its asset portfolio nor did it accept government bonds in payment for capital stock, which represented a logical business decision since the risks of default and repudiation remained so great in the early 1780s. In short, the bank's value to the federal government, while not insubstantial over the short run, was inconsequential in terms of extricating the nation from its long-term financial difficulties.

The BNA's impact on the private sector was much more lasting. The bank's organization and its operations served as a stimulus, and also a useful model, for the subsequent spread of American commercial banking. The importance of the precedents it established can hardly be exaggerated. The BNA was organized as a corporate enterprise with numerous stockholders, who held transferable shares that could be traded at market prices. No similarly organized joint-stock firms had been permitted in the colonies by Parliament. The BNA obtained the privilege of issuing its own paper currency, which represented a departure from English practice since, except for the Bank of England and royally chartered banks in Scotland, only proprietorships and partnerships with six or fewer partners were allowed to issue money in the British Empire. Under English common law, the liability of partners for the redemption of currency and deposits in specie was unlimited. American organizational innovations in the financial services markets were thus highly significant. They opened the door for the creation of a financial system of currency-issuing banking institutions chartered throughout the states and capitalized by pools of private investment funds that could, through the authorization and sale of additional stock, be expanded again and again to correspond with the growth of the economy.

Did stockholders in the BNA also depart from English custom and receive the privilege of limited liability? To be more precise, were stockholders liable for debts exceeding the size of their investment in the corporation? The de jure answer in the late eighteenth century was probably yes—the existing English rule of unlimited liability still applied; but de facto, American investors do not appear to have been exposed to the same degree of personal liability as in Great Britain. Under English common law, shareholders in corporations chartered by Parliament, both as a group and individually, typically had no different responsibilities than members of partnerships—that is, they assumed unlimited liability for all corporate debts in bankruptcy.

The charter of the BNA avoided the whole stockholder liability issue. However, in the absence of any explicit wording about liability limitations, the presumption of legal scholars has been that the precedents of English common law still held sway in the United States during the last decades of the eighteenth century unless altered by statute. In the charters of most subsequent banks, members of boards of directors were typically singled out and assigned liabilities ranging from two to three times the par value of their investment in corporate shares if they voted to approve any activity that violated the charter terms, such as the issuance of unauthorized currency. But the general liability of passive owners, who were not involved in management, was not stipulated in any of the early charters that I reviewed. The extent of stockholder liability in early American banks and corporations is examined at somewhat greater length in the Appendix. In scanning the literature on the topic, I blithely assumed that legal historians had settled the issue long ago, but I soon discovered my error. All things considered, I believe we may safely conclude that the prospect of limited liability does not appear to have been among the inducements attracting investors to place their funds in the shares of commercial banks and other corporate ventures.

Governance of the BNA was placed in the hands of a board of twelve directors, duly elected by stockholders at regular annual meetings. The board was dominated by persons nominated by Philadelphia merchants holding the largest number of shares. Everyday management was in the hands of two bank officials. The board named Tench Francis to the position of cashier, at one thousand dollars per year. He was responsible for performing routine transactions, including the handling and safekeeping of currency and coin, and the supervision of five subordinate employees. The bank's president was selected from within the membership of the board. Thomas Willing, Morris' former partner, who later headed the First Bank of the United States, became the first president. His duties were important, but the discretionary powers of presidents were circumscribed in the early banks. The board of directors retained firm control over lending operations. Willing negotiated with potential borrowers on a regular basis, but final decisions regarding the granting or denial of loan applications and renewals came at the weekly or biweekly meetings of the board of directors.

The BNA was the first American financial institution to maintain continuous specie convertibility for its currency issue. Holders of bank notes always had the option of exchanging them for specie coins of equal value at the teller window during regular hours. In establishing convertibility at the holder's discretion, the BNA adopted the procedures followed by all currency issuers in Great Britain, large or small, ranging from the Bank of England to mercantile proprietorships and partnerships that dabbled in banking. The convenience and safety of the service was undeniable since paper that could be continuously exchanged for specie was unlikely to suffer serious depreciation. Of course, bank managers had to exercise good judgment to ensure that sufficient specie was always on hand, or in reserve nearby, to meet customer demands. American commercial banks invariably operated with fractional reserves, which allowed them to expand the money supply beyond the value of their specie holdings but made them vulnerable to runs during general financial panics.

During the preceding era—the late colonial period—the steady public demand for the paper monies placed in circulation by the assemblies, either to pay taxes or to repay loans at governmental land offices, had supported currency values fairly well after 1750. Yet the exchange ratio between specie and sterling bills of exchange was subject to periodic fluctuation, usually linked to shifts in a given colony's international balance of payments. During the war years, the currency emissions of Congress and most state legislatures were useful as a medium of domestic exchange but proved disastrous as a store of value. Privately issued currency supported by adequate specie reserves for conversion purposes promised a more reliable device for sustaining values, thus the founding of the BNA was the crucial first step in the creation of a more privatized system of money and banking.

Another advantage of bank notes over the paper monies created by the colonial legislatures was the prospect of constantly recycling bank notes back into the economy. All colonial issues had deadlines for final redemption, and some were subject to regular amortization schedules. The volume of colonial currency in circulation could not be adjusted from month to month or from year to year to correspond with the volume of local economic activity. Bank notes were much more flexible instruments. When customers repaid their outstanding loans, the bank could normally reissue the cash to new borrowers within a few days. Indeed, banks could expand and contract the volume of currency in circulation within a period of weeks in response to trends in the local economy and specie flows. The only interruption threatening the continual recycling of bank notes back into the economy was the impending expiration of a bank's charter since few corporate enterprises were granted the privilege of perpetual life in the early national period.

The process of substituting private for governmental currency was accepted with little controversy or heated public debate in Pennsylvania in 1781. The plan received approval not only because of its practical advantages, namely continuous convertibility, but it could also draw upon the British and continental heritage that had condemned in no uncertain terms the issuance of unconvertible fiat paper. The BNA was a welcome innovation because it merged practicality with principles considered intellectually and even morally sound in most of western Europe.

One prominent supporter of the plan for chartered commercial banking was Thomas Paine, the fiery author of "Common Sense" and other influential revolutionary pamphlets. A vocal defender of the political rights and privileges of artisans and common laborers, Paine defended the BNA against charges that it was an elitist organization unsuited to serving the public interest. He promoted the bank as a potentially egalitarian institution offering credit facilities to a wide spectrum of citizens. In publications addressed to artisans and day laborers, he extolled the advantages of sound money for every level of society, especially the middling and poor. Paine deplored the excesses of fiat paper and advocated a strictly metallic standard or the next best alternative, namely a private banking system issuing paper money convertible to specie at will. Indeed, in the eighteenth century, unlike the nineteenth, most public figures who advocated hard money positions were inclined to endorse the introduction of commercial bank notes into the economy because bank notes were viewed as vastly superior to the fiat monies that had been issued in the colonies and states during most of the preceding decades. In the early national era, few political commentators on financial matters were uncompromising hard money bullionists.[4]

The most telling criticism of the BNA and other urban commercial banks focused on the public's limited access to credit facilities. The stockholders and their elected representatives on the board of directors were mostly Philadelphia merchants, and the loan applicants approved were invariably from the local community. Large stockholders received special consideration; indeed, for many owners, ready access to credit was the chief motivation for investing in the bank. Self-dealing was also common; the directors did not hesitate to draw upon bank resources to meet their own periodic financial requirements. The bank's interest-earning assets in the 1780s were largely short-term loans used to finance mercantile working capital—accounts receivable and inventories. The lending function of the bank was oriented toward only a small segment of the general population—the friends and business associates of stockholders. Farm families in outlying regions failed to qualify for accommodations from the BNA since bank directors had decided to grant no loans with long maturities, and farmers normally required credit for six to twelve months.

Some representatives of farming districts protested because the BNA promised no credit facilities for the agricultural sector. But defenders of the bank, such as Paine, argued that farmers, artisans, and other citizens would benefit from the bank's lending operations in indirect, but nonetheless very substantial, ways. By lending to firms in the Philadelphia mercantile community, the bank fostered an expansion in the overall volume of regional credit. In response, merchants extended more favorable terms to small shopkeepers and storekeepers, and they in turn could allow their farm and artisanal customers to purchase more goods by increasing the volume of outstanding book credit. The pyramiding argument makes good economic sense to us today, but its convoluted nature produced a number of skeptics in the 1780s. Although the BNA made the majority of its loans to local merchants, some artisans and shopkeepers had limited access to credit facilities. Of roughly seventy-five hundred heads of households in Philadelphia in 1790, about twelve hundred different citizens were granted loans in the early 1790s. Listed among them were more than one hundred identifiable artisans.

Loans were normally granted for thirty to sixty days, and renewals were normally frowned upon unless the borrower was a
prominent stockholder. The interest rate applied to loans was uniformly the legal maximum of 6 percent. The main justifications for
the preponderance of short-term loans were the reduced risk of
lender default and the maintenance of a high degree of liquidity.
By holding a loan portfolio with an average maturity of thirty to
forty-five days, the directors would be able to build up specie reserves fairly quickly in an impending crisis, thereby increasing the
probability of maintaining bank note convertibility.

Generally speaking, the conversion principle was the feature
that elicited broad public support. The farm majority was willing,
at least initially, to forego the opportunity for direct access to bank
credit from urban financial institutions in return for reasonably
strong assurances that bank notes would serve not only as a convenient medium of domestic exchange for every occupational group
but as a reliable store of value as well. The latter attribute was exceedingly important in the early 1780s, and it paved the way for the
American adoption of procedures prevailing in the British banking
system—procedures that had, surprisingly, failed to develop when
the former colonies had been members of the British Empire. The
subsequent founding of the First Bank of the United States was the
culmination of the movement toward the widespread adoption of
English precedents, but the contours were already laid out between
1781 and 1785 by the BNA and two other commercial banks in New
York and Boston.

The BNA offered another new financial service unavailable in
colonial times. It accepted deposits of specie and bank notes, either
for safekeeping or as a convenient means of expediting a customer's payment transactions through check writing (often spelled
"cheque" prior to the twentieth century). Financial historians writing before World War II generally believed that the settlement of
accounts by checks drawn against deposits was uncommon until the
second half of the nineteenth century; but deeper digging since
midcentury has pushed the inception of routine check writing by
business enterprises back in time further and further.

The origins of settling accounts through the transfer of checks,
in fact, coincided with the very origins of American commercial
banking. In 1784, for example, BNA bookkeepers made up to 450
entries per day related to customers' checks and deposits. Some
merchants generated as many as 50 items per month. By 1789 the
BNA maintained more than 640 accounts; the median balance was

in the vicinity of $250, with less than 15 percent carrying balances over $1,000. Few accounts maintained high balances since the bank paid no interest on deposits. Nonetheless, aggregate deposit liabilities at nearly $900,000 in 1792 exceeded capital stock by one-fifth. In fact, bank records indicate that the value of bank notes in circulation was generally less than deposit liabilities, and often lower by 50 percent.

The data suggest that Philadelphia business firms had already started the procedure of holding cash balances in a mix of currency, deposits, and specie—three completely interchangeable forms of money after 1781. Yet to place those developments in the proper perspective, it should be noted that the BNA was clearly a bank ahead of its time in regard to the aggregation of funds in deposit accounts relative to currency and capital. Most commercial banks in the early national and antebellum periods did not concentrate on deposit growth as a key means of expanding the volume of loanable funds but looked instead to the augmentation of capital, according to historian Naomi Lamoreaux.[5]

The BNA directors ran a very conservative financial institution in the 1780s and throughout the early national period. Although many supporters of the charter application had predicted that emissions of bank notes, linked to liberal lending policies, would exceed by two or three times the amount of paid-in capital, the volume of currency outstanding in the 1780s and 1790s was often less than stockholders' equity. Additional sales of stock increased capital from $400,000 in 1781 to more than $850,000 in 1784. Some stockholders later sold shares back to the bank, perhaps to offset loans, and reduced the capital account to about $750,000 by 1790. Bank notes outstanding averaged about $350,000 in the 1780s.

The directors ranked safety above the goal of profit optimization. The bank was an experimental venture, and management realized that the success or failure of the enterprise would not only affect the value of their investment in its stock but would likely have a major impact on the future of the American financial system in Philadelphia and throughout the new nation. The bank maintained substantial specie reserves, normally somewhere in the range of 20 to 40 percent, against bank note and deposit liabilities. The policy of maintaining high liquidity was the outcome of managerial decisions, not statute law, since the charter had specified no minimal reserve requirements.[6]

The BNA issued only modest amounts of currency in the 1780s.

The average volume of bank notes outstanding in the 1780s, for example, was only about half the aggregate value of the Pennsylvania assembly's outstanding paper in 1766. Given the growth in population, bank note circulation on a per capita basis in Pennsylvania by the mid-1780s was about one-quarter the figure recorded for colonial paper money two decades earlier. The actual volume circulating inside the state could have been even lower, however, since an undetermined portion of the BNA's currency was paid out to settle the federal government's accounts in the other twelve states; and that money may not have flowed back into the Philadelphia area for several months.[7] Meanwhile, customer deposits, which often equaled or exceeded the circulation of bank notes, helped boost the bank's contribution to the postwar money stock. The privatization of financial services moved quickly, but it was far from complete in the postwar decade.

Government still had a vital role to play in local financial markets in the immediate postwar era. From 1780 to 1783 the Pennsylvania assembly authorized three separate currency issues, emitting a total of about $2 million in fiat paper. Most of those monies had been taxed away by 1785.[8] That same year, the legislature authorized another $400,000, with one-third reserved for issuance through the reconstituted loan office. For more than a decade, the BNA and the state legislature coexisted as suppliers of paper monies to the Pennsylvania economy and as sources of loanable funds. If we presume that the citizens of Pennsylvania had retained their former preference for currency as the most convenient means of holding money—so long as its value was adequately supported—then opportunities clearly existed for an expansion of commercial banking facilities in the 1780s. Meanwhile, state government helped to fill the gap by providing limited financial services in emulation of the colonial tradition.

Despite its conservative management style, as reflected in the holding of a relatively modest portfolio of interest-earning loans and discounts, the BNA generated healthy profits in the first decade of operations. Corporate earnings were typically paid out fully in dividends during the eighteenth and nineteenth centuries, thus dividend rates are good indicators of overall profitability. The directors paid out 8.75 percent to investors on the par value of shares in 1782, the first full year of operations. In 1783 and 1784, dividends averaged 14 percent. The rate fell to 6 percent during the mid-1780s, after the bank sustained loan losses associated with a few substantial debtors during a mild business downturn, but dividends rose as high as 12.5 to 13.5 percent in the early 1790s. Low operating costs contributed to profitability. The bank paid no interest on deposits, and its managerial expenses were minimal since members of the board of directors, who met regularly to act on loan applications, served for modest honorariums.

Meanwhile, the founding of the BNA was the catalyst for the nascent commercial paper market that emerged in Philadelphia in the 1780s, according to historian Thomas Doerflinger. Before independence, merchants had rarely converted book credits into formalized debt instruments, not unless an old account was past due or a sterling bill of exchange was required to transfer funds to another port. However, the bank's preferred mode of negotiating mercantile loans had a sudden impact on standard business procedures. The BNA directors preferred to discount the commercial paper of its borrowers; thus merchants frequently converted receivables into formal instruments with thirty- to sixty-day maturities and offered the signed paper to the bank as collateral for their debt obligations. The bank thereby gained two-name paper as security—first, the name of the original mercantile debtor and second the endorser, who was the bank's loan customer. Doerflinger described the use of commercial paper and the bank's lending procedures as a "nut and bolt; neither made sense without the other, and the thread that engaged them was the process of discounting."[9] In this context the discount was the amount of interest deducted in advance; the proceeds were less than the face of the note, based on the interest rate applied and maturity date. Moreover, as a result of its routine lending activities, the BNA ended up acting as an important clearing house for the city's commercial paper, and that function aided in generating a fair amount of credit information on loan customers.

As commercial banks went into operation in other American cities in the late eighteenth and early nineteenth centuries, the practice of converting open book debts into formalized notes continued to spread among mercantile firms. *Discounting* soon became the term most commonly used to describe the routine lending activities of banks. The system of advancing funds to borrowers had British antecedents. In London, numerous banks and discount houses, most of them unincorporated firms, made cash advances to holders of sterling bills of exchange that were generated in the course of conducting British foreign trade, which was substantial by the eighteenth century. Americans had been party to those sterling instruments for decades but only as drawers and drawees. No American firm offered discounting services on a steady basis, nor indeed had any reason for doing so since colonial accounts were invariably maintained and settled on the British side of the Atlantic. After achieving political independence, American merchants, partly out of a desire for greater freedom and partly out of necessity, sought to gain a larger degree of economic independence from the domination of the providers of British financial services. The rise of commercial banking and the emergence of domestic commercial paper markets were two logical responses.

The general acceptance of discounting as the standard method of bank lending in urban markets had an impact on prevailing theories about sound banking principles. The adoption of that procedure was compatible with the so-called real bills theory of commercial banking. It was promoted as a valuable tool for the prudent management of financial institutions from a microeconomic standpoint and as a useful mechanism for dampening fluctuations in regular business cycles. Proponents of this school of economic and financial analysis eventually dominated intellectual circles in the United States, and their influence lasted well into the twentieth century.

The assumption behind the real bills doctrine was that adherence to its dictates would translate into mechanisms of internal regulation and control. If banks loaned strictly against commercial paper generated by actual mercantile transactions, then the size of the money supply would automatically adjust to the "needs-of-trade" and never become excessively inflationary. The aim was to eliminate from the commercial banking system virtually every other type of loan transaction—foremost among them all speculative ventures in distant, unimproved lands. If every bank prudently stuck to real bills and thereby protected itself from the presumed dangers of a rash of bad loans, proponents of the doctrine predicted the moderation, or even the wholesale elimination, of boom-and-bust cycles in the general economy. Despite its simplistic appeal, the theory was seriously flawed. It failed to take fully into account the possibility of excessive inventory accumulation based on the discounting of mercantile bills in urban areas and, secondly, it failed to acknowledge the role of rural banks which, by necessity, secured most of their loans with crops and farmland.

In its infancy, however, American commercial banking was largely an urban phenomenon; and advocates of the real bill hypothesis, including influential financial historians in the nineteenth and early twentieth centuries, took their cue from the generally safe and successful records of the BNA and its cautious imitators. In truth, early urban banks rarely restricted themselves to discounting mercantile paper. Many institutions including the BNA made intermediate-term loans to persons with good credit and a reportedly large net worth, typically stockholders, who participated in vast speculative purchases of frontier lands. Morris himself received liberal credit for land speculation, and then proceeded to lose a fortune. But banking theorists and financial historians, without access to internal bank documents, assumed as an operational reality what they wanted to believe in order to equate the presumed facts with their pet theories. In truth, commercial banking was safe and sound for three decades after 1781 because boards of directors were careful to limit the volume of outstanding loans to correspond with a bank's capital and to restrict all manner of advances to persons offering adequate collateral, multiple signature notes, substantial personal net worth, or some combination of all three margins of safety.

Meanwhile, undaunted by fact or fancy, later proponents of the real bills doctrine invariably cited the overall performance of the early banking system as surefire proof of the validity of their far-reaching hypotheses. That dubious intellectual heritage became another of the legacies of the first era of American commercial banking, and the continuance of vehement political debate over the functional segmentation of financial services in the twentieth century reveals that shadowy images of the real bills doctrine still haunt the organization and structure of U.S. financial markets.

External Challenges to the BNA

The BNA got off to a hugely successful start in 1782. The public accepted its bank notes readily in trade, and the loan volume generated instantaneous profits. The directors operated throughout the next year without any major distractions. In 1784 and 1785, however, the bank became embroiled in three public controversies that threatened its privileged status. The first challenge centered around the plan to organize a rival commercial bank in Philadelphia; the second arose from the state's decision to revive the public loan office, which had functioned so smoothly in colonial times; and the third challenge—linked to the second—stemmed from a rurally organized movement to repeal the bank's Pennsylvania charter. The outcome of these three contests, once again, set precedents that influenced the future development of the nation's commercial banking sector.

The profitability of the BNA encouraged its organizers to propose an expansion of capital. In January 1784 the directors approved a plan to issue an additional one thousand shares, thereby doubling the number outstanding. Since the bank had operated profitably during the last two years, the directors decided to raise the issue price to five hundred dollars, an advance of 25 percent over the subscription price in 1781. Although priced higher, the new shares possessed no greater claim on earnings and dividends than the shares previously issued. From the modern perspective, the directors' decision to offer new shares at a higher issue price, which reflected the success of the enterprise over the previous two years, seems fully justified. Indeed, based on the second-year dividend rate and an expectation of its continuation, investors seeking a 9 percent return on their investment should have been willing to pay more than six hundred dollars to acquire BNA shares on the open market. In retrospect, five hundred dollars appears to have been a bargain price to lay equal claim on the earnings of a firm that had quickly established a solid record of sound management.

But a policy that might seem fair and reasonable to modern analysts elicited a different reaction from critics in the 1780s. In valuing the shares of this corporate entity, many contemporaries refused to take into account management performance and the greater degree of risk associated with launching a completely new venture. To critics, the seemingly identical assets merited equal valuation irrespective of the degree of managerial expertise applied in past years. They believed the two-year difference in the timing of stock issues was trivial and irrelevant. Others believed it verged on the unethical for directors to seek a premium price from new investors.

Within a fortnight a group of Philadelphia merchants who had not been among the original investors in the BNA announced plans to establish an independent financial institution to be known as the Bank of Pennsylvania.[10] Quaker merchants provided much of the leadership. In addition to unfavorable comments about the higher asking price for BNA stock, they complained that the directors' partiality to stockholders and other insiders had prevented outsiders like themselves from gaining legitimate access to credit facilities. Stock in the new bank was offered to investors at four hundred dollars per share, the same offering price as the original BNA issue, and by 5 February organizers announced that $280,000 had already been raised and further stock subscriptions were anticipated. A board of directors was elected and a charter application promptly went forward to the Pennsylvania legislature, where the initial response was positive.

After the newly elected directors of the Bank of Pennsylvania had formally applied for a corporate charter to the state legislature, members of the BNA board expressed mounting fears about the possibly devastating consequences of the introduction of competitive commercial banking into the Philadelphia market. Having operated as a monopoly for two years, management was uncertain about what might transpire under competitive conditions. The greatest fear was that the presence of a rival might drive both institutions to ruin—bankrupting the BNA and leaving the business community without access to reliable financial services. As a consequence, BNA spokesmen requested the opportunity to appear before the appropriate legislative committee to oppose the issuance of a corporate charter for a second commercial bank.

A good many of the danger warnings of BNA investors were mere verbal tactics designed to protect local monopoly profits. Yet there can be little doubt that several otherwise very knowledgeable people were genuinely confused about the possible consequences of competitive banking—for example, Robert Morris and Alexander Hamilton. What had sparked their concern were reports about the precipitous depletion of the BNA's reserves resulting from the conversion of bank notes into specie by persons investing in the newly organized Bank of Pennsylvania. The BNA faced something approaching a mild run—a threatening development for any institution relying for safety on fractional reserves. Perhaps, the two financiers wondered aloud, an insufficient stock of specie circulated in regional money markets to support two competitive banks.

Hamilton had initially favored the plan for a second Philadelphia bank, but after receiving reports about the loss of gold and silver from the BNA's vaults and the virtual halt to discounting during the following two weeks, he withdrew his endorsement and confessed probable error. "On a superficial view, I perceived benefits to the community, which, on a more close inspection, I found were not real," Hamilton admitted to one correspondent in early April. In a letter to Thomas Jefferson, Morris concluded: "The struggle to get such capital places these institutions in a degree of opposition to each other injurious to them all."[11] Morris was, of course, a major investor in the BNA, thus his motives may not have been pure; but the thrust of his correspondence suggests that he was genuinely concerned about promoting the development of a healthy American financial system.

In an atmosphere of conflict and confusion, a compromise was hastily arranged. The directors of the BNA agreed to reduce the offering price for new shares to four hundred dollars, and in return the organizers of the Bank of Pennsylvania agreed to withdraw their charter application and disband the whole enterprise. Most subscribers to shares in the new bank quickly transferred their investment into the BNA. The threat of bank competition in Philadelphia dissipated and monopoly was perpetuated. A merger of interests seemed the more prudent course in what contemporaries considered a fragile financial atmosphere. Along with the expansion of its capital base, the number of BNA stockholders increased sharply, since few of the new investors had acquired large blocks of stock. By 1786 the list of investors included the names of more than 1,200 Philadelphians, plus 650 additional U.S. citizens residing elsewhere and 285 foreigners (90 percent Dutch).[12] The BNA became an enterprise with the support of most factions within the Philadelphia mercantile community, including many Quakers, after 1785.

The fears of Morris, Hamilton, and other commentators about the long-term consequences of competitive banking were grossly exaggerated, although in fairness they had fortuitously raised an important issue about following sound procedures in managing the transition from monopolistic to competitive banking within a given community. Morris and Hamilton were usually clearheaded about financial matters but they were not omnipotent. The argument that the country possessed too little coin and specie to support numerous commercial banks in Philadelphia and elsewhere was nonsensical. By the mid-1780s the nation's money stock was composed largely of specie—perhaps as much as $15 million was scattered throughout the thirteen states. Pennsylvania probably had as much, or more, hard money in general circulation in the 1780s than in any decade during the last half century.

What had caused alarm among merchants dependent on the BNA for routine credit accommodations had been the bank's sharp curtailment of loan commitments and the retirement of bank notes in response to the anticipated drain on reserves. The drain occurred as investors transferred funds into the coffers of the Bank of Penn-

sylvania in late January and early February. However, the new bank
did not commence lending operations at once but waited instead for
the state legislature to take action on its charter application. During the prolonged interregnum, the specie transferred out of the
BNA was temporarily frozen; it was unavailable to provide the base
for continuous banking services, including the creation of currency
liabilities and the discounting of mercantile commercial paper. If,
instead, the Bank of Pennsylvania had started to discount paper
and issue currency against accumulated reserves in mid-February
while awaiting final legislative approval, then the aggregate volume
of banking services in Philadelphia would not have diminished significantly.

In short, the difficulties that Hamilton, Morris, and their co-
horts interpreted as a serious threat to the city's evolving financial
system were, in retrospect, merely the temporary consequences of
bad timing. Generally speaking, a lag of several weeks between the
accumulation of capital and specie for the establishment of a new
competitive bank and the commencement of its projected lending
operations could disrupt financial services in a local economy, and
that chain of events had occurred in Philadelphia in 1784. Frozen
reserves were unproductive for everyone concerned. On the other
hand, given a smooth transition, nothing was fundamentally destabilizing about the introduction of competition among several institutions into the commercial banking sector.

Doubters finally realized the viability of competitive commercial banking after the First Bank of the United States (First BUS)
entered the Philadelphia market in the early 1790s. The BNA and
First BUS did not undermine each other's operations, and indeed
with the calming of exaggerated fears, the old proposal to create a
Bank of Pennsylvania was resuscitated in 1793. By the mid-1790s,
Philadelphia became the first American city to possess three commercial banks—all thriving and profitable.

In 1785 two additional threats to the BNA's position emerged.
This time the opposition had its genesis in the political sphere.
The establishment of the BNA led to improved financial services in
Philadelphia, but it had done little to benefit directly other citizens
of the state, particularly farmers who constituted the major occupational group. The BNA made no loans to the farm sector, and
the circulation of its bank notes in rural areas was insufficient to
meet the monetary demands of farm families. Remembering the
financial successes of the still recent colonial past, rural constituents

put pressure on their elected representatives to provide more financial assistance for agriculture. In response, the state's unicameral legislature had authorized three issues of fiat currency totaling $1.9 million between 1780 and 1783, which significantly augmented the money supply. However, it had promptly taxed all the new monies out of existence by 1785. Farmers cried again for monetary relief.

In the spring of 1785 the Pennsylvania legislature authorized a fresh currency issue of $400,000. Two-thirds of the new monies went to meet the interest currently due on the state's public securities, with this portion of the total issue scheduled for retirement through general taxation. The remaining $135,000 was allocated to the reconstituted loan office. The former colonial mechanism for providing long-term funds to the agricultural sector was suddenly reinvigorated after a lapse of more than a decade. The terms were similar to previous public programs. Borrowers could obtain from $65 to $265, at 6 percent interest over eight years, against real property with a market value at least three times greater than the outstanding loan. Modest upper limits were again placed on borrowers to ensure that the funds were widely distributed throughout the state. The reopening of the loan office in 1785 signaled the reinvolvement of government in financial markets and to about the same extent of participation as in the prewar era. Some rural voters hoped the state government would reassert itself and reemerge as the provider of continuous financial services to the regional economy.

During the public debate over reviving the loan office, the BNA made a series of tactical maneuvers that provided critics with the ammunition to place its status in jeopardy. Sensing that the state might try to reclaim supremacy in financial markets, bank directors initially opposed the bill authorizing issuance of new monies. When that tactic failed, they threatened to refuse acceptance of government currency at teller windows either for deposit or the repayment of bank loans. Their justification for rejection was the inconvertibility of government paper into specie at the issuing offices—a perfectly legitimate concern for a competing private institution maintaining convertibility based on fractional reserves. If holders of government paper could freely exchange their fiat money for bank notes and specie at tellers' windows, then logic dictated that the bank could be drained of reserves very quickly through no fault of its own. But rural voters interpreted the directors' decision as a slap in the face since the bank's policy implied that private firms had seized the power to judge the legitimacy of public monies. From the perspective of its critics, the BNA directors had assumed an unreasonable and arrogant stance regarding the management of local monetary affairs. A similar superior position had previously been enunciated by Parliament's intransigent Board of Trade.

In retaliation, long-standing opponents of the bank introduced a bill into the Pennsylvania legislature that called for the revocation of the bank's corporate charter. The movement toward privatization was suddenly threatened. The spring session ended before any action could be taken, but when legislators reconvened in September 1785, the bill was quickly approved. Opposition to the bank came largely from persons living outside the Philadelphia region. Critics presented a laundry list of complaints: alleged usury, favoritism in approving loans, discrimination against artisans and farmers, failure to make loans longer than sixty days to honest borrowers, insistence on absolute punctuality in paying debts, admission of foreigners to stock ownership, chasing specie out of the state, and the bank's steadfast refusal to accept provincial paper at its teller windows.

Hoping to expand the operations of the government's loan office as an alternative system of finance, rural legislators argued that the state treasury should be the prime beneficiary of interest income on borrowed funds, not private investors. For decades, the interest income on hundreds of first mortgage loans had provided Pennsylvania government with a large percentage of its total revenues, and supporters of the loan office aimed at recapturing that source of income for public purposes. A few years later, the complaint about lost public revenues, which followed the withdrawal of government from the mortgage market, was voiced often and loudly by John Taylor of Caroline, who became a leading opponent of the spread of private enterprise in the commercial banking sector during the late eighteenth and early nineteenth centuries.

Detractors who believed that revocation of the charter would soon put the BNA out of business were overly optimistic. The bank simply reverted to noncorporate status, becoming in effect a large joint-stock partnership with transferable shares. After the legislative vote, the banking office remained open as usual, and the directors continued to issue bank notes and discount mercantile notes.

Although the loss of the Pennsylvania charter had a minimal impact on daily operations, stockholders were determined on principle to regain corporate status. In the spirit of compromise, the bank withdrew its opposition to the reestablishment of the state's loan office. Robert Morris acknowledged the validity of arguments about the need for more access to long-term credit in agricultural areas. It would, he stated, "promote and encourage the landed interest and operate as much in its favor as a bank does in favor of commerce." [13] In addition, the directors reversed their earlier stand and expressed their willingness to accept deposits of fiat monies so long as all receipts were recorded in special accounts maintained separately from transactions involving bank notes and specie.

The new policy increased the burden of record keeping, but by eliminating the possibility of intermingling fiat paper and bank notes, the BNA believed it could sustain its specie reserves. The bank's more cooperative attitude came too late to affect the outcome of the legislative vote in the fall of 1785, but the directors had high hopes about the prospects of obtaining a reversal in the first scheduled session of 1786. Supporters published stirring defenses of the bank's conduct and pointed out its contribution to the general welfare, emphasizing the soundness and usefulness of its circulating bank notes as a medium of exchange and store of value for the whole population. They refuted the claim that the presence of banks caused specie to flee the local economy. Meanwhile, the directors entered into negotiations with members of the Delaware legislature about obtaining a charter from that contiguous state and transferring banking operations to nearby Wilmington or New Castle if necessary.

Having altered its position on the handling of fiat currency to mollify vocal critics, and with a charter offer in hand from rival Delaware, the BNA was optimistic about its ability to turn around the Pennsylvania legislature in 1786. New elections produced a political realignment more favorable to the bank. The vote to restore a Pennsylvania charter sailed through with a solid majority; however, one important change was made in the charter terms. The original incorporation act specified no limitation on the life of the charter. Bank defenders had claimed the charter was perpetual and inviolate, but victorious legislators in 1785 argued that the corporate charter was revocable and remained in force merely at the pleasure of the legislature. The issue was resolved with the specification of a charter term of fourteen years, granting the bank the privilege of incorporation through the end of the century.

For the next half century, until the adoption of general incorporation laws for commercial banks beginning in New York in the late

1830s, bank charters invariably contained expiration dates ranging from ten to thirty years. With the prominent exceptions of the two nationally chartered banks in 1812 and 1836, few banks with governmental charters failed to win renewals; although in later decades they typically paid special tax assessments, or license fees, for the privilege of gaining another lease on their corporate lives.

After the turmoil of 1785 and 1786, the BNA settled into a long span of steady, uneventful operations. The most experimental half decade in American commercial banking, involving the operations of the new nation's original bank, had passed. The precedents established in Philadelphia from 1781 to 1786 exerted a tremendous influence on the subsequent development of the nation's financial system. The BNA and its principal sponsor, Robert Morris, led the way toward the privatization of crucial financial services previously performed by provincial governments. On the advice of Alexander Hamilton, organizers of the Bank of New York sent several representatives to Philadelphia to seek information about the BNA's routine procedures and lending policies before opening the doors of their own unchartered bank in 1784.[14] Because of its great capital base and its geographical expanse, the First Bank of the United States was likewise a crucial and innovative institution; but most of the principles of successful commercial banking on a modest scale were already established before Hamilton became secretary of the treasury in Washington's first administration.

The founding of the BNA was a vehicle for the introduction of financial intermediaries into the North American economy. Previous loan transactions were invariably directly between parties seeking accommodations and those with surplus funds to lend. The Philadelphia bank and its imitators in New York and Boston in the 1780s carried the financial system in a radically new direction. The early banks accumulated specie through the sale of stock or the acceptance of deposits, and they issued fully convertible bank notes in the process of discounting the debt instruments of their mercantile customers. In sum, they became financial intermediaries between savers and borrowers—the suppliers and users of capital surpluses.

Like the colonial and some confederation legislatures, commercial banks created new monies for distribution into the economy. Because they operated on fractional reserves, these financial institutions had the power to multiply severalfold the volume of money in circulation beyond the value of specie locked away in their vaults.

The early urban banks preferred lending against two-name paper, and they stimulated thereby the common use of formal debt instruments, as opposed to open mercantile accounts, and the subsequent emergence of an organized commercial paper market.

The BNA was crucial to the subsequent institutional development of the entire American financial system. The effect did not arise from the scope of its operations, but because the bank's sound record encouraged the founding of a host of imitators, a series of independent financial institutions of small to intermediate size at the state and local level—plus one heavily capitalized national bank with branch offices in several states. The BNA emerged as a highly visible symbol of the nation's renewed commitment to financial responsibility. Its founding coincided with the general movement toward greater fiscal conservatism at the federal level. Except for the indents issued to federal bondholders, congressional disbursements after 1782 were in specie or in the bank notes of the BNA, which were themselves convertible into specie upon demand. Morris purposely identified the financial standing of the federal government with the fortunes of the bank; consequently, the proven soundness of the bank's paper money reflected favorably on the Treasury as well as bank directors.

The federal government's sponsorship of bank notes—a novel financial instrument in the American economy—as a useful medium of exchange, a form of legal tender, and a reliable store of value was an important first step along the road toward rehabilitating the reputation of currency as a viable form of money after the total collapse of the ill-fated Continental issues. Indeed, the relationship between the government and its chartered banking institution was mutually reinforcing since both sides were seeking respectability and financial legitimacy. Meanwhile, the success of the BNA gave a strong boost to the public's perception of chartered commercial banking as a mainstay in a newly restructured American financial system, and the bank's profitable record reflected the wisdom and prudence of its two prime sponsors—the Philadelphia mercantile community and the U.S. Treasury—both of which were under the direct influence of Superintendent of Finance Morris.

Given the circumstances of the prior decade, namely the irreversible depreciation of congressional paper, the directors of the nation's early banks put great emphasis on maintaining the soundness of their respective currency issues. With few exceptions, chartered banks held ample specie reserves, and their ratio of paid-in capital to loans outstanding was likewise strikingly conservative. During the first three decades of commercial banking, financial institutions were rarely viewed as prime agents for promoting the growth of the local economy. Their role instead was to lay the foundation for monetary stability by providing citizens with a superior medium of exchange—that is, paper money that was convenient to hold, universally accepted, and, equally important, a reliable store of value.

The private commercial bank was an innovative institution in the immediate postwar period, but its debut came in only three major port cities along the Atlantic coast during the 1780s. The nascent privatization movement did not preempt the participation of state governments in financial markets. Even in the three states with chartered banks, the governmental sector actively provided various financial services, while in the other ten states, government played the same domineering role that it had exercised during the prior decades.

7

The States in the 1780s

THE TRANSFORMATION of the British North American colonies into thirteen independent states, loosely tied together under the national confederation government, did not end their involvement in the financial services sector. That involvement continued throughout the war and into the 1780s. Most state legislatures felt public pressures to perform the same financial functions as their colonial predecessors. All thirteen issued fiat currencies to raise and supply troops and to assist Congress in financing the war effort. In the postwar decade, the legislatures faced challenges very similar to those they had faced in the aftermath of the Seven Years' War.

During the War for Independence, the thirteen separate states acquired mutual financial liabilities associated with the currency and debt issues of the Continental Congress. In addition, they incurred voluminous obligations of their own, consisting of varying mixtures of fiat paper monies and interest-bearing obligations. Most legislatures tried to deal with the situation by drawing upon their immediate experience: the lessons of the previous war. The challenge was vastly greater, however, because the net financial burden borne by the domestic population in waging the War for Independence was up to ten times greater per capita than that borne by the previous generation in the war with France for an expanded continental empire.

The states, acting individually, had voluntarily shouldered financial responsibility for approximately 60 percent of the aggregate American military expenditures from 1775 to 1783. By various methods they had settled about three-fourths of the obligations by

137

1790, when Congress assumed most of the remaining debts totaling just over $18 million in outstanding state obligations. In the final accounting—after the comprehensive congressional debt assumption program had taken effect and relieved their legislatures of some of the burden—the several states ended up assuming about 45 percent of overall war costs, somewhere around $75 million in specie funds.

By the mid-1780s, most state legislatures had adopted multi-year fiscal programs designed to meet their accumulated war debts. In most states, political leaders initially voted to adopt a program of heavy taxation, with the aim of retiring their obligations over a seven- to ten-year period. They were moving on a fast track. By comparison, the federal government under its new Constitution took nearly a quarter century to extinguish more than $70 million in war debts, which it officially funded in 1790.[1] Not every state legislature was prompt in reducing its outstanding debts. Some like Massachusetts and South Carolina were dilatory, but most adopted sundry programs to press forward on debt reduction, hoping to return to the normalcy of low taxation and limited government as soon as possible. A few states like North Carolina were reticent to increase tax revenues for debt retirement because the leadership believed that their state would emerge as a net creditor and thus receive financial reimbursement from the debtor states once the final apportionment was determined.

The achievements of the several states were, overall, highly commendable if assessed from the standpoint of responsible fiscal management. The sale of loyalist properties eased the burden substantially in some regions. Loyalists reported to British officials in 1784 that the value of their confiscated estates was £10.8 million (about $50 million).[2] While that figure was certainly overstated, if those properties brought in about one-quarter of that amount at public auction, loyalist losses covered perhaps as much as 15 percent of the military expenditures of the several states. Taking their cue from the successful postwar policies of the 1760s, the states considered a host of proposals, ranging from write-offs or write-downs of depreciated currencies to new and higher taxes on persons, property, and goods moving across state boundaries. The debates in the early 1780s were often acrimonious because the financial challenge was formidable—five times greater at the state level alone than after the Seven Years' War—and no group of taxpayers, or potential taxpayers, wanted to be assigned an unfair burden.

In the debates of the 1780s, several divergent views emerged regarding the disposition of outstanding debts. The protagonists may be divided into two broad groups—the urgency faction and the gradualist faction—with the criterion for membership centered on conflicting beliefs about the proper length and scope of debt reduction programs. The urgency faction, which represented the majority of the political leadership in the early 1780s, aimed at extinguishing all state obligations within a decade or so. Members were willing to face up to the difficult task of redeeming the public debt with all deliberate speed. The issue was more complex, however, because under its umbrella, the urgency faction provided room for persons espousing alternative routes for reaching the common goal of a quick settlement. The mainstream majority, the "honor-one's-debts" coalition, wanted to extinguish the debt in four to ten years through crash programs of heavy taxation, irrespective of the temporary hardships imposed on the general population. The radical wing of the urgency faction was composed mostly of indebted farmers who wanted to scale down drastically, or even repudiate, outstanding public obligations. Their approach would force public creditors, disproportionately urban merchants and other persons of accumulated wealth, to absorb capital losses. Irrespective of their differences over the implementation of debt reduction programs, all members of the urgency faction were acting squarely within the tradition of the previous generation of political leadership.

While they may have differed over whether to impose stiff taxes, rely heavily on repudiation, or settle on some mixture of the two, members of the urgency faction were in general agreement about one fundamental proposition regarding the future character of American society. They were united in their opposition to the perpetuation of a large public debt, since they associated such bloated financial systems with the alleged corruption of powerful European monarchies. The urgency faction feared that, if it failed to press ahead with a redemption program, however painful in the short run, the outcome could very well be the establishment of a similar system of European public finance in the United States.

A permanent national debt would foster the creation on American shores of a class of aristocratic parasites who lived for generations in luxury off the interest income generated from their investments in government securities. From the perspective of the urgency faction, a permanent floating debt was an unsavory device for allowing a monied elite to live indefinitely off the tax revenues collected from middling farmers and artisans. Contemporaries were already aware that a small group of urban investors was actively acquiring large portfolios of public debt instruments. Thomas Jefferson was an articulate spokesman for the aspirations of the urgency faction; he argued that every generation ought to be made wholly responsible for redeeming its accumulated public debts—even if the pursuit of that policy required personal sacrifice for a brief time.

The gradualist faction, on the other hand, was in no rush to sink the principal of the public debt. Its members were more concerned about obtaining legislative recognition of the taxpayer's obligation to repay all public debts at face value in specie. Repudiation was their greatest fear. They advocated postponing full retirement of the outstanding debt until an unspecified future date. Their revenue program called for modest levels of taxation—just enough to cover the payment of interest. Gradualists also opposed high taxes because they feared social and political dangers, from their perspective, of overly ambitious programs aimed at generating sufficiently large budget surpluses to make inroads on the outstanding principal. In contrast to the attitude of the urgency faction, leaders in the gradualist camp also saw potential benefits in maintaining the good will of a clientele of government security holders dedicated to the permanence of a republican form of government. Alexander Hamilton was the recognized leader of this contingent, and his outlook eventually prevailed in the funding program at the federal level.

At the state level in the early 1780s, however, a sense of urgency prevailed in almost every legislature, and political leaders took steps to rid their governments of the dark clouds of public debt. In a stance that seems at first glance contradictory, but which in fact made perfect sense, leaders of the mainstream wing of the urgency faction realized that, if they wanted to eliminate the overhanging war debts and pave the way for the return of low taxes a decade hence, it would require a heavy dose of high taxes in the short run. Steep poll and property taxes, in particular, would probably be required for four to eight years to meet annual interest payments and simultaneously sink the debt principal. By steadily retiring these public obligations, taxpayers could avoid paying hundreds of thousands of dollars in future interest to avaricious debt holders. Those considerations led most state legislatures, despite their abhorrence of taxes in general and their fear of the heavy hand of government, to enact sweeping revenue programs designed to produce large surpluses in statehouse budgets—surpluses that could be applied to debt redemption. By the mid-1780s every state had formulated a tax program designed to reduce the outstanding principal, consisting of the face amount of the debt plus, in most cases, several years of past-due interest.

In about half the states, legislators had visions not merely of rapidly retiring state obligations but of moving on to sink a portion of the overhanging federal debt as well. In response to the pressure from federal security holders residing within their respective borders, some legislatures voted to absorb a portion of congressional debt. Congress had suspended interest payments on the federal debt in 1782, and two years later it authorized the issuance of "indents," or certificates of accrued interest, to federal debt holders in lieu of genuine monies. Since the indents were not backed by any credible taxing authority, they immediately plummeted in value and left in their wake thousands of dissatisfied federal creditors. After the failure of two congressional attempts to generate a federal revenue by imposing a uniform tariff on imports into the United States, and with little prospect of achieving unanimous agreement on any other tax plan under the Confederation government, federal debt holders began to petition their state legislatures to assume financial responsibility for the payment of the interest due them and perhaps even the redemption of the outstanding principal.

In most states various programs of increased taxation and federal debt absorption went forward on schedule, and much progress was made in extinguishing public obligations. The sharp hikes in taxes, mostly after 1785, imposed heavy burdens on American households, however. In Massachusetts an overly ambitious fiscal plan designed to wipe out the state's large accumulated debt in just four years precipitated Shays' Rebellion, an armed uprising in the western counties in 1787. As a result of that incident, the state's program of high taxes and planned debt reduction was abandoned and scaled back to more modest levels in the late 1780s.

In South Carolina, middling households complained about pressures associated with the repayment of massive private debts, including impending suits and property seizures, plus the heavy burden of upcoming state taxes. The state's debt redemption program stalled before it ever got off the ground. The South Carolina legislature acted to defuse smoldering resentments and prevent the possible outbreak of armed rebellion against governmental authority.[3] When Congress absorbed the remaining state debts in 1790, public

creditors in Massachusetts and South Carolina were strong supporters of the federal program.

States Reissuing Currency in the 1780s

More than half the states remained directly involved in the financial
services sector in the 1780s through the reissuance of fiat currencies. All thirteen states had issued fiat monies during the war. The
sums placed in circulation had a face value of about $210 million,
roughly equivalent to congressional emissions. But Virginia, which
experienced hyperinflation in the last few years of the war, was responsible for $128 million, or more than 60 percent of the total.
Currency emissions in the other twelve states were much more re-
strained. The issues were either taxed away during the war, allowed
to depreciate so heavily that the paper became virtually worthless—
like Continental currency—or were finally recognized as a portion
of a given state's continuing debt obligations at a wide range of
depreciated values. Virginia, for example, adopted a depreciation
schedule that wrote down its paper at the extreme ratio of one thousand to one, effectively wiping out millions of dollars in potential
future liabilities.

In the early 1780s, all thirteen states went through the process of
settling their own internal accounts and determining what amounts
were still owed to citizens holding fiat monies and debt certificates.
A reasonably accurate calculation of aggregate state obligations in
the early 1780s, based on the analysis of hard data, has eluded scholars to date because of the diversity of settlement techniques among
the thirteen governmental units and differing exchange ratios for
their paper monies. All we know with certainty is that outstanding
state debts were at least $18 million as late as 1790 since the federal
government assumed that total under Hamilton's funding program.
The amount absorbed by the federal government included undetermined amounts of accrued interest as well as original principal.
After concluding the swap program, Treasury officials estimated
in 1791 that state debts combined stood at $8 million. The mini-
mum total debt of the states combined, therefore, was $26 million
in 1790.

My guess—and at this point the number is no more than a
crude deduction based on circumstantial evidence—is that the several state legislatures had officially recognized a figure somewhere
in the neighborhood of $35 to $50 million specie as their outstand-

ing debts by the end of the war. It follows, therefore, providing my guess is reasonably accurate, that the several states had managed to redeem, or write down, from 25 to 50 percent of their outstanding debts by the end of the 1780s. Much of the debt reduction at the state level came in the second half of the decade when tax rates in some locales rose sharply and notes receivable associated with the sale of confiscated loyalist estates matured.[4]

Seven states emitted paper money after 1783. They were Rhode Island in New England; New York, Pennsylvania, and New Jersey in the mid-Atlantic region; and North Carolina, South Carolina, and Georgia in the South. As in colonial times, their legislatures issued currencies with two different mechanisms of retirement— either public taxation or the mortgage payments of private borrowers. In most instances, the same legislative package authorized one currency emission from the state treasury to meet certain public expenses, plus a second companion emission, usually a lesser amount, allocated to loan office administrators to fund a series of mortgage loans to eligible borrowers. The emissions in the 1780s normally contained legal tender provisions, and the subsequent record of those monies as a store of value was reasonably good. In short, several states in the postwar era tried to reinstitute the monetary stability that had prevailed within their borders during the third quarter of the century, and for the most part the legislatures were successful.

The pressure to issue currency in those seven states came from several groups within society. A cross section of the population merely wanted to expand the stock of money through the addition of fresh paper, thereby supplementing the coinage in circulation. They viewed the new monies as a convenient medium of exchange that would stimulate the volume of economic activity. The lack of monies to lubricate routine transactions was a familiar eighteenth-century refrain. Some persons deeply in debt undoubtedly hoped the new monies would soon depreciate and allow them to pay off existing obligations with cheapened fiat paper. The goals of debtors were generally dashed, however, because the paper issued after the war tended to maintain its value relative to specie and foreign exchange. Also supporting paper money emissions were persons holding real estate who sought to raise funds either for consumption or investment by negotiating first mortgages at government loan offices.

Public creditors, a coalition of the holders of state and federal debt certificates, also ended up supporting the paper money movement in those seven states. Most public debt holders had received very little return on their investments for several years since regular interest payments on debt certificates were generally suspended in the late 1770s and early 1780s. Creditors would have preferred payments in specie, but many concluded that the receipt of monies from a fresh but limited emission of state currency was a satisfactory substitute. Even if the currency held up vis-à-vis specie for no more than a month or two, the initial recipients would still have time to use their monies to acquire other, more tangible assets.

When legislatures authorized currency emissions in the 1780s, most simultaneously approved comprehensive programs to raise substantial tax revenues during the next three to five years; and they generally stuck by those pledges in the second half of the decade. Budget surpluses were steadily applied to the redemption of the paper monies in circulation. The initial distributions of freshly printed currency typically went to cover the interest currently due on public debts. When those monies flowed back to the state treasury in taxes a few years later, some of the paper was immediately retired, while a portion was paid out of the public treasury a second time to redeem a given state's debts plus accrued interest from prior years. Meanwhile, citizens sometimes had the option of paying their taxes with public securities rather than currency or coin, which likewise translated into debt retirement.

The sweetener that elicited the support of public creditors, broadly defined, was the commitment to use new monies to pay claims related not merely to state obligations but on federal securities as well. Political leaders who supported state assumption of federal debts and those who advocated new emissions of paper money were thus able to find common ground. Paper provided a means of current payment that was otherwise lacking—or lacking without voting an immediate increase in taxes. The emission of fresh paper permitted citizens to delay implementation of higher taxes on their persons and property until the second half of the 1780s, and that margin of two or three years was critical in several states. Six of the states issuing currency in the mid-1780s had officially assumed at least a portion of the federal debt; assumption in New Jersey was de facto but not de jure. (Another four states assumed federal debts but did not emit fresh paper money to make interest payments on federal securities—Massachusetts, Connecticut, Maryland, and Delaware.)

The Constitution, which took effect in 1789, denied the states the right to emit any new issues of so-called bills of credit, or fiat monies. The reason most frequently cited for that provision was the poor performance of provincial and state currencies as a store of value during the prior decade and one half. Yet the states' overall record in managing their paper monies, excepting Virginia, was vastly superior to the ill-fated continentals issued by Congress. Even so, the states' performance was uneven. In most states, the fiat currencies issued in the 1770s suffered steady depreciation and were only partially funded.

As the ensuing state-by-state analysis clearly reveals, most governments retired or refinanced through debt obligations the fiat currencies emitted in the 1780s at face value, or thereabouts, through tax collections or the mortgage payments of private borrowers. Only North Carolina had a poor record. The performance of six of the currency-issuing states in the immediate postwar years was reasonably good, thus the constitutional ban on the continuance of currency emissions was not justified by the facts.

PENNSYLVANIA

During the early years of the war, Pennsylvania had issued substantial amounts of paper money. As a result of a vigorous program of taxation at the end of the decade, however, the state had retired almost all of its outstanding currency by 1779. Pennsylvania was typical of the other twelve states with regard to the application of tax monies during and after the war; the sums collected were used foremost in the effort to maintain the state's own reputation for fiscal responsibility. Congress had to settle for second call on most state treasuries. Pennsylvania was one exception, along with Massachusetts; it had a solid record at all levels, remitting approximately 85 percent of the sums formally requested by the federal government from 1778 to 1783. In 1780, 1781, and 1783, the legislature emitted additional rounds of fiat monies, and simultaneously approved taxes to sink the paper. Retirement proceeded on schedule, and the state had redeemed all its outstanding currency by 1785.

When Robert Morris halted the payment of interest on the domestic federal debt in 1782, after his failure to obtain unanimous agreement on a modest 5 percent national tax on imports, the Pennsylvania legislature stepped in to fill the void. The state began making interest payments to resident citizens holding federal debt certificates in 1783. Indeed, taxpayers were asked to bear a comparatively heavy tax burden throughout the late 1770s and early 1780s. In addition, public monies were raised from the sale of loyalist properties, which reportedly amounted to nearly $3 million in 1780 alone. Fines on persons failing to perform military duties brought in a few more dollars. The legislature allocated monies to meet congressional requisitions, to retire the state issues of currency, and to pay interest due on both state and federal debt certificates.

Meanwhile, the Bank of North America went into operation in 1782 and provided the state economy with paper currency convertible into specie upon demand. BNA bank notes were an excellent medium of exchange plus a reliable store of value. Since Superintendent Morris frequently used bank notes to meet the current expenses of Congress, many flowed into other parts of the nation. Pennsylvania, in sum, was a state with an innovative financial services sector that boasted two active currency-issuing components in the mid-1780s. From 1782 to 1784, the public and private systems were generally complementary; but the next year a serious conflict arose.

Following the scheduled retirement of the outstanding fiat paper in 1785, citizens demanded a replacement issue to supplement the bank notes and specie still in circulation. Pennsylvania was a governmental unit with a long history of issuing public monies dating back to the 1720s, and political leaders in the mid-1780s were not yet prepared to surrender the power to exert some influence over the money stock to the private sector. In accordance, the legislature voted in 1785 to issue £150,000 ($400,000) in new paper. Two-thirds of the emission was allocated to pay interest on state and federal debts, with retirement scheduled from future tax revenues.

When the issue was debated in the legislature, John Dickinson, president of the state's executive council, opposed the bill because it failed to provide monies for both the original debt holders and secondary investors. He wanted to pay a portion of the accrued interest to the original holders even though they had long since sold out to secondary buyers—often at rock-bottom prices. Dickinson argued that he did not want to reward unduly speculators who had acquired debt obligations at discount prices. He claimed payment of 6 percent interest to current debt holders would reward speculators with returns of up to 50 percent on their recent investments. In response, supporters of the bill pointed out that the so-called speculators were persons who had demonstrated superior faith in the viability of the existing government and confidence in its willingness to meet all debt obligations when others had doubts. Therefore, secondary investors deserved handsome rewards since they had assumed the risk of possible public default or payment long delayed.

The controversy over the wisdom and legality of discriminating between original and secondary debt holders arose again in the heated congressional debates of the early 1790s, when James Madison and Alexander Hamilton and their respective followers took opposing sides. The issue is discussed in detail in chapter 10 on congressional funding. Meanwhile, a brief overview of the situation at the state level, including Pennsylvania, must suffice. Whereas policies of discrimination against secondary holders were often proposed and debated in legislative bodies, in no instance were such programs ever enacted at either the federal or state level. Resolute respect for the sanctity of legal, voluntary contracts—part of the British heritage—prevailed despite some hesitation on the part of legislators in deference to the arguments of persons like Dickinson who sought what, they asserted, would be a more equitable settlement of financial accounts.

In 1786 and 1787, frustrated by the lack of progress at the national level, Pennsylvania formally assumed more than $6 million in federal certificates. Certain federal certificates became eligible for transfer into state obligations through a generous swap program. Local citizens were permitted to exchange all federal debts initially contracted inside the borders of Pennsylvania, as well as in the neighboring states of New Jersey and Delaware, for new state certificates. The federal securities that Philadelphia merchants had purchased from southern holders on secondary markets were deemed ineligible for the exchange mechanism. During the 1780s, the state paid $1.1 million in interest to former holders of federal securities; that sum was greater than the amount Congress requisitioned to cover Pennsylvania's assigned share of the federal indent program. Rather than sending tax monies to the national treasury for distribution to parts unknown, the state made interest payments directly to local citizens and later asked Congress to grant credit for those sums in the general settlement of accounts between the federal government and the states. Later, when Hamilton's funding program went into effect in 1790, Pennsylvania reversed the earlier transactions; it reissued federal securities to all participants in the earlier swap program.

One-third of the paper money that the Pennsylvania legislature authorized in 1785 was scheduled for emission through the reinvigorated loan office. The agency was permitted to make loans to citizens at 6 percent interest for up to eight years in the range of £25 to £100 ($65 to $265) doubly secured by real property—either in lands or residences. Retirement of the currency arose through the amortization of the mortgage loans over the life of the issue. The loan office allotted its £50,000 ($130,000) to the state's fifteen counties, and within six months most of the funds were in the hands of borrowers. The mean loan was about $175. Of the 750 borrowers, two-thirds were farmers, one-sixth artisans, and the remainder esquires and merchants. The rebirth of the governmental loan office received strong support from the rural population and many urban artisans.

While the money bill was being debated in the legislature, directors of the BNA expressed strong opposition to the state's efforts to maintain a prominent role in the financial services sector. In an effort to prevent a new emission in 1785, private bankers in Philadelphia threatened to refuse acceptance of the state's inconvertible fiat currency at teller windows. Since the new monies were to possess full legal tender status in private and public transactions, many legislators viewed the bank's refusal policy as a clear defiance of state law. In retaliation, politicians from rural areas headed the movement that led to the revocation of the bank's state charter in September 1785. As explained previously, farmers complained that the BNA, which operated from a single office in Philadelphia, provided no direct credit to the agricultural community, and they resented its campaign to deny them continued access to state funding. Many taxpayers cited the greater social benefits accruing from public as opposed to private lending since interest revenues went directly into the state treasury under the former arrangement rather than to the shareholders of private enterprises. In the colonial past, interest earnings had often been sufficient to cover the peacetime expenditures of the provincial government for years—even decades. The public loan office had functioned successfully in Pennsylvania for more than half a century, and potential borrowers had no intention of breaking with that long-standing tradition.

During the next several months, a compromise between the rural faction and Philadelphia bankers was arranged. Robert Morris, a leading stockholder in the BNA, came out in favor of a plan for public-private coexistence. He praised the loan office in particular as a legitimate and necessary service that complemented a chartered urban bank. Bank directors reversed themselves and agreed to accept the state's fiat currency in deposits so long as those monies were not intermingled with accounts denominated in bank notes and specie. After the political settlement was negotiated in 1786, the BNA received a new Pennsylvania charter that was good through the end of the century. Relations between the private and public sector were generally harmonious thereafter.

The state's fiat currency held its value relative to bank notes and specie fairly well in the first year after issuance, but it had depreciated somewhat, reportedly up to 30 percent, in 1788. The legislature remained faithful to its schedule of taxation and currency redemption, however, and by the end of 1790 all the paper monies issued by the state treasury had been retired at face value. The fiat currency issued through the loan office did not mature until 1793, and much of it stayed in circulation, complementing bank notes and coins. Meanwhile, the new federal Constitution had outlawed the states' participation in currency emission, thus paving the way for the complete privatization of that financial function beginning in the 1790s.

NEW YORK

Political events in New York were less tumultuous than in Pennsylvania; but a similar contest between urban merchants, who favored the encouragement of private commercial banking, and farmers, who wanted the state government to remain true to its heritage of public service in the financial sector, was played out in the mid-1780s. In 1784, the rural faction favored a fresh emission of government paper, while New York City's leading merchants looked to the prospect of obtaining a state charter for the new bank sponsored by Alexander Hamilton and business associates.

The legislative sessions during the next two years produced a standoff, however, and temporarily prevented the state from renewing its active involvement in financial services. The lower assembly, controlled by agricultural interests, passed two currency bills in 1784 plus another in 1785; but the upper chamber, where urban merchants held power, rejected all three. Members of New York City's mercantile community, who were usually creditors in the domestic market, raised the specter of inflation. The merchants had high hopes that the establishment of the Bank of New York, based on the model provided by the Bank of North America, might soon privatize completely the issuance of paper money within the state and provide citizens with a continuously convertible means of payment and a reliable store of value.

The Bank of New York began operations in 1784 with a capitalization of $800,000, twice the size of the Philadelphia institution. The directors planned to concentrate on short-term loans to the port's active mercantile community. In an effort to forestall the bank's possible preemption of the issuance function, the lower house balked at granting the Bank of New York formal charter rights. But that tactic proved ineffective and produced no tangible results. The bank opened its doors as an unchartered firm and operated for the next six years under the terms and conditions laid out in the bylaws, which the stockholders voted to approve at the initial organizational meeting. Unlike events in Pennsylvania, the state legislature never harassed the bank once it started making loans and issuing currency.

The issuance of bank notes by the Bank of New York, in the absence of a corporate charter from higher public authority, represented another American departure from the strict rule of British statute law. Parliament had prescribed that no partnership nor any joint stock company with more than six participants could emit paper money unless it had been granted explicit charter powers— which was rarely done in England, and never in the colonies.[5] The bank notes of the Bank of New York added a new component to the regional money stock, but because they were printed in large denominations and circulated mainly in the city and its hinterland, farmers continued to demand renewed governmental involvement in supplementing the money stock. Two years later, with the support of Governor George Clinton, the rural faction finally convinced the upper chamber to approve a comprehensive financial package that provided for an issue of currency more accessible to the agricultural sector.

During the 1786 session, the New York legislature approved the issuance of £200,000 in fresh currency with legal tender status in the payment of taxes but not private debts. Simultaneously, the state assumed full responsibility for interest and principal on some of the federal debt held by local citizens. Only federal loan certificates originally issued within state borders were eligible to participate in the swap program; eligible certificates amounted to $1.4 million of the approximately $5 million in federal securities held by New Yorkers.[6] The legislature assigned £50,000, or one-fourth of the new issue, to pay a portion of the interest past due through the end of 1784 on public securities. It represented a small start toward meeting the state's financial obligations; but the legislature soon launched an ambitious three-pronged tax program aimed at paying off the accrued interest, making inroads on the outstanding principal, and eventually retiring the most recent emission of fiat paper backed by public revenues. Up to half of the state's tax revenues in the mid-1780s came from customs receipts on imports, thereby lessening the need for direct assessments on persons and property.

The legislature allocated three-fourths of the currency issue authorized in 1786 to the revived government loan office. Borrowers could negotiate mortgage loans ranging from £20 to £300, at 5 percent interest for up to fourteen years, by offering as collateral either land valued at twice the loan amount or a residence valued at three times greater. The terms and conditions were virtually a replica of the loan office emission that had been approved by New York's colonial assembly nearly a half century before in 1737. The monies issued through the loan office remained in circulation throughout the 1790s and maintained their value vis-à-vis specie and bank notes until their scheduled retirement in 1800.

In New York, as in Pennsylvania, the state government and the unchartered Bank of New York coexisted as providers of financial services to the general public in the late 1780s. Bank notes were the preferred medium of exchange in New York City, while the government's fiat currency circulated widely upstate among farmers and artisans. Although some feared that such an arrangement was incompatible with what passed in the late eighteenth century as sound economic principles, the two monetary systems functioned in tandem without any discernible negative effects. Exchanges between the two currencies occurred at market rates; and the state's fiat paper, of which at least three-quarters was backed by private mortgages, passed at face value or minor discounts throughout the trading area. New York, therefore, possessed for decades a sound paper money system characterized by currency that served as both a useful medium of exchange and a reliable store of value.

Like Pennsylvania, New York also assumed federal securities as state obligations. The initial assumption totaled $1.4 million, but that figure had risen to $2.3 million by 1790 after the legislature voted to accept debt certificates issued to military personnel in 1783 in payment for the sale of state lands. When Hamilton's funding program was approved by Congress in 1790, the state returned the federal securities acquired in the initial swap program to the original owners, as happened in Pennsylvania.

One important factor contributing to the state's generally favorable finances in the 1780s was that New York had never assumed responsibility for its proper share of the cost of the war, which was based on a nationwide per capita assessment. The resources devoted to financing the state militia, the provisions provided to supply federal troops, and the state legislature's response to congressional requisitions for funding were in combination insufficient to meet New York's allotment. That deficit did not become publicly known until the final settlement of accounts among the thirteen states was announced in the mid-1790s. Meanwhile, at native-son Alexander Hamilton's urging, the federal government had agreed to assume up to $4 million of the outstanding wartime debts of every state, and New York benefited to the tune of nearly $1.2 million in 1790.

When the names of the debtor and creditor states were announced in 1793, New York showed a net deficit of just over $2 million, the largest aggregate deficiency for any state and the second largest per capita deficit at $6.75. In retrospect, New York should have never been permitted to transfer any of its debt burden to the U.S. Treasury since, as of 1790, it already owed creditor states nearly $900,000 and thus merited no relief at all. The federal assumption of the state's remaining wartime debts was undeserved because it increased even further New York's obligations to the union, although at the time few probably anticipated a shortfall of that magnitude in the final settlement. New York subsequently repaid a small portion of its huge debt to Congress, but the fact remains that the state's citizens managed to evade responsibility for upwards of $2 million of joint war costs. Since local citizens spent less per capita on the war effort than the vast majority of citizens in other states, it comes as no surprise that there were no serious threats of tax rebellions in New York in the 1780s.

NEW JERSEY

All the paper money in New Jersey in the postwar era was emitted through the auspices of government since no banks were founded in the state during the eighteenth century. Bank notes issued by the two organized banks in Pennsylvania and New York often flowed across the state's borders, however, and were used by the local population.[7] In the New Jersey legislature, a geographic split on the currency issue emerged, with representatives from the northern counties favoring paper and their counterparts southward mostly opposed to paper. Proponents cited the successes of currency issues in the colonial era, while the opposition criticized the proposal to make the monies legal tender in private as well as public debts. Critics contended that legislative majorities could be not be counted on to take the steps necessary, meaning raising taxes, to fight depreciation. Governor William Livingston was a prominent member of the antipaper camp, and he vetoed one currency bill in 1785.

Livingston finally agreed to a compromise in 1786. The agreement called for the emission of currency under two mechanisms: a lump sum to fund loans arranged through the governmental loan office and, second, a series of new monies issued annually to pay the interest due on public securities, both state and federal. The first half of the compromise plan satisfied the credit needs of middling farmers, and the second half received solid backing from the holders of public securities. A motion to assume full legal responsibility for the principal of the federal debt held by New Jersey citizens failed by a single vote; the legislature nonetheless issued so-called revenue monies amounting to more than eighty-five thousand dollars annually from 1785 to 1789 to cover the interest on federal securities. Thus, New Jersey, de facto, did as much to meet the financial demands of citizens holding federal obligations as the other states that passed formal assumption bills.

The New Jersey loan office, funded with £100,000 in fresh currency, began making loans in November 1786. Borrowers received amounts ranging from £25 to £100 at 6 percent interest for up to twelve years secured by real estate valued at twice the loan amount. For the initial seven years, borrowers paid interest only; beginning in the eighth year, they began amortizing the loan with five equal annual payments against the principal. Most of the mortgage-backed currency was retired from 1795 to 1799 in accordance with the original retirement schedule.

A small volume of public monies was retired early. In October 1788 the New Jersey legislature enacted an unprecedented law that permitted third parties to acquire outstanding loan office assets from the public agency at face value. In those cases borrowers owed all future interest and principal payments to private investors rather than to the state. One purpose of the legislation was to support the market value of the currency, which was passing at discounts of up to 25 percent vis-à-vis the fiat monies of Pennsylvania and New York. The program was designed to achieve that goal by stimulating demand for the currency among private parties investing in public assets and by simultaneously reducing the volume of outstanding monies. The loan office immediately destroyed the currency offered by third parties to settle debts in advance of their maturity dates.[8] As it happened, few private purchases of public loan assets occurred, probably because the 6 percent interest rate associated with the loans was lower than individuals with surplus funds could earn on alternative investments elsewhere in the private sector. Nonetheless, the New Jersey experiment represented another initiative designed to privatize, at least in part, the mortgage lending functions of state government.

RHODE ISLAND

Rhode Island was the only state in New England to issue paper money in the 1780s. Once again this small province lived up to its long-standing reputation for financial unorthodoxy. In the first half of the eighteenth century, before Parliament passed the Currency Act of 1751, Rhode Island had been among the most reckless colonies in regard to the management of its monetary system. The colony and its citizens had routinely failed to provide adequate backing for huge volumes of fiat emissions, and, as a consequence, its monies had suffered staggering depreciation. The colonial legislature refused to impose the requisite taxation, while private borrowers defaulted on collateralized mortgage loans without suffering the loss of landed property. After 1751 Rhode Island, along with the rest of New England, was forced by British statute to return to a specie standard, and the entire region's monetary systems were characterized by soundness for the next quarter century.

In the decade after American victory in the War for Independence, the Rhode Island legislature was almost constantly in turmoil over the twin issues of paper money and the settlement of state debts. A classic confrontation between elected officials representing urban merchants based in Providence and Newport, the major port cities, and a larger group of legislators representing the rural farm community erupted in the state capital. Farmers wanted cheap money to pay off personal debt obligations, while merchants tried to hold the line and maintain some semblance of a sound financial system.

In May 1786 the rural faction pushed through the legislature a bill establishing a government loan office with the authority to emit up to £100,000 of paper money. The funds were available for fourteen years at 4 percent interest secured by property valued at twice the loan amount. Borrowers paid interest only during the first seven years and then paid off the principal in seven equal installments beginning in 1793. Unlike most other states, Rhode Island set no minimum and maximum loan limits. The number of borrowers totaled nearly two thousand, with the median loan under £20 and the mean just over £50. The largest loan was £2,265 to the mercantile firm of Clark and Nightingale.

The most controversial aspect of the bill was the full legal tender status granted the monies, meaning that the currency had to be accepted at face value by private citizens as well as public officials. The debate over the granting of legal tender status in private debts had been an extremely divisive issue in the political contest between the Board of Trade in London, which protected the interests of English creditors, and several colonial legislatures in the 1760s and early 1770s. The issue was finally settled in 1773, when agents representing the colonial legislatures and Parliamentary leaders agreed to a modification in the law that banned legal tender status for paper money in the payment of private debts but not in public transactions. That precedent was favored by most domestic creditors as well, and the restricted legal tender rule was continued in the other six states that issued currency after the war.

Since Rhode Island was on a strict specie standard when those negotiations were ongoing in the 1760s and 1770s, its political leaders were unfamiliar with the logic that lay behind the earlier compromise. Moreover, the rural faction held the upper hand in Rhode Island government, and many farmers had anticipated that the currency would depreciate and thereby allow them to retire old debts at discount rates with cheap paper. In this state, a genuine struggle between debtors and creditors did, in fact, characterize the second half of the 1780s.

Rhode Island merchants resisted the legal tender provisions. Many defied the law and refused to accept paper money in all circumstances, whether in the settlement of old debts or in payment for current purchases. As a result the paper did not maintain its value relative to specie; the exchange rate fell precipitously to a ratio of 7:1 by August 1787. Farmers blamed merchants for undermining the monetary system, and they legislated a series of fines and penalties designed to force mercantile acceptance of the paper at face value.

The state never assumed any of the federal securities held by its citizens because voters were too busy battling over the disposition of the state's internal debt to consider broader issues. The rural faction enacted a bold legislative program designed to retire promptly the state's public debt in 1787. The two outstanding debt issues, nearly equal in size and carrying interest rates of 4 and 6 percent, respectively, totaled approximately $585,000. About one hundred public creditors held more than three-quarters of the state's internal debt. The legislature approved a plan to sink the principal virtually overnight by requiring holders to exchange their debt instruments for unsecured fiat currency at face value.

When merchants holding nearly three-fifths of the outstanding principal balked at participation in the involuntary retirement program because the market value of the existing currency had fallen so low, the rural faction, with vengence, arbitrarily canceled all the debt certificates that had not been presented to the state treasury for exchange. The prominent Brown family of Providence, which later provided funds to the university named in its honor, possessed about $70,000 of the forfeited certificates, or 12 percent of the certificates outstanding. Rhode Island farmers, in effect, had discovered a means of repudiating a huge portion of its state debt.

The state pursued a fairly rigorous tax program from 1785 to 1789. The treasury collected more than $400,000 in taxes plus $60,000 in interest earnings on loan office mortgages. Of that sum, about half was exchanged for state debt certificates. Most of the 750 public creditors who participated in the state's debt settlement plan were persons with only modest holdings of state securities; the mean value exchanged was only $325. The fiat money received in settlement was worth substantially less than the face value of the debt obligations—up to 80 percent less in terms of purchasing power according to contemporary estimates.

The public creditors holding the largest amount of Rhode Island debt lost all the legislative battles at the state level in the 1780s, but they benefited handsomely from the success of the constitutional movement and came out ahead in the end. Not surprisingly, given the voting power of the rural, anti-federalist faction, the first Rhode Island constitutional convention rejected ratification. The state did not reverse that decision and join the reorganized union until 29 May 1790, more than a year after the Constitution had taken effect.

When Congress agreed to fund the remaining state debts, the holders of the nearly $350,000 in forfeited state certificates looked to the federal government for recognition of their claims, and they received a friendly ruling from representatives of the U.S. Treasury. Unfortunately, Rhode Island received a federal allocation of only $299,000 for the settlement of its debts, which was insufficient to cover all claims. The state legislature ultimately made up the difference, but the negotiations extended into the first two decades of the nineteenth century. Most of the public creditors who had refused to cooperate in the currency settlement in 1787 received full payment of interest and principal in specie or its equivalent— or very nearly full payment.[9] As a result, public creditors in Rhode Island ranked among the strongest supporters of the new national government since they received partial compensation as a result of the federal absorption of state debts.

When the federal government's accountants announced the final apportionment of war costs in 1793, Rhode Island came out looking very good. The state ended up with a credit balance of $299,000. Although not all that much when considered as a lump sum, the amount translated into $4.60 per capita for the free population, making its citizens the second largest individual creditors of the new nation. The U.S. Treasury settled accounts by issuing new debt certificates to the state government, and the legislature used the unexpected windfall to satisfy up to three-quarters of the claims of the state's remaining public creditors. In total, the transfer of funds from the federal government to Rhode Island covered more than four-fifths of the state debt associated with the war. If citizens had anticipated the favorable outcome of the work of the congressional accountants, fewer Rhode Islanders would have likely opposed ratification of the Constitution in 1788 and 1789.

North Carolina

North Carolina, like Rhode Island, had a somewhat checkered history in managing its financial affairs. The state's aggregate obligations totaled over $40 million (the nominal value in state currency) by the end of the war—with that sum about equally divided between paper money and various debt certificates. The legislature imposed few direct taxes during the late 1770s and early 1780s, but chose instead, through the mechanism of steady and irreversible depreciation, to allow the tax burden to fall heavily on individuals who transacted business in its fiat currency. As a result of adopting an official devaluation schedule combined with a currency swap program, North Carolina reduced the volume of currency outstanding from a high of $20 million in 1783 down to $5 million by the end of the decade. Legislators adopted a descending scale of depreciation rates for the various currency issues in relation to specie values: for the emissions in the last months of the war, the ratio was set at an astronomical 800:1, but the overall mean was in the range of 200:1.[10] Most of the wartime paper still in circulation as late as 1789 was retired during the next decade, after the government agreed to accept the remaining bills in payment for the purchase of state lands at roughly one-thousandth of their face value.

The state had a more respectable record in regard to maintaining the purchasing power of two much smaller currency issues in the mid-1780s. It issued $250,000 in 1783 and the same amount again in 1785. Of the new monies, $180,000 went to pay past-due wages of the state militia; $70,000 was issued in exchange for wartime currency issues; $160,000 was targeted for the discharge of state and federal debts; and $90,000 was allocated for making a token contribution in response to a requisition from the federal government.[11] The first currency issue fell in value by 15 to 25 percent within a year of its emission and then stabilized at that level; the second issue had less success, dropping by one half and dragging down the former issue as well. By 1789 only 10 percent of the $500,000 of new monies had been retired. The poor performance of the state's fiat currency during the war and the legislature's failure to institute a program of steady retirement in the late 1780s damaged the reputation, and thus the market value, of the postwar emissions.

In addition to its fiat currency obligations, North Carolina accumulated a huge volume of state debt during the war. An appointed board later determined that $21 million of debt existed, at varying interest rates, in five certificate categories: currency, specie, bounty, loan office, and military. Undaunted, the legislature pressed ahead after 1783 to get out from under the dark clouds of indebtedness. It employed several techniques of debt reduction. The state treasury obtained funds from the disposal of confiscated loyalist properties and the sale of public lands on the western frontier and used the monies to retire some obligations. Second, the legislature repudiated a portion of the debt certificates by enforcing a depreciation scale. Third, it purchased outright public debts with new monies arising from the currency emission of 1785. The final method of debt redemption drew on budget surpluses generated from property taxes in 1787, 1788, and 1789. By 1789, through one means or another, approximately 60 to 80 percent of the wartime debt had been officially retired.

North Carolina also assumed almost all the federal debt certificates held by citizens. Since few loan office certificates had been sold to local investors during the war, the assumption program encompassed mainly quartermaster's certificates issued to local suppliers during the southern campaigns of 1780 and 1781 plus wage certificates issued to soldiers at the end of the war. The nominal value of the absorbed federal debt was roughly $7 million. Government records are inconclusive about how much state citizens received in past-due interest and principal repayment, as measured either in the state's fiat currency or in specie values. Whatever the case, North Carolina first rejected ratification of the Constitution, and gave its approval only in November 1789. Citizens hesitated to join a more permanent union in large part because they feared becoming saddled with taxes to sink the overhanging obligations of the other political units—the federal government's accumulated debts plus the remaining obligations of other dilatory states. Their fears proved unwarranted, however, because in the final settlement of wartime accounts reported in 1793, North Carolina itself ended up as a debtor state rather than a creditor. In the 1780s, most local political leaders believed the state had contributed more than its share to the common cause, but the numbers showed otherwise. North Carolina came up $500,000 short overall—or minus $1.90 per capita for the free population—ranking below only New York and Delaware in terms of its per capita debt to the union.

Generally speaking, however, North Carolina faced up to its postwar financial crisis with little hesitation. The legislature had adopted a comprehensive program to deal with the critical issues by the mid-1780s. Minor squabbles between rural and urban contingencies were fought over scaling down debts on the basis of accelerated depreciation schedules and about granting full legal tender status for the currency emissions of 1783 and 1785. For the most part, however, legislators followed the precedents established during the previous postwar period. The urgency faction held sway, and the leadership adopted programs aimed at quickly retiring the state debt plus the federal certificates held by North Carolina citizens, thereby making it possible to return to the glory days of low taxes and small government.

SOUTH CAROLINA

South Carolina, along with its northern counterpart Massachusetts, made only modest progress in erasing accumulated debts during the 1780s. It did, however, respond positively to congressional requisitions for financial assistance. The free population sent about $4.50 per capita in specie to Congress from 1781 to 1788, more than four times the mean for the thirteen states and over twice the contribution of Maryland, the second ranking state. Since the record in South Carolina contrasts so sharply with how analogous problems were handled by the political leadership in Massachusetts, the course of events surrounding issues such as taxation, debtor relief, and the issuance of paper money are worth examining in some detail.

Courthouse demonstrations, described by some contemporaries as full-fledged riots, also occurred in South Carolina to protest the combined impact of private debt collection and taxation on citizens of middling wealth. In this instance, the legislature responded by enacting a series of stay laws, thereby defusing a grass-roots movement that might have accelerated into open rebellion. The state soon put the brakes on its program of public debt retirement. Advocates of a more gradualist approach were able to temper the overly ambitious tax programs of the urgency faction. That early departure from the colonial norm—namely, the hasty settlement of overhanging state debts—eventually generated enthusiastic support for the Constitution. South Carolina became one of the prime beneficiaries of the centralization of taxing power and debt policy after the Washington administration took office.

During the first three years of the War for Independence, the South Carolina legislature issued fiat monies amounting to £1.7 million. The monies held their value fairly well through 1777, but influenced by the downward trend of the continental dollar, South Carolina currency depreciated heavily versus specie beginning in 1778. When the British army occupied Charleston in May 1780, the exchange ratio was reportedly about 65:1 and sinking. During the war years, total currency emissions were in the neighborhood of £8 million—a figure 75 times greater than the total amount Parliament had allowed the colony to print from 1731 until independence. Taking into account depreciation schedules, the purchasing power of the state's wartime emissions in specie was somewhere around £500,000, or $2.2 million. None of the wartime currency emissions were recognized as part of the official state debt in the postwar era, thus the burden of taxation associated with the mechanism of depreciation fell on the multiplicity of currency holders between 1776 and 1780.

In contrast, the state made a determined effort to pay off in specie most of the holders of its recognized debt certificates. From 1775 to 1777, the treasury had managed to borrow up to £200,000 from local investors at interest rates ranging from 6 to 10 percent. The majority of the claims against the state treasury arose from soldiers uncompensated for military service from 1780 to 1782 and from citizens who had provided American troops with supplies during the campaigns of 1780 and 1781. The state also assumed a portion of the federal debt by instituting a securities swap program for military personnel holding congressional debt certificates issued by Superintendent of Finance Robert Morris in 1783. After evaluating and assessing the claims of creditors, the state issued debt certificates carrying 7 percent interest, with the repayment of principal pledged in specie values at some undetermined date.

The urgency faction in the South Carolina legislature pushed forward a revenue program in the 1783 and 1784 sessions that was designed to extinguish the state's recognized debt obligations with all deliberate speed. Revenues came from two sources. The state treasury collected the amounts due from the sale of vacant and confiscated estates, and the legislature assessed new taxes on persons, property, and imports, including slaves. Meanwhile, to demonstrate its good faith and honorable intentions, the legislature issued interest certificates (indents) to security holders. The indents were legal tender in the payment of tax assessments in 1784 and 1785, and were, in truth, merely another form of fiat currency.

To ease the financial strain associated with the repayment of existing private debts, the legislature enacted a stay law that called for delaying the maturities of all pre-1782 obligations until 1 January 1786, when those debts were rescheduled for settlement in four annual installments with interest accruing at the rate of 7 percent. Given a respite from debt repayment, state residents freely imported a vast volume of foreign goods, plus more than five thousand slaves, in 1784. Because of a poor harvest in 1785, exports fell short, leaving a substantial balance owing both foreign and domestic creditors.

The threefold combination of higher taxes, unpaid debts linked to the postwar import boom, and the impending due date for the first scheduled installment against pre-1782 debts precipitated civil unrest in South Carolina in 1785. Facing the possibility of the seizures of their lands, several hundred citizens assembled in Camden, a town about fifty miles northeast of Columbia, and defiantly prevented the courts from sitting and adjudicating cases related to indebtedness and unpaid taxes. By August the court system was no longer functioning, except in Charleston, because of threats against judges and jurors.

Rather than calling out the state militia to quell the unruly crowds, Governor William Moultrie summoned an emergency session of the legislature to deal with the crisis. The urgency faction listened intently to the reasoned arguments of the gradualist camp. Rapid retirement of the state's outstanding obligations, under existing conditions, was deemed imprudent and potentially revolutionary. Private debtors and delinquent taxpayers were granted extensions in meeting their obligations. Under the Pine Barren Act of 1785, debtors had the right to make payments in kind rather than in monies. The statute ordered the courts to recognize as legal tender the transfer to creditors of real estate listed at two-thirds of the estimated market value, including unimproved pine forests on the western frontier where appraisals were often of questionable accuracy—thus the name "pine barren."

In October 1785, in response to the demands of rural voters, the legislature reopened the governmental loan office and authorized the issuance of £100,000 ($440,000) in fresh paper money. Borrowers could obtain between £30 and £250 for five years at 7 percent interest collateralized by land or specie at least three times greater in value. The revival of the loan office pleased the rural constituency since it provided farmers with a new source of mortgage credit and simultaneously augmented the local money supply. The new currency exchanged at face value, or near par, for specie after a united front of leading Charleston merchants promised to support its market value. The paper remained in circulation for years thereafter, with isolated bills reportedly presented to the state treasury as late as 1815.

South Carolina politicians were determined to keep the peace after the Camden riots of 1785, and they bent over backward to appease an aroused citizenry suffering acute financial pressure. One consequence of the implementation of liberal stay laws was that the original plan to redeem the bulk of the public debt within a decade of the peace treaty was jettisoned. The legislature never repudiated its obligations, but the treasury went forward more slowly in redeeming outstanding securities. Much of the state's revenues went to meeting congressional requisitions; and with the payment of nearly $450,000 in specie during the decade, South Carolina had an outstanding record in meeting its responsibilities to the Confederation.

Historian Robert Higgins estimated that the state retired approximately one-quarter of its obligations in the 1780s, or about $1.25 million, which appears a reasonably accurate deduction on the basis of scattered and imprecise information on state finances. More than $4 million dollars in unretired state debts remained on the books when the U.S. Treasury assumed responsibility in 1790. That sum translated to about $40 per capita for the free population or about five times greater per capita than Massachusetts, the second ranking state in terms of aggregate debtor relief.

Some critics complained that South Carolina taxpayers had been unduly rewarded. After dragging its feet on debt redemption in the 1780s, the state had instructed its congressional delegation to support federal assumption, and thereby evaded financial responsibilities that others had met. But those accusations proved unwarranted when the final settlement among the states was announced in 1793. Even after factoring in the federal assumption of war debts, the citizens of South Carolina ranked as the new nation's major creditors on a per capita basis at $12.

GEORGIA

Georgia's financial experiences during the war and its aftermath stood in sharp contrast to events in neighboring South Carolina since it operated more on a pay-as-you-go basis than perhaps any other state in the union. In the early years of the war, the legislature authorized a sizable issue of fiat currency. Although the exact amount of Georgia's wartime issues has remained elusive, Congress agreed to redeem $400,000 worth of the state's paper in Continental dollars in 1777 and simultaneously provided an additional $300,000 for future military contingencies. In the effort to come up with a precise accounting of postwar obligations, the legislature adopted an official depreciation schedule for all its wartime issues in 1783, which listed exchange rates with specie; the ratio was 3:1 in 1778, 8:1 in 1779, and more than 800:1 in June 1780 when the schedule ended.

Governor Edward Telfair presented a long-delayed but fairly

comprehensive report on the state's financial status to the legislature in 1786. The public debt, including claims arising from all sources, totaled £205,000, or less than $1 million specie. The governor estimated that no new taxes would likely be required to extinguish the outstanding obligations because the sale of confiscated properties alone had generated notes receivable of £220,000 in the state treasury; if all those notes were collected at maturity, the revenues would cover the whole public debt. Apparently, about one-quarter of those receivables went sour or were delinquent for one reason or another, because in the federal assumption of 1790, Georgia transferred about $250,000 of its state obligations to the U.S. Treasury. The unredeemed state debt at the end of the decade was low on a per capita basis as well, and Georgia often lined up with opponents of the congressional bill to authorize federal assumption of state debts.

Meanwhile, the legislature remained active in the financial services sector. It authorized the issuance of £50,000 of fresh fiat paper in 1786. The stated purposes of the monetary program were twofold: to prepare for possible military action against the Creek Indians (the dispute was eventually settled without war) and to pay wages, long overdue, to citizens who had served in the state militia during the War for Independence. The currency emission was approved as a stopgap measure, with redemption supposedly arising from the sale of thousands of acres of state lands, not from general taxation.

Following the negotiation of a peaceful settlement with the Creeks in 1788, the legislature voted to postpone land sales, undermining the backing for the most recent currency emission. Local merchants, fearing depreciation, had resisted acceptance of the bills from the outset. As a result, the currency depreciated by up to 75 percent within a year of issue. Finally, in January 1789, the legislature officially devalued its currency by one-third and established an orderly retirement schedule extending over a five-year period that drew on the state's general tax revenues.

The seven states that issued currency in the postwar era were a fairly diverse group geographically. New York, Pennsylvania, and New Jersey represented the mid-Atlantic; the two Carolinas and Georgia were southern, while Rhode Island was the lone representative of New England—and the most exceptional in the group. In the first half of the eighteenth century, Rhode Island had experimented freely with paper money—indeed too freely to prevent precipitous, irreversible depreciation. But dating from Parliament's passage of the Currency Act of 1751 until American independence, the colony had stayed on a strictly specie monetary standard. Thus, the state's embrace of a renewed system of fiat currency, after a hiatus of nearly a quarter century, was a departure from the experiences of its immediate past. In the other six states, however, the emission of currency in the 1780s was the continuation of long-established legislative policy. Those political units remained heavily involved in the financial services sector, both as issuers of new monies and, except for Georgia, as providers of loanable funds to citizens with real estate for collateral.

In five states, the legislatures maintained their monopoly on currency emissions, but in two others privately organized banking enterprises arose to issue competitive monies. In Pennsylvania and New York, two commercial banks emerged to challenge the dominant position of the legislature in the monetary sphere. The Bank of North America in Philadelphia and the Bank of New York in New York City were warmly welcomed by the local mercantile communities, but they met opposition from the residents of outlying areas. Rural residents feared that, if financial markets were completely privatized, all the benefits linked to an enlarged money stock, plus access to loanable funds, might accrue solely to the urban population.

In both states compromises that fostered coexistence were reached. Both governmental agencies and private banks issued currency and made available credit facilities to qualified borrowers. The commercial banks issued paper monies convertible into specie upon demand. Fiat monies backed by the power of taxation were emitted by the states' treasuries, while government loan offices issued a second variety of unconvertible currency secured by first mortgages on the real property of citizens. What some contemporaries had feared were two fundamentally incompatible financial systems proved instead to operate in reasonably complementary fashion in Pennsylvania and New York in the 1780s. Public and private monies circulated in tandem throughout the two states, and they were exchanged freely in their respective home markets at rates very close to face value, according to contemporary reports.

Specie States in the 1780s

Six states refrained from issuing currency after the signing of the peace treaty in 1783 and relied solely upon hard money for the negotiation of financial transactions, large and small. As was true during the colonial era, the coinage was almost exclusively foreign in origin—mainly Spanish, augmented by some Portuguese and French coins, plus a fair amount of English coinage left behind by the British army. Half of the strictly specie states were in New England—Massachusetts, Connecticut, and New Hampshire; the other three were located in the upper south region—Maryland, Delaware, and Virginia. Those six states formed the core of the political bloc that pressed for the restrictive phrase in Section 10 of the Constitution that denied state legislatures the right to issue bills of credit, meaning inconvertible fiat currency. Five states are covered in this chapter; Massachusetts follows with a chapter of its own.

Since the New England states were all on a hard money standard after passage of the Currency Act of 1751, the reintroduction of paper money to prosecute the war effort was typically justified as a mere expediency and a system to be abandoned as soon as conditions allowed. Farther southward, Virginia had relied solely on coin for decades, and its experience with paper money had been relatively brief. Virginia waited until 1755 to issue its first round of fiat currency. It had never created a mortgage loan office, and it had subsequently suffered a major defalcation involving Assembly Speaker John Robinson that was not discovered until after his death in 1766. Only Maryland and Delaware had records of sustained, largely successful paper emissions in the colonial era, but each chose to forego that option in the postwar decade.

The hard money states differed with regard to the settlement of their respective war debts in the 1780s. Initially, all six legislatures had hoped to press forward with the retirement of their outstanding obligations, but in Massachusetts the redemption program ground to an abrupt halt following Shays' Rebellion. Although historians have offered a myriad of explanations for the suddenness and strength of the rebellion, the prime cause was the mismanagement of fiscal policy in the mid-1780s. The legislature's attempt to accomplish the near impossible—namely, the retirement of a substantial debt in the period of only half a decade—led to what was, in retrospect, a fairly predictable outcome. Political leaders in several other states—notably Virginia, Connecticut, and South Carolina—ran into analogous problems in the same period, but backed off and followed the path of fiscal restraint. In Massachusetts extremists in the urgency faction refused to listen to the voices of reason.

When trouble predictably arose, they voted to respond to civil unrest with military force. Within a year gradualist politicians gained control of state government, and Massachusetts implemented a revised program of debt redemption with more distant and realistic horizons.

VIRGINIA

Virginia's program of debt extinction consisted of a mixture of increased taxes and partial repudiation. The legislature was firmly in the hands of the urgency faction, but there was no herculean effort to pay off every obligation in specie values. Instead, the state aimed at reducing its financial obligations in systematic fashion, and legislative leaders pursued generally viable, and politically acceptable, fiscal policies. After revaluing sharply downward its obligations in the mid-1780s to satisfy the radical wing, a vigorous program of tax collection in 1787 and 1788 made huge inroads in the outstanding principal. As a result, Virginia ended the decade in fairly good financial shape, and its leaders were mostly lukewarm about the proposed federal assumption of state debts.

At the start of the war, Virginia still had roughly £150,000 in colonial currency outstanding. It added much more as the conflict proceeded. The early emissions were reasonably moderate—$350,000 of fiat paper in 1775 and $500,000 in 1776—but the situation soon got out of control. In parallel with the fate of congressional dollars, the state's fiat currency began depreciating sharply in the late 1770s. In a self-defeating effort to maintain purchasing power, the value of subsequent issues escalated. The hyperinflation culminated with an emission of $35 million in 1781 when the exchange rate with specie was more than 1,000:1 and sinking into oblivion. Virginia emitted $128 million during the war—more than 60 percent of the total for all thirteen states and almost one-third of the total for the states and Congress combined.

In the immediate postwar years, the legislature tried to formulate a comprehensive program of debt retirement. Most of the monies issued in the hyperinflation of 1780 and 1781 were valued at next to nothing. Some of the interest-bearing certificates issued during the war—quasi money/quasi loans—were not repudiated in whole but written down to more realistic levels—that is, closer to prevailing market prices. Several tax laws that applied stiff assessments on property and persons were enacted in the 1780s, but complaints from constituents about pressing private debts and slow economic recovery led to recurring suspensions, so-called tax relief, from 1781 through 1786. Modest revenues arose from the imposition of a 2 percent tariff on imports plus higher duties on wine and spirits.

Once everyone had agreed on the extent of the state's obligations, the leaders of the urgency faction looked for the right opportunity to retire a huge chunk of the debt. With tobacco sales on the upswing by mid-decade, the time seemed ripe for a substantial, bite-the-bullet assessment. Heavy direct taxes were finally applied in 1787, generating a treasury surplus of roughly $1 million for debt reduction. The state also set aside some of its revenues to meet congressional requisitions; overall it had sent a total of nearly $2 million (specie) to the U.S. Treasury by 1790. Under the federal debt assumption program, Virginia was relieved of just under $3 million of its outstanding debts, and that amount proved just about equal to the state's creditor position vis-à-vis the other twelve states in the final settlement of 1793. Along with five other states, Virginia came very close to balancing its books for the wartime era, ending up with a paltry deficit of $100,000, or $.25 per capita for its free population.

MARYLAND

Dating back to the 1730s, Maryland had a long history of successful management of its paper money issues, all of which were backed solidly by tax revenues and private mortgages. Thus its suspension of new currency emissions after 1781 stands as one of the most noteworthy reversals of the Confederation era. The decision to retire paper and revert to specie was not unanimous, however, for the two branches of the legislature split over financial policy. The lower chamber, which represented middling farmers and planters, voted to emit currency at least twice in the mid-1780s, but the senate always rejected the idea.

Despite their differences over fiat currency, the leadership in both branches of the legislature agreed about the urgency of retiring the public debt; and Maryland had an outstanding record in that regard. The data are inconclusive, but it appears that the state eventually retired most of its wartime obligations—currency and debt certificates—at very close to face value in specie equivalents. From 1774 to 1776, the treasury issued nearly $950,000 of fresh fiat currency to finance the military effort, while another $480,000 at 5 percent interest was authorized in 1780. The emission of £200,000 in 1781 was secured by notes receivable from local purchasers of confiscated loyalist properties and was sunk as planned by 1785.

Maryland also applied heavy taxation. In 1782 property taxes netted £265,000, of which less than 10 percent went toward the payment of current interest. Most of the remainder went to retire outstanding obligations. In addition, the legislature invited citizens to swap their holdings of federal securities for state certificates paying 6 percent interest as early as 1782, and the state treasury eventually accumulated $660,000 in federal debt certificates. In the federal assumption program, the state transferred to the U.S. Treasury around half a million dollars of its remaining liabilities. By reducing its public debt to the neighborhood of $2.50 per capita for the free population in 1790, Maryland ranked among the most conscientious states in cleaning up its wartime obligations. In the final settlement among the thirteen states, Maryland's net position was reported at very close to equilibrium, showing a slight deficit balance of $151,000, or $.70 per capita for the free population.

DELAWARE

The information on Delaware's finances in the eighteenth century is exceedingly sketchy. In colonial times Delaware issued only small volumes of currency, and its monies passed at values very close to Pennsylvania paper. During 1775 and 1777, the legislature authorized £55,000 in new monies, of which £45,000 was issued through the government loan office and secured by private mortgages. Later, in the federal assumption program of 1790, the state asked the U.S. Treasury to take over its wartime debts totaling $59,000. Three years later, the final settlement board listed the state's deficit to the union at $612,000—the second largest negative number for any state. On an individual basis, Delaware's free population owed citizens of the seven creditor states nearly $11 per capita, more than 50 percent greater than the shortfall in New York. Since the deficit was never repaid, Delaware taxpayers were the nation's main free riders, making the smallest per capita contribution to the American victory in the War for Independence.

CONNECTICUT

Connecticut was among the most fiscally responsible and prudently governed states throughout the independence era. The legislature redeemed a substantial share of the obligations incurred during the war at specie values, employing mostly direct taxes on persons and property rather than relying heavily on the mechanism of currency depreciation. According to Henry Bronson, the most authoritative historian of Connecticut currency, who published his treatise more than a century ago in 1865, the state "was moderate and conservative . . . compared with . . . the other states . . . ; her leading statesmen were, after the standard of that day, shrewd, considerate and wise."[12] In the early 1780s, a majority of legislators felt a keen urgency about retiring the state's outstanding obligations. Many in the Connecticut legislature were still under the spell of the principles espoused in the Currency Act of 1751, which stipulated that emergency emissions of fiat paper and all other extraordinary wartime debts should be settled within, at most, five years.

Even before the outbreak of hostilities with the mother country, Connecticut had departed from its recent monetary past. From midcentury until 1770, the colony had been on a specie standard, and yearly budget deficits were financed through the placement of two-year interest-bearing notes. In 1771, 1773, and 1774 combined, however, the legislature authorized the issuance of £39,000 of two-year paper in various denominations, some reportedly as low as 2.5 shillings, which carried no interest component. Since the bills paid no interest to holders at maturity, the funds were presumably intended to enter the money stock. As the political crisis with Britain deepened, Connecticut issued larger sums of fiat currency to finance military preparedness. In 1775 and 1776 the rebellious colony emitted two separate issues of fiat monies totaling £260,000 with maturity dates staggered over the next two to five years. Political leaders justified suspension of the specie standard as an emergency measure.

After two years of indecisive fighting, with its fiat monies depreciating steadily and an empty treasury, Connecticut reverted to financing governmental deficits through public loans. In May 1777, the state began exchanging fiat currency—accepting both state and continental paper at market rates, not face value—for promissory notes with one-year maturity dates paying 6 percent interest issued in amounts of £30 or greater. From 1777 to 1779, the treasurer negotiated loans of £205,000; a substantial share of the borrowings in the last two years brought in no new funds but represented the refinancing of the previous year's loans.

Unlike most other states, which typically postponed programs of rigorous tax collection until the resolution of the war, Connecticut maintained at least a modest level of direct taxation throughout the late 1770s and into the early 1780s. In 1780 the state participated in the congressional currency swap program and emitted £190,000 in new tenor bills that bore interest at 5 percent after 1785.[13] From 1777 forward, Connecticut revealed a determination to finance its share of the war effort with financial instruments ultimately redeemable in specie values and with funds raised through taxation or the sale of loyalist assets—not through depreciation or partial repudiation.

By the signing of the peace treaty with Great Britain, Connecticut's state debts had been calculated fairly precisely at £1,135,000. The bulk of the debt, more than 70 percent, was accounted for by securities issued to the state's disbanded military forces and its outstanding treasury notes. In May 1783, the legislature approved a financial package designed to lengthen modestly the maturity dates of half the state's obligations. It authorized the state treasurer to seek investors for a loan totaling £609,000 at 6 percent interest and maturing in stages during the next three to ten years. The minimum investment was £10, an amount probably close to the median income in the state. Tax rates were simultaneously increased with the goal of retiring the whole principal during the next decade.

But citizens began protesting about strained financial conditions immediately thereafter, and the legislature quickly retreated. It voted in May 1784 to suspend for three years the collection of new taxes voted the previous year. At the first sign of trouble, the gradualists in the legislature prevailed on the urgency camp to retrench and retire debt at a slower pace. The revised policy called for generating sufficient revenue to meet ongoing interest payments on the debt plus only modest redemptions. When the federal assumption of state debts took effect, Connecticut had redeemed about half the debt burden listed in 1783. In the final settlement of 1793, the state was rated as the third largest creditor of the union on both an aggregate and per capita scale. Given its policy of retiring obligations incurred after 1776 at specie values, Connecticut achieved a solid record of fiscal rectitude; and it did so without displaying the political and judicial rigidities that led to armed rebellion in neighboring Massachusetts.

NEW HAMPSHIRE

A review of New Hampshire's public finances in the 1780s likewise reveals the application of fairly sound and sensible principles. Like the other three New England states, it had operated on a specie standard from 1751 until independence. From 1775 through 1778, the legislature issued £230,000 in fiat monies to fund the war effort, with two-thirds carrying an interest component of 6 percent. The onset of heavy depreciation in 1777 convinced political leaders to shift back to a greater reliance on borrowed funds. The treasury was authorized to contract loans totaling £300,000 by 1779, but cautious lenders had advanced only £96,000 by the early 1780s. When Congress allowed the states to swap continental dollars at the exchange rate of 20:1 in 1780, the legislature took that opportunity to issue another $142,000 of new tenor currency.

New Hampshire began shifting back to a hard money standard in the summer of 1781. The treasury adopted a scale of depreciation covering 1777 to 1781 that converted the outstanding fiat currency into specie values. The urgency faction was determined to sink the public debt in no more than five years—the old rule of thumb inherited from the Seven Years' War—but citizen protests led to a revision of that aggressive policy. In response to complaints about an inadequate medium of exchange, the legislature permitted debtors to make tax payments in kind, mainly grains and livestock, beginning in 1781. Tax collections fell from £110,000 in 1782 to only £22,000 in 1785, with the arrearages of some towns canceled outright. During the last half of the decade, the gradualists controlled fiscal policy. They raised sufficient revenues to cover interest charges and redeem from 5 to 10 percent of the principal annually. When the U.S. Treasury assumed the state's obligations in 1790, the modest sum of $283,000 was outstanding, or roughly $2 per capita, suggesting that the state had redeemed about 40 percent of its debts in the 1780s. The settlement committee granted New Hampshire creditor status amounting to $75,000, or about $.50 per capita.

8

Massachusetts and Shays' Rebellion

❖ ❖ ❖

THE DISCUSSION OF the financial situation in Massachusetts in the postwar decade is purposely last for one reason: Shays' Rebellion. An understanding of the financial histories of the other twelve states is an absolute prerequisite for comprehending the underlying reasons for the outbreak of violent public protest in western Massachusetts in early 1787. Because of its timing, that armed rebellion has been cited in most accounts of the Confederation era as the single most important event in convincing a majority of the nation's political leaders of the need for some readjustment of the powers of the central government under the Articles of Confederation. That reform movement, in turn, led to the drafting of the new Constitution and a much stronger central government. Most historical explanations of the causes of Shays' Rebellion concentrate on rivalries between various classes or groups within society—debtor versus creditor, cosmopolitans versus rural communities, agrarian as opposed to commercial visions of society, soft money (paper) versus hard money (specie), or some combination of them all.[1] The various approaches contain elements of truth, but the most powerful explanatory force has been overlooked by most historians.

The interpretation offered here is that the rebellion was primarily the predictable outcome of the gross mismanagement of the public debt redemption program by extremist elements that dominated the state legislature, particularly the upper chamber. Members of the extremist wing of the urgency faction set out to accomplish the impossible—retirement of the entire debt within the decade—and they predictably ran into strong opposition and seri-

173

ous difficulties. Their failure to comprehend the magnitude of the task before them, accentuated by a strong dose of human intransigence, was more responsible for what transpired in western Massachusetts than alternative analyses focusing on underlying social or political conflicts. By nature, farmers living in western Massachusetts were no more restive or confrontational than their counterparts in other regions—nor was the elite governing class any more paternalistic and domineering than its peers in other states. The magnitude of financial miscalculations was simply greater in Massachusetts and persisted much longer. Exaggerated optimism about what could be accomplished in the short run was at the root of the problem. Given that thirteen separate political units were trying to cope with the settlement of public debts on an unprecedented scale, it was not surprising, in retrospect, that the process would break down in at least one state and potentially several others as well.

Much of what occurred in Massachusetts through 1786 had clear parallels with events in other states. In the other twelve states as well, legislatures, remembering the successful debt repayment schedules established after the Seven Years' War, were initially prone to press ahead with speedy redemption programs. But whereas the political leadership elsewhere was able to readjust programs and policies in the light of public protest and financial realities—namely, a public debt many times greater per capita at the provincial level than in the 1750s and 1760s—their counterparts in Massachusetts were rigid, unrealistic, and uncompromising in their effort to retire the public debt too rapidly given the magnitude of the state's obligations.

When the tax burden imposed to redeem the debt proved too onerous for middling property holders in other states, gradualist factions were usually able to sponsor legislative reforms that stretched out the maturity dates of public securities. That extension came in Massachusetts too, but not until after public discontent had escalated into armed conflict. Meanwhile, the adherence to an irresponsible, impractical, and ultimately unnecessary program of fiscal policy in this solitary, critical state contributed to the renewed movement for a more permanent and more centralized national government with enhanced taxing power.[2]

Like the other twelve states, Massachusetts began issuing fiat currency in the early years of the war. Abandoning its long-standing policy of funding budget deficits solely through the placement of short-term loans in local financial markets, as dictated by the Currency Act of 1751, the legislature authorized the issuance of non-interest-bearing paper monies to support the state militia beginning in 1775. Simultaneously, the treasury sold interest-bearing notes to raise additional funds for the military effort as it had done for the last quarter century. The emission of currency and treasury notes escalated rapidly, however. Tax revenues trailed governmental expenditures by a wide margin. In 1776, for example, the legislature authorized the expenditure of more than £1.35 million, but it assessed no new taxes at all during the calendar year.

Given the widening gap between cash outgo and inflow, citizens holding the state's financial obligations began to doubt the depth of the legislature's commitment to generating the tax revenues necessary to back the issues fully. By 1777 the fiat currency had gone into a tailspin, and treasury notes were exchanging hands at sharp discounts as well. Dual efforts to stop rampant inflation through the imposition of price controls and legal penalties on persons passing monies at less than face value proved ineffective. Massachusetts had not witnessed financial disarray on this scale since the late 1740s.

In another effort to dampen inflationary expectations, the legislature authorized the conversion of all fiat monies denominated in amounts of $1 or more, a total of £439,000, into treasury notes paying 6 percent interest and maturing in 1781 and 1782. Hoping to reassure skeptics about its commitment to redeem financial obligations, the political leadership simultaneously raised taxes. Indeed, few state legislatures attempted to tax citizens as heavily both during and after the war as Massachusetts—in that respect the accelerating tax rates that precipitated the Shays' unrest were no anomaly. During the next four years, the legislature assessed $3.6 million (specie value) in direct taxes, mostly in the poll and property categories. From 1777 through 1786, Massachusetts made a patriotic effort to tax its citizens to provide financial support for the war, and it probably achieved more success on that front than any other state in the union. Nonetheless, the strategy of converting fiat currency into treasury notes and simultaneously increasing taxes failed to stem the inflationary tide. The implementation of the anti-inflation plan recalls to mind the old adage—too little, too late.

The market value of treasury notes continued to erode after 1777. Those financial instruments lost their status as a vehicle for prudent investment and quickly degenerated into another form of fiat currency. Treasury notes were rarely sold to investors after 1778 but were paid out directly from the state treasury to settle current accounts, thereby sustaining the military campaign. Historian Whitney Bates calculated that Massachusetts issued treasury notes with a face value of £11 million between 1775 and 1780, but their specie value was only about £1.15 million or $3.7 million. In other words, the state's treasury notes had surrendered 90 percent of their purchasing power during the six-year period.[3] The issue of December 1779 traded at an exchange ratio of 25:1 vis-à-vis specie.[4]

In 1781 the legislature began the recall of its outstanding financial liabilities and moved toward the reinstitution of the specie standard that had prevailed during the third quarter of the eighteenth century. Outstanding paper monies and treasury notes were subject to adjustment based on an official depreciation schedule that converted each chronological series into specie values at progressively lower conversion ratios. The residue of the reevaluation process became the core of the state's consolidated debt. Some contemporaries in rural areas complained that state officials had favored creditors in formulating the depreciation schedule and argued, in turn, that a higher percentage of the potential debt should have been repudiated—as happened, for example, in Virginia. According to historian E. James Ferguson, the net effect was "to double, at least, the state debt."[5]

The state adopted a new constitution in 1780, and thereafter all taxes were payable in hard money—or the equivalent value in other mediums of exchange. The rapid deflation damaged debtors —especially farmers—and rewarded creditors, public and private. During the transition from paper to coin, the legislature occasionally allowed persons who claimed difficulties because of monetary shortages to pay obligations in kind with marketable crops and livestock products. Over the years the treasury received payments in various combinations of specie, legal commodities, Morris notes, and bank notes issued by the three organized American financial institutions.

During the early 1780s Massachusetts completed the task of consolidating all its various financial obligations into a single debt issue that paid 6 percent interest annually in specie. The total came to just over $5 million; per capita debt was roughly $11 to $15, or about one-third of prevailing incomes. In general conformity with the fiscal policies adopted in most of the other twelve states, the urgency faction enacted a tax program designed to generate sufficient revenues to meet not only interest payments on the existing debt but also to produce budget surpluses that could be applied against the outstanding principal. Not all the tax levies were collected on schedule, however, and delinquencies contributed to the subsequent crisis. Despite occasional outcries from hard-pressed taxpayers, in the five years from 1781 through 1786, the debt reduction program moved along generally according to plan. Owners of state securities received regular interest payments, and about $1 million in debt obligations was redeemed, the equivalent of nearly 20 percent of the outstanding principal.

Once the legislature had put its internal affairs in order, the state collected a fair amount of tax revenue for the benefit of the federal government in response to congressional requisitions for assistance. From 1781 to 1788, the state sent Congress more than $800,000, of which $363,000 was in specie and $453,000 in federal indents. Only four other states—Pennsylvania, Virginia, South Carolina, and Maryland—made larger financial contributions to sustaining the national government in the 1780s.

Based on its overall performance during the first half of the decade, Massachusetts would not have appeared to be a likely candidate to undergo an imminent major political and economic crisis. Based on its heavy military expenditures during the war on behalf of the union and a laudable record in meeting periodic congressional requisitions, it seemed very likely that the Bay State would emerge as a creditor of the federal government in the final apportionment of war costs among the thirteen states. Thus, the financial outlook was by no means bleak in 1785. On the contrary, Massachusetts had won the battle against inflation, and most legislators believed the state was once again on the path toward fiscal respectability.

Perhaps the state's success in raising tax revenues in the early 1780s went to the heads of legislators in the populous eastern half of the state and produced overly optimistic expectations about the prospect of redeeming the state's outstanding obligations. A similar feat of debt reduction had been accomplished in the 1760s at the end of the previous war. Whatever the underlying rationale, the extremist wing of the urgency faction was in full control of the legislature in the mid-1780s, and its leaders were determined to rid the state of its overhanging debts posthaste.

Public officials had no reliable method of determining how much taxation a given population could reasonably carry relative to current income and accumulated wealth since statistical information of that nature was not available in the eighteenth century. Leaders of the urgency faction realized that taxpayers might suffer financial stress over the short run, but they believed a heavy tax burden could be borne for four or five years. Some also were under the illusion that thankful citizens in the 1790s would, in retrospect, praise the legislature for its resolve in facing up to a mountain of debt. Having freed themselves of the debt yoke, taxpayers would soon celebrate the return of very low prewar rates associated with an unimposing government. Few legislators in Massachusetts, not even those persons that some historians have labeled as hard-headed political conservatives, wanted to perpetuate the state debt or to nourish thereby an "elite monied interest" living in aristocratic style off their investments in government securities. Indeed, their aim was just the opposite. On that score, the attitude of the political leadership in Massachusetts was in harmony with the rest of the nation in the mid-1780s.

While the legislature was consolidating its debts and debating tax policy, the state witnessed the opening of the nation's second chartered commercial bank in Boston in 1784. The Massachusetts Bank was modeled on the Bank of North America, but unlike its predecessor, it attracted little controversy either at birth or during the early years of operations. The bank was not viewed as a rival of state government in the financial services market. When Massachusetts reverted to a specie standard early in the decade, the legislature had forsworn the issuance of fiat paper for any purpose whatsoever, including the making of mortgage loans to private citizens.

Since the Massachusetts Bank promised to maintain continuous convertibility for its bank notes into coin, few objections, either philosophical or practical, arose to challenge its legitimacy. The capital invested was fairly small as well—only $100,000 had been accumulated by 1785—and dividend rates were rather modest, averaging only 5 percent annually the first five years. The emergence of a system of privately owned, state-chartered institutions to provide financial services to the general public went forward smoothly in Massachusetts in large part because the legislature had no tradition of sustained involvement in financial markets, particularly the mortgage sector. The Massachusetts Bank was never a competitor of state government but rather a potentially complementary entity; therefore, it received relatively free rein from the outset.

Dissatisfied with what seemed to them slow progress in terms of debt retirement—only a 15 percent reduction by the middle of the decade—leaders of the urgency faction formulated a coordinated program of staggered maturities and matching tax revenues designed to retire the entire outstanding principal in five annual installments beginning in 1785. The general plan called for citizens to bear a heavy tax burden for five consecutive years in order to generate a series of huge budget surpluses: 1785, $350,00; 1786, $1.1 million; 1787, $1.2 million; 1788, $1.1 million; 1789, $750,000; in total, $4.5 million.[6] Then, with the principal retired, state tax rates could fall again to low, prewar levels in the 1790s. From an organizational standpoint, the Massachusetts leadership had done a great deal of advance planning—ordinarily a laudable strategy; but in this case foresight was not rewarded because the plan itself was fatally flawed.

Some legislators who identified with the aspirations of middling farmers and artisans went along with the accelerated debt retirement program because, over the long run, it promised to lower the amount of public monies expended on interest and thus to relieve the burden on taxpayers. Not every legislator who supported the program was aligned with debt holders in the eastern half of the state. Some believed in the wisdom of taking a strong dose of fiscal medicine in order to speed along financial recovery in the not too distant future. Indeed, if state debt per capita had been 80 percent lower—that is, comparable with the level in the 1760s—the legislature's five-year plan would have likely gone forward with scattered protests but no civil uprising.

To gain a better understanding of what was in store for Massachusetts taxpayers in the late 1780s, consider what would happen today if Congress voted to pay off the entire U.S. national debt—more than $3 trillion in 1990—during the next half decade. To accomplish that goal federal income taxes would have to be raised by 50 to 75 percent. Federal revenues would rise from roughly 20 to 30 percent of GNP, and the federal budget would show a surplus of $600 billion for five years in a row. Based on our understanding of modern economics, the U.S. economy would sink into a depression so deep under those circumstances that the Great Depression of the 1930s would seem mild by comparison. While the agricultural-commercial economy of the 1780s was perhaps more resilient in the face of such financial mischief, there were practical limits even in that earlier era.

Some historians have suggested that weak markets for foodstuffs and high household debts were the underlying causes of the strained finances of western Massachusetts farmers, but com-

parative analyses of the agricultural sector and debt levels in other
northern states have failed to generate corroborating data in support of that hypothesis. On the contrary, studies by Gordon Bjork
and Merrill Jensen indicate that the American economy had fully
recovered from the impact of postwar deflation and recession by
the mid-1780s.[7] The demand for New England products was strong
at home and overseas, and Massachusetts farmers should have been
full participants in the broad postwar recovery. But starting in 1785
the state treasury began implementing an ill-considered fiscal policy
that drained excessive monies out of the pockets of ordinary taxpayers in an effort to produce a huge budget surplus in the state
treasury.

Taxes scheduled for collection in 1786—to pay the current interest on the state debt, to retire one-fourth of the principal of that
debt, and to meet congressional requisitions for financial assistance—totaled between $1.3 and $1.6 million, or approximately
8 to 11 percent of aggregate state income. In the prewar years, provincial taxes had rarely climbed above 2 percent of income, thus
the revenue demands in the second half of the 1780s were unprecedented and for much of the population unmanageable. The state's
fiscal policy alone was capable of inducing a recession in the most
vulnerable sectors of the state's economy, irrespective of private debt
levels or the effect of any other internal or external factors.[8] High
taxes were the prime cause of calamities on two fronts: a depressed
local economy—the result of curtailed aggregate demand—plus
hundreds of financially-strapped taxpayers facing foreclosures on
farm mortgages. Moreover, the interplay between those two negative factors caused the economic situation to deteriorate steadily
during 1786 and into 1787.

The general hypothesis offered here is not wholly original, although it is perhaps more strongly buttressed because of its presentation within a comparative context. Charles Bullock, Whitney Bates, and Forrest McDonald are three historians who earlier
stressed the heavy burden of taxation in the late 1780s as the underlying reason for Shays' Rebellion. Bullock was an eminent turn-of-
the-century financial historian, and one of the first U.S. scholars
to venture into this specialized field of historical inquiry. Writing
during the first decade of the twentieth century, Bullock set out his
views about causation in a volume devoted to Massachusetts financial history between 1780 and 1905.

Bates completed a brilliant master's thesis at the University of

Wisconsin in 1948, shockingly still unpublished, that spelled out in detail the state's fiscal policies throughout the 1780s and their consequences.[9] Although he identified taxation as the main precipitant of civil unrest, Bates linked high tax rates to the application of a questionable depreciation schedule in converting paper obligations to specie debts because, he alleged, it unfairly rewarded public creditors. The consolidated debt figure of $5 million was probably too high given the extent of paper depreciation from 1777 to 1780. In short, Bates never challenged strongly the prudence or necessity of a crash program to retire the debt before the end of the decade. He merely raised doubts about the fairness of the formula used to establish the magnitude of the debt, with the inference that if the consolidated principal had been smaller in 1784, then the direct taxes imposed from 1785 to 1789 would have been at lower rates and more tolerable.

The application of a flawed depreciation schedule may, indeed, have granted public creditors more than their due. However, it seems unlikely that any error was egregious, as borne out by the release of the final report of the congressional settlement commission in 1793. It showed that the Congress owed Massachusetts $5.2 million to reimburse taxpayers for their generous contributions to the war effort—a number that exceeded marginally the size of state debt at its high point. The state later received an advance against that total when the U.S. Treasury assumed $4 million in state debt in 1790. Bates came very close to putting his finger on the fundamental cause of the fiscal and political crisis, but like many contemporaries, he was too willing to accede to the power of the rhetorical flashes of extremists in the urgency faction.

To date, McDonald has probably come closest to unearthing the truth of the matter. A distinguished political and constitutional historian who has focused much of his work during the last quarter century on the confederation and early national periods, including a biography of Alexander Hamilton, McDonald stressed the importance of high tax rates in causing unrest. In an essay written jointly with his wife, Ellen, and published in 1988, McDonald dismissed interpretations that emphasized the burden of heavy private debts as the proximate cause of turmoil in the western counties. In response to citizen protests, they noted that the legislature suspended new suits for debt collection for eight months during its fall session in 1786, yet the rebels did not lay down their arms or disband their military units. The most persuasive evidence on the

issue is that current and overdue taxes were five times greater at
ten pounds per capita than private indebtedness at two pounds per
capita in the three most rebellious counties. The McDonalds concluded: "In 1786 the government of Massachusetts, having taken
on and mismanaged a huge burden of public debt, levied and set
out to collect an oppressive and, in fact, unpayable array of taxes to
service that debt." [10]

The thrust of that argument is on the mark, although the term
service is misapplied in this instance, because in financial circles it
normally implies the generation of sufficient revenue to pay the
current interest plus the amortization of a small fraction of the
outstanding principal. In the 1790s Hamilton adopted the strategy
of merely servicing the public debt at the federal level, with principal retirement strictly optional, whereas the Massachusetts legislature had plans to extinguish all its obligations by the end of 1789.

A few contemporary political leaders questioned, at least momentarily, the wisdom of trying to sink the Massachusetts public
debt so rapidly. Oddly, one was Governor James Bowdoin, who
later declined to back away from a military confrontation with the
Shays' rebels. In a speech to the legislature in October 1785, soon
after taking office, he recommended that the retirement period
be stretched from five to fifteen years.[11] But extremists, who had
supported him for governor, refused to reconsider the imminent
implementation of the crash program already debated and decided.
Incredibly, legislative leaders were so confident of their ability to
generate tax revenues from dutiful citizens that they vowed to heed
as well the congressional requisition of 1785 for more hard money.
Bowdoin, in an act of utter folly, proposed a special specie tax of
£325,000 in September 1786 to meet another congressional requisition. At a time when most other states were hesitant in responding
to congressional pleas, the Massachusetts extremists were determined to live up to their ongoing financial obligations to the federal
government while simultaneously paying off the state's creditors
in full. From 1781 through 1788, Massachusetts sent more than
$350,000 in specie to Congress—the fourth highest amount among
the thirteen states overall and tenth ranking on a per capita basis.

Many legislators thought the speedy elimination of the debt was
not only commendable public policy but that a positive collateral
effect would be the financial discipline extended to the middling
and lower classes. The lazy and chronically idle would be forced
to put their noses to the grindstone and pursue more productive

activities to pay their taxes. Moral improvement was always among the expressed goals of public policy in Puritan New England. To make the imposition of an admittedly heavy tax burden from 1786 to 1789 more palatable, the legislature decided to assess no new taxes in 1785—none beyond those amounts already scheduled for collection during the calendar year, thereby allowing citizens some respite from the coming storm.

Despite the resolve of the urgency faction to coerce citizens into meeting the state's financial obligations in short order, signals of impending difficulties emerged in the mid-1780s. Tax arrearages grew year after year. Of the $930,000 assessed against persons and property between 1780 and 1782, nearly half was past due as late as December 1785. Between 1782 and 1786 additional taxes of $3.3 million were scheduled for collection, yet by October 1787 more than $1.4 million, or 40 percent, were past due. Under the state's internal revenue system, the locally elected tax collector in each town was held personally liable for the quota assigned by the state treasurer; and after July 1786 county sheriffs became liable for arrearages as well. To escape governmental claims against their own assets, collectors and sheriffs were forced to file suit against tax delinquents and to seize farms, crops, livestock, and other property when payments were not forthcoming.

Sometime in 1786 or 1787 tax arrearages were approaching, or even possibly exceeded, the amounts scheduled for collection during the upcoming twelve months. Due dates for tax payments under different legislative programs increasingly overlapped. Some taxes due in 1786 and 1787 had been scheduled for collection years earlier as a consequence of debt consolidation and the lengthening of maturities for treasury notes. Meanwhile, new tax assessments were enacted to finance ongoing expenditures. The treasury department anticipated tax revenues of $1.15 million in 1786, with $960,000 arising from direct assessments on persons and property and the remainder coming from tariffs and excise taxes. The state planned to allocate 40 percent of that amount to meet the congressional requisition of 1785, 25 percent to pay the current interest on the outstanding state debt, and a similar percentage for principal retirement.

No single piece of legislation alone was responsible for triggering a series of civil disturbances aimed at frustrating the activities of public officials involved in the collection of public taxes and private debts. Instead, it was the cumulative effect of past and present legislative decisions regarding the implementation of fiscal policy that generated civil unrest. The difficulties in meeting tax assessments were unquestionably compounded by the overhanging private debts that contributed to the atmosphere of desperation. Taxpayers everywhere were feeling the pinch, but the pressure was most intense in the western counties; Hampshire, Worchester, and Berkshire had the highest percentage of delinquencies. Farmers in those regions were hard pressed to catch up with the previous years' assessments and were in no position to contribute to the retirement of the state debt by the end of 1789. Petitions for relief poured into the state legislature in the first half of 1786, all to no avail.

Bands of rioters closed the courthouses in several inland towns during the second half of 1786 in a sustained effort to prevent evictions and the forced sales of properties. Under the leadership of Daniel Shays, a disgruntled and embittered farmer, armed civilians, numbering perhaps two thousand, marched on the federal arsenal at Springfield in January 1787. In the brief battle, cannon fire killed three rebels and drove off the rest, but they soon regrouped. Rather than responding to the crisis in a spirit of compromise, as had happened in every other state where civil unrest to protest taxes had persisted, Governor Bowdoin raised an army of more than four thousand troops to put down the rebellion, a task accomplished by the end of February.

The rebels lost on the military front but won a huge political victory. The elections in 1787 sent new blood to the legislature and a new governor, John Hancock, who had served an earlier term as governor from 1783 to 1785 and then retired from office. Shaken by the threat to popular government, Hancock and legislative leaders belatedly abandoned the program of accelerated debt retirement and suspended the tax collections associated with that program. They sponsored tax reductions and private debt relief laws that gave middling citizens some breathing room. Tax assessments on persons and property dropped significantly from 1787 through 1790.

In the end, Massachusetts public debt stood at about the same level in 1790 as originally formulated in 1784—about $5 million. Approximately 20 percent of that total had been redeemed through 1786, but accruals of unpaid interest on outstanding securities during the next three years canceled out the earlier gains. The seesaw policy of very high taxes followed by very low taxes had accomplished nothing. The misconceived plan to sink the whole amount in half a decade produced a nearly catastrophic political crisis and virtually no progress in terms of debt retirement.

Looking back from the final settlement date in 1793, financial conditions in Massachusetts and South Carolina in the 1780s were quite similar in several critical respects. Both states had acquired substantial wartime debts in the course of making major financial sacrifices to support the war effort. That they later became the chief beneficiaries of the federal assumption of 1790 is perfectly understandable. The transfer of their debt obligations to the U.S. Treasury, which amounted to more than 40 percent of the total, was a partial restitution of monies to which they were genuinely entitled. Despite outward appearances, neither South Carolina nor Massachusetts taxpayers reaped windfalls in the assumption program, as happened in Delaware and New York. The $8 million in state debts that Massachusetts and South Carolina combined transferred to the federal government in 1790 ultimately proved insufficient to settle their accounts with the Continental Congress, and they received another $2.4 million in direct payments from the federal government in 1794.

The supreme irony of the whole Shays' affair is that, if the Massachusetts legislature had never taken any action to retire any of the outstanding debt after 1784, but merely maintained interest payments, its creditor position vis-à-vis the confederation government would subsequently have generated sufficient funds to cover the whole principal. The state treasury received financial assistance totaling $5.2 million—$4 million indirectly through assumption and $1.2 million directly through the receipt of U.S. government securities. Massachusetts taxpayers had already done more than their share to finance the unified effort against the British, and citizens of the other states had the collective responsibility for making full restitution.

Hindsight, of course, is always more lucid. Certainly Massachusetts political leaders in the 1780s were justified in expressing doubts about when, if ever, the national government would actually be in a position to live up to its own huge debt obligations, much less deal with reimbursements to creditor states. Exactly when Congress would become sufficiently solvent to resume interest payments on its own outstanding debt was anybody's guess, but the prospects as of 1785 did not look encouraging. Thus, the fact that most states decided to proceed with debt reduction was a reasonable and prudent course of action. Nonetheless, Massachusetts legislators exceeded the bounds of sound fiscal management by adopting a program of accelerated debt reduction in 1784 and holding steadfastly to it for so long. Slow but steady progress in retiring the state's huge debt would have been sufficient under the circumstances and especially since reimbursement, partial if not full, in some form was anticipated at some future date—provided the union held together.

In fact, the main emphasis, in retrospect, should not have been on debt retirement at all but rather on the maintenance of interest payments on a regular and steady schedule; and that could have been accomplished with tax rates 75 percent lower than those enacted in 1784 to cover the period from 1785 to 1789. Hamilton realized that the mere resumption of interest payments was the key to resurrecting the nation's credit standing when he assumed authority over the federal debt policy in 1789. If Hamilton's policies fall within the dictionary definition of financial conservatism, how then would the policies of Massachusetts extremists in the mid-1780s be labeled?

9

Financial Services in Transition

FOR THE THIRTEEN newly independent states, the 1780s were a transitional decade in terms of their involvement in financial affairs. Initially, most states tried to maintain the basic policies of the recent colonial past. With the exception of Delaware, which linked its monetary system with neighboring Pennsylvania, each colonial legislature had developed a distinct financial system; and that diversity was evident in the postwar era as well. Seven legislatures continued to issue paper monies after Yorktown—three in the lower south, three in the mid-Atlantic region, plus maverick Rhode Island. That practice came to an abrupt halt in 1789, however, because the Constitution prohibited the state governments from emitting bills of credit, which contemporaries interpreted to mean all forms of inconvertible currency. Meanwhile, all thirteen states had to face up to their lingering debt obligations, and the majority made substantial progress in retiring the outstanding principal. Nine states assumed a portion of the federal debt held by residents, and several states began paying the interest due on those securities. Responsibility for sinking the joint war debts incurred by Congress was passing steadily into the hands of state governments in the mid-1780s, and thereby threatening the prospects of securing a stronger central government under the revised Articles of Confederation.

The most radical departure from the colonial past was the establishment of chartered private banks in Philadelphia, New York City, and Boston, which issued currency supported by fractional specie reserves. The constitutional ban on fiat monies in combination with

the emergence of chartered banks fostered the increasing privatization of financial services in the 1790s and early nineteenth century.
The creation of chartered commercial banks represented a significant break with institutional patterns prevailing in colonial times.
Under British law, no enterprise with more than six partners, or
stockholders, was permitted to issue currency anywhere within the
empire unless Parliament granted charter privileges. As a practical
matter, permission was rarely granted—and never in the colonies.
On several occasions large groups of investors in Massachusetts and
Connecticut sought approval for so-called land banks—institutions
that issued paper money backed by private mortgages—but Parliament always denied charter status and, when necessary, it ordered
the recall of monies already placed in circulation.

In addition to providing the legal climate for planting the seeds
of private commercial banking, the thirteen states also had to face
up to the monumental debts associated with the war. Unlike the federal government, which suspended interest payments on its domestic obligations, most states made progress in retiring their outstanding debts in the 1780s. Nine states not only sunk a fair amount of
their obligations but even voluntarily resumed interest payments
on portions of the federal debt held by residents. While Congress
floundered, the state legislatures pressed forward with a variety of
debt reduction programs.

The superior performance of the several states is understandable for two key reasons. First, the states had the power of taxation;
they could impose a whole range of taxes on imports and exports,
on luxury items, on property, and directly on persons. Congress
could merely ask its political subunits for more revenue, whereas
the states could demand the collection of monies from taxpayers
and pursue the delinquent through the courts. Second, the state
legislatures had more experience in coping with the problems of
public debt retirement since the leadership could draw upon the
lessons learned in the aftermath of the Seven Years' War. With few
exceptions—New Jersey was one—the former British colonies had
extinguished their postwar debts in a decade or less through emergency programs of heavy taxation. The success of debt retirement
in the 1760s provided the model for legislative action two decades
later. As a result, leaders who felt a similar urgency about the elimination of public debts sprung to the forefront in every state legislature in the early 1780s. The universal aim was to rid the states
and their citizens of the burden of indebtedness as soon as humanly

TABLE 9.1
State Requisition Payments to Congress, 1781–1788
(in hundreds of thousands of dollars)

	Paid in Specie	Per Capita in Specie	Paid in Indents	Per Capita Specie/Indents
South Carolina	$ 445	$4.50	$—	$4.50
Maryland	400	1.90	—	1.90
Pennsylvania	645	1.50	435	2.50
Virginia	600	1.45	390	2.40
Rhode Island	75	1.15	—	1.15
New Jersey	150	.90	—	.80
New York	250	.80	400	2.10
Massachusetts	360	.75	450	1.70
Connecticut	180	.75	70	1.05
Delaware	32	.55	45	1.35
New Hampshire	20	.15	85	.80
North Carolina	28	.10	—	.10
Georgia	—	—	—	—
Total	$3,185	$1.00	$1,875	$1.55

Note: Per capita figures based on estimated free population in 1790. Based on "Schedule of Requisition Payments of the Several States," March 1788, Papers of Continental Congress, 1774–1789. The printed schedule lists quotas and payments on congressional requisitions of October 1781, September 1782, April 1784, September 1785, and August 1786.

possible. The problems of dealing decisively with the federal debt would be addressed after the general settlement among the several states revealed which individual states were debtors and which were creditors of the union.

If public officials throughout the nation had known in the mid-1780s what they subsequently learned in the summer of 1793, the financial history of certain states would have been dramatically different. Beginning in 1786, after congressional clerks had settled the claims of individuals, they began gathering pertinent information related to each state's contribution to the united military effort against the British from 1775 to 1783. The settlement committee took into account a host of factors. Among them were how much money each state treasury had spent from its own internal resources on the war, including the value of the provisions supplied to American troops, how much interest a given state had paid to holders of federal debt certificates, and how generous each state legislature had been in responding to congressional requisitions for financial

TABLE 9.2
Apportionment of War Costs among the States
(cost in millions of dollars in specie)

	Population	Cost	Percent of Cost
Virginia	699,265	$15.4	20.0
Massachusetts	475,327	10.5	13.7
Pennsylvania	432,879	9.5	12.4
North Carolina	353,523	7.8	10.2
New York	331,590	7.3	9.5
Maryland	278,514	6.1	7.9
Connecticut	236,841	5.2	6.8
South Carolina	206,235	4.5	5.9
New Hampshire	141,722	3.1	4.0
New Jersey	179,569	3.1	4.0
Georgia	70,842	1.6	2.1
Rhode Island	68,446	1.5	1.9
Delaware	55,540	1.2	1.6
Total	3,530,293 [a]	$76.8 [b]	100.0

Source: Benjamin Ratchford, *American State Debts.* Durham: Duke University Press, 1941, table 5, p. 63. Ratchford reproduced the official government document in its original form; he alerted readers to two other mathematical errors. The report was titled "Abstract of the Balances Due to and from the Several States on the Adjustment of their Accounts with the United States, by the General Board of Commissioners for That Purpose, under the Several Acts of Congress, for the Final Settlement of the State Accounts, per their Report of June 27, 1793."

[a] These population figures are about 200,000 below the census counts for the thirteen states in 1790 and about 400,000 below the overall count for the states plus territories.

[b] The official government document has a column footing of $77,666,678; my addition of the figures assigned to the states produced a revised number of $76,766,678. The most likely explanation of the discrepancy is that accountants transposed the numbers six and seven and produced an error of $900,000.

assistance. From 1781 to 1788, the thirteen states overall had sent Congress $3.2 million in specie and $1.9 million of indents issued to holders of federal securities.

The settlement committee calculated the total expenditures by the thirteen states for the general welfare at $114.4 million. It then deducted all federal advances to the states, including the $18 million in debts assumed in 1790, leaving a net balance of $76.6 million for the common expenses. Each state was assessed its proper share of the aggregate cost on a per capita basis. From each state's assessment, all its various contributions were deducted. This was a zero sum game in which six debtor states ended up owing $3.5 mil-

TABLE 9.3
Final Settlement of War Costs among the States
(in thousands of dollars)

	Status as of 1790	Assumption of State Debts	Final position as of 1794	Final position per capita for free population
Debtors				
Delaware	− 553[a]	59	− 612	−10.75
New York	− 890	1,184	−2,074	− 6.75
North Carolina	+1,294[b]	1,794	− 500	− 1.90
Maryland	+ 366	517	− 151	− .70
Virginia	+2,843	2,934	− 91	− .25
Pennsylvania	+ 702	778	− 76	− .15
Creditors				
New Jersey	+ 744	695	+ 49	+ .30
Georgia	+ 266	246	+ 20	+ .40
New Hampshire	+ 357	282	+ 75	+ .50
Massachusetts	+5,230	3,982	+1,248	+ 2.70
Connecticut	+2,219	1,600	+ 619	+ 2.70
Rhode Island	+ 499	200	+ 299	+ 4.60
South Carolina	+5,205	4,000	+1,205	+12.00

Source: Paul Trescott, "Federal-State Financial Relations, 1790–1860," *Journal of Economic History* (1955), table 2, p. 229.

Note: The seven creditor states received payment from the federal government in the form of U.S. government securities, including an additional $700,000 to cover accrued interest. The six debtor states never repaid the $3.5 million due to the federal government, although New York made a modest reimbursement.

[a] Minus sign indicates debtor position vis-à-vis Congress.
[b] Plus sign indicates creditor position vis-à-vis Congress.

lion to seven creditor states. The U.S. Treasury was designated to serve as the intermediary, charged with the duty of compensating creditors with emissions of freshly drawn U.S. government bonds and supposedly collecting the deficiencies from debtor states. Six states came out surprisingly close to balancing their books; their debit or credit balances were less than one dollar per capita. New Hampshire, New Jersey, and Georgia showed small credits, while Pennsylvania, Virginia, and Maryland came up slightly short.

The three largest debtors were Delaware, New York, and North Carolina. On an absolute basis New York had the largest deficit at over $2 million, followed by Delaware at $612,000, and North Carolina at $500,000. On a per capita basis, however, Delaware topped the list; each of its roughly fifty thousand free citizens owed their counterparts in the creditor states nearly $11. Delaware devoted few of the state's resources to the military effort, and it responded halfheartedly to congressional requisitions for funds in the 1770s and 1780s. Citizens in New York and North Carolina owed about $7 and $2, respectively. Except for New York, which reimbursed the federal government for a portion of its deficit, none of the other five states sent forward any funds to cover their remaining joint obligations.

The four major creditor states were Massachusetts, Connecticut, Rhode Island, and South Carolina. Both Massachusetts and South Carolina were owed $1.2 million, while Connecticut was due $619,000 and Rhode Island $299,000. All the creditor states received payment from the federal government to balance their books. The big winners were the citizens of South Carolina; the state treasury received federal securities worth $12 per capita for the free population. The per capita payments for the others were $4.60, Rhode Island; $2.70, Connecticut; and $2.70, Massachusetts.

How differently might events have unfolded if the settlement committee had begun sorting through the claims of the thirteen states in the early 1780s and then granted political leaders access to fairly reliable progress reports on its deliberations? In actuality, the committee started to investigate state claims in 1786 and it functioned in strict secrecy, leaving unlimited opportunities for outsiders to engage in guesswork based on incomplete facts and imperfect suppositions. As is predictable under such circumstances, some states realized they were likely to come close to balancing their books in terms of debits and credits, but others were either overly optimistic or too cautious in judging their probable standing. In legislatures where working assumptions proved wide of the mark, political leaders would have undoubtedly planned their fiscal strategies quite differently if they had been better informed about their status relative to the other twelve states in the union.

North Carolina and Massachusetts stand out as states that could have benefited significantly from a measure of advance knowledge about their relative status in the ongoing settlement process. North Carolina politicians assumed in the 1780s that the state would end up a major creditor of the union. Several units in the Continental army had been quartered within the state in the late stages of the war, and the legislature had authorized the shipment of provisions to supply the troops. The monetary value of the amounts advanced was sufficiently great that most legislators intuitively believed the state's credits would exceed its per capita allocation of joint war costs by a wide margin. Meanwhile, the state had steadily reduced its debt obligations, which had fallen below $2 million by the late 1780s.

Misperceptions about North Carolina's financial status vis-à-vis the other twelve states was an important factor in convincing a strong anti-federalist coalition to resist acceptance of the Constitution for nearly two years—until ratification in November 1789. Anti-federalists feared that a strengthened central government would assume the remaining debts of the several states, and that, as a consequence, North Carolinians would be forced to pay a disproportionate share of the costs of independence—covering not only their own obligations but also the reportedly staggering debts of delinquent states such as Massachusetts and South Carolina.

The anti-federalist argument in 1788 contained an element of truth, but the state's favorable position was grossly exaggerated. Prior to the federal assumption program, North Carolina was, as popularly alleged, a creditor of the union on the order of $1.3 million. But what local politicians failed to realize was that four other states—Connecticut at $2.2 million, Virginia at $2.8 million, and Massachusetts and South Carolina at $5.2 million each—were vastly greater creditors. Moreover, Georgia and Rhode Island were larger creditors on a per capita basis. North Carolina was not the shining star of fiscal virtue that so many of its inhabitants had concluded—at least not in comparison with other states.

Soon after the state's entrance into the union in late 1789, the federal debt assumption program took effect and North Carolina was relieved of its remaining wartime obligations of $1.8 million. Most legislators believed federal debt relief in 1790 represented a mere downpayment and that additional inflows of funds from the central government would be forthcoming after the settlement committee had completed its work. That optimism proved unwarranted. The committee ultimately listed North Carolina as the third largest debtor state on both an aggregate and per capita basis. In truth, federal debt assumption had transferred an extra $500,000 to the state treasury to which local taxpayers were not strictly entitled, a deficit that North Carolina never covered.

In retrospect, many members of the strong anti-federalist faction, which had delayed ratification for more than two years, seem to have been guilty of looking a gift horse in the mouth. The federal assumption program granted more benefits to North Caro-

lina than to ten of the thirteen states in the union. Rather than
leading the opposition to the Constitution, North Carolina should
have joined with Delaware and New York, the two main financial
beneficiaries, in supporting the document that called for a stronger
national government with the taxing power to relieve the states of
their postwar debts.

The story in Massachusetts was very much the reverse. If Massachusetts legislators had realized the magnitude of the state's creditor
position in relation to the other states in the mid-1780s, they would
have likely been less determined to make such rapid reductions
in the outstanding principal. The extremist wing of the urgency
faction almost certainly would have tempered its demands for increased taxation. Based on their experiences after the Seven Years'
War, most legislators believed that speedy retirement of the state
debt was an absolute requirement and that sky-high taxes were unavoidable. Had the state's financial status been more fully compre-
hended, however, it would have suggested to any objective participant in the political process that there was no reason to rush ahead
with debt retirement—none, that is, if they believed in the future
of the new United States and the fair allotment of the aggregate
costs of achieving independence among all the nation's citizens.

At the time Massachusetts consolidated its debts in 1784 and
approved the tax legislation to sink the entire principal by the end
of the decade, the state's credit balances with Congress already exceeded its debt obligations. Moreover, in the midst of the massive
effort to generate huge budget surpluses for debt retirement, Governor Bowdoin twice convinced the legislature, in 1785 and 1786, to
approve extra taxes in order to respond favorably to congressional
pleas for further funding. Those sums simply swelled the state's balance on the credit side of the ledger; by the end of the decade the
state was a $5 million creditor of its peers. Massachusetts had be-
haved so responsibly from a financial standpoint from 1775 to 1785
that its legislature did not know how or when to call a halt to the
policy of fiscal rectitude.

It took Shays' Rebellion to produce a gradualist approach to
debt reduction. Federal assumption led to the transfer of $4 mil-
lion worth of debt obligations to the U.S. Treasury, but even after
deducting that amount from the state's account with the federal
government, it still showed a healthy credit balance. When the settlement commission released its long-awaited report in 1793, Massachusetts received $1.25 million in additional monies. If the state

legislature had raised sufficient revenue to cover only the annual interest on the debt in the 1780s and had made no further voluntary payments to Congress to meet its quota, the settlement due the state treasury from the six debtor states was large enough to cover the state's entire outstanding debt.

Shays' Rebellion was, in retrospect, an unnecessary and preventable revolt because the taxes that triggered its outbreak were themselves an unnecessary and unbearable burden placed on the shoulders of Massachusetts taxpayers who had already contributed as much as citizens anywhere in the nation to the victory in 1783. Yet, without that minor rebellion, the movement to reform the Articles of Confederation might have never been transformed into a closed-door convention to draft a stronger Constitution. From that strange perspective, the mismanagement of financial affairs in Massachusetts during the late 1780s had a silver lining—namely, the beneficial effect of strengthening the nation as a united political force under a more powerful central government.

Even though their own debt obligations were pressing, eight state legislatures also assumed at least a portion of the federal burden. Pennsylvania, New York, Massachusetts, Connecticut, Delaware, Maryland, and the two Carolinas exchanged state obligations for existing federal debt certificates. The New Jersey legislature missed authorizing a swap program by a single vote, yet it agreed to pay the current interest on federal debts until the national government was in a position to reassert fiscal responsibility. In every instance, citizens had the option of participating in the swap program. No forced conversions were in store for persons who preferred to wait for Congress to act, and some holders of federal securities held back because they did not want to go on record as receiving interest payments in the state's fiat money rather than in specie.

As a result of the absorption activities, responsibility for servicing the federal debt, which totaled $27 million at the end of the war and was expanding at the rate of 5 percent annually because of accruing interest, began to pass steadily from the federal government into the hands of its political subunits. At one point in the 1780s, three states—Pennsylvania with $6 million, Massachusetts with $4 million, and New York with $2 million—had assumed a minimum of $12 million in federal debt. Comparable numbers for the other states are less firm, but it seems likely that at least half of the federal domestic debt had been absorbed by the states by 1787.

In Massachusetts the absorption was primarily a symbolic gesture rather than the assertion of fiscal responsibility since federal debt holders received little from the state in terms of interest payments. But Pennsylvania paid $1.1 million in interest on the federal debt in the 1780s, and New Jersey paid more than $400,000. New York covered the interest payments on federal securities eligible for its swap program from 1786 through 1790.

This analysis suggests that historians may have exaggerated the importance of Secretary of the Treasury Hamilton as the creator of a funding program for the national debt during Washington's first administration, since several states had already assumed those financial responsibilities and were carrying them out. Some states— Virginia was one—even talked about the possibility of redeeming the principal of the federal debt held by residents after all the state's obligations had been retired, presumably in the early 1790s. The idea had great appeal in certain southern states because by 1787 only a small share of the federal debt was owned by persons living in the region.[1]

The repayment of the national debt, which appeared to be a potentially powerful unifying force among the thirteen states at the end of the war, was rapidly eroding as a compelling reason for greater political centralization in light of state activities in the mid-1780s. Nationalists like Morris and Hamilton were becoming increasingly alarmed about the eroding prospects for a more powerful national government given the ambitious financial programs of several key states. When Shays' Rebellion dashed the plans of Massachusetts legislators to pay the interest on federal securities held by its residents, nationalists rejoiced. That singular event renewed the hope in some quarters that financial concerns, which had been fading as a potentially cohesive force from 1783 to 1786, would lead increasing numbers of influential political leaders to look with greater favor on the blessings of a stronger union with independent taxing power.

Part III

The Early National Era

❖ ❖ ❖

10

Funding the National Debt

D URING THE first decade under the new Constitution, the American financial services sector underwent significant institutional development. The innovations provided needed economic, and later even political, stability for the experimental form of federal, republican government. The two most important events in the financial sector were the creation of a nascent capital market at the national level and a reaffirmation of the political commitment to commercial banks under private control, but sometimes with partial governmental investment, as the sole issuers of a circulating currency. Those banks became a key source of credit for urban merchants and, in the early nineteenth century, for increasing numbers of farmers in market-oriented regions.

The emerging capital market was intertwined with the funding of unpaid wartime debts, and there were linkages to increased capitalization in the banking sector as well. The institutional structure of American commercial banking soon took on a dual character. One highly capitalized national bank received charter privileges from the federal government in 1791, while the states granted multiple charters to banks, mostly medium-sized institutions, operating strictly within their borders. Rivalries over the chartering powers of the federal government versus those of the several state governments emerged in 1791, and that legacy has more or less continued throughout the nineteenth and twentieth centuries.

The political leader most closely associated with the implementation of innovative financial policies at the federal level was Secretary of the Treasury Alexander Hamilton. Consequently, his ini-

tiatives during President George Washington's first term in office
have been grouped together and dubbed the Hamiltonian financial program by historians. The main components were funding
the outstanding debt and establishing a strong national bank with
interstate branching privileges. The Hamiltonian label is fully merited, since no other individual at the time, or since for that matter,
had such an immediate impact on shaping the structure of the U.S.
financial system. Nonetheless, after granting recognition of the secretary's preeminence, the tone here is perhaps less adulatory in
assessing the innovative character of the treasury secretary's contributions to the American financial structure than generally found in
many previously published historical accounts.

Many of Hamilton's ideas and proposals had obvious precedents
in the colonial and Confederation periods. Therefore, his exalted
reputation has arisen very much as a consequence of our limited
knowledge of the financial histories of the colonies and their successor states prior to ratification of the Constitution and, second,
because of the reigning periodization of U.S. history, which has
split specialists into the distinct subfields of either colonial history
or early national history. Few historians of the new nation famil-
iarized themselves with financial conditions at the state level before
1789, and especially not before 1770. Previous scholars have also
tended to look overseas to France and England for influential ideas
that inspired Hamilton's outlook on financial reform, whereas this
study stresses the domestic origins of the secretary's policies and
especially the contributions of his mentor, Superintendent of the
Treasury Robert Morris, under the Articles of Confederation.

This revised interpretive framework is an outgrowth of the over-
arching periodization of this study, which traces events from the
turn of the eighteenth century through the early years of the nineteenth century. To be fair, however, Hamilton must be accorded his
full due. He selected a particular package of financial reforms and
used all his consummate political skills, including the art of compromise, to push the enabling legislation through Congress during
President Washington's first term. He then implemented the comprehensive program before leaving office in 1795.[1]

The most innovative feature of American finance under the
newly strengthened federal government was the emergence of a
functioning capital market. The securities that formed the core of
the early market were U.S. government bonds and the stock certificates of the First Bank of the United States. Together, that combi-

nation of government debt and corporate equity totaled nearly $90 million, a figure roughly one-third of U.S. gross national product in 1790. Those securities paid steady returns to holders, and they soon attracted a host of European investors—a sure sign that American securities had achieved international standing. Organized auction markets—infant stock exchanges—for the securities arose in Philadelphia and New York; and other issues, frequently the stocks of other local financial institutions, were often found on the lists of securities dealers as well. By the turn of the century, the American capital market was established, expanding, and ready to assist in the nation's economic development. Indeed, the origins of American commercial banking and investment banking virtually coincide, and the two sectors developed more or less in tandem during the new nation's first quarter century and beyond.

Origins of Capital Markets in Europe

In pondering the underlying causes for the phenomenon of sustained economic growth in western Europe and North America during the eighteenth and nineteenth centuries, what immediately leaps to mind is the snowballing effect of technological breakthroughs and industrial advancements. Yet, innovations in the financial services sector were perhaps equally vital. In several European nations, the development of organized capital markets generally accompanied rapid industrialization and enhanced agricultural productivity. Whether a cause-and-effect relationship between financial innovation and improvements in other, more tangible economic sectors actually existed is one of those abstract concepts always difficult to prove—or to deny. Although the larger debate cannot be engaged in this limited space, a small boost can nonetheless be given to proponents who assert the importance of broadening financial markets in establishing the conditions for increases in living standards over the long term.

Scholars usually trace the origins of sophisticated international banking transactions to northern Italian merchant bankers in the thirteenth and fourteenth centuries. Those initiatives eventually waned, however, and for a more appropriate context we must race ahead to the rejuvenation of the European financial sector in sixteenth- and seventeenth-century Holland. The Dutch government nurtured a growing capital market in Amsterdam, and it successfully funded the national debt at Europe's lowest interest rates by attracting thousands of private investors, large and small. To quote historian Eric Schubert, the city "had large markets in commodities, securities, and foreign exchange; trade flows and trade financing centered around the Bank of Amsterdam with its large cache of gold and silver; and the Amsterdam stock market, the busiest and most sophisticated in Europe, handled such operations as forward sales and options."[2] The success of Amsterdam provided a model for two major rivals—London and Paris—to emulate. London ultimately caught up with Amsterdam and pulled ahead, but Paris fell by the wayside when the John Law debacle left in its wake the French monarchy without a major bank or a viable market for securities.

When King William of Orange and Queen Mary were invited to assume the throne in 1689, they carried across the English Channel plans to strengthen the financial markets in London based on their experiences in Amsterdam. The largest issue trading at the time was the English East India Company, the profitable joint-stock company initially chartered by Queen Elizabeth in 1599, which had offered its shares to the public in 1657 with no restrictions on ownership by foreigners. According to historian P. G. M. Dickson, more than fifty joint-stock firms were regularly listed on price sheets circulated among dealers and brokers in the early 1690s as well as numerous government issues with short and long maturities.[3] In 1694 Parliament chartered the Bank of England, a privately owned bank organized to invest primarily in government securities, and an active market in its shares quickly developed.

During the eighteenth century, London's capital market demonstrated increasing sophistication. The South Sea Company, a joint-stock company with transferable shares, received a parliamentary charter in the second decade of the century, and it copied the Bank of England by becoming a large investor in government debt issues. South Sea shares later became the vehicle for an unfortunate speculative mania, but even after the bubble had burst in 1720, the company survived and continued to participate in the financing of government securities. Larry Neal has explored the increasing integration of the Amsterdam and London financial markets by the mid-1720s, highlighted by the cross-listing of the most actively traded securities on both sides of the English Channel.

The so-called financial revolution in the public sector led to the issuance in the 1720s of perpetual governmental debt instruments called consols. Their popularity, in turn, laid the groundwork for an enormous expansion in the British national debt fueled by escalating expenditures related to war, defense, and empire. According to historian John Brewer, the increasing effectiveness of the tax system, especially the collection of a myriad of excise taxes by an efficient public bureaucracy, generated the increasing revenues necessary to cover the annual interest on a mounting public debt. Although passage in 1720 of the Bubble Act, which outlawed limited liability for all business firms without an explicit corporate charter voted by Parliament, placed somewhat of a damper on the formation of new joint-stock enterprises, the London financial markets were thriving by the mid-eighteenth century.[4]

American Colonies

In British North America, on the other hand, a capital market developed very slowly. The limited size of the colonial market discouraged innovation. In the seventeenth century, the settled population was exceedingly thin, just reaching 250,000 or thereabouts by 1700. Although population rose rapidly during the next half century, climbing to 1.2 million by 1750, the colonists continued to defer to London as the financial center of the British Empire. Americans drew on the London houses involved in overseas trade to finance a persistent trade deficit; and the accumulated debts, linked mostly to southern planters, were normally rolled over year after year—with unanticipated requests for settlement during the financial panic of 1772 the most notable exception.

In chapter 3, we cited the figures of Jacob Price and Alice Hanson Jones who independently estimated that British mercantile credit might have run as high as £6 million on the eve of independence. A fair share of that trade credit, perhaps one half, had passed from one generation to the next; over the decades it had evolved into a more or less perpetual British investment in the future prosperity of the colonies. Although the debts were primarily in the form of periodic extensions of book credit running up to eighteen months and were always subject to a creditor's nonrenewal, from a practical standpoint the aggregate was so high that it would have been impossible to collect the balance due in full in any less time than several consecutive growing seasons. (The Crisis of 1772 ebbed before Americans were able to clean up their accounts, although many southern planters encountered financial setbacks in their efforts at partial compliance.) Under the circumstances, any prolonged retrenchment of trade credit was impractical for other commercial considerations as well; its withdrawal would have undermined the continued sales of British manufactured goods in the extremely lucrative colonial market. On another front, historian Mira Wilkins estimated the total British investment in other, more tangible assets—land, shipping, iron plantations—at roughly £1.1 million in the mid-1770s. Those numbers suggest that as much as £7 million of British capital was committed to North America on the eve of independence, and it financed perhaps 6 percent of the aggregate physical wealth of the colonies.

Precision in estimating the numbers is impossible given the tentative nature of the data, but the important point in this context is that capital transfers to North America were made almost exclusively at the initiative of British citizens. Only Europeans were in a position to draw upon the facilities in London and Amsterdam to raise funds for investment in the colonies. The thirteen provincial governments had no prospect of floating loans in the London market, nor could Americans with visions of future profits expect to gain access to long-term financing in the English capital—not unless they were involved in joint ventures with British investors in projects such as developing raw land on the frontier. The colonies were thousands of miles across the ocean, and given slow communications and unreliable intelligence about their diverse economies, British investors considered the very idea of purchasing colonial securities, public or private, too risky to contemplate, even momentarily. To raise private investment capital or the funding to cover provincial legislative deficits, Americans had to look almost exclusively to their own resources. A key reason why the Continental Congress turned to fiat currency as the primary means of financing the War for Independence was that no viable alternative existed; domestic capital markets were still small, regional in character, and concentrated in a few northern states.

The effort to identify the roots of the nascent capital market that emerged in the 1790s is frustrated by the lack of knowledge about investment patterns in the colonial era. Only limited information has come forth, and about all that we can do at this date is to cite scattered evidence suggestive of future developments. The best data come from New England. Following Parliament's passage of the Currency Act of 1751, the four New England legislatures were denied the option of emitting more fiat currency. Those colonies returned to a specie standard, and coins were again the prime medium of exchange for the general population. To finance periodic budget deficits, their legislatures raised the needed specie by selling treasury notes paying interest at the legal rate, typically 5 to 6 percent, to local citizens for terms running up to the mandated two-year limit—or as many as five years for shortfalls resulting from wartime emergencies such as occurred during the Seven Years' War.

From 1751 to 1772, historian Leslie Brock calculated that Massachusetts issued treasury certificates in varying maturities totaling £2.3 million, or a mean of about £100,000 annually. From 1750 to 1753 and later from 1771 until independence—after virtually all of the lingering debts from the Seven Years' War had been retired— the treasury recorded no outstanding debt at the end of the fiscal year. A carryover debt from one year to the next totaling £13,000 first appeared on the ledgers at the end of fiscal 1754. It rose during the war to £454,000 in 1762 (roughly $1.5 million at the lawful rate), which represented somewhere around 20 percent of the colony's annual gross output. The ability of the treasury to raise such substantial sums of money over the short to intermediate term was a notable achievement, demonstrating that a provincial market for government securities, centered in Boston and drawing upon its hinterlands, could be developed and sustained under the proper circumstances.

In compliance with parliamentary regulations and its own desire to escape the burden of debt, however, the Massachusetts legislature embarked upon a resolute program of abnormally heavy taxation in 1760. Within a decade the treasury had reduced its annual reliance on borrowed funds to less than £100,000, and the maturities of all its certificates were for periods shorter than one year. As a result, the market for public securities in Massachusetts was rapidly dissipating in the early 1770s because of the legislature's success in redeeming its outstanding debts—just the opposite of what was happening across the ocean in London where the British national debt kept rising to new heights year after year.

The data on the other three New England colonies is more fragmentary, but they also issued interest-bearing treasury certificates to finance occasional deficits from midcentury until independence. From 1755 to 1764, for example, Connecticut issued a total of £359,000 at 5 percent interest—a mean of £45,000 per annum. At the end of the Seven Years' War, the colony had £260,000 in debts still outstanding, or from 12 to 15 percent of the colony's annual gross output. New Hampshire owed more than £50,000 at the end of the war, or about 10 percent of its annual production, while Rhode Island owed more than £80,000, or somewhere around 15 percent of its annual gross output. Like Massachusetts, these three New England colonies also made substantial progress in reducing their outstanding obligations, and their credit rating with local investors was presumably very high.

More early signs of an emerging capital market in Massachusetts have been identified by historian Winifred Rothenberg, who focused on Middlesex County, the agricultural hinterland of Boston, beginning in 1730 and ending in the 1830s. Based on a sample of estates, of which 80 percent were those of farmers, she found that over the years individual credit networks thickened and widened— meaning that the number of credit partners steadily increased and their geographic dispersion was greater. In the colonial era, the obligations consisted of open book credit, signature notes, and mortgages. In the period 1730–50, the number of creditors of the average decedent totaled about eighteen; during the period 1751– 70, the figure rose to twenty-two; and in 1771–90 it had climbed to twenty-six. Moreover, in the 1780s various negotiable securities started turning up on estate lists for the first time, including Massachusetts state bonds, congressional debt certificates, and bank and insurance company stocks. All the evidence indicates that many New England farmers with surplus funds, as well as urban merchants and professionals, were becoming increasingly accustomed to including financial assets among their wealth holdings.

In her massive study of wealth patterns in the colonies on the eve of independence, Alice Hanson Jones calculated that 56 percent of all estates listed some financial assets. Wealth holders with estates greater than £400 possessed more financial assets than liabilities, while the reverse was true for lesser estates. Aggregate financial claims comprised 13 percent of wealth holders' net worth for the whole colonial population, but the figures for New England at 19 percent and for the middle colonies at 27 percent were far higher than for the southern colonies, where only 4 percent of wealth holders' net worth consisted of financial claims.[5] The low southern percentage is a telling number, for it suggests why capital markets developed so unevenly on a regional basis after independence. Growth was much slower in the southern states, an area where most wealth holders had long concentrated on land, slaves, and other tangible property and had generally foregone investments in financial claims.

The southern reticence to make large investments in financial assets was reflected in the pattern of congressional bond sales during the War for Independence. Although loan offices were established in every state, the southern states generated only 10 percent of the original subscriptions to the federal debt. Three northern states took more than 60 percent of the total. Pennsylvania alone produced about one-third of bond sales, while Massachusetts accounted for 20 percent and Connecticut 11 percent. Funds raised through the sale of securities to citizens generated about $11.6 million in specie for the Continental Congress—or about 7 percent of the total cost of the war. When the proposal to grant the federal government the exclusive right to collect a 5 percent ad valorem tariff was killed by Rhode Island in 1782, Superintendent of Finance Robert Morris suspended interest payments on the domestic debt, and the market value of congressional debt certificates plummeted. (Some interest was later paid in so-called indents, really a form of fiat currency; but indents themselves passed at discounts of 85 to 90 percent in the marketplace.) The assigned maturity dates for outstanding securities were likewise suspended and no new dates stipulated, since predicting when the federal government would have sufficient financial resources to meet its obligations was too problematic.

Congress was almost as successful in tapping capital markets overseas as at home. Foreign loans, mainly in France and Holland, brought in another $10 million from 1775 to 1789.[6] That favorable outcome was not too surprising since the underwriting and placement of long-term loans to governmental units had become fairly routine in the leading European financial centers by the last quarter of the eighteenth century. The most remarkable and encouraging news for the U.S. representatives on the continent was that the credit standing of the federal republic ranked so high among knowledgeable and sophisticated private investors in Amsterdam. During the eight years following the victory at Yorktown, Dutch investors acquired a total of $3.6 million in U.S. debt certificates at 4 to 5 percent, interest rates that were fully competitive with those commanded by some of the leading European powers. In comparison, Parliament had raised most of the millions of pounds required to cover its military expenditures in North America between 1775 and 1783 through increases in the national debt. Borrowing huge sums to fight wars around the globe had become all too easy in England as a result of the mutually reinforcing cooperation between the Exchequer and the rapidly maturing London capital market.

The individual states also sold bonds to local citizens during the war. Chapter 7 estimates the total of interest-bearing securities issued by the states as falling somewhere in the broad range of $35 to $50 million in the 1770s and 1780s. However, it is difficult to even guess at how much of that total represented direct sales of securities for specie compared to the volume of certificates issued to acquire military supplies of all varieties, to pay soldiers' wages, and to swap debt for previous currency issues. In this context only debt certificates issued to acquire private specie holdings were legitimate capital market transactions since they represented strictly voluntary exchanges. All the other debt transactions fail to qualify because of some measure of unilateral government action—for example, the offer of IOUs versus depreciating currency to suppliers—or because currency holders were simply given the opportunity to swap depreciated paper for more formal debt obligations. The aggregate debts incurred by state treasurers in attracting specie from private lenders were certainly a small percentage of their total outstanding obligations as of 1783, especially in the southern states; but how much smaller? One possibility, however chancy, is a guess in the range of 10 to 20 percent overall.

Hard evidence on specie loans at the state level is sparse in most instances. The published data are best for Massachusetts, which, for the purposes of this discussion, is unfortunately probably the least representative state in the union. From May 1775 through April 1781, the state authorized treasury notes totaling more than £4 million at interest rates varying between 5 and 6 percent. Of that figure, £1.15 million ($3.8 million) represented specie borrowed directly from private individuals to finance budget deficits. The solicitations to local lenders were often published. On 8 May 1776, this announcement appeared in the *Boston Gazette:* "Any persons disposed to lend, may apply to the Treasurer, at his Office in Watertown. Said Money is wanted immediately." The borrowings in 1775 and 1776 came due in two years or less. Starting in 1777 and thereafter the maturities lengthened but never exceeded five years—the old maximum under Parliament's currency regulations enacted in 1751 for New England. The outstanding balance on loans contracted for specie was £250,000 at the end of 1776, fell to £100,000 in 1777 and 1778, and climbed to £300,000 in 1779, where it remained for two years until the grand debt consolidation totaling £1.1 million took effect in the early 1780s.[7]

Overall, specie borrowings accounted for just over one-quarter of the treasury notes issued in Massachusetts before debt consolidation in the 1780s. On a relative scale, the Bay State had greater success in the domestic money market than Congress, which is not surprising given the state treasurer's involvement in arranging similar short-term to intermediate placements during the last quarter century. Indeed, the aggregate specie borrowings for the state of Massachusetts totaled $3.8 million compared to the congressional figure of $11.6 million for the whole nation. Comparing specie borrowings per capita for the free population, citizens of Massachusetts had a record three times better than American citizens generally, and it must be remembered that $2.3 million of congressional securities were sold in the Bay State as well. Elsewhere, it is doubtful that any other state legislature, except possibly in Connecticut, had such an outstanding record in regard to its ability to draw on local capital markets to finance wartime deficits. The mid-Atlantic states raised a modest percentage of their funding from specie loans, but the southern states generated only minute amounts.

During the mid-1780s, after the fighting had ended and the peace treaty was signed, several states faced up to their financial responsibilities and took action to foster the development of local and regional capital markets. All thirteen state legislatures took steps to recognize their respective obligations and, under the urgency ideals in vogue at the time, made progress in addressing the financial chaos left over from the war years. Taxes went up almost universally. Most states began paying interest on their debt certificates, in some instances past-due interest as well as current interest. Legislators generally endorsed optimistic programs for redeeming the outstanding principal during the next five to ten years. None achieved the goal of total debt redemption, but most states had made progress by the end of the decade; and many legislative leaders looked forward to a final payoff sometime during the 1790s. Meanwhile, the federal government, without an independent revenue, was drifting further and further into debt. The interest accruing on congressional domestic securities accumulated year after year and thereby increased the aggregate of its financial obligations.

For nationalists like Morris and Hamilton, the most troubling financial development in the mid-1780s was the movement by some states to assume as their own obligations significant portions of the federal securities held by local citizens. Congress protested the legality of the assumptions but it could not halt or reverse them. Eight states formally took that route, including Pennsylvania, New York, Massachusetts, Connecticut, Delaware, Maryland, and the two Carolinas. In the mid-1780s those states plus New Jersey, which never officially assumed ownership, began paying at least a portion of the interest due on various federal securities with a face value of approximately $9 to $11 million—or up to two-fifths of the total federal debt. Meanwhile, Virginia made so much progress in redeeming its state debts after 1785 that legislative leaders there also began talking about the assumption of federal debts. No state actually retired any of the federal principal, but the interest that each state had paid on congressional securities in the 1780s was credited to its respective account in the final settlement of 1793.

Morris, Hamilton, Madison, and their political allies realized in the mid-1780s that if the subunits continued their financial programs unimpeded for another five to ten years, the successes in several key states might undermine the nationalist movement. Thus, they wanted not merely to reform the Articles of Confederation in 1787 but to substitute a more centralized form of national government before financial pressures had eased and the states had started to lift the debt burden from congressional shoulders. In a letter to Morris back in April 1781, Hamilton had declared: "A national debt, if it is not excessive, will be to us a national blessing. It will be a powerful cement of our union." He never changed his mind.

From the Hamiltonian perspective, a national debt also translated into the likely emergence of a sizable capital market that could be nourished and systematically drawn upon to provide the financing for a host of worthwhile developmental projects in both the public and private sectors. A thriving capital market in government securities, as existed in Amsterdam and London, might prove extremely useful in the event extraordinary financial resources were required to fight another major war on land or at sea at some future date. Given the congressional experience with Continental dollars, the possibility of relying on fiat currency as a means of financing any future war effort had probably passed for the foreseeable future. A centralized, sustainable capital market was not to be shunned or scuttled as the debt-averse followers of Thomas Jefferson loudly proclaimed.[8] To Hamilton's way of thinking, the case was just the reverse: a capital market, with all the accompanying securities dealers, brokers, and, yes, even speculators, was a prospective national asset rather than a prospective malady. If, however, the federal debt were eventually dispersed in some fashion among the thirteen political subunits, the opportunity to create a national capital market centered in one of the nation's leading commercial cities—Philadelphia, Boston, and New York were the main candidates—would probably be lost for decades.

This discussion leads naturally to a subject that cannot be easily skirted in any examination of late eighteenth-century economic issues, namely, an ideological struggle that arose soon after ratification of the Constitution between political leaders who identified with Jeffersonian ideals versus their rivals, the Federalist Hamiltonians. The argument centered on two critical issues: the role in American society of an organized capital market consisting largely of public securities, and the legitimacy of a potentially large national, quasi-central bank.[9] Jeffersonians opposed the creation of the new institutions, and by and large they had colonial tradition on their side. First, the Jeffersonians argued that the American economy (actually the sum of thirteen economies) had moved forward successfully in the past without the presence of either a capital market or private commercial banks, large or small, and therefore few compelling arguments existed for initiating such major institutional alterations, which were likely to promote social divisions.

Most Americans in the 1780s still expressed an aversion for the burden of public debt, particularly any hint of perpetual indebtedness. Under their former colonial status, the legislatures had acted decisively to redeem in timely fashion the abnormally high debts— abnormally high in the American context—incurred during the Seven Years' War. After the War for Independence, the dominant urgency factions in state legislatures had likewise moved to extinguish the wartime obligations of the respective states. Although the task had proven more difficult than anticipated, since the most recent war debts had risen to such unprecedented heights, most Americans probably still agreed with Jefferson's rule of thumb that every generation should assume responsibility for repaying its own outstanding public debts—meaning within fifteen to twenty years at the outside. In a letter to President Washington in 1792, Jefferson summed up his differences with Hamilton: "I would wish the debt paid tomorrow; he wishes it never to be paid, but always to be a thing where with to corrupt & manage the legislature."[10]

Most members of the Jeffersonian camp were also in varying degrees captives of a conspiratorial interpretation regarding the underlying causes for the breakaway from Great Britain. According to the general line of argument, crown and Parliament had strayed from the maintenance of upright constitutional processes during the third quarter of the eighteenth century because of rampant corruption. Among the forces contributing to decaying public morals were the allegedly devilish influences of the so-called urban monied elite. Who constituted the elite? Prominent in that parasitic circle were stockjobbers and other speculative elements who encouraged Parliament to sink deeper and deeper into red ink and then made huge profits underwriting the loans required to prop up the bloated ship of state. In his study of the British political economy in the eighteenth century, historian John Brewer reported that some domestic critics of government policy expressed similar reservations, but in England they constituted a distinct minority.[11] In the United States, the heightened suspicion of persons involved in the operation of financial markets, who were routinely accused of excessive greed and questionable patriotism, had its origins in the rhetoric of the independence movement. That outlook remained alive for decades, surviving through the administration of President Andrew Jackson and well into the twentieth century.

The Jeffersonian opposition to the creation of a permanent national capital market was based in part, therefore, on persistent fears that a small group of wealthy financiers might worm their way into the political structure and reincarnate the undefined, but undoubtedly dangerous, disease of European corruption on American shores. If that happened, U.S. citizens would never escape the burden of public debt. Instead, their indebtedness would likely escalate in future decades, producing more profits for financiers—the monied elite—and more miseries for the typical taxpayer. Since most participants in the London and Amsterdam capital markets in the late eighteenth century were dealing primarily in government securities, not company bonds and stocks, the Jeffersonian reservations about the long-term implications of Hamiltonian policies were rational.

Underlying concerns about the link between political corruption and capital markets were also elements in the Jeffersonian opposition to the proposal to establish the First Bank of the United States, a large institution with $10 million in capital resources modeled on the Bank of England. The British financial institution had been founded in 1694 with the explicit charge of assisting the government in financing the growing national debt. The Bank of England invested its private resources mainly in government securities and conducted only a limited commercial business with London merchants. Its origins suggested that the impetus for its founding was to create a reliable vehicle to support the English national debt. In short, a powerful national bank and a strengthened capital market were integral parts of a British financial system that was geared to serve the requirements of an expanding, primarily military, governmental sector. Consequently, public policy was highly susceptible to the influence of stockjobbers, speculators, and other manipulative elements. The congressional debate over a national bank for the United States will be discussed in the next chapter. Meanwhile, we should keep in mind that linkages clearly existed between Hamilton's overall plan to fund the national debt and then to establish a large chartered bank—and both were based on English precedents.

Hamilton's Funding Program

The first Congress and first president inaugurated under the new Constitution took office in March 1789. A few months later, President George Washington appointed Alexander Hamilton as secretary of the treasury. In January 1790 the new secretary presented the extensive *Report on the Public Credit* to Congress recommending a comprehensive program designed to fund the national debt, which meant in this case merely the resumption of interest payments in specie (no more indents). Principal repayment was deferred until an unspecified date, with the possibility of minimal annual reductions in unusually favorable years. The federal domestic debt was roughly $40 million, consisting of $27 million in original principal plus $13 million in accrued interest, which had accumulated at the rate of 6 percent annually over the last eight years. Overseas, Congress owed just over $12 million, mostly to the French government ($8.4 million) and private investors in Holland ($3.6 million). Only the latter had received interest payments in specie regularly throughout the 1780s, and for that reason the Dutch continued to advance fresh monies to the U.S. government during the early 1790s.

Among the most controversial features of Hamilton's debt plan was the proposed federal assumption of a large proportion of the remaining wartime debts of the several states. The treasury secretary argued that the military expenditures from 1775 to 1783 were common expenses to be shared among the thirteen states united against Great Britain, and therefore, given the structure of the new government, it was entirely appropriate for the central government to assume responsibility for all unpaid debts. Hamilton's proposals made good sense from two perspectives. First, the secretary desperately wanted to reverse the previous trend toward state assumption of the federal debt, which he believed threatened the viability of the new nation by promoting political dissolution. If the national debt were to become the cement holding the union together, as he had asserted back in 1781, then a wholesale consolidation under the auspices of the federal government was the only means of accomplishing that nationalistic goal.

Left largely unsaid in that context was the collateral argument that inclusion of the state debts would increase the initial size of the envisioned national capital market on the order of an extra $15 to $25 million. If the federal government could meet the interest payment on that additional sum as well, then its credit rating at home and abroad would receive an extra boost. Hamilton was interested primarily in enhancing the credit standing of Congress and was generally unconcerned about the status of the various states, none of which had significant debts beyond those overhanging from the war. Despite the states' superior record in meeting their public obligations in the 1780s, none had attracted a sizable number of private investors beyond its borders, either in neighboring states or overseas. Thus, their international credit rating was low or, perhaps more accurately, nonexistent. For the time being at least, Hamilton was satisfied with the states' unrecognized status since he did not want any major domestic political rivals while trying to establish a high credit rating for the national government at home and particularly abroad.

Another reason for assuming the states' debts in 1790 was that the federal government was already destined to become involved in the financial affairs of its subunits sooner or later no matter how slowly Congress responded during Washington's first term. The delay in congressional involvement was occasioned by the glacial work schedule of the congressional settlement commission, which had been created in the early 1780s and charged with the task of auditing all the debits and credits affecting each state's account. After the grand total was accumulated, the cost was to be apportioned on a per capita basis according to state population. From each state's monetary assessment for military costs the commission planned to subtract all its various and validated credits, leaving a surplus or deficit. The final accounting would almost certainly show that some states were net creditors and others net debtors since the apportionment was a zero sum game. According to the original plan, the federal government was to act as intermediary—collecting monies from the delinquent states and using the funds to reimburse the creditor states.

TABLE 10.1
Federal Assumption of State Debts, 1790

	Amount	Per Capita Free population
Delaware	$ 59,161	$ 1.05
Pennsylvania	777,983	1.85
New Hampshire	282,595	2.00
Maryland	517,491	2.40
Rhode Island	200,000	3.10
New York	1,183,716	3.85
New Jersey	695,202	4.10
Georgia	246,030	4.90
North Carolina[a]	1,794,803	6.80
Connecticut	1,600,000	6.95
Virginia[b]	2,934,416	7.15
Massachusetts[c]	3,981,733	8.50
South Carolina	3,999,651	40.00
Total	$18,272,781	$ 5.75

[a] If Tennessee population included = $6.00 per capita
[b] If Kentucky population included = $6.10 per capita
[c] Includes Maine

Hamilton proposed that Congress intervene prematurely in the ongoing settlement process by making what amounted to progress payments to the states. Several states temporarily burdened with high debts seemed virtually certain to prove major creditors of their peers and deserved temporary relief. Massachusetts and South Carolina were the most prominent in the probable creditor category; one of the key reasons those two states had accumulated such monumental debts was that their citizens had contributed more than their fair share to financing the war. Other states, confident of their creditor status, also had visions of receiving huge reimbursements to help in redeeming their debts, including Virginia and North Carolina. The settlement commission's work was far from finished in 1790, and its membership estimated that the end still lay years ahead.

Fearful of the negative reaction in Congress if he proposed progress payments to some states while denying equal treatment to probable debtors, Hamilton followed the path of least political resistance. The treasury secretary suggested that advances covering the vast majority of the remaining state debts be assumed and incorporated in the federal total. Many historical accounts continue to report that all remaining state debts were eligible for assumption, but a limit of $4 million per state was applied. Only Massachusetts and South Carolina received near the maximum federal assistance in 1790, and federal accountants later proved in 1793 that those advances were fully justified. Two states, Delaware at $59,000 and New York at $1.2 million, received debt relief that was completely undeserved since their citizens were, in retrospect, already deficient in their contributions to the common cause. Four other states that merited a measure of debt relief came away with more than their due; the excesses were $500,000 for North Carolina, $151,000 for Maryland, $100,000 for Virginia, and $76,000 for Pennsylvania.

Did Hamilton contemplate at the time that adoption of his magnanimous premature assumption program would likely benefit his home state unduly once all the accounts had been sorted out? Perhaps, but the evidence is lacking. Critics of the assumption plan did complain that certain states might realize unwarranted gains, but, given the absence of any solid financial data, no one could identify exactly which states might reap windfalls or what the magnitude might be. According to historian Forrest McDonald, the treasury secretary planned to reward creditor states with payment in federal government securities, but from the outset he had no intention of demanding restitution from states that proved debtors in the final accounting.[12]

Hamilton's appointment as head of the Treasury Department and the implementation of his funding program for the wartime securities of the federal and state governments represented the final triumph of the gradualist approach to debt repayment. Perhaps the word *triumph* is too strong in this context; the term *confirmation* might be equally appropriate since the movement toward the gradualist position had been under way in most quarters for several years after the magnitude of the financial challenge began to sink in. Hamilton absorbed the state debts and made gradualism official government policy. His measured approach to debt management was in sharp contrast to prevailing public attitudes less than a decade earlier. At the beginning of the 1780s, urgency factions generally controlled fiscal policy at the state level, and they were determined to emulate the successes of their immediate predecessors after the Seven Years' War. Most state legislatures adopted ambitious tax programs to redeem fully their wartime obligations in reasonably short order—generally within five to ten years. Some states made substantial headway, but others floundered when citizens protested the heavy taxation required to retire the outstanding principal. In most states the political leadership quickly reassessed the financial situation and then adopted steps designed to string out the redemption period well into the 1790s. No state, however, was prepared to go as far along the gradualist path as Secretary Hamilton: namely, suspending principal repayments more or less indefinitely except for token retirements designed to create favorable publicity and to enhance thereby the reputation, not to mention the market prices, of U.S. public securities.

The essence of the Hamiltonian fiscal program was to hold federal taxes to the minimum level required to pay the annual interest on the government debt, plus all military and other incidental expenses. No surplus for genuine debt redemption would flow into the Treasury's coffers for the foreseeable future. The strategy was ingenious because it appealed so blatantly to one of the two conflicting views swirling about in the rival Jeffersonian camp. The Jeffersonians hated a perpetual public debt, but they simultaneously detested high taxes. In the 1780s their hatred for debt was the stronger emotion; indeed, they were even prepared to suffer high taxes in the short run in order to sink the outstanding principal. The aim, of course, was to revert as soon as possible to the idyllic world of low taxation that had prevailed during most of the colonial era. But after more than a decade of abnormally high taxes linked to the past war, the debt-averse Jeffersonians were ready for a measure of long-term tax relief.

Progress had been made at the state level, but the original federal debt of $27 million was approaching $40 million and still mounting as a result of the accrual of unpaid interest. Despite the sacrifices of local taxpayers in some regions, state and federal indebtedness *combined* had changed little during the last decade. Hamilton's debt management policy signaled an end to exaggerated retirement expectations; and, in turn, it promised a lighter tax burden distributed more evenly throughout the nation, which appealed to persons concerned about equity and fairness. Jeffersonians temporarily gave up the dream of debt extinction in return for immediate tax relief plus the assurance that the resumption of interest payments would prevent any further unintended increases in the overall level of indebtedness through mounting arrearages.

Hamilton was able to offer the prospect of a lower tax burden by proposing a debt package aimed at reducing the cost of public borrowing. The secretary proposed the issuance of an array of

new bonds that produced an effective interest rate lower than the
6 percent stipulated on most of the public securities outstanding in
1789. The plan was somewhat intricate, but it lowered the federal
government's interest expense to under 4 percent on the outstanding principal through the 1790s. The federal domestic principal of
$27 million retained the official 6 percent rate, but one-third of the
bonds were not eligible to start collecting interest until 1800.

Prior to Hamilton's presentation of his report to Congress,
many informed congressional leaders, including persons drawn
from across the political spectrum, believed the secretary might recommend a partial repudiation of the accumulated past-due interest. Instead, he proposed full funding for the $13 million in ar-
rears, including outstanding indents, but at a reduced interest rate
of 3 percent. For the outstanding state debts assumed by the U.S.
Treasury, Hamilton suggested this mixture: interest at 6 percent on
four-ninths of the total immediately, interest at 3 percent on three-
ninths immediately, and interest at 6 percent on the final two-ninths
beginning in 1800. The net interest cost was 3.66 percent through
the end of the decade, rising to 5 percent in the next century. All
the securities paying 3 percent were redeemable by the government
at any time, but only a fraction of the 6 percents could be retired in
any given year, irrespective of the size of the government surplus.
Hamilton made the majority of the bonds in his funding program
noncallable in any given year because he wanted to ensure that a
market in U.S. government bonds would survive for up to thirty
years at a minimum, thereby laying the groundwork for the issuance
and trading of other securities. Otherwise, he feared that the Jeffersonians might seize control of the government sometime within the
next decade or so and reintroduce a crash redemption program
designed to pay off the whole national debt in a decade or so.[13]

Hamilton hoped that the success of his funding program would
soon produce market rates as low as those unilaterally imposed
on frustrated debt holders by his department in 1790. Once Congress resumed interest payments on a regular basis, he anticipated
a sharp decline in market yields on government loans, placing U.S.
credit on comparable footing with the great European powers by
the turn of the century. Again his judgment proved correct. Not
long after the funding program went into effect, U.S. government
bonds paying 6 percent interest traded at premium prices, and
yields to investors had fallen to 5 percent or less by 1795.

Hamilton had instituted the ultimate gradualist program. He

needed to raise tax revenues that amounted only to about 2 percent of U.S. national income in 1790 to meet the annual interest
expense. Few state debts remained outstanding to drain away additional tax dollars. After fifteen years of disruption and uncertainty,
the treasury secretary had reestablished the continuity of American
taxation policy; the low-level tax rates of colonial times were once
again a reality.

The federal government's debt structure in the 1790s was vastly
different from its modern counterpart. In the late twentieth century, the U.S. Treasury financed the national debt through a host
of securities with maturities ranging from short-term bills (three
months), to intermediate notes (two years), and long-term bonds
(thirty years). None of the government's debts in 1791 had fixed
maturity dates. U.S. securities were essentially the equivalent of
British consols, perpetual debt instruments introduced with great
success by successive exchequers in the second quarter of the eighteenth century. Consols were an important factor in the overall
structure of parliamentary debt, helping to finance persistent budget deficits over the decades; but securities with indeterminate
maturations never constituted the whole of British indebtedness as
was true of the American government under its new Constitution.

Hamilton concluded that the most crucial element in supporting the debt was the regular payment of scheduled interest. But to
further enhance the new nation's credit standing, however, he also
promoted in rather vague fashion the establishment of a sinking
fund. Its purpose was to provide a measure of reassurance to debt
holders concerned about the ultimate redemption of the outstanding principal. The general idea was to set aside revenues associated
with a specific tax or with surpluses, when realized, associated with
the operation of a specific government department—in the American case the U.S. Post Office—and then to apply the funds to purchases of public securities in the open market.[14] The interest earned
by the sinking fund was, in turn, to be used to acquire more public
securities. Finally, over a period of, say, twenty-five to forty years,
the sinking fund would acquire virtually the entire public debt—
at which point an executive branch of government would own all
the liabilities of the legislative branch, so to speak, and the whole
national debt could be blissfully canceled. (The monies accumulating in the social security fund in the 1990s represent a roughly
similar proposition, although they are scheduled to be paid out to
retirees after 2010.)

The monies accumulated in the sinking fund from year to year were supposedly considered inviolate; that is, they could not be diverted by a legislative body at a later date for other expenditures but had to be devoted strictly to debt reduction. The creation of a sinking fund was one means of ameliorating an otherwise bad situation, namely a debt structure with no regularly scheduled maturity dates. The Treasury's plan promised a high degree of flexibility since it took effect only under certain favorable conditions such as the realization of departmental surpluses. When deficits arose, the sinking fund purchases were automatically suspended.

The implementation of a sinking fund as a mechanism for systematically reducing national indebtedness dates back to a parliamentary initiative in 1717. The British fund was operational through the 1720s and 1730s, and it achieved a certain measure of success in lowering the nation's public obligations by £6 million during a twenty-year period. Unquestionably, the fund was a factor in promoting Parliament's good credit rating and lowering the cost of borrowing. With the military costs of maintaining and expanding the British Empire escalating after 1740, the temptation to raid the fund to gain access to additional financial resources— by selling its assets back to the general public or diverting its interest revenues to other purposes—proved irresistible. But under the urging of the indefatigable propagandist Dr. Richard Price, Prime Minister William Pitt rejuvenated the sinking fund in the 1780s. Monies were diligently used to acquire portions of the outstanding debt, while even more fresh borrowings in escalating amounts were simultaneously being negotiated on the other side of the ledger.[15]

Financial historians have differed in their assessment of the motivations for the creation of a sinking fund for servicing the U.S. public debt. Some experts have cited the adoption of a sinking fund as clear evidence of Secretary Hamilton's devotion to the principle of the retirement of the national debt. He included a sinking fund in his proposals of 1790, shepherded it through the Congress, and later in his farewell statement when leaving the Treasury post in 1795 called for its vigorous application in the years ahead. Those actions, admirers of the Hamiltonian program have claimed, disprove the Jeffersonian charge that the treasury secretary was wedded to a permanent national debt. His support of the sinking fund allegedly indicates his genuine dedication to the traditional colonial principle of public debt eradication.[16]

Other scholars have expressed a more skeptical attitude, and

I too have cast my lot with the doubting-Thomas camp. The lineage of skeptics includes Adam Smith, who observed in the *Wealth of Nations* in 1776: "A sinking fund, though instituted for the payment of old, facilitates very much the contracting of new debts."[17] What Smith meant in that context is that the sinking fund was a means of maintaining a steady demand for public securities in the market, thereby holding up their price, lowering the cost of future borrowing, and paving the way for the government to float ever-increasing amounts of new securities. For every dollar retired, so to speak, another two—or three or four—were added to national indebtedness. Biographer Forrest McDonald echoes the same skeptical tone about Hamilton's motivations. In my view, the treasury secretary included a sinking fund provision in his financial package because of its anticipated public relations benefits; he hoped it would influence positively the financial markets. News of its existence might help in raising the prices of $70 million in public securities with indeterminate maturity dates. If that was the intent, the plan worked marvelously well, since prices for the 6 percent bonds paying immediate interest quickly climbed above par value.

A sinking fund could generate favorable publicity, while its probable impact on net federal indebtedness was deemed marginal at best since the Post Office was not expected to realize substantial surpluses over the years. Perhaps $100,000 annually might become available—a drop in the bucket. Something could be gained and little lost by creating a sinking fund, for its existence did not seem to threaten, but rather to enhance, the development of a thriving capital market in governmental securities. In 1792 aggregate U.S. debt totaled $80.4 million. When Hamilton left office in 1795, the figure had risen to $83.8 million, and it essentially remained flat at $83 million until the Federalists relinquished political power in 1801.

Discrimination against Secondary Holders

The political storm that surrounded Hamilton's funding program related to a substantive amendment offered by Congressman James Madison, who proposed that the Treasury Department discriminate between the original holders and final holders of federal securities. Hamilton and Madison had been longstanding allies in promoting the institutional changes necessary to create a strengthened national government, and their published essays defending the Constitution had been instrumental in its ratification. In the 1780s, their approach to most financial issues had been generally in harmony, thus Madison's effort to modify the implementation of his friend's comprehensive funding program caught most contemporaries unawares. Historians have been perplexed as well; some have suggested that Madison was insincere in advocating discrimination and that he acted only to mend political fences in his home state of Virginia, where many constituents were agitated about reports of allegedly rampant speculation in public debts in the late 1780s.[18] Knowing his proposed amendments would fail to draw a majority— they garnered about one-third of the House vote—Madison was, by some accounts, simply grandstanding in an effort to appease his critics, rivals, and constituents back in Virginia.

The issue that Madison raised on the House floor sparked heated debate in early 1790. Hamilton's message called for the issuance of new securities to whomever presented the old certificates for exchange, with the presenter receiving full value. But Madison offered an alternative method of distribution. He proposed that, in issuing new federal securities, the Treasury should devise a formula for dividing the proceeds between the original recipient of an outstanding debt certificate, whether in the 1770s or 1780s, and its final holder in all cases where the two names differed.

Madison's recommended division was to offer secondary holders the highest market prices attained for their security issues at some arbitrary date, with the differential between those prices and nominal face value of the securities refunded to the original recipients. Accordingly, both parties would realize some of the gains associated with the upswing in security prices that had occurred since the new federal government had been organized under the Constitution. His suggestion ran counter to the terms explicitly printed on the outstanding debt instruments and the English law of contracts. Madison argued, however, that the situation was extraordinary because of the exaggerated depreciation of the 1780s, and therefore it deserved an irregular but nonetheless more equitable solution. Many original holders had sold out to speculators at only a fraction of the face value of their certificates—discounts of 75 up to 90 percent were not uncommon for some federal certificates. Those who had sold in desperation after Congress suspended interest payments had been shortchanged and treated badly, in Madison's opinion, and he urged the government to make some form of restitution.

In that context it should be noted that Madison's amendment

offered nothing for any of the intervening holders—that is, temporary owners between the initial and final owners—since determining how many persons might fit into that category and at what price
they should be compensated was simply impractical given the absence of records related to multiple transactions. Meanwhile, even
if the new securities were divided between the original and final
holders of the certificates, most speculators would likely still realize a profit on their investments, although less than anticipated at
the time of purchase. Under his plan both parties stood to gain
something, and Madison extolled its overall fairness and equity.

Hamilton objected vigorously to Madison's proposal. He cited
law and precedent. The treasury secretary expressed particular
concern about how potential foreign investors might react to such
a major deviation from standard financial procedures. He feared
it might discourage Europeans from purchasing American securities in future years. This radical idea threatened to undermine the
secretary's grand strategy for creating an active U.S. capital market. Hamilton rejected the unsavory speculative label, arguing that
secondary investors in public securities were true patriots who had
supported the credit of the national government when others had
demonstrated little faith. Those patriotic investors deserved their
just rewards since they had willingly borne the risk of partial or
even full repudiation. But the key Hamiltonian argument was, to
repeat, the sanctity of legal contracts and the well-established customs and procedures governing the operations of European capital
markets.

The question of whether to include some form of compensation for the original recipients of federal certificates in any funding
bill that authorized the assumption of state debts prompted a vigorous debate. The split in the House was largely sectional. Except
for South Carolina, whose members favored immediate assumption
without conditions, most southern representatives supported Madison's proposal to discriminate between original and final holders,
and they controlled enough votes to prevent the enactment of the
Hamiltonian plan. Southerners knew that, during the last half decade, northern investors had acquired large volumes of federal
securities originally issued in their region, and they resented the
fact that those speculators would soon reap all the gains associated
with funding.

How the impasse was resolved ranks among the most famous
backroom political deals in the nation's history, and three of the

nation's most prominent leaders were the main participants. Hamilton pledged to provide sufficient northern votes to create a new permanent capital city on the border between Maryland and Virginia, as opposed to naming New York or Philadelphia. Madison and Jefferson agreed to withdraw their objections and to persuade a few southern representatives to change their positions on the funding bill, thereby granting the treasury secretary virtually all the provisions that he wanted for the funding act.[19] In this instance, Hamilton revealed another of his masterful attributes: the art of compromise. Although he had hoped in the mid-1780s for a revision of the Articles of Confederation that would produce a form of government more squarely under the control of the propertied classes, he was able to put his reservations about an excess of democracy aside and write numerous articles favoring ratification of the Constitution. When compromise was called for again in 1790, Hamilton calculated that creating a strong capital market for the United States was more important for the nation's survival than the final location of the federal government. Thus, he was amenable to negotiating a swap of votes linking assumption with the establishment of the District of Columbia.

Hamilton held out for nondiscrimination and assumption, and he finally won in the political arena. Final holders received full value in new government securities irrespective of the acquisition price, while most of the unredeemed state securities became the immediate obligations of the U.S. Treasury. This review of the confrontation between Madison and Treasury Secretary Hamilton provides the proper foreground for tracing developments in the emerging American capital market with reference to the trading of public securities in the 1780s. The definitive historians remain E. James Ferguson and Whitney Bates, and their publications have outlined the parameters of these developing markets.

In heated congressional debates, advocates of discrimination between original and final holders cited recent reports of rampant speculation in public securities and lamented the prospect of parasitic speculators making quick and "undeserved" profits at the expense of impatient and ill-informed holders who had sold out perhaps a little too hastily—that is, just prior to when the federal government was on the verge of resuming interest payments on its outstanding obligations. The critics of speculative activity had in mind mostly the flurry of transactions in 1788 and 1789, after ratification of the Constitution; but trading in government securities had occurred throughout the 1780s. Many of the initial recipients of federal certificates transferred their rights to third parties for cash or other assets; and many of the latter, in turn, sold their security holdings to subsequent rounds of investors—sometimes realizing gains but at other times suffering losses. Since no records of intervening sales and purchases were maintained, it is not possible to know what percentage of securities in the hands of final holders were acquired from original holders versus other intermediary investors.[20]

The best guess, however, is that the vast majority of transactions from ratification until Congress adopted the funding program in August 1790 occurred among secondary holders. Presumably, few of the original holders who retained their securities through the bleak mid-1780s decided to dump them in the final months before the funding program took effect. In other words, it seems unlikely that more than a handful of original owners were among those who missed profit opportunities by selling out to speculators in 1789 and early 1790, the assertions and lamentations of Madison and his legislative supporters notwithstanding. Speculators who profited the most did so largely at the expense of their less informed or less audacious counterparts who made different judgments about the risks and rewards associated with continued ownership of debt certificates at prevailing market prices in the period from ratification through the implementation of funding.

Three main types of federal debt instruments were traded in the 1780s, and they tended to command differing prices in the marketplace. The three categories were bonds ($11.6 million), certificates ($17 million), and indents ($3.6 million). Those obligations hit their lows sometime in the mid-1780s and then rose in price, although at differing rates, starting with the calling of the constitutional convention, ratification by nine states, the submission of Hamilton's report in January 1790, and congressional approval of the funding program eight months later. The most highly regarded federal securities were the bonds sold directly to investors for cash—for specie at first and later for depreciated currency that was subsequently readjusted to a specie basis.

Contemporaries believed bond obligations would claim first call on future congressional surpluses and that redemption at par was highly likely. Still, market prices for bonds fell precipitously after Treasurer Morris suspended interest payments on the domestic debt in 1782. Yet they rarely fell below twenty-five cents on the dollar even in the darkest days of the mid-1780s. As plans for the new government moved forward after 1787, the prospects for redemption improved significantly, and the bonds had climbed back to near par by 1790. Bond owners were generally wealthier individuals who were accustomed to holding portfolios of financial assets, and Treasury Department records indicate that high-value instruments remained in the hands of original holders more frequently than other securities.

Debt certificates issued to soldiers and military suppliers were seen as obligations likely to claim a second call on congressional coffers, and they traded at lower prices than bonds. Many traders worried that the instruments might suffer partial repudiation, and those fears were reflected in the marketplace. Certificates sold for as low as ten to fifteen cents on the dollar at their low point, and even as late as 1789 they had not risen much above the level of fifty cents. Most of the speculative activity in 1789 and 1790 centered on the $17 million in debt certificates. Indents were also considered vulnerable to repudiation, and they too traded at prices lower than bonds. As it happened, outstanding indents were fully funded, but at the 3 percent rate associated with the arrearages of interest on the federal debt.[21]

Who exactly maintained active markets in these securities is difficult to state with any certainty except in Philadelphia, Boston, and New York, where several firms were involved in negotiating sales. Some even advertised their brokerage services and announced their willingness to trade on their own account. Elsewhere, scattered mercantile firms around the country presumably negotiated transactions in debt instruments on an irregular basis. Despite their ad hoc nature, markets in public securities existed after 1783 in all thirteen states, according to Ferguson.

Most of the original holders of federal certificates who sold out to secondary investors likely did so soon after receiving them in payment for goods or services. The vast majority of the $11 million in securities issued to common soldiers when the Continental army disbanded in 1783 quickly passed into other hands.[22] The same was true of persons who received certificates totaling about $6 million in payment for military supplies. Those citizens typically had little interest in holding financial assets, public or private, to an undetermined maturity date. They needed whatever cash could be raised immediately either to buy goods for immediate consumption, pay off private debts, or to invest in more tangible assets such as land, livestock, inventories, structures, or bonded workers.

The prices sellers received for federal certificates were undeniably extremely low in the early and mid-1780s. Ten to fifteen cents on the dollar was not uncommon. That sum was as much as investors were willing to pay—and for good reason. The debts had no assigned maturity dates, just sometime in the future when Congress could secure the financial resources to make good on its obligations. Meanwhile, the Treasury could not even pay the current interest. Under the circumstances, an investment in federal obligations was highly risky, even if most holders believed full payment, plus accrued interest, was fairly certain at some future point. Informed guesses about how many years might pass before Congress took action exerted a continuing influence over prices. In all financial calculations, the timing of future returns is invariably reflected in market values. Present value theories hold that a given amount of money received in an earlier period is always valued more highly than the same sum received at a later date since the former can be reinvested to earn interest during the intervening months. Eighteenth-century financiers did not resort to the sophisticated formulas routinely used by modern analysts to evaluate the timing of returns on investments, but they nonetheless were familiar with the general principle that monies received within a few days were more valuable than identical amounts collected years into the future.

This mildly technical discussion leads directly to a perennial historical question: were the original holders of government securities who sold out to secondary investors unduly exploited and thus entitled to additional compensation in 1790? Most modern financial analysts would argue in the negative—opposing Madison and supporting Hamilton. Let us assume that on average sellers of certificates received about twenty-five cents on the dollar from 1783 to 1785. For example, the soldier who received $25 for certificates with a face value of $100 in 1784 had the use of that money for seven more years than the investor who was forced to wait until the resumption of interest payments in 1791. If the soldier invested the money in productive assets that returned 8 percent compounded annually, by 1791 the proceeds from that sale would have climbed steadily in value to about $43. Meanwhile, the investor in the soldier's certificates received no interest payments or any other form of remuneration during those same seven years.

When investors swapped their claims on the states for new federal securities, they received an investment package consisting of three components: first, securities covering two-thirds of the original principal that paid 6 percent immediately; second, securities covering one-third of the principal that paid 6 percent starting in 1801; and third, securities paying 3 percent immediately that covered the interest in arrears since 1782. Only bonds in the first category rose in price to face value ($100) and above in 1791. The bonds in the second and third categories traded in the range of $60 to $70, or thereabouts. If we assume that the market value of the entire package of securities held by a given speculator in 1791—which included past-due interest—averaged approximately $130, it follows that the present value of that investment seven years earlier, again assuming an 8 percent discount rate, was roughly $75. Under those conditions, the adjusted profit realized on a speculator's $25 purchase in 1784 was $50, not the $75 difference in unadjusted dollars. Of course, some speculators acquired debt certificates at even lower prices than twenty-five cents on a dollar, and they, in turn, earned higher rates of return.

Further reflection suggests that perhaps lower adjusted profits accrued to most investors. The investor had no means of determining when interest payments would be resumed and at what rates. Indeed, if political considerations had delayed the resumption of interest payments for four additional years—until 1795—then the adjusted investment value of the exchange at the same 8 percent discount rate would have fallen to $55, which brings up another related issue. Were the risk and reward assumptions the same for buyer and seller in 1784? Probably not. If the investor's rate of return expectation is raised to 15 percent to compensate for uncertainty about the timing and adequacy of funding, then the adjusted value of the investment in 1784 falls to $49; at 25 percent the adjusted value drops to $28 and produces a generally fair and equal exchange between original holder and secondary buyer. I believe the 25 percent criterion is reasonable under the circumstances and therefore have concluded that little exploitation of original owners occurred. Viewed from another angle, investors in public securities from 1783 to 1785 had no superior knowledge about when their investments were likely to rise in value, and there was considerable evidence to suggest that the process might take several more decades. Overall, it seems fair to conclude that in most instances the actual profits realized on speculative investments were a far cry from the exaggerated multiples alleged by Madison and his supporters.

Madison pointed to an allegedly gross inequity between the financial returns realized by original holders of federal debt instruments who sold prematurely and the returns of secondary investors who held to 1790. However, modern techniques have narrowed that gap—and perhaps even eliminated it altogether, depending on varying assumptions about the profit and risk expectations associated with investments in the federal debt and other forms of productive assets in the mid-1780s. Madison erred on two accounts. First, like many contemporaries unaccustomed to analyzing financial data (plus many people in the late twentieth century as well), he failed to consider fully differences in the timing of financial returns. Secondly, most of the trading in government securities in 1789 and 1790 occurred among secondary holders themselves. Some decided to take their profits on federal certificates, which had risen, for example, from thirty cents on the dollar in 1789 up to the fifty-cent level in 1790. Numerous prudent investors feared that political rivalries might delay actual funding for several more years, lower the final interest rates, or even produce partial repudiation.

The most frenzied trading in public securities in the years just prior to funding occurred in the obligations of the states. Those obligations commanded widely differing prices, depending on the records of their respective legislatures in the payment of interest and retirement of principal. In states such as Pennsylvania and Maryland where debt reduction had proceeded generally on schedule throughout the 1780s, the prices of their securities remained reasonably close to par. (Indeed, nationalists in Congress found it discouraging to note that the credit standing in the domestic market of some of the nation's subunits in 1787 ranked vastly higher than that of the federal government itself.) In states that had had difficulty in generating sufficient tax revenues to service their debts—as in Massachusetts and the two Carolinas—the prices of their public securities had fallen to very low levels by the late 1780s.

As soon as rumors about the possibility of an immediate assumption of state debts began to circulate—that is, years in advance of the final report of the interstate settlement commission—the trading in heavily discounted state securities picked up and prices began to move upward. Still, as late as the fall of 1789, just prior to the release of Secretary Hamilton's report to Congress, various securities issued by Massachusetts, Virginia, and the two Carolinas could be bought for as little as ten to thirty-five cents on the dollar. Here was an opportunity for genuinely quick and substantial profits. By this late date Hamilton had been named treasury secretary and the risks of governmental inaction had significantly diminished. The rewards were potentially great if the prices of securities climbed to within striking distance of par over the next few months—as actually happened by 1791.

Historian Whitney Bates has chronicled the vigorous purchasing programs of several prominent northern investors in the debts of three southern states—Virginia, North Carolina, and South Carolina—in 1789 and 1790. For the three states combined, out-of-state investors ended up holding slightly more than half of their federally funded state debt, which totaled $8.6 million. Virginia, the most fiscally responsible of the group, had the least nonresident holders of its outstanding debt—just under one-third. The percentage of nonresident investment was highest in North Carolina securities—more than 80 percent—in part because the state hesitated before entering the union in November 1789, and many local holders decided to sell out in the face of a rise in prices that might not be sustained. A mere eighty investors who put up $10,000 or more accounted for 90 percent of North Carolina's out-of-state holdings.

Merchants in the large port cities of Baltimore, Philadelphia, and New York who had decided to specialize, at least temporarily, in financial services maintained fairly steady markets in these issues after 1788. In cooperation with their agents in southern commercial centers, they bought and sold for their own account and performed brokerage functions for third parties. New York City was the hub for speculation in southern state debts. Among the major investors and traders were two firms headed by Andrew Craigie and William Constable; in the latter instance the ubiquitous Robert Morris was listed as a partner. About 5 percent of the aggregate debt of the three southern states was acquired by foreign investors, with British residents claiming $347,000 of the total $428,000.

The group of speculators who bought state debts during the eighteen months prior to funding realized the greatest percentage returns on their investment. In fact, profits could be made after Hamilton's proposal to fund the state debts was first announced publicly in January 1790, after congressional passage of the funding bill that summer, and also during the intervening months before actual implementation. Why did profit opportunities last so long? One explanation suggests that some holders, after waiting years for interest payments in specie, remained skeptical about the federal government's ability to generate sufficient tax revenues to make its intentions a reality. Another factor was likely persistent worries about the outlook for interest rates on any new issue of U.S. securities. Hamilton boasted that yields would eventually fall to around 4 percent, and that was fast approaching by mid-1791—even sooner than the secretary could have anticipated. But in late 1790, no one could be sure how the market might receive the $70 million in new domestic debt. Some astute traders believed that yields might settle in the range of 8 to 10 percent, in which case the prices of the highest quality Treasury bonds, those with coupons paying $6 annually for each $100 in principal, would fall below face value and into the price range of $60 to $75.[23] Instead, prices climbed to more than $120 by June 1791. One of the main reasons speculators in federal and state securities in the 1780s generally came out ahead was that yields to investors on U.S. government bonds almost immediately settled in the 4 to 6 percent range after funding. Only in England and Holland were contemporary national governments able to borrow at comparably low rates.

A key factor to remember in this context is that the volume of trading in the fledgling American capital market was already heating up in the late 1780s—well in advance of Hamilton's program to create a more sustained and substantive market for public securities. In one bold stroke the treasury secretary had formulated a financial program that elevated the credit rating of the relatively new United States to first rank among nations. Almost all of the outstanding debts of the political subunits—the several states—were cleared away, although moderate amounts remained in some locales even after assumption. Just as the former colonies had escaped a heavy debt burden within a decade after the Seven Years' War, their successor states were in roughly an analogous position less than ten years after Yorktown. Taxes at the state level plummeted everywhere in the 1790s—as they had from 1765 until the Declaration of Independence. Meanwhile, the federal government had assumed the burden of a debt of $70 million; and a lively, functioning capital market consisting primarily of U.S. government bonds but supplemented by shares in the new First Bank of the United States, plus a small assortment of public and private securities, had rather quickly taken shape.

By the last decade of the eighteenth century, the U.S. government was issuing bonds with indefinite maturation dates, virtually the same as British consols, with the prospect that portions of its existing debt would remain outstanding for at least thirty years and possibly much longer. Only 2 percent of the principal of the outstanding bonds carrying a 6 percent interest rate was eligible for recall and redemption in any given year, irrespective of budget surpluses. The Hamiltonian fiscal program was fully in place by 1792 and already basking in its glory since the yields on U.S. securities had fallen to within the secretary's target of 4 percent by the end of Washington's first term. The gradualist approach to debt reduction had lowered the tax burden to tolerable levels and simultaneously produced a nascent capital market at the national level. That strategy remained intact through the Federalist presidencies of Washington and Adams, but it was steadily eroded after Jefferson assumed office in 1801.

To generate the revenues to cover the interest on the national debt during the 1790s, Hamilton proposed a tax program noted primarily for its light burden on citizens. He hoped to raise about $5 million for the federal government annually, with up to $3.5 million of that amount, or 70 percent, required to maintain interest payments on the debt. The $5 million figure represented only about 2 percent of GNP in 1792, an extremely low tax burden for a central government in comparison with contemporary European standards. The level of taxation recommended to Congress in 1790 was firmly in line with the colonial tradition of imposing minimal taxes during peacetime. That was one feature of the overall Hamiltonian financial program with which the Jeffersonian contingent could readily identify. The Federalist party staked its reputation on its ability to avoid the repudiation of any of the outstanding principal of remaining federal and state wartime debts as of March 1789, while simultaneously holding down taxes to modest, traditional levels.

As the prime source of federal tax monies, the treasury secretary decided on the tariff—a tax on imports. The system was easy to administer through customs houses in major ports, and the incidence of taxation was conveniently hidden from consumers in the final prices they paid for foreign goods. The imposition of a federal tax was expected to help in lowering rates at the state level where levies were applied chiefly to properties and persons (polls). A uniform national tax was touted as being more geographically equitable. That argument had merit, but remnants of inequity remained since its incidence fell thereafter on the shoulders of the purchasers of imported goods—mostly the middle and upper classes. The tariff act prescribed differing rates on various goods and on the distances goods traveled before reaching American shores. Included in the bill were some mildly protectionist features, but the aim was to generate revenues equal to about 10 percent of import values.

Hamilton's plan was fundamentally a resurrection of the impost bill that Superintendent of the Treasury Robert Morris had proposed under the Articles of Confederation in the early 1780s. After Morris had failed to obtain the unanimous consent of all thirteen states, the original plan never went into effect. Hamilton came back to Congress roughly a decade later with the same strategy, but he asked for tariff rates twice as high, and now he needed only a majority in both houses to gain passage. The rates initially enacted failed to generate sufficient funds for the central government to pay the interest on the outstanding debt and other incidentals, however. Customs receipts were so low in 1791 and 1792 that Hamilton convinced Congress to approve a slight increase in overall rates. In 1793 tariff revenues jumped by a quarter, up to $4.3 million, and they revealed a fairly steady upward trend thereafter. The overall federal tax burden remained relatively light, however. The free white population paid, on average, only about $1.25 each—a figure less than 3 percent of per capita income.

Two years after presenting his congressional report on the public credit, Secretary Hamilton submitted a second report on the status of manufacturing in the new nation in December 1791. Among his recommended policies to promote manufacturing were high tariffs on certain "infant industries" until manufacturers could reach a level of reasonable international competitiveness. Some historians have asserted that Hamilton was an avowed protectionist who was more than willing to provide indirect public subsidies to budding manufacturers through high tariff walls. But a careful analysis of his actions in the 1790s suggests that Hamilton's support was mainly rhetorical, not substantive. While strongly committed to promoting the industrial sector in the abstract, as a practical matter Hamilton simply could not afford to forego the collection of revenues on virtually every class of goods passing through American ports. If tariff walls locked out some items, then the lost revenue would have to be made up elsewhere. He wanted industry, yes, but creating a thriving American capital market was his first priority; and to accomplish that outcome, the secretary had decided to generate a steady flow of customs duties to cover the government's interest payments.

The revenue bill that Congress enacted in 1790 also included internal excise taxes on alcohol, plus small levies on an assortment of items. Excise taxes were designed to pull in perhaps $500,000 annually, or less than 15 percent of anticipated federal revenues. A key reason for their implementation in the early 1790s was to establish a precedent for the enactment of internal federal taxes. An astute follower of trends in British taxation, Hamilton undoubtedly knew that excise taxes had become a huge source of parliamentary revenue during the eighteenth century, and he wanted to keep them on the books as a possible source of future monies. British taxes on beer and spirits were major revenue producers after 1750. The U.S. rate on whiskey, up to thirty cents per barrel, was an anomaly in the American context—an instance of a genuinely highly visible rate on a specific product. It generated about $350,000 in revenues in the mid-1790s, but cost from $50,000 to $100,000 to enforce.

Vigorous efforts to collect taxes on distilled spirits led to the so-called Whiskey Rebellion in western Pennsylvania in 1794. The outbreak provided the Washington administration, urged on by a militant Secretary Hamilton, with a golden opportunity to demonstrate its commitment to suppressing domestic disorder. The U.S. army routed the frontier distillers, but the Federalists handed their political rivals a recurring campaign issue for upcoming elections. Indeed, President Thomas Jefferson had eliminated all excise taxes by 1805.

11

The First Bank of the United States

THE SECOND pillar in Secretary of the Treasury Alexander Hamilton's grand strategy for developing an American financial sector that would one day rival the money centers in England and Holland was the creation of a large nationally chartered financial institution. The capitalization of the Bank of the United States was $10 million—an enormous sum by contemporary standards. The Bank of North America, by comparison, had started in 1782 with a capital of only $400,000. By July 1791, when the First BUS opened its books for stock subscriptions, the total capital of the five state banks already operating in Boston, Philadelphia, New York, Baltimore, and Providence was less than $3 million combined. Throughout the life of its twenty-year charter, the First BUS remained the nation's largest business enterprise; but its initial overwhelmingly dominant position in American commercial banking was steadily eroded because of the establishment of more than one hundred state-chartered institutions. When the First BUS wound up its affairs in 1812, its capital accounted for less than 15 percent of the aggregate American investment in the commercial banking sector.

As most historians have claimed during the last two centuries, the First BUS was inspired by the example of the Bank of England. Yet some important differences existed in the organizational structure and scope of operations of the two banks. The Bank of England had been established in 1694 to serve almost exclusively the needs of the national government, including not only the granting of short-term loans to smooth over temporary cash shortages but also continuing the support for the intermediate- and long-term debts of the Exchequer. During the eighteenth century, most of the earning assets in the Bank of England's portfolio were consols and other debt obligations with maturity dates of one year or longer. By providing a steady demand for parliamentary debt issues, the English bank supported security prices, lowering yields and interest rates as a consequence—thereby providing Parliament with the leeway to finance a long series of persistent budget deficits. Operating under a corporate charter from Parliament, ownership was strictly a private affair, which theoretically made its directors and managers less subject to political pressures; and its shares traded regularly on the securities exchanges in London and later Amsterdam.

The fundamental difference between the First BUS and its English counterpart was that the American version was a mixed enterprise—both in terms of its ownership pattern and the range of customers served. The U.S. government reserved the right to acquire 20 percent of the shares, yet it agreed to waive voting rights in stockholders' elections for members of the board of directors (a provision altered in the charter for the Second BUS in 1816). The government did reserve, however, the right to inspect the bank's books regularly. The treasury secretary was authorized to request a balance sheet listing assets and liabilities as often as once per week.

The United States decided to deviate from the practice in England and allow partial public ownership for several reasons. Some have explained the public-private mixture as one means of assuring that the federal government would have ready access to credit facilities. With a bank capital so large relative to the size of contemporary business firms, the U.S. government loomed from the outset as one of the most welcome customers at the discount window. It alone had the capacity to negotiate loans totaling in the hundreds of thousands of dollars or even millions—loans that could generate large inflows of interest revenues with little administrative work, provided, of course, the new federal governance system proved workable and the Treasury Department could raise sufficient tax revenues to keep its head above water.

The fractional public ownership was motivated in part by the desire to maintain some degree of continuity with the colonial heritage of legislative loan offices. During the half century before independence, those publicly owned financial institutions managed by public employees produced steady profits that alleviated the burden on taxpayers. Many political leaders wanted to preserve a measure of that tradition of public involvement in the financial sector. Thus, in an attempt to forestall criticism that the proposed national bank would cater strictly to the "selfish" interests of wealthy urban investors, as opposed to the welfare of ordinary citizens, Hamilton recommended a mixed enterprise—government ownership of 20 percent of the shares with 80 percent going into private hands.

Critics bemoaned the fact that private investors would reap the vast majority of the bank's anticipated profits in contrast to the institutional arrangements that had existed in every colony prior to political independence. The opposition raised a pertinent issue since the former loan offices had generated sufficient interest revenues to make substantial contributions to legislative budgets in several locales. In the colonial era, the loan offices had been viewed as mechanisms for introducing currency into the economy, expanding the credit available for capital building, and, equally important, producing a steady revenue for provincial governments. Later, through investments in bank stocks, chartering fees, and annual taxes on bank capital, state legislatures were able to recapture a share of that lucrative source of revenue derived from the financial services sector.

To thwart possible objections, Secretary Hamilton was able to assure Congress that, according to his plan, a portion of the bank's dividend payments would come directly to the U.S. Treasury and accrue to the benefit of taxpayers. He also pointed out that dividends from the government's investment in bank stock would aid in reducing the overhanging wartime debts. As it happened, though, the first obligation that required repayment was the bank's loan to the Treasury of the entire $2 million purchase price for the acquisition of its quota of five thousand shares of stock over a scheduled ten-year period.

The movement toward privatizing banking services was already well under way by the early 1790s. However, many voters were not yet prepared to forego public ownership and governmental involvement at the federal level, especially in light of the constitutional prohibition on new issues of paper currency by state legislatures or their agencies such as mortgage loan offices. The mixed banking enterprise, which remained prevalent throughout the early decades of the nineteenth century at the state level, was another compromise between the proven, but now outlawed, practices of earlier decades and the promise of an ever-expanding financial sector based primarily on the initiatives of private citizens. The First BUS was predominantly a private institution, but it retained an element of governmental ownership—at least until President Thomas Jefferson, who had challenged the bank in 1791 on constitutional grounds, decided to wash his hands of the whole affair and unload the remaining 2,220 shares of the government's stock holdings in 1802. Jefferson authorized the sale to Baring Brothers, the eminent English merchant banking firm, at a premium of 45 percent over par, earning a tidy profit of $670,000.[1]

Despite the contemporary criticism about his Anglophilia, Secretary Hamilton did not envision the First BUS serving as the handmaiden of an expansive government in a fashion similar to the role played overseas by the Bank of England. While he anticipated relying on the national bank for assistance in financing temporary shortfalls in the collection of tax revenue, the secretary was not expecting the First BUS to accumulate millions of dollars of unpaid loans without assigned maturity dates in its portfolio of earning assets. Although he had no plans to reduce the principal of the funded debt by any significant degree in the foreseeable future, Hamilton likewise did not anticipate a series of large budget deficits in the 1790s that would cause the national debt to rise to even greater heights. Of course, the possibility existed of being drawn into a major military confrontation with one of the European powers, which might elevate the national debt—as happened two decades later during the War of 1812. Nonetheless, Hamilton did not envision the First BUS as an institution that would provide a convenient vehicle for expanding the debt-carrying capacity of the federal government. That aspect of the Bank of England's status in the English financial system was not part of the overall strategy in formulating the details for the establishment of an American national bank.

To make that fact plain to all, the charter terms expressly prohibited the First BUS from adding long-term government securities to its portfolio beyond the contributions of stockholders—an effective limit of $8 million. The bank could sell the bonds acquired from stockholders who submitted them as partial payment for stock subscriptions, but liquidated federal securities could not be subsequently repurchased. That provision alone virtually guaranteed that the First BUS would not evolve into an engine fueling the growth of the national debt. Hamilton always had one ear tuned to the warnings of critics who were suspicious of the motives of allegedly avaricious financiers. Therefore, he voluntarily placed severe limitations on the latitude of bank directors—limitations that were designed to preclude the federal government's reliance on the First BUS to soak up millions of dollars in additional long-term debt. Promoting economic stability—as an antidote to the instability of the 1780s at the federal level—was the prime Federalist motivation for establishing a national bank in the early 1790s.

As it happened, the bank's creation proved timely because the Treasury was forced to rely fairly heavily on its resources for intermediate-term funding in the early and mid-1790s. The bank loans had assigned maturity dates, and Hamilton's successor made a sincere effort to clean up the bank debt before the end of the century. Hamilton was forced to resort to bank financing soon after the bank's doors opened in December 1791 because income from the tariff, which provided the bulk of federal revenues, proved lower than anticipated, and expenses were somewhat over budget. The initial government loan in May 1792 was for a modest $400,000. But later the secretary had to ask for more financial assistance. During the next few years, military expenditures rose to cover increased costs on several fronts: conflicts with Indian tribes on the frontier, raising an army to quell the Whiskey Rebellion in western Pennsylvania, and a naval construction program designed to meet threats at sea from warring European states.

By 1796 loans to the federal government totaled $6.2 million—more than 60 percent of the bank's capital—and the new treasury secretary, Oliver Wolcott, was pressed by bank directors for repayment of at least a portion of the $4.4 million coming due during the next twelve months. After considering and rejecting the possibility of floating a new public issue of $5 million in long-term securities to refinance the bank loan, the Treasury decided instead to sell off some of its stock holdings in the First BUS and apply the money to bank loan reduction. Altogether, the government sold twenty-eight hundred of its shares in the First BUS, more than 55 percent of its holdings. The entire proceeds of $1.5 million, which included a profit of $380,000 because of the premium price at which First BUS stock traded in the financial markets, was turned over to the bank.

In 1798 and 1799, the Treasury went ahead with the earlier plan to issue new securities, and it used the proceeds from the new issues to reduce its outstanding bank debt to less than $3 million. Because of the tense political situation surrounding American relations with France and Britain, potential investors in the 1799 loan would not subscribe until the interest rate was raised to 8 percent, a much higher rate than the Treasury had paid in the past. Indeed, the rate was nearly double what Hamilton had forced upon debt holders in the early 1790s.[2] Soon thereafter financial conditions noticeably improved. Budget surpluses in the early years of the Jefferson administration gave Secretary of the Treasury Albert Gallatin sufficient funds to pay off the bank debt in its entirety.

The First BUS also differed from the Bank of England in terms of the mix of public versus private paper in its loan portfolio. The bank directors started pressing the Treasury for curtailment of its loans in the mid-1790s in large part because of the heavy demand for credit facilities from private borrowers. Beginning with the John Adams administration and solidifying with the election of Thomas Jefferson in 1800, the bank steadily shifted its customer base away from a heavy reliance on government toward the mercantile sector.

During its second decade of operations, the First BUS became almost exclusively a commercial bank—in the true sense of the word—and its loans to the U.S. Treasury were much less important.[3] From 1800 until the War of 1812, with the exception of the embargo year of 1809, the Treasury ran consistent surpluses and thus had no need for bank financing. The First BUS had the flexibility to shift its primary orientation from accommodating the needs of the U.S. Treasury to granting loans to private parties in the eight port cities in its branch network.

The evidence is not clear about whether Hamilton, on an intellectual plane, intended the First BUS to serve mainly the credit needs of government or to meet the requirements of private business firms. Perhaps he had in mind equal or flexible accommodations for both groups, which explains the request for such a large initial capitalization. In public reports and pronouncements, he cited the inherent advantages for all economic units—merchants to farmers to legislatures. As an abstract political and economic theorist, Hamilton was free to consider a whole range of possibilities for constructing the best possible environment for the new nation. But from a practical standpoint, his responsibilities as secretary of the treasury forced him to think of the First BUS mainly as an institution on which he could lean heavily for assistance in establishing an impeccable credit rating for the United States among long-term investors in securities. He certainly expected to have first call on the First BUS' loanable funds. As treasury secretary, Hamilton could not afford to miss any interest payments on outstanding U.S. securities without doing the nation's credit rating irreparable harm in the domestic and European capital markets. No prudent secretary—no matter who it had been—including, dare I suggest, even Thomas Jefferson himself, once the constitutional debate had been settled and the bank had become a reality—could have, or should have, adopted any different attitude about the advantages of having so close at hand this powerful financial institution with the largest credit lines in the nation.

A second default on interest payments after the adoption of the new funding program would have been an unmitigated national disaster, and the margin for error was small because of the uncertainty surrounding how much revenue would actually be generated by the tariff and excise taxes during the early presidential administrations. Hamilton had tried to hold tax rates as low as possible to promote the popularity of the new centralized governance system under the Constitution. As it happened, revenues were, in fact, slightly lower than required to pay the interest and meet all the other pressing government expenditures; and Hamilton, and his successor Wolcott, turned on several occasions to the directors of the First BUS to provide the financial resources to keep the government solvent. The secretary was also able to raise additional funds simultaneously in the Amsterdam capital market. He might have been able to bring in even more money from the continent if necessary, but the presence of the First BUS was reassuring; it prevented the likelihood of too many sleepless nights worrying about how to stave off bankruptcy in the event of a major shortfall in tax collection. Robert Morris had not had similarly solid support in 1782—neither institutionally nor politically—and, of course, he was forced to suspend interest payments on all U.S. securities held in the domestic market.

The desire to keep the First BUS as a more or less captive source of funding for the U.S. Treasury during the uncertainties of the 1790s may go a long way in explaining one of Hamilton's policy positions that previous historians have listed as somewhat baffling, namely, his expressed opposition to the establishment of branches of the First BUS in other major commercial cities throughout the several states. Based on his nationalistic ideology, most historians calculated that Hamilton figured as a likely advocate of an extensive branch system that would extend the influence and power of the central government across a broad geographical expanse and tie together more tightly the nation's economy. The directors, who were elected by stockholders residing in all thirteen states, made the establishment of several branch offices one of the first items of business on their agenda at the board meeting of January 1792.

Four branches were opened that very year in New York, Boston, Baltimore, and Charleston, and they received an initial allocation of $1.28 million of the bank's capital. By 1800 those four branches claimed $3.7 million, or 37 percent, of the aggregate capital—with the New York office rising from $550,000 to $1.8 million. In later years, the directors added offices in Norfolk, Savannah, Washington, and New Orleans. By 1805 the seven branches commanded slightly more than half the bank's capital resources and thus made more loans than the main office in Philadelphia.

Like the widespread and persistent use of fiat currency in the colonial era, the adoption of a full-scale branching strategy was an innovative feature of the American financial services sector. The offices outside of Philadelphia performed all the main functions of the parent. No other contemporary business enterprise with such a sizable capital had created a branch network to dispense its services or market its goods. Administering a bank so geographically dispersed presented unique and challenging managerial problems. As the vote of the directors so amply demonstrates, Americans were in an experimental mood in several respects in the late eighteenth century—including the creation of a vast system of interstate branches in the field of commercial banking. Across the Atlantic Ocean, two Scottish banks operating under parliamentary charters had established branch offices throughout Scotland earlier in the eighteenth century, thus Americans were not the first to test the feasibility of the branching concept. Still the branches of the First BUS were spread out over a much larger territory than their Scottish counterparts and had much more capital resources at their disposal. American offices also possessed much more managerial autonomy under the auspices of local boards of directors that made independent decisions on loan applications.

Hamilton opposed the branch system for several reasons—some stated publicly, others kept in reserve. He expressed openly his fears that the lack of management expertise in other cities, coupled with inadequate control mechanisms emanating from the main office in Philadelphia, might allow branch officers to make a sufficient volume of bad loans or take other questionable actions that could threaten the whole institution. Given the novelty of branch offices in banking firms and the relative novelty of commercial banking in general, that reservation seems fully justifiable.

Among Hamilton's unstated reservations, because its utterance would expose publicly his Anglophilia, was the example of the Bank of England, headquartered in London and possessing no branch offices. The English national bank admittedly accommodated the loan requests of a few wealthy mercantile customers, but it remained primarily an institution oriented toward serving the needs of the Exchequer. If adopted in the United States, a branch network had the potential of diverting the attention of bank directors away from what Hamilton saw as their primary task for the immediate future— namely, stabilizing the American political and economic system in the nation's capital, then located in Philadelphia.

In addition, the treasury secretary may have retained some lingering doubts about the feasibility of two or more commercial banks operating profitably in a single market. A similar issue had arisen in Pennsylvania in the mid-1780s. Several concerned proponents of private commercial banking, among them Hamilton and Robert Morris, had questioned whether the Bank of North America, which issued convertible bank notes, could coexist with a revived state loan office that would issue unconvertible fiat currency or whether it could compete with a second privately funded commercial bank without causing both institutions irreparable damage. A plan to establish a rival bank had been quashed when its organizers were invited instead to invest additional capital in the Bank of North America. After considerable political controversy and the negotiation of a compromise solution, the public loan office in Pennsylvania eventually reopened its doors and, despite some trepidation, the bank suffered no negative consequences.

Old fears about the consequences of competitive banking likewise contributed to public debate in the spring of 1792 regarding the possible absorption of the three existing independent banks in Philadelphia, Boston, and New York into the First BUS.[4] That absorption strategy would have eliminated all the fancied problems associated with multiple banking. In addition, it would have given the First BUS a monopoly at the national level and conceivably would have resulted in protected markets everywhere in the United States, depending on how the several states treated future charter applications.

Once Hamilton was reconciled to the creation of a branch network, he toyed with the idea of recommending the absorption of the Bank of New York, an institution he had helped to create in 1784. His own holdings of bank stock in 1792 were minor, but he had influential friends who had a substantial stake in the Bank of New York. The secretary was plainly concerned about the loss of

U.S. government deposits, mostly linked to tariff collections at the customs house, that the Bank of New York would suffer once a branch office of the First BUS was functioning. But the thought of absorption soon passed, and with it went any possibility of creating a nationwide banking monopoly. If the absorption proposal had taken hold, the institutional development of the American financial services sector would unquestionably have been arrested. Instead, existing banks continued to thrive and compete with the First BUS, and during the next two decades many eager banking entrepreneurs received charters for new institutions from their respective state legislatures.

Hamilton may have also been worried that local resentment of the sudden presence of an out-of-state bank with exclusive interstate branching privileges might turn local voters against the whole concept of a national bank or, worst of all, alienate them from the national government itself. In a society so suspicious of central authority, the branch offices would serve as a constant reminder of the financial power of a giant corporate enterprise chartered by the U.S. government, which many Americans, especially in the southern states, had argued was unconstitutional and therefore illegitimate. For a combination of reasons, therefore, Hamilton preferred to maintain the lower profile of a single Philadelphia office. Given the persistent opposition that the chartered national bank and its 1816 successor encountered for the next four decades—political opposition that ultimately led to their untimely demise—the secretary's hesitancy to attract too much unwanted attention through the strategy of branch banking, in retrospect, probably represented the wiser choice.

Hamilton may have genuinely envisioned the First BUS developing an active commercial business at some future date; but for the time being he did not want to risk the possibility that loan requests from hundreds of mercantile firms, large and small, in the branch offices might soak up a healthy share of its loanable funds in the mid-1790s. The bank was already extending credit facilities to Philadelphia merchants in competition with the Bank of North America, and a third commercial bank opened in the city in 1793. The treasury secretary needed to retain ready access not just to a mere several hundred thousand dollars in loan funds, but possibly to millions of dollars in the event tax collections did not match expected inflows and the revenue laws had to be adjusted— as occurred in 1793 when Hamilton sought and obtained a modest increase in tariff rates.

In retrospect, the outcome of the vote at the board of directors' meeting dismissing the secretary's objections to a system of branch offices was an important defeat. Coming on the heels of a long string of Federalist successes, it marked the initial victory in the Jeffersonian effort to dilute the impact of the Hamiltonian financial program and to hold it in check. The rival Republicans were opposed to the creation of an artificial national financial center ruled by the alleged narrow and selfish motives of stockjobbers and speculators; and the vote to break up the concentration of bank capital in Philadelphia was a step designed to prevent, or slow down, the movement to create a small-scale replica of London on American shores. The branching strategy was doubly welcome to Jeffersonians because it transferred capital away from the political capital and out to cities in other states that hoped to mount challenges to the Philadelphia financial community.

Hamilton got virtually everything he wanted during his first two and one-half years in office, but starting in 1792 his power to control events began to ebb. The pendulum swung slowly away from the principles of Hamiltonian finance during the remaining years of the decade and then picked up speed with the election of President Jefferson in 1800.

Given the charter limitations on purchases of U.S. government securities in the open market, the closest link between the funding of the national debt and the establishment of the First BUS, the two main pillars in the Hamiltonian program, was the provision that allowed prospective owners to acquire shares in the new bank by paying one-quarter of the amount subscribed in specie and three-quarters in government securities. Based on that formula, the treasury secretary expected the bank to begin operations holding as much as $6 million in government securities, or about 8 to 9 percent of the outstanding federal debt in the domestic market.

Subscriptions to First BUS shares were accepted from the public beginning on 4 July 1791, a date picked specifically because of its significance in the independence movement. The offering price was $400 per share, a high minimum designed to appeal exclusively to wealthy investors. The twenty thousand shares available to the general public were oversubscribed that very morning, proving that Americans had the willingness and capacity to create a financial institution with a capitalization as large as $10 million. How times had changed! Just a decade earlier in 1781, sponsors found it difficult to raise a mere $400,000 to capitalize the Bank of North America. The proximity of Philadelphians gave them an advantage in the acquisition of subscription rights, but local brokers and agents had worked for several months to solicit applications for shares from wealthy households in other states. Many residents of the other major port cities—Boston, New York, Baltimore, Charleston—also invested substantial sums in the First BUS.

The rush to purchase shares was reassuring on two fronts. It virtually guaranteed that the bank would get off to a flying start with specie inflows of approximately $2 million. At the same time, the mechanics of acquiring shares boosted the demand for U.S. securities. The debt series paying 6 percent current interest was already trading above par, and the bank's stock subscription plan helped to sustain those elevated prices. With prices on the rise, prudent investors had incentives to own both U.S. government securities and shares in the federally chartered Bank of the United States. Indeed the date—4 July 1791—must rank as among the most celebratory points in Secretary of the Treasury Alexander Hamilton's distinguished career, and perhaps its pinnacle. His comprehensive plan for funding the national debt and creating a national bank with a large capitalization were both in place, and the economic and financial prospects for the nation under its new federal form of government had never looked so optimistic as in the summer of 1791.

As promised in the treasury secretary's report of December 1790, the First BUS also issued a highly acceptable form of paper currency which, thanks to the branching system, spread fairly widely throughout the United States. Its bank notes were convertible into specie at the branch of original issue, and they proved a useful medium of exchange and a reliable store of value.[5] The directors considered the possibility of allowing the holders of bank notes issued by one office to exercise the conversion privilege at tellers' windows anywhere in the branch system. That proposition was dismissed because of concerns that an unexpected inflow of currency might deplete local specie reserves and force a temporary suspension of payments, which would likely damage the reputation of the bank.[6] In regard to the volume of bank notes issued, bank directors emphasized safety by maintaining substantial reserves.[7] For most of the period, the First BUS placed in circulation between $1.00 and $1.50 per capita for the nation's free population. Other chartered banks added to the supply of bank notes in circulation. In *Economica*, the contemporary statistician Samuel Blodget compiled estimates of the contributions of coin and bank notes to the money stock:

	Metallic medium (million)	Bank notes (million)	Total (million)
1792	$18.0	$11.5	$29.5
1800	17.5	10.5	28.0

Assuming those numbers are fairly accurate, the money supply for the free population in 1800 was $6.50 per capita, with bank notes contributing more than one-third of the total.

The bank notes issued by the First BUS did not circulate freely among the general public, however, because the $5 minimum was high relative to prevailing income levels. Bank notes were used more commonly in the wholesale trade than in retail transactions. As in colonial times, the typical farmer and worker still relied on foreign coins in small to intermediate values for routine exchanges. (The U.S. mint played a minor role in augmenting the money stock.) The level of specie reserves that directors of the First BUS held against bank note liabilities is difficult to calculate with any precision on a monthly basis because of the irregularity of the surviving data. Somewhere in the neighborhood of 50 to 80 percent seems a fair guess—a figure far more conservative than the practices of many London goldsmiths in the seventeenth century and most state-chartered American banks. As a result, the First BUS made only modest net additions to the money stock through its issuance of currency.

On the other hand, the bank accepted lodged deposits from governments and individuals, and it may have created deposits in the process of making loans to borrowers.[8] Calculating the reserve ratio for the five dates listed in table 11.1 by combining deposit and bank note liabilities, the procedure routinely followed by modern banks, the figures range from a low of 23 percent to a high of 39 percent, with 33 percent the overall mean. Those ratios represent a relatively safe and conservative figure for a large interstate bank with substantial responsibilities to the federal government and for the maintenance of monetary stability in general. The directors sacrificed the potential of increased earning power by holding a tight rein on their institution's credit expansion. The holding of fractional reserves, nonetheless, permitted a threefold increase in the aggregate money supply—one of the advantages of a privatized commercial banking system cited by Hamilton in his public report of 1790.

Whether by accident or design, bank directors steered a careful,

TABLE 11.1
First Bank of the United States:
Reserve Ratios on Selected Dates
(in millions of dollars)

	A	B	C	D	E
					Reserve
	Deposits	Bank Notes	A +B	Specie	Ratio
Dec. 1793	$3.3	$2.0	$ 5.3	$1.2	.23
Jan. 1799	5.2	4.1	9.3	3.0	.32
Nov. 1801	8.4	6.5	14.9	5.3	.36
Jan. 1809	8.5	4.5	13.0	5.0	.38
Jan. 1811	7.8	5.0	12.8	5.0	.39

Source: Table compiled from data in James Wettereau, "New Light on the First Bank of the United States," *Pennsylvania Magazine of History and Biography* (1937), 263–85.

prudent course for the nation's largest commercial bank from 1792 to 1811 both in terms of the volume of bank notes issued and the quality of its loan portfolio. Their managerial philosophy generally conformed with the policies later followed by Nicholas Biddle, the nation's premier national banker in the nineteenth century, during his tenure as president of the Second BUS. The directors of the First BUS were not profit maximizers; even at that early date they adopted some of the policy initiatives that we later came to associate with central banking.

During its twenty-year charter period, the First BUS averaged net earnings of approximately 9 percent on its capital base and paid out annual dividends of just over 8 percent. Indeed, the directors set the maintenance of an 8 percent dividend rate as their goal and then let that consideration dictate the size of the outstanding loan portfolio, which fluctuated around the $16 million mark most years. The bank's stock was a good investment vehicle for persons seeking a steady return with a modest degree of risk. The shares became a favorite investment of fiduciaries overseeing the financial affairs of widows, orphans, and various charities. From the first day of issue, bank stock soared to a premium. During most of the next two decades, it generally traded at between 115 and 150 percent of the par value of four hundred dollars, thereby providing later investors with respectable yields of 5 to 7 percent—not much different from yields on U.S. government securities.[9]

The First BUS' stellar performance—in terms of the safety of its currency issue and its consistent, if unspectacular, profitability during the first few years of operations—was another crucial factor in solidifying and further legitimizing the movement toward the complete privatization of commercial banking services. The three chartered banks in Philadelphia, New York, and Boston all had unblemished records in the 1780s, thus demonstrating the advantages of banks organized and financed by private capital. But the First BUS made a greater impression nationwide because of the larger volume of bank notes and their wide geographical dispersion.

The soundness of its convertible paper money verified the claims of the proponents of chartered private banking. We can speculate on the contrary outcome if, for example, the First BUS had started out by expanding its loans and bank notes too quickly, as happened after the Second BUS received a national charter in 1816. Suppose, as a consequence of mismanagement, the First BUS had been forced to suspend payment (refuse to convert bank notes to specie). At that point the whole concept of chartered banking might have been seriously discredited. A movement to amend the Constitution and allow the states to reissue their own paper money would not have been out of the realm of possibility. After all, the right of legislative issuance had only been recently surrendered; and some critics, especially in rural areas, remained dubious about the judiciousness of granting that exclusive privilege to private interests. Instead, the directors of the First BUS proceeded cautiously. Its record for soundness set an excellent standard and thus went far in sustaining the trend toward privatization. During the next two decades, more than one hundred commercial banks throughout the nation received charters from state legislatures.

The First BUS also served as an unofficial regulator of the operations of the increasing number of state banks. That valuable function had not been envisioned by advocates of a national bank, but it evolved in response to changing circumstances. Because of its great size and its geographically distributed branch network, the First BUS regularly accumulated a substantial quantity of bank notes issued by state institutions. By presenting those bank notes routinely for conversion into specie, the national bank kept sufficient pressure on the reserves of state banks to prevent them from making an excessive volume of loans and imprudently expanding the volume of currency in circulation.

Scattered evidence suggests that directors occasionally aided state banks vulnerable to the possibility of runs and the prospect of suspended payments because of temporarily inadequate reserves. The national bank either refrained from presenting bank notes for conversion or made outright specie loans to state banks desperately in need of breathing room. When it made such loans, the First BUS was acting as a lender of last resort, a function usually associated with so-called central banks. Although never assigned broad, supervisory duties in the charter terms, the national bank did perform a number of central banking functions. In that context, the label "quasi-central bank" seems appropriate, and the First BUS merits designation as a legitimate forerunner of the Federal Reserve System that emerged in the twentieth century.

Despite its operational successes that blazed the trail for additional privatization, the First BUS developed two vexing problems that stymied its supporters and ultimately led to the failure to gain a congressional extension of its charter in 1811. The most critical issue related to its alleged unconstitutionality. That subject matter has been adequately covered in the existing historical literature and is briefly recapitulated here. Two articles written more than three decades apart by Wayne Morgan (1956) and Benjamin Klubes (1990) examine the confrontation between the pro-bank and anti-bank factions in 1791. The outcome was ultimately decided by President George Washington in favor of the expansive interpretation of constitutional powers put forward by Secretary Hamilton.

Klubes documents that participants in the battle divided mostly along sectional lines, with bank opponents who questioned its constitutionality and propriety overwhelmingly representing the southern states. That division seems logical and predictable, given that four of the existing state-chartered banks were in the northern states and a fifth in Baltimore had just received authorization from the Maryland legislature. Chartered banks financed by private capital were still a distinct novelty from Virginia southward, and some opponents were almost certainly influenced by understandable fears and suspicions about the dangers of unfamiliar economic institutions. Once the Jeffersonians became accustomed to enjoying the superior services offered by chartered commercial banks, however, their attitudes softened. With a few exceptions, most eventually became staunch supporters and defenders of the privatization process—at least until the Panic of 1837.[10]

The only factor that perhaps needs slightly more emphasis in this context than accorded in previous historical accounts is that the constitutional issue was already old hat when it reemerged in the early 1790s. As discussed in chapter 6, that topic had already arisen in connection with the issuance of a charter for the Bank of North America. After substantial controversy, Superintendent Robert Morris initially obtained a federal charter in 1781; but once the bank began operating in 1782, the debate about the proper limitations on congressional powers resurfaced. Critics reasserted that the Articles of Confederation had not explicitly authorized the issuance of corporate charters by Congress and hammered away at the alleged illegitimacy of the BNA's legal status. Morris mooted the issue by convincing the Pennsylvania legislature to offer a substitute state charter, and several other legislatures proved equally accommodating. The federal charter was then withdrawn to satisfy the complaints of constitutional purists, and there the whole matter rested until revived in 1791.

Because of the earlier political division, everyone active in political life knew, or should have known, that a similar controversy was likely to arise in any discussion about a national charter for the First BUS. Madison, Jefferson, and the others who attacked the constitutionality of granting congressional corporate charters were, in other words, on solid ground in regard to the precedent set in 1782.[11] Advocates of limited powers had won that first round, and they believed the same principles prevailed in the 1790s—and in perpetuity for that matter. The proponents of expanded powers held sway during the Washington administration, but it was a premature and ultimately false victory. The failure of nationalists like Hamilton to insert a provision granting corporate charter powers to the federal government in the final constitutional draft of 1787 came back to haunt them—in this case not in 1791, but decades later in the recharter votes of 1811 and 1832.

A second issue that arose belatedly could not have been so easily anticipated by the Federalist camp. Indeed, what at first appeared a positive development became instead an unfortunate liability— namely, the foreign ownership of stock in the First BUS. During Hamilton's tenure in office, foreign demand for bank stock was a welcome sign of the nation's resurgent financial respectability. Along with steady purchases of U.S. government bonds by overseas buyers, the willingness of foreign nationals to acquire ownership rights in the American national bank, invariably at a premium above the original issue price, was a trend fully in accord with the secretary's plan to boost the standing of American securities in European capital markets. Many Europeans possessed surplus capital, and rather than earn lower returns on investments of roughly identical risk in their home markets, they sought out better opportunities in the United States. Moreover, the inflow of capital to purchase bank shares was beneficial to the overall economy as well. Americans presumably took the proceeds of stock sales, which typically included a tidy profit, and reinvested the monies in other productive investments in the domestic market that yielded even higher returns than the 6 to 7 percent available on bank stock.

Throughout most of the remainder of the 1790s, foreign ownership of bank stock progressed. The directors started paying regular semiannual dividends in the second half of 1792, normally 8 percent annually, and their steady performance attracted the notice of securities brokers in London, Amsterdam, and other European money centers. By 1798 foreign residents held title to just over half of the shares outstanding; in 1809 their share had risen to more than 70 percent. The degree of overseas participation validated the attainment of the Hamiltonian goal of enhancing the prestige of the U.S. securities in world markets. But it was another example of having too much of a good thing.

Opponents of the First BUS were able to use the pattern of foreign ownership to launch stinging attacks in the congressional recharter debates of 1811. Critics charged that the bank profited mainly foreigners, not American citizens—an undeniable fact that incensed politicians prejudiced against British investors, who held most of the foreign stock, and stirred up latent xenophobia. Proponents countered that U.S. borrowers benefited from access to the loanable funds supplied in large part by foreigners, but they could not convert enough doubters. Foreign stockholders were not permitted to vote their shares in elections for directors under the charter terms, but that provision did little to dissuade opponents about the dangers of majority foreign ownership in an institution that closely resembled an agency of the U.S. government.

The rhetoric in 1811 was exaggerated but understandable and, in retrospect, not completely unreasonable. For example, how would Americans in the late twentieth century likely react to the news that Japanese nationals had quietly acquired a majority of the outstanding shares, even without voting privileges, in the existing Federal Reserve System? The analogy may be strained, but not all that much. (Shares in the Federal Reserve System are closely held by member banks and not traded—a prudent arrangement.) In retrospect, bank supporters would have been politically astute to rule out foreign ownership altogether or at least limit it to a decidedly minority position—say, one-quarter or one-third of the outstanding shares. Restrictions on foreign ownership would have run counter to the general plan to elevate the status of the American capital market, and the absence of overseas buyers would have acted, in theory, to restrain price increases in bank stock because of lowered demand. But over time tighter rules on foreigners might have helped to prolong the charter life of the First BUS. The same mistake was repeated in drafting the charter terms for the Second BUS in 1816—and with equally disastrous results.[12]

During Hamilton's tenure at the Treasury Department from 1789 to 1795, the First BUS conformed reasonably closely to the image that the secretary had in mind—namely, a mixed enterprise with numerous similarities to its inspiration, the Bank of England. Approximately half of the bank's earning assets were government securities and loans. Starting with the $2 million term loan granted the Treasury to purchase 20 percent of the initial public offering—a 100 percent margin transaction with no equity—plus the $6 million in long-term U.S. bonds surrendered by private shareholders to take advantage of the three-quarters payment option for privately held shares, the bank received a minimum of $480,000 in interest annually from the U.S. government from 1792 through 1795. That sum alone covered about 60 percent of the annual dividend since the administrative expenses incurred in managing the government portfolio were minimal.[13]

Through 1795 the directors simultaneously authorized loans of roughly $6 to $8 million annually to commercial customers— an informed guess based in part on the scattered information in table 11.2.[14] Many of the transactions—the majority according to some accounts—were so-called accommodation loans, which were not always supported by collateral such as mercantile inventories or improved real properties but which were secured instead by the signature of a second credit-worthy endorser, thus the term *two-name paper*. A fairly continuous record of commercial loan activity at the Charleston branch during the 1790s has survived, and it reveals mean loans outstanding of $637,000 for the three years 1793–95.[15] That figure was slightly more than double the allocated capital for the branch. If the directors of the other three branches followed similar policies, the outlying network would have generated annual loans of $4.8 million by late 1795, leaving the Philadelphia headquarters with just under $2 million, or around 30 percent of all the

TABLE 11.2
First Bank of the United States:
Assets on Selected Dates
(in millions of dollars)

	Public Securities	Loans to Treasury	Commercial Loans	Total Assets
Dec. 1793	$6.0	$2.8	$ 5.3	$14.1
Jan. 1795	6.0	3.9	6.4	16.3
Jan. 1796	3.5	6.0	7.0	16.5
Jan. 1799	3.3	3.8	9.4	16.5
Nov. 1801	3.1	2.9	13.3	19.3
Feb. 1809	2.2	—	14.6	16.8

Source: Table compiled from data in James Wettereau, "New Light on the First Bank of the United States," *Pennsylvania Magazine of History and Biography* (1937), 279.

bank's total commercial business. These figures seem quite plausible, and so with a proper warning to scholars about their partially assumptive character, I offer them as reasonably valid representations—valid until subsequent historians can reveal flaws in fact or interpretation.

Because of modest but persistent budget deficits, the Treasury was forced to seek financial assistance from the First BUS throughout most of Washington's second term. By the end of 1795, in addition to the original $2 million term loan extended to purchase bank stock, the government had outstanding loans of more than $4 million that were routinely rolled over on their assigned maturity dates. In an effort to reduce its holdings of Treasury obligations and thereby to free more loanable funds for private customers, the directors decided to sell off $2.4 million in long-term government bonds, a reduction of 40 percent from its opening position in 1791. The charter terms dictated that these sales could never be reversed; thus open market operations, so common to modern central banks, were never an option. By November 1801, long-term government bonds in the bank's portfolio had dropped to $3 million. Thereafter, the directors reduced their holdings only slightly. The next surviving date is February 1809, when $2.2 million was still on the books, representing 13 percent of earning assets.

The bank's directors had already started to back off from an increasing dependence on government obligations in the last year of Washington's second term. Meanwhile, Oliver Wolcott, who as-

TABLE 11.3
First Bank of the United States:
U.S. Treasury Deposits at Branch Offices
(December 31—in thousands of dollars)

	1803	*1804*	*1805*	*1806*
Philadelphia	$ 996	1,130	554	878
New York	1,244	703	1,097	1,341
Boston	588	667	819	1,174
Baltimore	617	227	431	295
Charleston	430	306	159	245
Washington	230	178	72	306
Norfolk	472	188	332	181
Savannah	139	150	120	62
New Orleans	—	—	121	237
Total	$4,716	3,549	3,705	4,719

Source: John Thom Holdsworth, *First Bank of the United States* (Washington: Government Printing Office, 1910), 60.

sumed the duties of treasury secretary in early 1795, eventually curtailed the linkage even further. Wolcott was a carryover in the Adams administration, and he took steps to float a new issue of securities, described earlier, and to reduce the government's short-term obligations to the First BUS. By January 1799, aggregate government debt in the bank's portfolio totaled $7 million—down from more than $9.5 million in 1795 and 1796. Under President Thomas Jefferson and his treasury secretary, Albert Gallatin, the government borrowed only rarely from the national bank. In 1809 the only federal obligations listed on the bank's balance sheet were $2.2 million in long-term bonds.

During the second decade of its operations, the working relationship between the First BUS and the Treasury underwent a profound reversal. Whereas the government had leaned on the bank for continued financing in the 1790s, in the next decade the Treasury left much of the excess revenue produced by budget surpluses on deposit in the First BUS, its official fiscal agent. Again the data are incomplete, but surviving December reports for 1803 through 1806 list mean government deposits of $4.16 million (see table 11.3). For those four dates, 72 percent of the deposits were listed on the books of just three offices. Treasury deposits at the New York branch exceeded the main office in Philadelphia on three occasions, and twice at the Boston office. Indeed, the evidence tends to suggest that the sharp increase in deposits during the second decade of operations was fueled largely by the money management policies of Treasury Secretary Gallatin. Bank managers presumably took advantage of the interest-free government deposits to make loans in the private sector. The federal branch of the American governmental system had returned, although indirectly through the services of a financial intermediary, to making additions to the aggregate money stock and providing loanable funds to citizens. However, in the latter case the financing went mostly to urban merchants rather than mostly to landholding farmers and a few artisans as in colonial times.

The net result of all the alterations was that, after 1796, the volume of business handled by the First BUS shifted more toward the private sector. Commercial customers accounted for somewhere around 40 percent of earning assets in 1793, more than 55 percent in 1799, nearly 70 percent in 1805, and more than 85 percent by 1809. The mixed character of the enterprise—the orientation toward both government and commerce—had dissipated. Increasingly, the First BUS evolved into a large bank with a strong commercial orientation, little different except in terms of size and scope from more than one hundred competing state-chartered institutions. Indeed, if the directors had chosen to liquidate their remaining $2 to $3 million in U.S. securities during the first decade of the new century, the only important remaining connection with the Treasury would have been the routine maintenance of deposit accounts to process the collection of taxes and pay the checks covering government expenditures.

The realignment of its loan portfolio beginning in 1795 signaled the end of that early phase in the bank's history, the years when its operations paralleled most closely the role of the Bank of England. The full-throttle Hamiltonian program did not survive long his resignation from office in January 1795. During his tenure, the First BUS had been primarily an institution that gave first call on its loanable funds to its prime sponsor, the federal government. On Hamilton's departure, the bank still looked to the Treasury for more than 60 percent of its interest revenues; by 1799 the comparable figure had fallen to less than 45 percent, and by 1809 to just 13 percent.

The Treasury's good fortune to generate sufficient budget surpluses to avoid reliance on outside financing also in a peculiar way became a decisive factor in the congressional decision to allow the charter of the First BUS to expire in 1812. Although Secretary Gallatin pointed out repeatedly that the bank had provided a safety net for the federal government during his long tenure in office, he could not make a powerful argument in favor of its continuance on the basis of current necessity. All he could do was to refer vaguely to the help it would be able to offer in some unspecified emergencies that might arise at some future date.

In fact, the controversy over recharter was debated mostly on an abstract plane. Opponents raised the constitutional issue, a rehash of positions argued twenty years earlier, and appealed to xenophobia by citing the huge majority of foreign stockholders. In a speech to the House in January 1811, Representative John Eppes (Virginia) pointed to the close connection between Parliament and the Bank of England. The "union of a monied interest with a government," he warned, was "dangerous to republican principles." Eppes rebutted the assertion that the national bank was necessary to the "management of the finances of the United States." The necessity argument might have had some merit in the early 1790s, he conceded, when few banks had been organized, but the situation in 1810 was vastly different since more than one hundred chartered banks now served the nation. In February, Senator William Crawford (Georgia), who favored recharter, emphasized performance and other more practical matters in his congressional speech. The national bank had performed admirably during the last two decades—as had the American economy. The federal government was financially sound, so why, he asked rhetorically, would anyone want to "abandon a well-tried system."[16] The threats to liberty that Jeffersonians had articulated so forcefully in the 1790s had never materialized, Crawford observed.

The vote on recharter was extremely close. President Madison took no official position, leaving the matter for the legislature to decide. In private, however, Madison had dropped his earlier opposition to the bank on constitutional grounds, an old position dating back to the congressional debates in 1791. Fellow Republicans had heard his former arguments against the bank's legitimacy again and again. Most politicians who survive in office long enough eventually find that some of their earlier pronouncements come back to haunt them. Madison wanted the bank rechartered, but he refused to exert pressure on friends and allies to save it from an untimely extinction. He advised everyone to vote his conscience. In the Senate, Vice-President George Clinton cast the final negative vote to break a tie.

The directors proceeded with the liquidation of the national bank's assets. Its bank note and deposit obligations were all paid promptly and in full. Stockholders received reimbursement for their capital plus a small premium from retained earnings. Up to three-quarters of the capital was due to foreigners. Some of that money was reinvested in the United States but several million dollars flowed overseas. The closing of the First BUS created entrepreneurial opportunities in the nine cities where it had left the market, and numerous state-chartered banks rushed in to meet the loan demand from mercantile customers. From 1811 to 1812, the aggregate number of state banks jumped from about 115 to more than 140. Moreover, the capital invested in American banking enterprises rose as well, climbing from just over $75 million in 1811 to $84 million one year later. By 1815 the nation had more than 200 banks with authorized capital of $115 million. Indeed, the transfer of capital and accounts from the national bank to other institutions went smoothly, without causing a significant disruption in the functioning of the financial system.

When the charter expired in 1812, the First BUS was a far cry from its inspiration, the Bank of England. The institution was no longer closely aligned with the federal government in terms of the extension of credit facilities, and it had not been critical to the success of treasury financing for more than a decade. The bank had provided the nation with an extremely safe currency backed by substantial reserves of specie, and it had provided leadership and some oversight over the operations of mushrooming state banks. Many Republicans were convinced that the bank was unconstitutional and therefore illegitimate on principle. Moreover, from a practical standpoint, it had outlived its usefulness and was superfluous in light of the continued growth of the decentralized system of state banks. Most critics changed their minds about the need for a large national bank in the aftermath of the War of 1812, but before the outbreak of hostilities many Jeffersonians and future Jacksonians celebrated their belated victory over one of the major planks in the Hamiltonian program.

Conclusion

The Hamiltonian financial program, designed to rejuvenate the moribund American capital market and solidify the trend toward the privatization of currency issue through chartered commercial banks, was an instantaneous success. The funding program for the national debt proceeded smoothly, and shares in the First BUS sold out within hours. The prices of government securities and bank stock rose above par almost immediately—a sure sign of a welcome reception by investors. Yields on U.S. securities paying current interest (one series did not resume payment until 1800) settled at between 4 and 5 percent—a rate that compared favorably with yields on securities issued by most contemporary governments in Europe. The credit rating of the United States climbed from its lowly ranking in 1787 up to an elevated status within a relatively short time. Foreigners were so strongly attracted to the investment opportunities that they eventually owned a majority of the outstanding government debt and shares in the First BUS. In the early 1790s all signs were positive regarding the possibility of creating an active and expanding market in securities, public and private.

Hamilton's dream of shaping the American financial services sector in the image of the British model went mostly according to plan during his tenure as treasury secretary from September 1789 to January 1795. Federal tax rates, mainly the tariff and excise taxes, were intentionally set at low levels to generate just enough revenue to cover the interest on the debt, which frequently accounted for more than half the budget, and other routine expenses. No surpluses that might become available to pay off the outstanding principal were anticipated or desired since Hamilton viewed the national debt as a great cement of the union, a device to retain the allegiance of the propertied classes. The gradualist approach to debt reduction came to the fore in the early 1790s and proved a welcome antidote to the financial sacrifices advocated by the urgency faction at the state level during the 1780s.

The treasury secretary also received permission to organize the nationally chartered Bank of the United States after a lengthy and vitriolic dispute over its constitutionality. Sixty percent of the initial bank capital came in the form of U.S. securities, thereby linking closely the two main elements in Hamilton's grand scheme for American economic revival. The bank's unblemished safety record

TABLE 11.4
Foreign Investors in American Securities, June 1803
(in millions of dollars)

	English	Dutch	Other	Combined
U.S. government bonds	25.1	15.2	3.0	43.3[a]
First BUS stock	4.0	2.0	.2	6.2[b]
State bank stock	5.0	3.0	1.0	9.0[c]
Total	34.1	20.2	4.2	58.5

Sources: Samuel Blodget, *Economica: A Statistical Manual for the United States* (1806) and reprinted by Augustus Kelley, New York, 1964; data compiled from table on p. 198. J. Van Fenstermaker, *The Development of American Commercial Banking, 1782–1837*, (Kent, Ohio: Kent State University Press, 1965), 111.

[a] The combined foreign investment in U.S. government bonds represented exactly half the total outstanding federal debt at the end of 1803.

[b] The combined foreign investment in First BUS stock represented 62 percent of outstanding shares.

[c] The combined foreign investment in state bank stock accounted for approximately one-third of their aggregate capital.

confirmed and deepened the earlier movement toward private chartered banking that had gotten off to a promising start in the mid-1780s and then became a vital necessity following the constitutional ban on fiat issues by state legislatures. The bank was created as a mixed enterprise with a substantial amount of flexibility in regard to the composition of its loan portfolio, yet while Hamilton was in office it maintained a strong identification with the Treasury.

Tax revenues were inadequate to cover expenditures in the mid-1790s, and the Treasury turned to the First BUS to maintain solvency. Across the Atlantic Ocean, the Bank of England had served as the government's financial savior for decades. But the charter terms of the First BUS, which ruled out the purchase of long-term government securities, guaranteed that its American counterpart could never duplicate that role. The bank chartered by Congress was purposefully denied the means of assisting directly in a permanent expansion of the national debt, although it could make intermediate-term loans (bridge loans) that might later be refinanced through new issues of long-term securities—as happened in 1798–99.

Until very recently most accounts of the early national period have conceded the successes of the Hamiltonian system and explained that, by and large, the Jeffersonian Republicans came to accept its necessity and recognized its significant contributions to American economic stability. The nation's credit standing in international financial markets was quickly revived and all Americans, whatever their political or ideological persuasion, could be proud of that accomplishment. But that interpretative framework has been challenged within the last few years by those who argue that following the presidential election of 1800, the Republicans began to undermine systematically the Hamiltonian foundations. Federalists believed more strongly in the efficacy of state intervention and control over the economy, whereas the Republicans were drawn to the advantages of freer markets and the encouragement of individual initiative—less government, rather than more.

This study confirms the existence of a growing counterrevolution in the financial services sector, although it places the crucial turning points earlier in the story. The Hamiltonian program, which rested so heavily on the English example and ignored American colonial traditions, began to weaken and unravel during the Federalist decade itself. Its decline took place in four stages. The first sign of its eventual unwinding was the vote of the directors of the First BUS to establish a network of branch offices. The second crucial development was the bank's shift away from a dependency on government obligations for interest revenues toward a greater reliance on commercial loans in the private sector. The third event was the steady reduction of the national debt during the administrations of Thomas Jefferson and James Madison. The final event, which led to the virtual dismantlement of Hamilton's grand strategy for American parity with European money centers, was the failed effort in 1811, on an extremely close congressional vote, to recharter the First BUS for another twenty years. Soon thereafter, the outbreak of the War of 1812 revealed that the Republicans had gone too far in their repudiation of the national bank.

The financial crisis surrounding the war rejuvenated the Hamiltonian vision. The national debt spurted upwards from $45 million to $127 million and in 1815 Congress voted to exhume the BUS. Developments beyond that date lie outside the time span of this volume, although we can quickly note in passing that during the mid-1830s the national debt was completely erased and the Second BUS was denied recharter and went into liquidation.

When the First BUS directors voted to establish a network of branch offices in 1792, they were engaging in institutional experimentation. Europe had no precedents. Secretary Hamilton opposed the idea on principle. Branches could be used either to centralize or, equally likely, to undercut the power of the main office in Philadelphia. It all depended on the administrative rules established and on the leadership personnel in the parent office and branches. If some of the branches performed poorly, they might dilute the capital of the entire enterprise. Even if they proved successful, Hamilton was concerned that the branches might divert the attention of bank directors away from their principal task, as he saw it, of standing ready to loan the Treasury sufficient funds to prevent any interruption in the payment of interest on U.S. securities. Throughout his term in office nothing went awry on that score; the First BUS advanced enough monies to cover budget deficits. Nonetheless, the seed of decentralization had been planted.

During Secretary Wolcott's administration of the Treasury Department (1795–1800), however, the First BUS turned its attention away from serving the needs of its number one customer, the U.S. government, and more toward the commercial end of the business—primarily loans to mercantile customers in the major port cities. When supposedly short-term and intermediate-term loans to the Treasury were not cleaned up but continued to mount, reaching $6 million in 1796, bank directors pressed for a curtailment, and Wolcott responded. The Adams administration was averse to raising tax rates sufficiently high to generate a budget surplus, thus other means of drawing down the loan were employed. The government sold nearly half its stock in the First BUS on the open market at a profit and used most of the proceeds for loan reduction. Through that action, the Treasury had simultaneously lowered its equity position in the institution and lessened its dependency on bank financing. Retreat from the Hamiltonian system occurred within months after its originator had departed government and several years before the election of 1800.

Meanwhile, the First BUS started liquidating the U.S. securities acquired from original stockholders. In 1795 alone, the directors sold off $2.5 million, more than 40 percent of their holdings. Bank directors reallocated loanable funds toward the private sector. Between 1794 and 1801, interest earnings from government loans and U.S. securities dropped by 40 percent. During those same seven years, loans outstanding to merchants and landowners with solid collateral or reliable endorsers more than doubled—from $6.4 to $13.3 million. Bank capital was steadily reallocated from Philadelphia, which possessed two other commercial banks, to other ports in the branch network where loan demand was strong and rising. From the initial allocation of $1.28 million in 1792, aggregate branch capital climbed to $3.85 million by 1800, with nearly half that figure assigned to the New York office. It was becoming increasingly clear that the vote to establish branch offices in other major cities had had a decentralizing effect on the nation's financial system, a development that coincided nicely with the outlook of the newly dominant Republican party.

By the turn of the century, the private commercial business conducted at the First BUS's seven branch offices (New Orleans, the eighth, was added in 1804) was in full swing. The bank had evolved from an institution with a strong government orientation in the period from 1792 through 1795 into a large commercial bank with active offices in major port cities. The BUS was vastly different from the Bank of England by the time the institution entered its second decade of operations. By cutting its close ties with the U.S. Treasury, the bank had become an institution with a strong local focus and a business enterprise more in harmony with Jeffersonian ideals of service to the local community.

After the election of President Jefferson in the fall of 1800, the counterrevolution against the Hamiltonian program continued apace, and it now focused on the retirement of long-term government debt. Hamilton had restricted the right of the Treasury to recall the 6 percent bonds to only a fraction of the securities outstanding, but there were no restraints on the retirement of the 3 percent bonds arising from the funding of past-due federal interest and the assumption of state debts. For the decade starting in 1801, Treasury Secretary Albert Gallatin trimmed the net federal debt from $80.7 to $45.2 million, despite the addition of $15 million in new debt in 1803 to acquire the Louisiana Territory from France.

The reductions were possible because of the sharp jump in customs revenues, which averaged $12.2 million from 1801 to 1811 after hitting a high point of $7.5 million in 1797. During Jefferson's two terms, the Treasury ran a deficit only once—the embargo year of 1808—and surpluses averaged $4.2 million annually. Investment bankers and loan contractors had little government business during Jefferson's eight-year presidency. What emerged was a compromise of sorts between the aims of the urgency faction, which held power in the early 1780s, and gradualists who supported the maintenance of the status quo in the 1790s. Jefferson's earlier assertion that every

TABLE 11.5
U.S. National Debt, 1791–1820
(in millions of dollars)

	Increase	Decrease'	Balance
1791	$	$	$ 77.2
1792	3.2		80.4
1793		2.0	78.4
1794	2.3		80.7
1795	3.1		83.8
1796		1.7	82.1
1797		2.9	79.2
1798		.8	78.4
1799	4.6		83.0
1800			83.0
1801		2.3	80.7
1802		3.6	77.1
1803	9.3		86.4
1804		4.1	82.3
1805		6.6	75.7
1806		6.5	69.2
1807		4.0	65.2
1808		8.2	57.0
1809		3.8	53.2
1810		5.2	48.0
1811		2.8	45.2
1812	10.8		56.0
1813	25.5		81.5
1814	18.3		99.8
1815	27.5		127.3
1816		3.8	123.5
1817		20.0	103.5
1818		15.0	95.5
1819		5.5	91.0
1820		1.0	90.0

Source: Paul Studenski and Herman Krooss, *Financial History of the United States,* (New York: McGraw-Hill, 1963), 54, 68, 77, 93.

generation should assume responsibility for repayment of its accumulated war debts—calculated at roughly fifteen to twenty years—became more or less official policy once he took up residence in the newly constructed White House.

Hamilton may have had visions of an American financial capital capable of competing with the leading European money centers, but that flowering was derailed and delayed in the first quarter of the century. Not until the rise of active capital markets first in Boston and later in New York in the 1840s and 1850s to finance the construction of thousands of miles of American railroad tracks under private ownership did the Hamiltonian dream begin to take on new life and press forward toward its ultimate fulfillment.

These developments in the financial sector square generally with historians Joyce Appleby and John Nelson's hypotheses about the strong capitalist/free market orientation of the Jeffersonian philosophy. The result came about in a rather backhanded manner, but it was real nonetheless. With the possibility of state-issue currency outlawed by the Constitution, the Jeffersonians shifted to the next best alternative—soundly managed private commercial banks under the guidance of local directors, including even the branch offices of the national bank headquartered in Philadelphia. They had been ideologically opposed to the establishment of a nationally chartered bank with a single office catering strictly to the enhancement of the financial power of the central government, since the Jeffersonians feared at all costs concentrated money power. But following the allocation of more than half the total capital of the First BUS to the seven branch offices, Hamilton's goal of transforming Philadelphia into a rival of London and Amsterdam in the first quarter of the nineteenth century was effectively thwarted.

12

State Banks in the New Nation

Following the successful funding of the national debt and the establishment of a large national bank in the early 1790s, American financial services underwent a broad, yet measured, expansion during the next quarter century. The economy grew sufficiently to support a fair degree of specialization by an increasing number of financial intermediaries. Merchants, planters, and lawyers had, of course, dabbled in providing credit facilities as a sideline since the seventeenth century, but the growth of more formalized financial institutions had been stymied. British law was one impediment, for it discouraged or forbade the mobilization of capital in corporations and the conduct of banking operations by firms with more than six partners.

With political independence the slate was wiped clean, and the U.S. legal structure was generally conducive to institutional innovation. Limits on the liability of passive investors (nondirectors) in corporate enterprises encouraged the marshaling of large pools of capital. Bankers, securities brokers, exchange dealers, and insurance agents were among the new full-time occupational categories that had not existed in the colonial period. Indeed, starting in the 1790s an identifiable financial services sector of the economy emerged. Most firms acted as intermediaries; they came between bank depositors and borrowers, between securities buyers and sellers, and between the insured and underwriters. Financial firms earned their profits either from commissions, with the fees generally diminishing over time, or in the case of commercial

266

bankers on the differential between the cost of acquiring funds and interest revenues on loans.

In the commercial banking field particularly, prudence and conservatism were the bywords of the era; and historians active in the late nineteenth and early twentieth centuries who were seeking a model for emulation often cited the period between 1785 and 1815 as something of a golden age. Because they used soundness as virtually the sole criterion for judging the performance of commercial banks, they exaggerated the accomplishments of the period in comparison with the results of later decades. Many historians writing before World War I also claimed that the early banks made loans based strictly on so-called real bills, meaning loans secured by self-liquidating inventories that were nonrenewable beyond sixty to ninety days. More systematic examination of scattered loan records suggests that those assertions, while true for some institutions in certain periods, were largely a question of wishful academic thinking.

The alleged purity of early banking was a myth designed to persuade bankers in a later age to adopt more cautious lending policies—a perfect example of the misuse of history to achieve goals judged laudatory in a subsequent era. In truth, bank directors often permitted rollovers beyond ninety days; and they sometimes granted accommodation loans, renewable for indefinite periods and secured by tenuous mortgages, to finance speculative land development projects on the frontier. When some projects collapsed, such as the one involving former Treasurer Robert Morris in the mid-1790s, banks seem to have been able to proceed against the assets of endorsers with enough success to avoid massive losses. Despite the lurid tales of good men gone wrong because of speculative excesses—Morris ended up in debtors' prison—what happened in the early national era nonetheless pales in comparison with the savings and loan scandals of the 1980s.

Generally speaking, modern economic historians, writing from the perspective of the late twentieth century, have argued that most bankers in the early national period were overly conservative. Bank directors paid too little attention to the societal advantages of promoting faster economic growth through an expansion in loans and the money supply. Safety was vastly more important than economic efficiency to the directors who set policy for the more than two hundred chartered banks, although a few banks were founded explicitly to offer partial financing to specific transportation projects. As a rule, however, bank directors made a sufficient volume of loans to generate just enough interest revenue to pay annual dividends of 8 to 12 percent to stockholders. They rarely tried to earn additional profits with the aim of boosting a bank's capital base through the retention of earnings. As a consequence of their limitations on loan volume, the currency issues of chartered banks were, as a rule, exceedingly sound. One phrase in Secretary of the Treasury Albert Gallatin's report to Congress in March 1809 reflected the thinking of many contemporaries: "Moderate dividends, . . . which check the circulation of bank paper, are the best evidence of the safety of the institution, and the wisdom of its direction."[1] Only a few banks failed before 1815, and all were linked to a single individual in New England who engaged in a series of fraudulent activities.[2]

Still, there remains a strong ring of truth to the older laudatory accounts of the accomplishments of the first generation of American bankers. Compared to the institutional immaturity of the colonial past, the early national period witnessed some impressive gains. The innovative activities of entrepreneurs in various financial fields created an institutional infrastructure conducive to rapid economic development in transportation, manufacturing, and agriculture after 1815. The slowdown in per capita income growth during the period from 1775 to 1810 provided a good opportunity for Americans to adjust to a privatized system of currency issuance that still left room for substantial citizen involvement through direct investment in bank stock and the exercise of legislative power to approve or disapprove of charter terms and limitations.[3] To compete with the British and Dutch in the long run, as Treasury Secretary Hamilton had envisioned, American entrepreneurs needed time to acquire financial skills—and time to accustom the public to transacting business with new financial intermediaries.

The creation of a banking system based on soundness was likewise important from a political standpoint. The rectitude of bank directors went far in blunting the skepticism of Jeffersonian Republicans about the societal consequences of encouraging and abetting the expansion of the financial services sector. The ideological bias against anyone who made a living by specializing in financial activities, persons often derisively labeled as social parasites, never completely disappeared and remained sufficiently strong to thwart recharter of the First BUS. Yet the harshest criticisms were gradually modulated. American bank directors did not seem to be cut from the same mold as the Republican image of reckless European speculators who allegedly made fortunes by manipulating the securities markets. Directors of chartered banks were typically successful local merchants, and their reputation for caution and probity became a genuine asset since their reputation for reliability rubbed off on the institutions they served.

The alteration in attitudes toward banks was not all that great a leap for many Republicans. Back in the 1780s, pamphleteer Thomas Paine had broken ranks with many fellow revolutionaries over the issue of privatized commercial banks when he applauded their potential beneficial effects on the lives of average citizens as well as members of the wealthier classes. Paine was attracted by the convenience and stability of convertible bank notes and the potential expansion of credit facilities for artisans and shopkeepers. Over the years other political figures became more comfortable with the idea of tolerating and sometimes encouraging the emergence of state-chartered financial institutions.

By the first decade of the new century, most Republicans had been persuaded that, under the proper circumstances, banks could provide valuable services that coincided with the public welfare. Banks in smaller towns were increasingly accepted as legitimate enterprises and were particularly welcome in communities distant from major port cities. The financial intermediaries could, through a reliance on fractional reserves, increase the money supply, expand credit facilities, and promote economic development. Banks that included among their customers—in some cases because of the dictates of the charter terms—artisans, mechanics, and farmers were not institutions that seemed overly threatening to society. Moreover, state legislatures retained the power to draft charter terms on an ad hoc basis that could be tailored to meet the objections of critics.

Some states outlawed the issuance of bank notes in denominations of less than five dollars, with the aim of protecting the lower classes from the potential risk of unexpectedly getting caught holding the currency of a failed bank. With small bank notes branded as illegal, citizens were expected to conduct most of their everyday business by relying on book credit or coins in denominations ranging from pennies, or fractions thereof, up to one or two dollars. As discussed in chapter 6 and at greater length in the Appendix, the public received added protection when legislatures made individual bank directors partially liable for an institution's debts in the event of bankruptcy.

Legislatures were likewise able to draft corporate charters that forced institutions to provide funding for socially useful projects such as turnpikes or bridges, and they could dictate the allocation of a given bank's loanable funds to state treasuries as well. The states could no longer make direct mortgage loans, but they could profit from the collection of dividends on investments in bank stock and the assessment of various fees, which held down general tax rates. Experience soon revealed that government was not falling under the thumb of ambitious financiers. Instead, prospective bank organizers were often at the mercy of state legislatures that had the power to approve or deny charter applications.

As a result of the generally favorable performance of commercial banks, for the most part the political system maintained a laissez faire attitude toward entrepreneurial initiatives in financial services generally, and that permissive environment carried over into the subsequent decades. Thanks to a steadily declining national debt, which had reached a low of $45 million on the eve of the War of 1812, and a geographically dispersed commercial banking system, no American city approached the elevated status of London or Amsterdam as a hub of the nation's financial community. As a consequence, the ambitions of stockjobbers and speculators, who were always few in number, were held at bay. Likewise, special interests representing the so-called monied elite made virtually no inroads in terms of polluting the political process as Jeffersonians had feared and frequently predicted when the Federalists held national power in the 1790s.

Despite the relaxation of Republican vigilance, which sprang mostly from southern roots, the development of indigenous American financial services occurred predominantly in the northern states. Southerners continued to rely heavily on the financial services provided by European firms, in particular the extension of credit against the shipment of cash crops—mostly tobacco and, increasingly in the 1790s and early 1800s, cotton, the emerging southern staple. The region had received reliable financial services from overseas sources in the colonial era, and that tradition was maintained during the early national period as well. Whether planters shipped to Scottish or English houses or instead to firms in France, Holland, and other continental destinations, liberal credit facilities, which were often one element in an overall package of marketing services, were invariably forthcoming. Less urbanization in the southern states meant less incentive to establish chartered banks to serve the requirements of local merchants in carrying inventories and receivables. With a greater supply of services emanating from overseas and less demand for mercantile loans, the development of financial firms in the southern states trailed the North.

When the First BUS opened its doors in late 1791, only five previously state-chartered commercial banks were already conducting business. They were located in New York, Boston, Philadelphia, Baltimore, and Providence. The establishment of four branches of the national bank early the next year in New York, Boston, Baltimore, and Charleston nearly doubled overnight the number of banking offices serving the major port cities. During the remainder of that decade, twenty-six more banks were established, and more than 90 percent were located north of the Maryland-Virginia border. New England led the way in the 1790s with sixteen new banks scattered throughout the region. The New York legislature chartered four corporations that entered the banking field. One, the Manhattan Company, started out in 1799 as a water company but soon diversified into commercial banking through an expansionary clause in its corporate charter. Pennsylvania, Delaware, Maryland, and the new District of Columbia added one bank each in the 1790s; the same was true for the only two southern states on the list, Virginia and South Carolina.

Overall, including the five branch offices of the First BUS, the nation possessed thirty-seven banking offices in more than twenty-five different locations that issued bank notes, accepted deposits, made loans, and performed other related services at the turn of the century.[4] All the major port cities along the Atlantic Coast had at least one banking office. Nine communities with less than five thousand inhabitants in the 1800 census situated between Alexandria, Virginia, and Portland, Maine, also boasted a chartered bank; the smallest, Bristol, Rhode Island, had less than two thousand residents. Banks in small towns were not unusual in New England before 1815, but that trend did not spread to the rest of the nation until a generation later.

When John Adams left office in March 1801, the United States had experienced more than fifteen years of privatized commercial banking, and none of the bank notes issued by any of these institutions had ever been repudiated or undergone steady depreciation. The monetary stability that had characterized the colonial economy in the third quarter of the eighteenth century was generally restored by the mid-1790s, but in a more uniform manner than during the previous era when varying mixtures of coins and fiat currencies had comprised the money stocks in nine of the thirteen original colonies. As Adam Smith had argued in *Wealth of Nations,* after acknowledging the success of some colonies in managing their fiat paper, privatized banks issuing currency against sufficient specie reserves represented a superior monetary system. American banking during the early national period reinforced the wisdom of Smith's proposition.

During the next decade and one half under Presidents Thomas Jefferson and James Madison, the system of state-chartered banks continued to expand at a steady pace. New banks appeared in all eighteen states, including the southern and western regions. The number of institutions climbed fairly steadily to about 115 in 1811; then the closing of the First BUS in 1812 triggered a burst of new charter applications to fill the gap left by its departure from financial markets. By 1815 the nation boasted around 210 chartered banks; that translates into one commercial bank for approximately every thirty thousand free citizens, a respectable figure even by modern standards. A disproportionate percentage of bank charters were in New England; that region, with about one-quarter of the U.S. population, was home to roughly one-third of all chartered banks, many located in small to medium-sized towns. In terms of size, however, New England's banks lagged the rest of the country, accounting for just one-fifth of total capital. The mean capital of New England banks was around $325,000, whereas bank directors elsewhere around the country, on average, had more than $650,000 in capital resources at their disposal.[5]

The data on capital resources highlights a distinctive feature of early American banks—their uniformly high capitalization in comparison with the modest sums invested in many banks in later periods. In the post–Civil War era, for example, federal and state governments combined chartered literally tens of thousands of new banks, some of which had capital bases as low as $10,000 to $25,000. On that score banking in the early national period was sounder and safer. The majority of commercial banks operating between 1790 and 1815 had substantial capital resources relative to the size of the local economies they served. Chartered banks in 1815 had total capital resources of $115 million, which translates into a mean of $540,000 per bank. Not all of the authorized sums were paid in by subscribers, so calculations of the actual amounts invested by stockholders must be lowered. However, recently published data on New

England banks suggests that 85 percent of the authorized capital in that region was subscribed and collected.[6] Medium-sized financial institutions were the rule in the early national period. There were few disproportionately large banks—the exception being the First BUS from 1792 to 1812—and only a handful of very small banks, mostly in a few New England towns. In 1815 the nation's largest commercial bank, created simultaneously with the liquidation of the First BUS, was New York's Bank of America with capital resources of $4 million—and no branch offices. Indeed, the overall structure of American commercial banking from 1800 to 1815 was probably superior to the organizational system that developed in the ensuing decades.

Not surprisingly, the capital invested in commercial banking was greatest in the nation's largest commercial cities. A review of data on the ports of New York, Boston, Philadelphia, and Baltimore reveals that those four cities combined had a total of thirty state-chartered banks in 1815, or just under 15 percent of the national total (see table 12.1). Those institutions had capital resources of $35 million, accounting for 30 percent of U.S. banking capital. The average size of institutions was nearly $1.2 million, double the national average. With just under $12 million in aggregate banking capital, New York City had already pulled away from its two main rivals, Boston and Philadelphia, which had $8.5 million and $7.7 million, respectively, invested in commercial banking.[7]

In short, the leading commercial cities were also becoming money centers—as Federalists had anticipated and Republicans had feared. Yet given the absence of extensive intrastate or interstate branch networks, no institution or group of institutions was able to dominate a regional economy or, by definition, the national economy. A concentration of financial power in a single urban market, as had happened in London and Amsterdam, showed no signs of replication on American shores. Indeed, the places where monopoly power was exercised most visibly were not the most commercially developed urban areas at all. Instead, the greatest degree of monopoly power was wielded by tight circles of bank directors in communities too small to support more than one financial institution.

Jeffersonians had feared the aggrandizement of the power of urban mercantile elites with the shift to privatized banking, yet the main increases in relative economic power flowed to the owners and officers of banks in rural communities since those institutions were

TABLE 12.1
State Chartered Banks in Northern Seaports:
Authorized Capital

Philadelphia		
1781	Bank of North America	$ 843,000
1793	Bank of Pennsylvania	2,500,000
1803	Philadelphia Bank	1,000,000
1809	Farmers and Mechanics Bank	1,250,000
1815	Commercial Bank	1,000,000
1815	Mechanics' Bank	500,000
1815	Schuykill Bank	400,000
1815	Bank of Northern Liberties	250,000
	Total	$ 7,743,000
New York		
1784	Bank of New York[a]	$ 1,000,000
1799	Manhattan Company	1,850,000
1803	Merchants' Bank	1,490,000
1810	Mechanics' Bank	2,000,000
1811	Union Bank	1,000,000
1812	Phoenix Bank	500,000
1812	Bank of America	4,000,000
	Total	$ 11,840,000
Boston		
1784	Bank of Massachusetts	$ 800,000
1792	Union Bank	1,200,000
1803	Bank of Boston	1,800,000
1812	State Bank	3,000,000
1813	New England Bank	1,000,000
1814	Manufacturers and Mechanics Bank	750,000
	Total	$ 8,550,000
Baltimore		
1790	Bank of Maryland	$ 300,000
1795	Baltimore Bank	1,200,000
1805	Union Bank	2,250,000
1806	Mechanics' Bank	600,000
1810	Marine Bank	600,000
1810	Commercial and Farmers Bank	700,000
1810	Farmers and Merchants Bank	500,000
1810	Franklin Bank	600,000
	Total	$ 6,750,000
	All four cities	$ 34,883,000
	U.S. bank capital in 1815	$115,000,000
	Four cities' share of U.S. total: 30 percent	

Source: Table compiled from Herman E. Krooss, "Financial Institutions," in *The Growth of the Seaport Cities,* edited by David Gilchrist, (Charlottesville: University Press of Virginia, 1967), table 16, p. 111.

[a] Founded in 1784, charter granted in 1791.

geographically isolated and thus protected from the competitive forces of the outside world. The most blatant form of market power was the rationing of credit to a limited number of favored customers—often persons connected to major stockholders through blood or marriage. By comparison, the old legislative loan offices of the colonial era had been vastly more democratic institutions because they had placed modest limitations on how much money any citizen could borrow.

With the formation of the new national government under the Constitution, ideological conflicts over the legitimacy of private chartered banking were less pronounced than in the 1780s. Some Republican diehards continued to assert that the emergence of a privatized banking system had usurped governmental powers by diverting interest revenues from state treasuries into private hands, but those charges fell on deaf ears. Partisan battles over banks continued at the state level—and some contests were frequently highly inflammatory. The debates typically addressed more practical matters, such as whether rival organizing groups backed primarily by Federalists or, alternatively, by Republicans could maneuver a charter bill through the legislature, and on what terms. For example, in the legislative debate over the proposed establishment of a chartered bank in northern Virginia in the early 1790s, John Taylor of Caroline voiced his usual warnings about the alleged corruptions of chartered financial institutions. Yet the Federalist-backed Bank of Alexandria received permission to begin operations in 1793 with only minor Republican opposition.[8]

Events in New York illustrate the new plane on which political battles over banking developed in the early national period. The first commercial bank organized in the state, the Bank of New York in 1784, drew its supporters mostly from investors with Federalist sympathies. That factor was instrumental in forestalling the granting of a formal corporate charter by the state legislature until 1791. When the First BUS opened a branch office in New York City, its local board of directors, elected by resident shareholders, was likewise dominated by loyal Federalists. Federalist directors at both banks made loans primarily to their friends, relatives, and business associates. Self-dealing was the norm and was encouraged so long as it was not imprudently abused, and surprisingly little abuse occurred—or at least not enough to cause a series of bank failures. Meanwhile, Republican-leaning merchants in the city felt denied. They wanted greater access to discount facilities, and the organization of a third local bank loomed as the best possible solution provided they could muster the votes to obtain a charter from the state legislature. They finally achieved that goal before the end of the century through a complicated and disingenuous route.

Aaron Burr, a leader of the state's Republican Party and a political rival of Alexander Hamilton (whom he later killed in a duel), was among the principals who proposed the formation of a chartered corporation to build a delivery system for safe drinking water to citizens of New York City. The Manhattan Company received broad charter powers from the state legislature and the authorization to raise $2 million in capital resources in early 1799. Soon after the company was formed, the directors, mostly Republican merchants, announced plans to scale back their investment in the waterworks and to use the "surplus capital" to create a new commercial bank. According to historian Beatrice Reubens, the bill was so skillfully drafted and lobbied through the legislature that some members of the Federalist opposition voted for the original charter bill and even invested their funds in company stock. When they discovered that Burr had double-crossed them, Federalists raised a howl and used the issue of political trickery to sweep the municipal elections of 1799. In attacking the Manhattan Company for stretching its charter powers to enter the commercial banking field, Hamilton derided the firm as "a monster in its principles."[9] But the political furor soon died down, and the Manhattan Company maintained its involvement in the financial services field—and it has continued to do so up until the present.

The Manhattan bank was innovative in several respects and merits further discussion on that account. Its prime customers were Republican merchants, but the directors also offered loan accommodations to a fair number of artisans, small manufacturers, and shopkeepers if they claimed the proper political affiliation. The original offering price for shares was set at only $2.50, a low denomination deliberately chosen to permit a few persons with modest savings to invest in the enterprise. Federalists complained that Republicans had politicized the banking issue by using the bank's more liberal lending policies to solicit votes from members of the lower and middling classes. In New York and elsewhere, banks were subsequently organized with the words *mechanics* and/or *farmers* in their formal titles. Reflecting Republican principles, charter terms sometimes dictated that certain middling groups receive minimal access to credit facilities—for example, 20 percent of all the names in the loan portfolio might be required to be mechanics or farmers. But the nonmercantile groups were not necessarily granted access to the same high percentage in terms of dollar volume. A bank could remain in compliance with charter terms if it loaned one mechanic just fifty dollars and four merchants ten thousand dollars each. Despite the continued opportunities for wide discrepancies and discrimination, the wider access to loan facilities dictated by law was more in harmony with the spirit of the legislative loan offices in colonial times. These more liberal rules contrasted with the clubby, exclusively mercantile atmosphere that prevailed at most institutions founded by Federalist elites.

Bank chartering remained a highly politicized game throughout the era in New York and elsewhere, with much competition between entrepreneurs affiliated with the two main political parties as well as rival factions within them. The battles were rarely over the legitimacy of state-chartered banks in American society but concentrated instead on which group of potential investors would receive organizing rights in certain locales. Republicans often were as active as Federalists, and probably more so after Jefferson's election. Vote swapping and bribery became common in some legislative bodies in the early nineteenth century when the number of applications for bank charters proliferated. As a consequence, the next generation of American political leaders finally forswore the ad hoc system of legislative chartering and converted the process into a nonpartisan mechanism with fixed rules for all applicants.

The Manhattan Company's banking division was also mildly innovative in terms of its overall strategies and administrative structure. The firm opened branch offices upstate in Utica and Poughkeepsie in 1809.[10] The directors of the First BUS had voted to establish an interstate branch network soon after its creation in 1792; banks in Pennsylvania, Vermont, and Delaware also had branch offices, so the concept was not exactly new. Still, only a handful of the more than two hundred banks chartered in the early national period created networks of intrastate branches. The maintenance of satellite offices under the day-to-day management of salaried employees was uncommon for firms in any line of business. The experiment in geographical expansion was not sustained, however; political opposition in the state legislature and economic reverses associated with the Panic of 1819 contributed to the decision of bank directors to abandon the branch system.

The Manhattan Company's brief experience in intrastate

branching was one of the exceptions that helped to prove the general rule—namely, that a unit bank conducting business from a single office location was overwhelmingly the norm. That pattern emerged because wealthy merchants and landowners strongly resented and resisted the entry of outside institutions with substantial financial resources into their local economies. The introduction of outside bank capital threatened the economic, social, and political dominance of local elites and was thus universally unwelcome. Local elites aimed to preserve for themselves the privilege of establishing, managing, and profiting from any financial institution functioning in the local market. They were generally able to exercise sufficient power in state legislatures to protect financial markets from the entrance of threatening outsiders in the commercial banking field. Most objections to the establishment of branches of banks headquartered elsewhere were fanciful and self-serving, but the arguments were nonetheless extremely effective in influencing the legislative and regulatory process. The atomistic commercial banking structure reflected the local orientation of most business enterprises in an era before the economy had felt the full impact of canals, railroads, and other improvements in the transportation system.

State legislatures lost the power to issue currency and collect interest from their mortgage loans in 1787, but they soon discovered the means of compensating for the loss of revenues from their direct involvement in financial services. They generated revenues from the financial sector indirectly instead. Revenues arose from three main sources: dividends on investments in bank stock, taxes on bank capital, and bonuses for granting and extending charters. Before independence, loan offices in the middle colonies had produced sufficient interest earnings in some years to cover all, or most, provincial expenditures. As a result, many voters had become accustomed to viewing the financial services sector as a legitimate target for public funding, and that tradition was perpetuated in the early national period.

The first response of legislatures seeking revenue from the evolving financial sector was to insist on provisions that allowed the state to acquire stock in the newly chartered enterprises. Like the First BUS, many state-chartered banks began as mixed enterprises. In most cases, a majority of the authorized shares went to private parties, with the state treasury purchasing a minority interest. Taxpayers could share in the profits of these private entities, which were licensed by government to promote the public welfare, through their state treasuries' regular collection of dividends. All the original thirteen states invested in bank stock. Vermont in 1806 and South Carolina in 1812 went one step further and created commercial banks wholly owned by state government. Despite their different organizational format, the two state institutions were reminiscent of colonial loan offices since they routinely emitted currency. The main difference was that, unlike the fiat paper of the colonial era, the state-owned institutions issued bank notes continually convertible into specie at tellers' windows.

The several states also generated revenues from banks by taxing capital and demanding bonuses for the extension of charters at their expiration dates, which typically ran for twenty years or less. Tax rates and bonuses varied from state to state and defy meaningful generalization. Every bank charter negotiation was an ad hoc affair. To measure the overall importance of banks in supporting state governments, economic historians Richard Sylla, John Legler, and John Wallis calculated the share of total state revenues that could be attributed to all dividends, taxes, and bonuses linked to chartered banks for the thirteen original states.[11] From 1811 to 1815, Pennsylvania led the way with nearly half its revenues generated from the banking sector, followed closely by Delaware (39 percent) and Massachusetts (38 percent). Only Rhode Island and New Hampshire reported no income from banks during the five-year period. The collection of public revenues from assessments on banks in the early decades of the nineteenth century started a trend that accelerated in most states after 1820. Drawing revenues from financial services, at first directly and later indirectly, was one of the key continuities between the colonial, early national, and antebellum decades.

State legislatures also used their power to grant or deny corporate status as a means of imposing other demands on applicants for bank charters. Since bank entrepreneurs were granted the privilege of entering a given market with some degree of limited liability and often exercised monopoly or duopoly powers, they were frequently expected to return the favor and aid their respective state governments in financing budget deficits. Charter terms sometimes called for the extension of loans to the state treasury as a condition for securing permission to conduct business as a corporation. In another arrangement, legislatures directed a bank to provide loans to assist a construction project deemed beneficial to the economy—usually turnpikes and bridges before 1815.[12]

In return for various financial benefits negotiated with the applicants for bank charters, some state legislatures passed laws forbidding private unchartered banks, or any other firm whether a proprietorship or partnership, from issuing currency. Restraining acts emerged in Massachusetts and New Hampshire in 1799. By 1815 nine states had enacted similar legislation. The laws prevented all other firms, including mercantile houses, from issuing private paper that might compete with the bank notes of legally sanctioned financial institutions. Private bankers could perform other financial services, only currency issuance was disallowed. State restraining acts helped to preserve the privileges of banking companies by outlawing competition from enterprises normally beyond the control of state government.[13]

The restraining laws on private parties were almost the reverse of the rules that had governed the financial services sector in colonial times. Under parliamentary law in the eighteenth century, all individuals as well as partnerships with fewer than seven partners were free to engage in unregulated currency issuance. Why the different policies on opposite sides of the Atlantic? In England, Parliament had not looked to the banking sector as a source of public revenues. Parliament had granted few corporate charters to banks after the South Sea fiasco in the 1720s, and thus it had no compelling reason to restrict the operations of private bankers. The American states, on the other hand, had discovered a means of generating revenues from banks in sums that were substantial relative to the size of their limited budgets. Consequently, they had strong incentives to protect the value of their licensing powers by prohibiting the circulation of all private currency within their borders.

The only large private, unchartered U.S. commercial bank in the early nineteenth century was the Girard Bank in Philadelphia. Its origins are noteworthy. When the First BUS closed in 1812, Stephen Girard, a wealthy Philadelphia merchant, thought he saw an entrepreneurial opportunity. He hired George Simpson, the former head cashier of the national bank, solicited many of its longstanding accounts, invested $1.2 million of his own money in the enterprise, and became the sole owner. Pennsylvania law forbade private bankers from issuing bank notes, and local bankers initially refused to accept his issue at their windows. Girard was persistent, however. He continued to defy the weakly enforced regulations—the state had no enforcement agency—and eventually worked out an arrangement with the other banks in the Philadelphia area to accept his currency in local settlements. Girard Bank held substantial specie reserves relative to its outstanding bank notes, and there was never any serious doubt about the owner's ability to make good on his outstanding liabilities. His Republican politics and the assistance provided to Secretary of the Treasury Albert Gallatin during the financial crisis surrounding the War of 1812 were undoubtedly factors that permitted Girard to flout the restrictions on private currency issues until the bank wound up its affairs soon after his death in 1831.[14]

Corporate chartered banking became the accepted norm during the formative years of American commercial banking. Except for the unending philosophical debate about the constitutionality of federally chartered private banking, the issue of privatized banking became progressively less controversial, and especially after the election of Republican Thomas Jefferson to the presidency in 1800. The role of the First BUS in the national economy likewise diminished. By 1812 it possessed less than 15 percent of the capital invested in commercial banking, and that percentage was sinking yearly. Commercial banks served primarily urban merchants, but the formulation of their original charter terms and the regular renewal of those terms every twenty years or thereabouts gave citizens, through their legislatures, the opportunity to make those private enterprises accountable to the general welfare. In the bargaining with financial entrepreneurs, legislatures sometimes forced banks to allocate a portion of their loanable funds to state treasuries, various transportation projects, farmers, and mechanics. Governments also used banks to alleviate the tax burden on individuals by generating revenues from investments in banks, taxes on bank capital, and bonuses for granting charters.

This was a calm era for American finance in general. It preceded the storm associated with the multiplying bank failures in the aftermath of the Panic of 1819. Except for the collapse of Andrew Dexter's banks in New England, the system was safe and reliable. Bank notes were esteemed both as a medium of exchange and store of value, and they circulated more widely as the years passed. The first fifteen years of the nineteenth century were, in fact, surprisingly harmonious for state-chartered banks and their myriad of customers.

13

Marine and Fire Insurance

In ADDITION to substantial institutional development in the commercial banking field, the colonies and their successor states witnessed a steady expansion of facilities in related financial markets. The sectors examined here are marine and fire insurance, with a quick glance at the embryonic life insurance market. The following chapter extends this general line of inquiry by focusing on a miscellaneous group of financial services, including lotteries, securities brokerage, and transactions involving foreign bills of exchange. Indeed, marine insurance and foreign exchange trading are functional activities with fairly close historical links since, until the emergence of organized companies in London, unspecialized merchants serving foreign markets were the primary underwriters of insurance policies covering risks at sea.

Marine Insurance

Marine coverage was the earliest type of insurance to develop organized, yet informal, markets. Issued to protect shippers against the risk of financial losses resulting from accidents at sea during peacetime or enemy sinkings and confiscation during wartime, marine insurance in one form or another dates back to antiquity. Because it rested on the principle of spreading risks among numerous shippers, this service was invariably confined to ports with substantial volumes of maritime activity. From Babylonian times, through the Middle Ages, and up until the seventeenth century, few, if any, specialized firms were devoted solely to underwriting insurance policies. Instead, prosperous merchants, and sometimes landowners with accumulated wealth in agriculture working in conjunction with insurance brokers, diversified their interests by underwriting marine policies as an offshoot to their main line of economic activity. Underwriters usually issued separate policies to cover in the first instance an individual ship and in the second instance its cargo. Cargoes with multiple owners frequently generated multiple policies.

In peaceful times, underwriters were able to calculate with a reasonable degree of accuracy, if not absolute precision, the likelihood of losses arising from such hazards as rough seas and ill winds on established trade routes. If the institutional setting was accommodating, marine insurance became available in port cities with a steady volume of seaborne traffic. Depending on the length of the voyage, the prevalence of pirates in certain waters, and the time of year—whether closer to the stormy or calm months—premium rates of 5 percent or less of the insurable value of ships and their cargoes were reportedly negotiated in Mediterranean ports on certain routes more than a thousand years ago. In more turbulent eras when overseas trading patterns were disrupted because of political divisions, potential underwriters were not able to measure risks accurately, and they withdrew from the market or insisted on prohibitive rates. Indeed, rates had a tendency to settle at either the lower or the higher end of the price spectrum.

In wartime, when ships and cargoes were subject to seizure by rival navies and armed privateers, rates could climb to as high as 30 to 50 percent of market values—in extreme cases as high as 75 percent or more. Under what circumstances would shippers pay premiums that approached the replacement cost of the merchandise itself? In those special cases, a few shippers willingly paid astronomically high rates because they hoped to realize profit margins of 200 to 300 percent or more when their merchandise reached a port cut off from its normal inflow of goods from the outside world because of a military emergency. Underwriting policies during wartime was a dangerous business—something that went beyond the rational calculation of a statistically measurable risk. War insurance was more akin to outright gambling and thus avoided by all but the most daring underwriters.

As early as Roman times, the so-called loan on bottomry was a common device for providing protection to shipowners against risks at sea. The system functioned in an odd manner, almost the reverse of modern business procedures, but the result was virtually the same. Owners negotiated collateralized loans in advance from underwriters at high interest rates for amounts limited only by the market value of a departing ship. The loan principal, plus interest, became due and payable when the ship arrived safely at its destination. If the vessel was lost at sea, on the other hand, the loan was canceled, thereby compensating for the loss. In effect, the interest charges applied to the loans served as the premium for providing insurance coverage.

As with commercial banking, financial historians generally trace the origins of modern marine insurance back to Italy in the fourteenth century. By the sixteenth century, Amsterdam and Antwerp were centers for underwriting in northern Europe. Underwriting was still uncommon in England in the sixteenth century, but demand rose steadily in response to the increased volume of English shipping in the North Atlantic. In 1575, during the reign of Elizabeth I, the crown established the Office of Assurances and required the compulsory registration of all marine policies. After 1650, London began to claim an increasing share of the North Atlantic insurance market.[1] Nonetheless, during most of the seventeenth century, the majority of British ships still sailed without adequate insurance coverage.[2]

The most common means of limiting accidental, noncommercial losses, and a system widely employed by both British and colonial American shippers in the seventeenth century, was the ageless strategy of dividing the ownership of vessels and their cargoes into fractional shares. Using that system to spread risk, a loss at sea did not fall on the shoulders of a single entity but on a group of investors, none of which was likely to suffer ruin because of one unfortunate incident. Shipowners seeking greater safety through diversification often took shares of one-third, one-eighth, one-sixteenth, and sometimes even smaller fractions in several vessels. Even when marine coverage became widely available on reasonable terms, the strategy of holding fractional shares was still followed by many cautious investors. On busy shipping lanes, a single merchant sometimes transported a large shipment of goods on two or more vessels sailing for the same port on different dates.

For protection from pirates or from belligerent vessels during wartime, merchant ships sometimes sought greater security by adding cannonry to their decks or by sailing in convoy under naval surveillance. In the eighteenth century, the navies of the major

European powers rooted out a high percentage of the pirates marauding in Caribbean waters, and insurance rates fell on the order of 10 to 20 percent to reflect the lower risk of loss due to robbery on the high seas.[3] Insurance underwriters typically gave rebates to the owners of vessels and cargoes that arrived in port under naval escort. While slow-moving convoys had a superior record in terms of protecting the physical safety of goods in transit, some merchants avoided them, preferring to book cargo space on vessels whose owners had announced their intention to forego protection and take their chances on the open seas. Those merchants claimed that a mass of goods simultaneously pouring out of the holds of vessels sailing in convoy produced glutted markets and low prices and that modest insurance rebates were insufficient to compensate for narrow profit margins.

In seventeenth-century London, persons seeking coverage for ships and cargoes secured policies through brokers who conducted business at various coffeehouses that served as news bureaus for the maritime trade and as informal insurance exchanges. Assisted by coffeehouse managers, brokers kept lists of individual underwriters willing and able to provide coverage up to certain monetary limits for specific kinds of risks. To protect themselves from the possibility of excessive losses linked to just one or two accidents at sea, most underwriters adopted the principle of risk diversification. They joined with peers to form a myriad of syndicates, with each participant accepting responsibility for only a portion of a potential loss and earning a proportionate share of the premium. The broker's function was to assemble a group of individual underwriters who, jointly, were able to satisfy the requirements of a shipowner or merchandise trader seeking coverage. Brokerage fees were in the range of .5 percent or less of the policy's value.

In the late seventeenth century, Lloyd's Coffee-House in London became the main meeting place for agents and brokers representing the largest number of private underwriters in the city. In 1720 Parliament granted formal charters to two corporations, London Assurance and Royal Exchange Assurance. They were the only two corporate entities authorized to underwrite marine risks in England throughout most of the eighteenth century.[4] The two corporations shared the marine market with numerous private underwriters who continued to issue policies at the coffeehouse exchanges, of which Lloyd's of London became the most renowned.

In the first half of the eighteenth century, the marine insurance sector centered in London developed very rapidly. Its development was as fast as, or faster, than any other sector of the financial services market. The net result was that during the same decades that London's capital market was emerging as Europe's largest and most sophisticated, the city's marine insurance sector was experiencing parallel advancement. Coverage on British vessels calling at ports throughout the empire was readily available by 1750. London underwriters sometimes covered ships and cargoes owned by the Dutch and other European traders as well; indeed, they offered policies on a large share of the maritime trade of other European sea powers and their colonies around the world. As members of the British Empire, Americans had direct access to those services, and their availability helped to provide underpinnings for the foreign trade sector of the thirteen colonies.

Like their counterparts in the mother country, Americans with shipments destined for overseas ports had limited access to maritime insurance during the seventeenth century. Surviving sources related to the scope of the insurance market in North America in the first century of settlement are extremely thin. Most information arises from sources dated after 1725. Generally speaking, colonial ships that regularly visited British ports, where they were subject to careful inspection to determine seaworthiness, were in the most favorable position to obtain coverage. The same generalization applies to cargoes entering or leaving English ports irrespective of the ownership of the vessel. A greater number of ships calling at southern docks, where they loaded tobacco, rice, and indigo, set sail for London and other British ports than the number routinely serving northern docks, which concentrated on supplying foodstuffs to the Caribbean and southern Europe. Therefore, a greater percentage of the maritime traffic on southern trade routes presumably obtained coverage from London underwriters. *Presumably* is the correct word here because the inference is based on deductive reasoning rather than on any hard data, which is scattered and scant.

By the mid-eighteenth century, when the historical record becomes more revealing, most colonial merchants habitually ordered insurance for shipments on routes deemed eligible for coverage by London underwriters. Americans typically requested insurance through the same British mercantile houses that handled their merchandise account and money balances in the mother country. The London market was highly competitive, and most underwriters charged roughly similar premiums on regular trading routes during peacetime. Whether a few colonial agents may have had the authority to issue policies binding on London underwriters is unknown. A few shippers may have chosen to save money in the short run by foregoing the purchase of maritime policies, in effect deciding by default to become self-insured; but business logic ran against such a strategy over the long term. By 1750 underwriters had determined with a fair amount of accuracy the probability of loss on any given voyage, and the premiums they charged generally reflected the underlying risk. If merchants or planters regularly shipped goods for sustained periods of time, the net financial burden, *on average,* of losses at sea equaled roughly the same amount whether one paid underwriters small amounts periodically in premiums or suffered major setbacks at random when tragedy struck. In the short run, two or three untimely losses could result in lost liquidity and financial ruin. For that reason, prudent colonials immediately took advantage of insurance services as soon as they became widely available. It was not an all-or-nothing proposition; some shippers bought insurance to cover half the value of the property at risk, or some other suitable fraction, and assumed liability for the remainder on their own account.

When premium rates climbed to 50 percent or higher in wartime, or because of the perceived threat of a naval confrontation, some shippers decided to forego coverage and tempt fate. For example, wealthy Philadelphian Stephen Girard, who later purchased the headquarters of the defunct First Bank of the United States and aided the U.S. Treasury in financing the War of 1812, objected strenuously to the high premiums demanded by underwriters in the embargo year of 1808. At such astronomical rates, "I prefer to run the risk of my own property," Girard told one correspondent.[5]

The emergence of an indigenous marine insurance business in the colonies came in the port cities of Philadelphia, Boston, and New York. By the second quarter of the eighteenth century, demand was increasing in northern ports for local underwriting facilities. Many vessels sailing out of northern ports headed southward and rarely, if ever, crossed the Atlantic to undergo inspection at docks in Great Britain, leaving them and their cargoes ineligible for coverage in the London market. Taking advantage of that market opportunity, a few American merchants ventured into the new field of insurance underwriting. The first advertisement in an American newspaper announcing the availability of marine policies underwritten by local merchants—persons unnamed, incidentally—appeared in Philadelphia on 25 May 1721 under the name of agent John Copson in the *American Weekly Merchant*. Copson invited interested shippers to apply for coverage at his office. The announcement claimed that he had made arrangements with several wealthy and responsible persons in the Philadelphia mercantile community who were ready to assume marine risks. But nothing is known about the actual extent of his business.

A similar announcement about the availability of marine coverage was placed by Joseph Marion in several Boston newspapers three years later. Marion was still running advertisements in the *Boston Evening Post* in 1745, claiming that his insurance office had been a going concern for more than two decades. But again no information exists about how many policies were issued at his office or on what terms. By the 1740s other firms had entered the market. According to insurance historian Edward Hardy, the premium rates generally in force in the Boston market in 1743 were: to Maryland, 6 percent; to London, 7 percent; to Guadaloupe, 8 percent; to Jamaica, 10 percent; to Holland, 10 percent; and to Madeira, 12 percent.[6] The rates provided no adjustments for departures at different times of the year, a common practice in London, thus their uniform application may be in doubt. Nonetheless, they provide guidelines suggesting the price structure for marine insurance when the American market was still in its infancy.

The letter book entries of the Beekman firm, a family of prominent New York merchants who diversified into the insurance field, also shed light on the origins of the marine market. The Beekmans were deeply involved in the mercantile life of New York City during the second half of the eighteenth century. Typical all-purpose merchants, they were involved in a multitude of business transactions, including the import and export of a wide range of goods. The Beekmans were simultaneously consumers and suppliers of insurance services. The partners routinely ordered insurance to cover shipments eastward across the Atlantic through the auspices of their London agent. At the same time, they participated as members of local underwriting syndicates for American merchants sailing to the Caribbean; alternatively, when declining to assume certain risks themselves, they acted as intermediaries between reliable out-of-town customers and other resident underwriters.

Three letters from the 1740s illustrate the Beekmans' performance of those three functions. In a letter addressed to the London firm headed by Robert Shaw and William Snell in 1747, Gerard Beekman ordered insurance to cover a shipment of flaxseed to Ireland on the *Four Brothers* and a second policy to cover a return cargo of finished goods from Liverpool. That same year in correspondence with Peleg Thurston, a merchant based in Newport, Rhode Island, Beekman promised prompt payment of three hundred pounds for the loss of the sloop *Defiance* that his firm had underwritten in conjunction with three other New York merchants, among them Philip Van Horne. A few months later, Beekman told Thurston that, because of a war scare in the West Indies, New York underwriters were asking for rates of 30 percent to cover shipments to the Caribbean—a premium Beekman believed unjustifiably steep given the circumstances.[7]

The first organized American marine insurance company with surviving bylaws was formed in Philadelphia in the late 1750s. Six merchants signed the lengthy partnership agreement: Thomas Willing, Charles Stedman, Alexander Stedman, John Kidd, William Coxe, and Robert Morris. The signators were, incidentally, the same Willing who later became president of the Bank of North America and the First Bank of the United States and the same Morris who served as superintendent of finance under the Articles of Confederation. Conducting business under the name Thomas Willing and Company, the partners informed correspondents that their combined fortunes, which were jointly pledged to cover underwriting liabilities, totaled eighty thousand pounds. The partners dissolved the firm within a year, however. Thomas Willing provided an explanation to one correspondent in September 1758: "We are Convinced . . . that Underwrit'g is a bad Business, and are determined to Drop a Company. . . . We dont expect any great Loss more than time & Trouble." He apparently soon changed his mind about the prospects, since a successor firm—Willing, Morris and Company—underwrote policies more or less continuously from 1760 to 1774.[8] Thus, in addition to his significant contributions to the early development of American commercial banking, Morris was also among the developers of the marine insurance field. Morris and Willing maintained a mutually beneficial business relationship for more than four decades with many complementary facets.

By midcentury or thereabouts, the three main northern port cities—Boston, Philadelphia, and New York—possessed the institutional framework to support the rise of an American marine insurance sector. Underwriters conducted business strictly on their own account or in partnership with others. Some mercantile under-writers tended to avoid agent intermediaries, inviting shippers to apply for coverage at their regular counting houses. In other instances, unaligned brokers maintained offices where they arranged policies to suit the requirements of insurer and insured. Insurance brokers rarely underwrote the policies issued through their own offices. The prevailing mechanism in North America was comparable to procedures in the London coffeehouses that catered to the maritime trade. In Boston, Hardy counted 19 different individuals who ran advertisements in local newspapers offering insurance services between 1724 and 1801. In Philadelphia, Harrold Gillingham counted 22 insurance offices between 1721 and 1796 and identified 170 persons who acted as underwriters—both individuals and partnerships—between 1759 and 1788. How many underwriters in the three main ports and other smaller ports participated in the American market in the eighteenth century is anybody's guess, but more than 1,000 names is certainly plausible.

Another clear sign of the rapid development of this financial sector was the emergence of reinsurance within the underwriting community. In a reinsurance transaction, the initial insurers of physical property purchase a second layer of insurance from third-party underwriters to protect themselves from the possibility of suffering extraordinary financial losses. In 1762, for example, Philadelphia underwriter Thomas Ritchie became extremely fearful that a slightly overdue vessel on which he had issued a policy some months previously had been lost at sea. To limit his potential liability, at the last minute so to speak, he paid another underwriter a premium rate 20 percent higher than he had originally collected from the shipper to assume half of his obligations if the worst in fact came to pass. The issuer of the reinsurance policy was lured by the premium bonus and decided to assume the risk. Whether that specific ship arrived in port is unknown and not particularly relevant in this context. The important point is that reinsurance—a policy issued by one underwriter to protect the exposure of another underwriter—was a sophisticated financial technique already in use in the Philadelphia market in the 1760s.

From the seventeenth to the end of the eighteenth century, the cost of marine insurance dropped on the order of 15 to 25 percent on major trade routes in the Atlantic Ocean. The reduced threat of piracy, more seaworthy ships, better navigational maps, and more experienced captains and crews were factors that combined to reduce the risk of losses; and premium rates fell accordingly. Greater competition among underwriters also played a role in giving buyers more for their money. In the previous century, reimbursements typically covered only 75 to 90 percent of actual losses, but by the mid-eighteenth century underwriters gradually assumed liability for 98 to 99 percent of the insured value of lost or damaged property.[9]

By the early 1770s, premium rates on routine shipments from the colonies to ports everywhere in the North Atlantic ranged from 2 to 5 percent, with seasonal variations. Longer, more atypical voyages to the South Atlantic or Pacific oceans elicited higher premiums. Few American merchants actually participated in the slave trade, but for colonial ships sailing to Africa to pick up a cargo and returning to the West Indies in the early 1770s, underwriters sought premiums of 8 to 11 percent on hulls and generally declined to assume any risk for the loss of slave lives in transit. When the China trade began in 1784, the quoted rate was 15 percent, but it fell to 7.5 percent by the end of the decade. Generally, maritime rates were not merely a function of the distance traveled. In peacetime more losses resulted from shipwrecks along shorelines than from flooded vessels on the high seas—excepting the losses during tropical hurricanes. Premiums skyrocketed during the War for Independence and in all confrontations involving naval powers. In the months just before the signing of the peace treaty in 1783, the rate on goods bound for France was reportedly as high as 55 percent.

After the adoption of the Constitution, state governments were anxious to develop a local insurance sector. Unlike the political debates related to the establishment of some commercial banks, the creation of corporations to issue insurance policies was rarely controversial. Marine underwriting steadily passed out of the hands of proprietorships and partnerships and into the arms of incorporated enterprises holding charters from state legislatures. Few firms were closely held; most had hundreds of shareholders. Initial share offerings were sold at low to moderate prices in many instances to encourage widespread public ownership and support. Organized insurance companies with vast financial resources and hundreds of stockholders captured an increasing share of the maritime market.

Numerous marine insurance companies received corporate charters between 1790 and 1815. The list in table 13.1 (see page 300) is not comprehensive since some mixed companies—fire, life, marine—specialized mainly in marine policies. The former system of private syndicate underwriting, which had prevailed in the colonial era and which was perpetuated in London, gave way in the United States to competition from corporate enterprises that mobilized large amounts of capital to meet potential loss liabilities. Most customers concluded that organized institutions with large capitalization possessed superior financial resources to pay extensive claims in the event of catastrophe; and, under the leadership of ambitious entrepreneurs, chartered insurance companies proliferated to meet the increasing demand. Some private parties who were already established in the field continued to underwrite risks in conjunction with marine brokerage offices after the turn of the century, but few new faces entered the market. Shippers preferred the new companies over private individuals even though the former had acquired the privilege of limited liability whereas the latter still did business under the rule of unlimited liability, personal as well as business.

Fire Insurance

Fire insurance was a highly innovative financial service that made a major impact on the American economy in the early national period. In contrast to the long lineage of marine coverage, fire coverage has relatively modern origins, having become available to a large number of property holders for the first time in England only about four hundred years ago. Fire insurance was also different from marine coverage because its initial market was consumer households, not business enterprises. It arose to cover structures at risk primarily in the residential market, not mercantile inventories or workplaces, although business properties became eligible for coverage in the early eighteenth century. The coming of fire insurance occasioned the emergence of a radically new form of business organization: the mutual company. Not owned by proprietors, stockholders, or government, the mutual company was owned instead by the policyholders themselves. Mutuals were cooperative, self-help enterprises; their civic-minded sponsors often stayed around to manage the companies as salaried employees. In addition, some fire insurance companies became financial intermediaries by accumulating substantial reserve funds, which were available for longer term loans and investments in stocks and bonds. Fire insurance companies were innovative in other ways. Some signed up large numbers of part-time brigades to battle blazes endangering insured properties, and they purchased pumps, hoses, ladders, and other fire-fighting equipment to aid in the efforts. Those public-safety functions were subsequently absorbed by municipal governments in the nineteenth century.

The first fire insurance companies were English, which helps to explain why the institutional mechanism for spreading the risk of financial losses associated with accidental conflagrations crossed to American shores so quickly. Protection against fire hazards was one of the new products associated with the consumer revolution that swept through eighteenth-century England. Fire policies were initially issued in the major urban areas but soon spread to rural markets as well. The firms that issued fire insurance policies were unique at the time because of the grand scale of their operations and the long periods over which customers contracted for their services. Excepting the postal system, which was primarily a governmental function, the earliest American fire insurance company, which was begun in Philadelphia in the 1750s, can claim the distinction of being the first large privately managed business enterprise in North America.

The inspiration for fire insurance as a modern financial service arose from a colossal tragedy: the Great Fire of London in 1666, which raged for four days and destroyed thirteen thousand houses inhabited by rich and poor. The idea of establishing some type of compensation system to protect residents against potential fire hazards in London actually predated the Great Fire, but organizers were unable to mount a successful drive to get the project off the ground. Prospective entrepreneurs had long ago concluded that large urban areas, where fire risks could be spread among several thousand structures, held out the best prospect for launching a successful venture. In 1638 Charles I granted a royal patent to William Ryley and Edward Mabb to establish a fire insurance company to serve London and its suburbs. The decree gave the two men monopoly rights for the next forty years; but the English Civil War intervened, and they failed to solicit enough subscribers to start the projected enterprise.

Compared to marine insurance, fire insurance was slow to emerge because the organizational requirements were much more formidable. The underwriters of marine policies assumed risks for a fairly short time, typically measured in terms of weeks or months—from the start of a specific voyage to its termination at a designated port. The owners of homes and rental properties, in contrast, thought about fire coverage in a totally different time frame—in terms of years and even decades. Independent marine underwriters working through brokers could enter and exit the maritime market every six months or so without damaging its overall structure, but maintaining the stability of a market for fire insurance was another matter altogether. Consumers expected a greater sense of commitment and permanence. Households wanted to insure their properties for longer periods, and they wanted greater assurances that the underwriters would still be present five to ten years later, or longer, to pay any claim. In an era when proprietorships and partnerships were tied strictly to the lifetimes of participants, few business entities had the organizational capacity to offer customers the prospect of longevity. Only entities with royal charters possessed the privilege of perpetuity, and Parliament granted few corporate charters to business enterprises during the seventeenth and eighteenth centuries.

After the London catastrophe, the first measures adopted to reduce fire risk and promote public safety were municipal building codes that encouraged brick and stone construction and restricted housing density. The events of 1666 had proven conclusively that a fire anywhere in the city was a potential threat to every household in every neighborhood irrespective of location. In the rebuilt city, the actual risk of fire was substantially reduced, which held out the prospect of lower premiums than what would have been required to provide similar coverage before 1666. During the next half century, the demand for fire insurance steadily increased while the rates for coverage kept falling—leading to the birth and rapid expansion of this financial service.

Beginning in the 1670s scattered evidence suggests that a few private underwriters began issuing fire protection policies on brick and stone buildings on an ad hoc basis. But the haphazard system of issuing fire policies by unorganized private parties was actuarially unsound and short-lived. Among the early underwriters was Nicholas Barbon, who had been one of the principal general contractors in the reconstruction of London and who frequently issued policies to owners of homes that he had built. Barbon was the prime mover behind the formation of the city's first fire insurance company in 1681, called simply the Fire Office. A joint-stock company that sought profits for investors, the Fire Office offered coverage for a minimum term of seven years, with initial premium rates of 2.5 percent annually for brick houses and 5 percent for wooden residences. Policyholders also had the option of prepaying for coverage lasting up to thirty-one years at rates discounted by two-thirds. The rates were high given the reduced risk of fire, and when competitors arrived on the scene a few years later, premium rates started falling dramatically.

By the mid-1680s Barbon claimed to have insured four thousand houses in the London area, and the enterprise was a going concern. Barbon recruited a brigade of fire fighters and marked insured houses with the firm's symbol for quick identification. After three years of operations, the firm had collected eighteen thousand pounds in premiums and paid out seven thousand pounds in claims. The Fire Office received a royal charter in 1688, which limited the liability of investors in the event of any huge losses such as a conflagration similar to the massive fire twenty years earlier. The firm later changed its name to the Phenix, and it remained in business until the mid-eighteenth century when competitive pressures dictated closure.

In 1683, two years after the establishment of the Fire Office, the Friendly Society for Securing Houses from Loss by Fire entered the London market. At its inception under the leadership of William Hale and Henry Spelman, the Friendly Society, despite its charitable name, was a profit-seeking firm. What was different in this case was the use of a clever marketing technique: the solicitation of memberships in an ongoing society. Once they had joined the private club, which was designed to provide a permanent customer base to spread risks, members could look forward to perpetual coverage on insured structures.

Persons joining the Friendly Society paid an initiation fee of 0.003333 of the face value of the policy, plus an annual premium of 0.000666. To cover a residence valued at £1,000, for example, the cost was £3.333 up front, plus two-thirds of a pound annually. (Those premium rates were for brick and stone residences; the numbers doubled for wooden frames.) Members were also contingently liable for an additional assessment of up to 1.5 percent of their policy value in the event of a rash of losses. Assessments, when necessary, were generally modest and never approached the maximum. Coverage was continuous until a member withdrew from the society. Members who resigned got back their initial fees, but the company kept the interest earned during the intervening period.

In 1696 a nontraditional competitor came on the scene with a nontraditional name. Called the Amicable Contributors for Insuring Houses from Loss by Fire, which indicated its self-help orientation, this London society's structure revealed a sharp departure from any financial service enterprise that had ever existed anywhere around the globe. A few years later its name was altered to a simpler title, Hand-in-Hand, after the symbol routinely displayed on its house markings. Hand-in-Hand was organized as a mutual company—a nonprofit, cooperative venture that blended the goals and functions of charitable organizations and mainstream business enterprises. The insurer and insured, acting in unison, were one and the same—a variation on the strategy of self-insurance. Policyholders were invited to general meetings held at least twice annually to vote on critical issues, among them the election of twenty directors who assumed the position of trustees. The directors engaged managers to run operations. Profits were distributed to policyholders as dividends, with payments divided according to the face value of the policies in force. By 1704 the company had issued more than seven thousand policies, the vast majority on brick and stone properties. The formation of Hand-in-Hand, the first mutual insurance company, marks the emergence on a significant scale of the nonprofit enterprise—a cooperative venture competing somewhat incongruously with profit-oriented firms in a predominantly capitalist economy.

By 1720, several additional fire insurance companies had been established in Great Britain, mutuals as well as profit-seeking enterprises. The two corporations that Parliament chartered in 1720 to issue marine policies—Royal Exchange and London Assurance—added fire insurance subsidiaries a year later. Companies sprang up in Bristol and Edinburgh. The policies they issued did not guarantee to cover the replacement cost of insured property, which became common practice in the United States in the late twentieth century. Underwriters were reluctant to promise replacement cost, irrespective of the face value of the policy, because of the incentive for arson by owners living in homes in deteriorating physical condition or located in deteriorating neighborhoods. Instead, they paid the estimated cash value at the time of loss.

The urban-based firms eventually extended coverage to rural residences and even recruited local fire fighters to help protect properties at risk. Home furnishings as well as structures became eligible for coverage. Mercantile inventories, factory buildings, and other commercial properties were likewise added to the risk pool. By the end of the first quarter of the eighteenth century, the fire insurance sector of the British economy, like the marine insurance sector, was well organized and well along the road to maturation.

The earliest fire insurance companies organized in North America were patterned on the model of the mutual society. The very first company had a short, unsuccessful history. The Friendly Society was organized in Charleston, South Carolina, in 1735. A huge blaze got out of control and spread from street to street in 1741, destroying most of the homes, which were predominantly wooden, in its path. The massive claims wiped out the company's modest financial resources; the venture went bankrupt and wound up its affairs.

The second attempt to establish a fire insurance company proved more lasting. Its main sponsor was Benjamin Franklin. After returning to Philadelphia in 1726 from a two-year sojourn in England, Franklin became a devoted advocate of improving the city's firefighting capabilities. City government was not unaware or unresponsive to the threat of fire, and it began appropriating funds for the acquisition of fire equipment in the 1720s and 1730s. Simultaneously, volunteer organizations of fire fighters sprang up in various neighborhoods. In 1750 Franklin spearheaded the plan to transform his local fire brigade into an organization that also provided insurance coverage. Initially, the Union Fire Company offered policies only to households that were active members of the local voluntary fire company.

Two years later, in 1752, the insurance company expanded its market and began offering policies throughout the city, thereby acquiring the economies of scale necessary for long-term survival. Renamed the Philadelphia Contributionship for the Insurance of Houses from Loss by Fire, the firm adopted the mutual ownership organizational structure inspired by Hand-in-Hand in London. Policyholders annually elected twelve directors to oversee operations. Before issuing a new policy, every structure was carefully inspected and brought up to fire safety standards. Premium rates were modest and roughly in line with the losses experienced.

The firm prospered and endured. By 1781 it had in force about two thousand policies covering properties valued at approximately $2 million in the Philadelphia area. In terms of the numbers of households regularly served, no other business enterprise in the colonies probably had a larger customer base. A man of innumerable talents, Franklin deserves special recognition for his entrepreneurial contributions as founder and dedicated overseer of this pathbreaking enterprise. Despite its shining example, no other similarly successful fire insurance company was organized anywhere in North America until after the War for Independence.

Beginning in the 1780s and 1790s, and accelerating rapidly after the turn of the century, the United States witnessed the establishment of numerous fire insurance companies, both mutuals and profit-seeking firms. Between 1794 and 1799 more than twenty-five firms received charters from state legislatures. The two organizational forms flourished side by side, which suggests to economic historians that the overall insurance packages offered to customers by mutuals and nonmutuals, their mix of premium rates and the quality of claim services rendered, were highly competitive. Otherwise, one of the two ownership patterns would have soon driven the other from the marketplace. The dual ownership system persists in insurance markets to this day. The mutual ownership system was confined to firms dealing strictly in fire insurance, however. As mentioned previously, many profit-oriented general insurance companies issued both marine and fire policies—a marketing strategy that proved harmonious in most instances.

The major urban centers along the Atlantic Coast were the headquarters of the largest number of firms issuing fire policies; but medium-sized inland towns such as Richmond, Virginia, and Hartford, Connecticut, attracted companies as well.[10] As the insurance field matured over the years, the number of risk classifications broadened considerably. Premium rates on structures varied according to construction materials, roof flammability, nearby landscaping, geographic location, and other critical risk factors. By the turn of the century, most rates fell within the range of .5 to 1 percent annually. Many firms insured rural as well as urban properties in order to generate a large and diversified risk pool. In 1800 Thomas Jefferson insured Monticello, his mountaintop home near Charlottesville, with Richmond Mutual Assurance Society, taking out four thousand dollars to cover the main house plus another thousand dollars for the outer buildings. While it was difficult to anticipate much help from organized fire brigades in fighting blazes in remote areas, a distinct advantage of rural properties was their relative immunity from the threat of wind-whipped flames leaping from nearby structures as often happened in densely settled urban areas.

Some newly formed fire insurance companies accumulated substantial cash reserves and joined commercial banks as financial intermediaries. Most banks focused on short-term loans to merchants, although there were frequent renewals and other exceptions to the normal lending rules. Cash-rich insurance companies invested in mortgages, other loans with longer maturities, public securities, and occasionally in the common stocks of commercial banks. The fire insurance company in Philadelphia, for example, had £7,090 out on loan in 1773.[11] Few governmental regulations dictated the composition of insurance company investment portfolios, leaving managers free to exercise their best judgment in choosing among the alternatives. As far as is known, no insurance company was forced to default on its obligations to policyholders because of bad investments prior to 1815.

One of the new companies organized in the postwar era instituted an innovative premium collection policy that had significant long-term repercussions. The Mutual Assurance Company, Philadelphia's second fire insurance firm formed in 1784, offered households a new type of policy beginning in 1800: a perpetual policy financed by a singular, prepaid premium. The upfront cost was relatively high, but after initial payment, policyholders were scheduled to make no annual payments for years thereafter—and, if everything progressed according to plan, possibly never again. Since financial resources at the outset were far in excess of anticipated claims during the next several years, the premiums collected from members created a substantial reserve fund.

Some marine underwriters in London may have established substantial reserve funds prior to 1800 so it is impossible to cite fire companies as the unchallenged pioneers, but the latter seem to have acted as financial intermediaries in a more systematic and sustained manner. In the case of the Mutual Assurance Company, the reserve fund was invested in various financial instruments, and the interest and dividends on the portfolio investments accumulated over time and became a form of retained earnings accruing for the benefit of policyholders. If the earnings on investments held steady and claims arising from fire losses were not abnormally high because of extraordinary conflagrations, coverage remained in force without the necessity of assessing additional premiums on policyholders.

Life Insurance

Some of the general insurance companies that received legislative charters between 1790 and 1815 obtained the right to issue

TABLE 13.1
American Insurance Companies, 1735–1810

Philadelphia
  1752   Philadelphia Contributionship
  1784   Mutual Assurance Co.
  1794   Insurance Co. of North America
  1794   Insurance Co. of the State of Pennsylvania
  1803   Phoenix Insurance Co.
  1803   Philadelphia Insurance Co.
  1804   Delaware Insurance Co.
  1804   Union Insurance Co.
  1809   Marine and Fire Insurance Co.
  1810   United States Insurance Co.

New York
  1787   Knickerbocker Fire Insurance Co.
  1796   New York Insurance Co.
  1796   Insurance Co. of New York
  1797   Associated Underwriters
  1797   United Insurance Co.
  1800   Columbian Insurance Co.
  1802   Washington Mutual
  1802   Marine Insurance Co.
  1804   Commercial Insurance Co.
  1807   Phoenix Insurance Co.
  1810   Fireman's Insurance Co.
  1810   Ocean Insurance Co.

Boston
  1795   Massachusetts Fire and Marine Co.
  1799   Boston Marine Insurance Co.

Baltimore
  1794   Baltimore Equitable Society
  1796   Charitable Marine Society

Norwich
  1795   Mutual Assurance Co.

New Haven
  1797   New Haven Insurance Co.

Hartford
  1810   Hartford Fire Insurance Co.

Charleston
  1735   Friendly Society
  1797   Charleston Insurance Co.

Sources: Compiled from data in Huebner, "Development of Marine Insurance";
Gillingham, *Marine Insurance in Philadelphia;* Hardy, *Early Insurance Offices.*
Note: Representative list of companies, not complete.

TABLE 13.2
Investment in Insurance Companies, 1792–1806

	Number of firms	Capital	% Change in Capital
1792	1	$ 600,000	
1794	4	1,200,000	100
1796	8	3,000,000	250
1798	9	3,000,000	—
1800	15	5,000,000	60
1802	29	7,500,000	50
1804	40	10,000,000	33
1806	50	15,000,000	50

Source: Mary Elizabeth Ruwell, "Eighteenth-Century Capitalism: The Formation of American Marine Insurance Companies," (Ph.D. diss., University of Pennsylvania, 1989), p. 109.

life insurance policies in addition to marine and fire. The policies were strictly term insurance with no forced-saving component to build cash-surrender value included in the premium as became more common after the mid-nineteenth century. Consumer demand for term life insurance proved extremely limited through the 1810s, however. The Insurance Company of North America, a large capital-stock firm founded in Philadelphia in the early 1790s, wrote only a handful of life policies during the next decade. The first company expressly organized for that purpose, the Pennsylvania Company for Insurance on Lives and Granting Annuities, was not incorporated until 1812, and sales were initially slow. This field of insurance remained in its infancy throughout the early national period.

Under the circumstances, a full-blown discussion of the origins and development of life insurance seems unwarranted in a book focusing mainly on the period from 1700 to 1815. This form of financial protection from the disruption of an income stream due to death only caught on with consumers beginning in the 1840s, and sales climbed rapidly thereafter. Suffice it to say that historians have traced the calculation of reasonably accurate mortality tables back as far as Roman times and discovered policies underwritten on lives for relatively short periods of time, typically one or two years at most. Several European governments used updated mortality tables as guides in the sale of life annuities to investors in the early modern period. In 1693 Sir Edmund Halley, for whom the famous comet is named, created one of the first scientific mortality tables based on an analysis of the municipal death records of Breslau, now in Poland, from 1687 to 1691. The Amicable Society for a Perpetual Assurance, a mutual company, began operations in London in 1706. Subscribers between the ages of twelve and forty-five paid an entrance fee and five pounds annually, with the benefits to survivors increasing over time. Edward Wigglesworth calculated one of the first American mortality tables for insurance purposes in 1793 from a sample of nearly five thousand recent deaths.

Particularly when it came to insuring human lives, many critics expressed concerns about the morality of the enterprise because of the financial rewards accruing to beneficiaries when another suffered the ultimate misfortune. In England after 1700, for example, some private underwriters regularly sold short-term policies, usually expiring in twelve months or less, on the lives of prominent politicians and other famous public figures. Speculators were eager buyers until the practice of sales to disinterested third parties —that is, to persons unrelated either by blood or marriage or without any formal business connections—was outlawed in 1774. Criticisms that life insurance underwriting was simply another form of gambling and not, therefore, a legitimate business venture were repeated in many quarters, especially religious quarters, starting in the eighteenth century and lasting well into the early twentieth century.

Despite its relative unimportance before 1815, two aspects of the development of life insurance are pertinent to this discussion and deserve some attention. First, the very earliest policies on lives were offshoots of marine underwriting. In addition to insuring vessels and cargoes, underwriters sometimes assumed risks on ship passengers—frequently a wealthy merchant accompanying his goods overseas or perhaps a close relative in transit. The main motive for purchasing the policies was far removed from our modern concept of life insurance, however; customers were thinking mainly in terms of financial protection to pay ransom demands.

The irregular marine policies were designed to spare the lives, or lengthy imprisonment, of wealthy persons captured by pirates or a belligerent political unit. If the worst came true, the proceeds went to the captors to gain the prisoner's release. By relying on ransom insurance, the captured merchant hoped to regain his freedom without impoverishing his family or business associates in the process. Like standard marine policies, the insurance was in force only for a limited period—strictly the length of the voyage or round-trip travel, typically just a matter of weeks or months.

The second pertinent fact was the establishment in 1759 of the Corporation for Relief of Poor and Distressed Widows and Children of Presbyterian Ministers. The organization was established by the Presbyterian synods in New York and Pennsylvania to insure the lives of their ministers. A similar corporation for Episcopalian ministers in the colonies arrived a decade later. Some financial historians have dismissed the organizations as essentially charitable in purpose and thus not legitimate precursors of modern insurance companies. Other scholars have labeled them "half-charitable, half-insurance" institutions. According to Viviana Zelizer, both "were structured very much as life insurance companies, except that they dealt with a specialized clientele and received gift contributions." [12] Subscribing ministers paid premiums based on existing mortality tables; additional monetary gifts to the fund from parishioners went primarily to assist the widows and children of deceased clergy who never bothered to take out a policy or who let their coverage lapse.

Conclusion

In addition to commercial banks, insurance companies organized as profit-seeking enterprises attracted large investments in their common stock. The Insurance Company of North America, founded in Philadelphia in 1792, began with a capital of $600,000; shares were priced at only $10 each and payable in installments to encourage widespread ownership. By 1806 investments in U.S. insurance companies exceeded $15 million. Unlike commercial banks, which attracted a large number of foreign investors, more than 90 percent of the capital invested in the insurance sector was domestic. Many U.S. investors in banks also owned shares in local insurance companies and served simultaneously on their respective boards of directors. Indeed, the vast majority of American capital invested in corporate enterprises from 1790 to 1815 was in firms that specialized in the provision of financial services. Commercial banks and marine and fire insurance companies were the first genuinely modern business enterprises in the United States.

Some of the large enterprises organized to underwrite maritime risks, including the Insurance Company of North America, one of the nation's first large corporate enterprises, were so-called general insurance companies. In addition to marine policies, they extended the scope of their operations to include fire and life insurance coverage as well. The creation of the general insurance company was an American innovation, an organizational schema unduplicated in London or elsewhere.

14

Lotteries, Securities, and Foreign Exchange

THIS CHAPTER focuses on three distinct financial markets: lottery tickets, stocks and bonds, and bills of exchange drawn in British pounds and other European currencies. The services were typically performed by separate enterprises, but a fair number of exceptions could be cited too—instances of institutional overlapping, particularly after 1790. Some private firms, for example, dealt in all three instruments. Lotteries were one popular means of financing public and private projects in an era when taxes were generally low and capital markets nonexistent or extremely immature. The rise of a national debt, beginning with the securities issued during the War for Independence and accelerating in the 1780s and 1790s, created new opportunities for specialists engaged in the brokerage field. Organized securities markets, with voluntarily agreed-upon trading rules governing the activities of the main participants, blossomed in the major financial centers in the 1790s, with New York leading the way. Other entrepreneurs in the largest port cities turned to developing more active markets for bills of exchange drawn in foreign currencies.

Lotteries

Lotteries were another feature of the financial landscape in the colonial and early national eras. Lotteries fell out of favor with public opinion later in the nineteenth century under the relentless pressure of the moral reform movement, but they made a major comeback in the late twentieth century, and for some of the very same reasons that had led to their previous popularity—which only goes to prove that, in human affairs, many practices once discredited later experience a rebirth and eventually come full circle. In the colonial period, lotteries were held regularly to serve both private and public purposes. The monies raised went to aid churches, charities, and schools or to provide funding for public projects at both the local and provincial levels.

With the exception of the Quakers, a minority everywhere beyond the borders of Pennsylvania, almost no organized group objected to lotteries on moral or religious grounds. The sale and purchase of lottery tickets was widely accepted as a normal social activity that aided the community. By the late eighteenth century, most private firms that provided brokerage services related to stocks, bonds, and foreign exchange also handled lottery tickets. Many citizens claimed there were only slight differences between the risks associated with buying lottery tickets and investing in stocks and bonds—a belief held by some financially unsophisticated people to this day.

Like so many of the financial services discussed in this book, lotteries have a long lineage dating back to Roman times, or even earlier. Buying a relatively inexpensive chance in a lottery, with the prospect of personal gain at long odds or, more likely, benefiting a worthwhile cause or the government treasury in the event of loss, has proven a popular fund-raising device in different societies around the world for hundreds of years. In the early modern period, Francis I of France was among the first reigning monarchs to tap into this lucrative source of public revenue beginning in 1539. Across the channel, Queen Elizabeth authorized a public lottery in England in 1566. When the Virginia Company, which planted a settlement at Jamestown in 1607, ran into serious money problems in 1612, it petitioned the crown for relief and received in return a new charter that granted the privilege of organizing lotteries to ease the financial burden. The company sold lottery tickets for a series of drawings for several years thereafter; in 1621 lottery proceeds of eight thousand pounds accounted for more than 40 percent of the company's net revenues. After 1709 the Exchequer of the Treasury and a vast array of smaller promoters throughout the country, private and public, were routinely in competition to attract lottery ticket customers. In response to complaints about alleged fraud and mismanagement, Parliament voted in 1721 to force all organizers to obtain licenses and conform to official regulations regarding lottery operations.

In the North American colonies, religious organizations and local governments were the main organizers of lotteries before the 1740s. Most private lotteries sought authorization from provincial legislatures before proceeding to issue tickets and announce drawings. Eventually, provincial governments themselves turned to lotteries as a means of generating revenues. Supporters hailed lotteries as an alternative to raising taxes that applied to the general public. Massachusetts was the first colony to take the plunge in 1744, with lottery proceeds used to assist in the military campaign against the French in Nova Scotia. The legislature hoped to raise £7,500 through the sale of tickets with a face value of £37,500, which translated into a 20 percent profit for governmental coffers. The lottery was a popular success and was soon imitated in other locales, particularly by Rhode Island officials.

By the 1770s all thirteen colonies had some experience with lotteries, with New Englanders leading the way. Only South Carolina and Georgia recorded no officially authorized ticket sales and drawings. The Virginia, Maryland, and Delaware legislatures approved just one each, and North Carolina only two. Even in those six colonies, churches and various charities held unlicensed drawings to raise funds. According to historian John Ezell, the number of lotteries receiving official recognition from 1744 to 1775 was much higher in the northern colonies: Connecticut held nineteen lotteries to raise more than £15,000; Massachusetts held twenty-two for more than £60,000; New Hampshire held eight for more than £14,000; New Jersey held seven for £7,550; New York held fifteen for more than £37,000; and Pennsylvania authorized five lotteries to raise more than £13,500. Rhode Island was the undisputed leader with more than eighty approved drawings to raise 190,000 in proclamation pounds and another 14,600 denominated in dollars.

For the most part, lottery proceeds provided a mechanism of raising monies to fund projects deemed too costly for local governments or beyond the immediate capacities of private organizations. Without commercial banks and other financial intermediaries to draw on as a source of funding, lotteries filled some of the gaps in the uneven financial system. Ezell classified the beneficiaries of 171 readily identifiable lottery-financed projects as follows: 58 were for internal improvements such as bridges, road repair, paving; 39 aided city and county governments; 27 were for churches; 19 for poor relief; 13 for schools; 10 for provincial governments, and 5 to benefit local industries—for example, a forge destroyed by fire. In Rhode Island in 1758, Joseph Fox was permitted to organize a lottery for the purpose of paying off three thousand pounds in personal debts, and presumably avoiding thereby debtors' prison.

In the summer of 1769, Parliament tried to discourage the practice of holding lotteries in the royal colonies. A circular letter went out to ten governors instructing them to decline to sign any bill authorizing a new lottery for whatever purpose without submitting the legislation to the Board of Trade for approval. The tone of the letter implied that approval would likely be withheld in the event applications were forthcoming. The text cited two main reasons for the imperial effort to curb lotteries: allegations of fraud and mismanagement plus broader considerations of the public welfare. The letter read in part: "such practice doth tend to disengage those who become adventurers therein from that spirit of industry and attention to their proper callings."[1] The colonists claimed the text reeked of hypocrisy since Parliament itself had scheduled annual lotteries for more than half a century to raise money for the crown.

The loudest critics asserted that the parliamentary directive was part and parcel of the overall plan to subject the colonies to arbitrary rule and, according to their analysis, the attempted prohibition of lotteries was simply another nail to close the coffin on freedom and self-government. If restricting colonial rights was indeed a prime motive, the plan was largely ineffective, since between 1769 and 1775 Rhode Island alone authorized thirty-five drawings. Connecticut scheduled another seven, and New York and New Jersey recognized one lottery apiece.

During the war years and throughout the confederation period, lotteries maintained their public appeal. Congress approved legislation in 1776 to raise a planned $1 million to pay for troops in the field through the sale of 100,000 tickets, with listed prizes running from $20 to $50,000. But sales were dreadfully slow, and little money was generated by the national government from that source. On the other hand, private lotteries to support worthy public and private projects went forward as usual at the state and local levels. Ezell counted at least eighty authorized drawings during the 1780s, with all thirteen states represented. Massachusetts and Rhode Island were again the leaders; but the Virginia legislature was active too, endorsing twelve lotteries for various improvements, including five schools and academies.

After the adoption of the Constitution, the most important institutional change in this field was the involvement of ticket brokers. They assumed some of the functions formerly performed by unpaid volunteers. The entrepreneurs expanded the size of the lottery market from its reliance on prospective buyers in a restricted locality to include customers throughout a region and sometimes much of the nation. Brokers bought huge lots of tickets at discount prices and then sold them to the general public through commission agents. By 1815 every town with more than one thousand inhabitants had agents who sold and traded lottery tickets. Solomon Allen, son of a Presbyterian minister, began selling tickets in Albany, New York, in 1808, and soon thereafter established a firm called S. Allen's Lottery and Exchange Office. A few years later he formed a partnership with his brother Moses and opened a branch in New York City titled Allen's Truly Lucky Office. By the 1820s the firm had outlets in nine major cities—as far south as Savannah and as far west as Pittsburgh. In addition to issuing and trading lottery tickets, the firm's outlets bought and sold bank notes drawn on out-of-town institutions, usually referred to by contemporaries as domestic exchange—a term used to distinguish those monies from foreign bills of exchange denominated in different currencies.

Some ticket brokers also sold what contemporaries called "insurance" or "policy" in connection with lottery drawings. Public drawings often extended over days or weeks, and the uncertainty prompted some persons to issue contracts that became operational contingent on whether certain numbers turned up or were left behind. Some purchasers of a block of tickets, fearing that none or few of their holdings might be drawn, hedged their position, so to speak, by negotiating a contract with underwriters providing for at least partial compensation—paying an appropriate premium for the service. In other instances, some speculators took chances on the numbers by trading tickets or ticket options while the drawing was ongoing. This latter activity was little short of outright gambling, although some people with knowledge of crude probability theory may have achieved an advantage over others. Today, we might classify those financial contracts somewhere within the broad category of futures options. The existence of such sophisticated mechanisms demonstrates how far financial services techniques had advanced by the first decade of the nineteenth century.

Stocks and Bonds

Among the new financial services to develop in conjunction with the emergence of an expanded capital market in the quarter century after the ratification of the Constitution were increased brokerage facilities for the exchange of securities among private parties. Brokers acted as intermediaries who arranged the purchase and sale of transferable securities already in the hands of investors—in what today is the secondary market. In that era, few brokers had the opportunity to perform investment banking services, namely assisting original issuers in the floatation of securities.[2] They did, however, become involved in trading the subscription rights to forthcoming issues. Current knowledge about the activities of securities brokers in the early national period arises mainly from scholarly studies of the New York market, the most prominent source being Walter Werner and Steven Smith's *Wall Street* published in 1991. Parallel activities were presumably taking place in Philadelphia and Boston, but they have not as yet been well documented.

From 1780 through 1815 the vast majority of traded securities were either U.S. government bonds or the common shares of commercial banks and insurance companies. Today the terms *shares* and *stock* are used interchangeably in reference to equities, but in the eighteenth century many contemporaries referred to public debt obligations as "government stock." Unless explicitly defined, a vague reference to stocks by contemporaries in the early national period could mean either equity shares or public debt. When critics complained about the alleged evils inflicted on society by the actions of "stockjobbers," they often meant persons who speculated in bonds as well as the shares of private firms. Securities brokers in New York City, and probably to an unknown extent in other leading commercial centers, occasionally ventured into much more speculative transactions such as futures contracts, short sales, and put and call options. In comparison with the growth of the U.S. capital market in later decades—starting with the boom in railroad securities after 1840—the trading volume in the early national era was relatively thin. However, in terms of the strategies employed by traders in swapping various types of financial instruments and the manipulative devices at their disposal, the markets were surprisingly advanced and highly sophisticated almost from the date of their emergence in the early 1790s.

The origins of modern capital markets are usually traced back to northern Italy in the thirteenth and fourteenth centuries; and from that base the techniques of issuing and trading various types of financial instruments migrated to northern Europe, where they were further refined. Financial historian Larry Neal has explored the rise of capital markets in Amsterdam and London from the sixteenth through the eighteenth centuries in a recently published book.[3] In addition to dissecting the tulip mania in Holland in the 1630s and the South Sea Bubble in England during the 1710s, Neal and his scholarly predecessors have demonstrated that many of the speculative techniques so prevalent today, mostly variations on futures and options contracts, were already routine transactions hundreds of years ago in the most advanced European financial centers.

In England, Parliament periodically cracked down on the most speculative types of financial activity. Most of the prohibitions were not directed at persons who actually took possession of securities, whether for long-term investment purposes or in the hope of making quick profits from short-term price movements. Instead, the restrictions were enacted primarily to curb transactions in futures, options, warrants, and other speculative devices that were appendages of capital markets. An Act to Prevent the Infamous Practice of Stock-Jobbing passed in 1734 and was known thereafter as Sir Barnard's Act in recognition of its prime sponsor. By the mid-eighteenth century, many similarities existed between the speculative activities promoted by brokers who dealt in securities and life insurance brokers who offered short-term policies to third parties on the lives of famous persons. For example, a daring speculator might decide to buy an insurance policy on the life of the current prime minister for the next six months. Alternatively, he might choose to purchase an option giving him the right to buy or sell a certain number of shares of a regularly traded security at an established price over roughly the same six-month period. In both instances, the speculator was taking a chance on the outcome of future events over which he presumably had no direct control. Critics asserted that persons who dealt in futures and options were not genuine investors and thus illegitimate participants in the operations of financial markets; but defenders countered that argument by claiming that the activities of speculators in peripheral, complementary areas helped to keep the mainstream securities markets functioning more smoothly.[4]

The unabashedly speculative sphere of the London market elicited loud public protests in the eighteenth century. Parliamentary efforts to curb speculative excesses by attacking the legitimacy of futures and options were ineffective, however. Restrictive laws simply drove the activities into other channels. Debts incurred in trading illicit financial instruments became uncollectable in the courts—falling into the same category as other gambling obligations—but trading in futures and options persisted based on mutual trust among participants. Except for denying access to the courts, the government did little to enforce the laws applicable to questionable financial transactions. A review of English precedent is pertinent here because several decades later similarly inspired legislative initiatives, designed to outlaw trading in various forms of futures contracts, were enacted in New York. Predictably, the response of brokers and their customers emulated the response of their counterparts in London; the speculative transactions persisted, but out of the public eye and without resort to the adjudication powers of the legal system.

Throughout the entire colonial period, no specialized securities brokers functioned in North America. Colonial business enterprises did not issue stocks, bonds, or transferable partnership shares. Few Americans held British securities, and those who did traded through the auspices of their London agents. Although the four New England colonies routinely issued two-year treasury notes after midcentury, most buyers held the investments to their maturity dates. Some transfers undoubtedly occurred, but they were isolated transactions negotiated without the assistance of recognized intermediaries. Futures and options contracts were nonexistent. As outposts of the empire, the colonies were thus exempt from the potential corruptions of aggressive stockjobbing and speculation— a decided advantage in the minds of many citizens who were subsequently drawn into the ideological camp of Jeffersonian republicanism.

The first American firms to advertise their willingness to act as securities brokers on a commission basis date back to the 1780s. Joshua Eaton placed an announcement in the Boston papers in 1784, while Archibald Blair was listed as a securities broker in a New York City business directory published in 1786. The exact securities traded are unknown but those individuals were likely involved in exchanges of the overhanging wartime debts of the federal government and the several states. By the mid-1780s the principal and accrued interest were somewhere in the neighborhood of $50 million, although the market value of the combined domestic debt was substantially less, perhaps as little as $10 to $15 million. According to financial historian E. James Ferguson, trading in the various public debt issues was common in major commercial centers throughout the nation.[5] Several prominent mercantile houses in New York and Philadelphia became aggressive purchasers of state and federal debt certificates—among them William Constable, Robert Morris, Gouverneur Morris, Andrew Craigie, Herman LeRoy, and William Bayard. Whether the investors bought exclusively for their own account or sometimes acted for third parties on a commission basis is undocumented and thus unknown. What is certain is that none of those prominent merchants eventually devoted a substantial share of their energies to brokerage services in the 1790s and thereafter. Those speculators may be listed as the forerunners of the specialized brokerage house but not genuine antecedents.

Because of the overwhelming preponderance of surviving data on the development of brokerage services in New York City, that market provides the focal point for the remainder of this discussion. The New York capital market came alive in 1790 with the announcement of Hamilton's funding program for the combined state and federal war debt. Prices for bonds scheduled to begin immediate payment of 6 percent interest fluctuated during 1791 and 1792 from a low bid of 84 in January 1791 to an asking high of 129 a year later, a rise of more than 50 percent, before falling back to a bid of 100 (par value) by the end of 1792. U.S. bonds paying only 3 percent interest and the 6 percent series scheduled to commence interest payments on a delayed basis both traded at lower prices. The common stocks of the First Bank of the United States and the Bank of New York, with the latter having operated as an unchartered firm since 1784, came to the market in 1791 and were quickly snapped up by investors. The Society for Useful Manufactures, the first American manufacturing company to offer its shares to the public, received a charter from the New Jersey legislature, and its stock was also traded in the New York market.

Brokers and auctioneers joined forces to organize regularly scheduled auctions of securities in July 1791. From August through March 1792, auctions were held at least twice a day to meet the demands of eager traders.[6] In response to the increase in trading volume and heightened public interest in securities markets, newspapers began reporting bid and ask quotations and the prices of recently consummated trades. In September 1791, a group of auctioneers and brokers met at a local coffeehouse and signed an agreement with fourteen specific rules aimed at establishing uniform procedures for the handling of securities transactions among themselves. That document, which was superseded by other joint agreements, marks the first step toward the formal organization of the New York Stock Exchange, which occurred in 1817.

The sudden emergence of active trading in government bonds and bank stocks in New York in 1791 stimulated local entrepreneurs to consider various proposals to tap into this fresh stream of liquid capital. Several new ventures were announced, and stock subscriptions were, in turn, solicited from interested investors. A subscription was a preliminary financial contract, typically acquired for a small fraction, say 5 to 10 percent, of the stated issue price. It gave the holder the privilege of purchasing actual shares at a fixed rate when the corporation was finally launched and the securities actually issued. (Subscriptions are similar in their functions to warrants.) Persons who anticipated a rise in the price of the shares of a newly proposed enterprise, when issued, were often willing to pay a premium for the subscription rights, and the so-called scrip was actively traded. In early 1792 three proposed new firms—Million Bank, Tammany Bank, and Tammanial Tontine Association—offered subscription rights to the general public, and their offerings were oversubscribed several times over. During the next few months, speculators drove the prices of the scrip offerings higher and higher. Meanwhile, a large number of futures and options contracts were written covering the eight to twelve securities routinely traded in the New York market.

In March 1792 the prices for securities and related contractual agreements fell precipitously, forcing many speculators into bankruptcy. Political insiders let it be known that the proposed Million and Tammany banks were unlikely to obtain corporate charters from the state legislature. Realists concluded that years might pass before the Society for Useful Manufactures would be in a position to pay dividends; indeed, it was possible that profits might never accrue. Scrip and stock prices fell sharply. Among those caught in the downturn was William Duer, one of Alexander Hamilton's key assistants at the Treasury Department and a person deeply involved in the Society for Useful Manufactures. Duer ended up in debtors' prison after losing his fortune in speculative activities in 1791 and 1792.

Financial historians Werner and Smith have referred to the collapse in prices in the spring of 1792 as the nation's first bona fide stock market crash. In labeling the episode a full-scale crash, a strong term, they have followed in the footsteps of most other chroniclers of prevailing conditions in the early stock market, including most notably Bray Hammond. But the use of the term *crash* is too strong and is unwarranted in this instance. The securities markets were in an embryonic stage in 1791 and 1792; American investors were still getting their feet wet in the new financial markets. The upswing was too short-lived and the number of issues traded and speculators involved were too few to justify the crash terminology. Rather than something approaching a genuine collapse, the episode was a justifiable market reversal. Admittedly, the prices of the securities and scrip associated with several untested and speculative ventures plunged fast and far. But other, more proven issues fared much better. The average prices for U.S. 6 percent bonds dropped from 123 in February down to 102 in April, a decline of more than 15 percent, but then held fairly steady throughout the remainder of the year, ending up at 103 in December 1792. Bond prices never dropped below 100 and were actually still higher in the summer of 1792 than during the same three months in 1791. The shares of the First Bank of the United States and the Bank of New York declined but they stabilized within a few weeks. Moreover, no evidence suggests that the panic in New York was paralleled by similar declines in Philadelphia, Boston, or any other major U.S. financial center. The price movements in March and April 1792 were a significant reversal of the upward trend in the New York market, but what occurred was not a crash because the magnitude was insufficiently great on either the local or national level.

The price reversal led to several important institutional adjustments, however. The New York legislature made public auctions of securities illegal. The same act outlawed futures and options contracts. Because those speculative transactions had been unenforceable in the judicial system under English law since 1734, the new regulations were perhaps redundant; but they reinforced the regulatory restrictions in the American context. Despite the new law, speculative devices such as futures, options, and short sales remained an integral part of the New York market, paralleling what had happened in London after the passage of Sir John Barnard's Act, according to Werner and Smith.[7]

Another noteworthy event following in the wake of the sharp market reversal was the signing of the so-called Buttonwood Agreement, named after the tree under which many securities were routinely traded, on 17 May 1792. The motivation for brokers and auctioneers alike "was to find an alternative to auctions that could preserve their market, while eliminating, or at least minimizing, the conditions that had brought on the panic." The goal was to "establish structured securities markets without auctions."[8] The signators agreed to charge fixed, noncompetitive commission rates on regular trades. They also pledged to give preference to each other in arranging swaps among customers, and that provision became the basis for transforming the leading brokerage houses into what amounted to a voluntary, yet exclusive, club. The agreement was not intended to create a legal monopoly; enforcement of the rules was an internal affair, not a matter for government regulators. Nonsignators retained the right to perform all the normal brokerage services, but most specialized brokerage firms, and most that aspired to specialization, decided to sign the Buttonwood Agreement. In this early period, the membership was open-ended, with no entrance fees for admission to the organization. Some brokers and former auctioneers who had been reluctant to sign in May 1792 decided to add their names to the document months or years later.

One of the leading brokerage firms in New York at the beginning of the new century was headed by Nathan Prime. Born in Massachusetts in 1768, he worked as a coachman for Boston merchant William Gray, who served as a director of the First Bank of the United States in the 1790s. Gray exposed Prime to the workings of high finance and reportedly loaned him the money to start his own business. Prime arrived in New York in 1795, entered the securities brokerage field, and almost immediately prospered. During the early years his firm brokered not only securities, but also out-of-town bank notes, mortgage loans, and insurance. Prime married the daughter of a wealthy local merchant and gained access to additional capital.

Nathan Prime was an important innovator in the New York securities field because by the first decade of the nineteenth century he had advanced from the status of broker to full-fledged securities dealer. Most brokers acted merely as intermediaries in negotiating securities transfers, which did not require them to put at risk more than small amounts of their own capital. When they required financing for two or three days, brokers relied on bank loans that were typically secured by the securities in transit. Dealers were more deeply involved in the market. They invested capital in acquiring a modest inventory of actively traded securities from which they could make direct sales to interested parties. Dealers usually established "bid and ask" prices for those securities in which they "made" continuous markets. By 1802, for example, Prime was publishing prices for ten securities on a weekly basis, and, according to Werner and Smith, "he was likely making a market in all of them."[9] His name was found frequently in the stock register of the Manhattan Company—the water company that shifted its focus and became a bank. In 1800 all dealers combined handled more than one-third of the recorded exchanges of Manhattan Company shares, and during the last five months of the year, Prime was a principal in 61 of 87 dealer trades, or 70 percent of the total.[10] In 1808 Prime added a partner and the firm changed its name to Prime and Ward. Successor partnerships were closely aligned with Baring Brothers and other leading Anglo-American merchant banking houses in the nineteenth century.

From 1792 to 1815, the number of securities publicly quoted in the New York market climbed from 5 to 23. At the outset, three federal bond issues and two bank stocks were actively traded. By the turn of the century, one additional federal bond issue, one more commercial bank, and two insurance companies were regularly quoted. By 1815 six bonds—four federal and two state and local issues—eight bank stocks, and nine insurance company stocks had their prices regularly reported in local newspapers; and they presumably headed the list of the most actively traded securities. These auspicious beginnings laid a firm groundwork for the subsequent growth of the New York market. By 1830 the number of publicly quoted securities had risen to 75, and by 1840, despite the disruptions of the Panic of 1837, the list had climbed to more than 115. After the War of 1812, more brokers made the transition to dealers and some gradually added investment banking functions. In connection with the railroad construction boom in New England during the 1840s, a few of the Boston brokerage houses briefly challenged their counterparts in New York. However, with the shift in construction to the Midwest in the 1850s, New York reclaimed and never relinquished the position of leadership in the securities field that had been solidly established during the early national period.

Foreign Exchange

The financial services available to participants in the foreign trade sector also improved steadily after 1790. The new lending facilities provided by hundreds of commercial banks made it easier for merchants to obtain funding to finance shipments and inventories. More intermediaries arose to smooth the sale and transfer of credit balances held overseas by American exporters into the hands of their importing counterparts who needed to acquire foreign monies to settle routine trade debts in distant lands. So-called merchant banking firms, which were typically involved in overseas merchandise trade on their own account and simultaneously provided specialized financial services to other foreign traders, expanded their operations both functionally and geographically after 1800.

The bill of exchange ranks as another financial device that had its origins in ancient times but became more commonplace in Europe during the early modern period. The payment mechanism operated in reverse order from today's check writing system. The person seeking funds initiated the process by drawing a draft on the person responsible for making payment. Once that draft had reached its final destination and had been formally presented for payment, the debtor accepted the draft as legitimate and simultaneously agreed to come up with the funds, either immediately (a sight draft) or within thirty to sixty days (a time draft). The bill of exchange did not require the maintenance of a bank account with a neutral third party to expedite the transfer of funds among merchants, which explains its popularity. Bills of exchange fell into two broad categories. Domestic bills of exchange were drawn in the same monetary units recognized as legal tender in the local economy, whereas foreign bills of exchange were drawn in differing monetary units. In North America, domestic bills were drawn in colonial pounds before 1776 and in dollars thereafter, while foreign bills of exchange were drawn in English pounds, French francs, Dutch guilders, and other European monetary units.

The fundamental transfer system for foreign bills of exchange that functioned in the seventeenth and eighteenth centuries can be outlined briefly for clarity. In the typical transaction, four parties played a significant role: an American exporter, an American importer, a foreign exporter, and a foreign importer. Two critical facts worth noting at the outset are that all financial transactions involving foreigners were ultimately settled on the books of accounts maintained overseas, not in the colonies, and that the location of settlement was most frequently London—although Paris, Amsterdam, Hamburg, and other continental cities sometimes were payment sites. By the late eighteenth century, a short-term financial market for accepted foreign drafts, which were commonly called acceptances, was active in London. That institutional development proved conducive to the expansion of British foreign trade and more indirectly to U.S. foreign trade as well.

For the most part, American exporters created the supply of foreign bills of exchange, and American importers provided the demand. A colonial exporter of tobacco, for example, selling to a buyer in Great Britain typically did not wait for payment until the shipment had arrived in port and the purchaser had arranged to send back silver or gold on a return voyage, a round-trip that might take from six to twelve months. Instead, around the date that this exporter placed his hogsheads of tobacco onboard ship, he initiated the accompanying financial transaction by drawing a single sterling bill, or perhaps a series of small bills, on the British buyer for an agreed amount. The tobacco exporter then sought out an American importer who had recently bought goods overseas and consequently needed to acquire sterling credits in London to offset outstanding debts. The colonial importer bought the sterling bill from the exporter at or near the prevailing exchange rate for local monies, whether coin or fiat currency. With that market transfer of financial instruments, the American exporter received immediate payment in local monies even though his tobacco shipment was perhaps not yet even halfway across the ocean. The American importer endorsed the newly acquired sterling bill and remitted it forthwith to his London creditor, who, in turn, took the steps required to collect the proceeds from the British purchaser of the American tobacco. That completed the whole financial transaction—unless the British tobacco purchaser refused to accept the bill for whatever reason. The refusal to accept, or honor, a bill of exchange led to all kinds of complications that will not be explored in the interest of conserving space and expediting the discussion.

The system of transferring foreign bills of exchange among colonists—usually denominated in pounds sterling but sometimes in francs, guilders, and marks—operated fairly smoothly in areas where the timing and monetary value of local imports and exports were fairly evenly matched. In the absence of market intermediaries, exporters and importers were forced to seek each other out to negotiate sales and purchases of the bills. Financial historian Arthur Cole originally suspected that newspaper advertising in major ports had probably served as a medium that brought together buyers and sellers of foreign exchange, but he conducted a thorough review of leading eighteenth-century newspapers and discovered little supporting evidence. Instead, the market presumably functioned mainly by word of mouth and other informal communications networks. As a rule, colonial foreign exchange markets were institutionally immature, with a decidedly local or regional orientation.

Eventually, some mercantile firms diversified their interests and began acting as foreign exchange brokers. For a commission or modest markup, they arranged transfers of sterling bills between buyers and sellers. Brokers were especially useful to agricultural producers in outlying areas who routinely exported foodstuffs and generated foreign credits sought by urban merchants importing finished goods. To cite one example, a few Baltimore mercantile firms acted as intermediaries for Virginia tobacco planters seeking sterling buyers. Sometimes brokers took a short-term position in foreign exchange, buying bills from impatient sellers at discount rates in the expectation that willing buyers would soon turn up. On most occasions, however, they refused to purchase a sterling bill until they had lined up an offsetting buyer.

The prices at which sterling bills traded hands reflected the current exchange rate between local money and sterling, with occasional modifications based on the credit standing of the local drawer or the prospective foreign acceptor. Most series of reported exchange rates, such as those listed in John McCusker's monograph covering all thirteen colonies over much of the eighteenth century, were generally prices for so-called first-class sterling bills drawn on parties believed reliable and who reportedly possessed sufficient wealth to cover their liabilities even in difficult times.[11] Even in areas with stable monetary systems, exchange rates fluctuated from month to month and year to year in response to shifts in trading patterns and other factors affecting the overall balance of payments. Deviations from par in both directions were typically of greater amplitude in the period from 1700 to 1815 than after 1820 when a more integrated national market began to take shape. Nonetheless, in the absence of governmental foreign exchange controls or any other type of regulatory intervention, periodically excessive premiums and discounts for foreign exchange were generally self-correcting over time since the colonies were full participants in the evolving international financial system based on the free, private exchange of silver and gold bullion.

Although New York and Philadelphia were more important financial centers in terms of the volume of transactions, the Baltimore foreign exchange market provides a good focus for analysis because of the survival of a critical document listing monthly prices for sterling bills of exchange from January 1791 through December 1829. Discovered tucked away in published government reports only in the early 1980s, the long-lost data were used by financial historian Lawrence Officer to calculate a pure exchange rate series on a quarterly basis for the entire early national period. He adjusted the reported prices to eliminate the distortions of interest rates and other extraneous factors. Officer's revised dollar-sterling exchange rate series reveals much less volatility than a predecessor series based on the less complete records of a Philadelphia merchant starting in 1803. Comparing exchange rates from the two series between 1803 and 1815 reveals other striking contrasts. The older series indicated that the dollar traded at below par more than 80 percent of the time, with a mean monthly discount of nearly 17 percent; Officer's series showed the dollar above par more than two-thirds of the time, with a mean monthly premium just shy of 3 percent. The greater stability of the more recent series suggests a higher degree of maturation in the U.S. foreign exchange market than scholars had previously assumed.

The first decade of the nineteenth century witnessed the emergence of one of the nation's earliest foreign exchange dealers. Alexander Brown, a linen merchant who had emigrated to Baltimore from northern Ireland at the turn of the century, was an innovator in this market. By the mid-nineteenth century, the House of Brown, as it was commonly known, had established branches in Philadelphia, New York, Boston, Mobile, and New Orleans, plus critical outlets in Liverpool and London. As early as 1803, Brown was corresponding with tobacco shippers in locales as distant as Petersburg, Virginia, about brokering bills of exchange in the Baltimore market. He dealt mostly in sterling, but Dutch guilders and French francs occasionally passed through his hands as well. Other merchants in ports along the Atlantic Coast frequently performed similar brokerage functions. Some firms advertised that they dealt in a whole range of financial services, among them stocks, bonds, out-of-town bank notes, lottery tickets, marine insurance, domestic exchange, and foreign exchange.

In 1810 Alexander Brown sent William, his second eldest son, to Liverpool to open a branch office of the family partnership. Soon thereafter the Baltimore office announced its intention to maintain a continuous market for foreign exchange, which meant that it would *always* be prepared to either buy or sell sterling bills of all valuations at its quoted daily rates. In making this public announcement, the Brown firm rose above the status of brokers to become a full-fledged dealer. The Baltimore office no longer brokered sterling bills drawn by third parties but drew drafts instead directly on its Liverpool office; the sterling bills it purchased from local exporters were not resold to local importers but remitted directly to the Liverpool partners for collection. Unlike the brokers with whom they regularly competed, the Browns felt less pressure to match fairly evenly their sales and purchases of bills in a given week or month. Instead, they adopted coordinated transatlantic strategies that took advantage of seasonal swings in exchange rates to boost profit margins. The Liverpool branch arranged access to the London acceptance market to provide financing during seasonal shortfalls. In sum, the Browns were near the forefront in the movement to integrate more closely the financial sectors of Great Britain and its former North American colonies after 1810. The First Bank of the United States and the vast majority of chartered state banks avoided involvement in the foreign exchange market in the early national period. In this sector, private merchant banking houses led the way. In subsequent decades, the Browns' sterling bills ranked at the very top of the international credit scale—on a par with those of the Second Bank of the United States and Baring Brothers.

The Browns' two branch offices, positioned advantageously on opposite sides of the Atlantic Ocean, also permitted the firm to offer an improved marketing and financial package to cotton exporters shipping to Great Britain on consignment. By 1810 cotton was already well on its way to becoming the main southern export. The partners sometimes speculated in the cotton market on their own account. Working through independent agents in Charleston and Savannah, the Browns also tried to lure the consignments of a substantial number of high-volume shippers. Because of its proximity to the Manchester textile manufacturing region, Liverpool was the key port for raw cotton shipments. To attract consignments to the Liverpool office, the Browns offered American exporters advance payments restricted to approximately 75 percent of the expected proceeds of cotton shipments, with the actual differential remitted after the conclusion of the sale. Exporters received sterling bills drawn on the Liverpool branch in payment, and they had the option of selling them immediately to the issuing branch or disposing of them elsewhere. Some chose the latter option because the Browns' bills usually commanded high prices from third parties, including other foreign exchange brokers. When exporters decided to allow the Browns to perform all merchandising and financial functions, the Browns were able to combine in a single transaction the making of advances and the negotiation of an exchange transaction. In expanding the scope of their services for foreign traders, the Browns were important innovators.

The Browns were involved in other financial markets as well and dabbled in marine insurance. Here again they performed the dual functions of broker and underwriter. The firm offered to arrange insurance coverage with other insurers for exporters consigning goods to the Liverpool branch; occasionally, the Baltimore office decided to assume risks on its own account. The partnership underwrote marine policies on ships as well as cargoes. In yet another field, the Browns began issuing letters of credit to American importers who wanted to enhance their buying power in overseas markets. For a fee, ranging from 2 to 5 percent of the amount contracted in this period, the Brown firm in essence guaranteed the overseas debts of trusted third parties. The U.S. letter of credit market was still in its infancy in the early national period, and a full discussion of its origins and operations is thus unwarranted here; but the scattered transactions occurring before 1815 blossomed into a substantial business later in the nineteenth century.[12] Generally speaking, merchant bankers were unspecialized enterprises typically involved in a broad array of mercantile and financial services. Several of the leading firms became more deeply involved in investment banking activities after the War of 1812.

15

Financing the War of 1812

THE WAR OF 1812, sometimes called the second war for American independence because it reaffirmed the break with Great Britain, immediately created serious difficulties for the Treasury Department. Congress eagerly voted to declare war to avenge British transgressions but hesitated to raise the taxes to pay for increased military budgets. As a result, Treasury Secretary Albert Gallatin was forced to turn consistently to debt financing to cover the cost of the conflict. From the outset he ran into resistance in securing adequate funding from the commercial banking community and private investors.

The war made heavy financial demands on the nation for four years, but unlike the earlier war against Great Britain, it did not last nearly as long. The cost of the war for the free population was just under $15 per capita, or roughly one-fifth of the comparable figure for the War for Independence. Military expenditures were nearly $95 million, of which $82 million, or 85 percent, was borrowed money. The per capita addition to the national debt was slightly less than half the comparable figure in 1790. The war ended with a diplomatic settlement in late 1814, although the news did not travel fast enough to prevent a major battle at New Orleans in January 1815 that gave a huge boost to General Andrew Jackson's political ambitions. Heavy expenditures on military accounts continued well into 1815 and put an added strain on congressional budgets.

The problems associated with financing the war effort breathed new life into the Hamiltonian financial program. Hamilton's grand plan for the development of U.S. financial markets had deteriorated under Republican assaults since 1801, culminating with the congressional refusal to renew the charter of the First BUS in 1811. At the outbreak of hostilities, the United States no longer possessed a large nationally chartered bank that could be relied upon to make more-or-less obligatory loans to the government in tight situations—a reverse of the situation prevailing in the 1790s. Meanwhile, the national debt, which Hamilton had proclaimed as the cement of the union, was a shadow of its former self and moving well along the road to extinction. Ignoring the $15 million purchase price of the Louisiana Territory, the Jefferson and Madison administrations had retired more than 60 percent of the debt inherited from the Federalists in 1801. At the end of 1811 the aggregate federal debt stood at only $45 million. Republicans congratulated themselves on their progressive dismantlement of the Hamiltonian system, namely a large national bank combined with a sizable and perpetual national debt.

The difficult wartime experiences challenged traditional Republican attitudes about the proper relationship between the nation's banking system and its capital markets. In the 1790s, Federalists had promoted a close connection between banks and public securities based on the British model. In contrast, Republicans, who often thought about financial issues in conspiratorial, moralistic terms, had viewed the Hamiltonian program as potentially dangerous to representative government because it seemingly enhanced the opportunities for political corruption. For example, close ties between the Exchequer of the Treasury and the Bank of England during the eighteenth century had promoted the escalating British national debt, Jeffersonians frequently asserted.[1] To prevent a repetition of that allegedly misguided institutional arrangement in the United States, they had worked assiduously since 1801 to diminish the role of the national bank in government affairs and to limit the influence of specialized securities dealers, who remained relatively few in number in the United States.

During the War of 1812, those rhetorical flourishes came back to haunt Republicans. They were forced to reassess the reasonableness and practicality of their views, and in most cases they reversed their earlier positions about the proper organization of the financial services sector. National banking proponents had argued in the congressional debate over recharter in 1811 that, despite the reservations of many critics, the nation had prospered and matured politically during the charter life of the First BUS. Having witnessed firsthand the problems associated with financing the war with a decentralized, leaderless institutional structure, Republican critics of the national bank were reluctantly forced to reconsider the fateful decision to deny recharter. With the memories of more stable times clearly in mind, Congress voted to resuscitate the national bank in 1816 and authorized a capital 3.5 times larger than its predecessor. For a decade or so after the War of 1812, political leaders everywhere willingly paid homage to Hamiltonian principles—principles that seemed less threatening to the Republican majority given the steady erosion of the polling power of Federalist candidates for public office.

When Secretary Gallatin sought to borrow money from the private sector in 1812, he met the first in a series of sharp rebuffs. His worst fears had come true. Gallatin had warned Congress on several occasions beginning in 1809 not to reject an application for recharter from the First BUS because, in an emergency, the Treasury might need the national bank's assistance in funding extraordinary governmental expenditures. The government had been generally free of bank debt for nearly a decade, he observed, but those favorable conditions might not last indefinitely.

Congress ignored Gallatin's pleas on behalf of the bank and then a year later declared war, placing him in the difficult spot that he had so accurately forecast. When war preparations began, directors of the First BUS were in the process of managing a smooth liquidation of assets. Most of its former branch offices were taken over by independent state-chartered banks with no ties or obligations vis-à-vis the federal government. When Gallatin appealed to the financial community for assistance, bankers gave only token responses to requests for short- to intermediate-term financing since the treasury secretary could give no assurances about when the loans might be repaid or subsequently refinanced through the issuance of long-term debt. Some large urban banks offered to purchase a limited volume of government bonds for their investment portfolios but not in sufficient quantities to accommodate the federal government's escalating requirements.

Not only was help from the banking community difficult to obtain, but Gallatin ran into resistance in trying to attract the investment of individuals in government securities. Congress authorized the issuance of $11 million in new bonds at 6 percent interest in March 1812, three months before it actually declared war. Optimists believed government securities could be placed at relatively low

TABLE 15.1
Quoted Prices and Yields for U.S. Government Bonds:
Boston Stock Exchange
(yearly averages)

	1801	*1805*	*1810*	*1813*	*1815*
Prices					
6% bond	93	94	103	95	85
3% bond	56	55	65	55	48
8% bond	110	105	paid	—	—
5.5% bond		93	paid	—	—
Current Yields					
6% bond	6.4	6.4	5.8	6.3	7.1
3% bond	5.3	5.4	4.6	5.4	6.3
8% bond	7.3	7.6	—	—	—
5.5% bond	—	5.9	—	—	—

Source: Joseph G. Martin, *Boston Stock Market,* (Boston: privately published, 1886),
p. 127.
Note: Average price is mean of Martin's reported annual high and low.

interest rates—meaning around 6 percent—given the gilt-edged
status of U.S. government securities that had generally prevailed
from the implementation of the Hamiltonian funding program in
the early 1790s. Since 1801, government bonds had typically yielded
from 5 to 6 percent according to quotations on the Boston securities exchange.[2] U.S. obligations had a solid international reputation
as well, with more than half of the bonds outstanding held by foreigners. The United States was one of the few nations that had
followed a consistent policy of paying off substantial amounts of its
national debt for more than a decade; less outstanding debt reduced
the interest drain on budgets and lowered the risk of any possible
default. So the outlook seemed reasonably good for generating a
strong demand for U.S. government bonds at modest interest rates.
But uncertainties surrounding the war altered the investment climate.

The American capital market had undergone development during the last quarter century, but it was still institutionally immature,
with barely a hint of a truly national base. Hamilton's successful
funding of the $80 million national debt in the early 1790s was not
an accurate gauge of the strength of the market since investors were
not asked to advance new monies but merely to swap old obligations
already in default for fresh securities judged more likely to resume

interest payments. In the first true test of the government's status as an issuer of new securities in 1799, Treasury Secretary Oliver Wolcott sold $5 million in bonds to private parties. Wolcott had hoped to place the bonds at 6 percent, but after lengthy negotiations with potential investors, he reluctantly agreed to raise the nominal rate to 8 percent in order to float the entire issue at par.[3]

Four years later, in 1803, Secretary Gallatin raised $11.25 million at 6 percent interest to assist in financing the purchase of the Louisiana Territory from France; most of the investors were foreigners.[4] Investors proved willing to advance funds with little encouragement since the purpose was to finance a moderately priced territorial acquisition in peacetime. After that date the Treasury ran huge surpluses and had no reason to return to the capital market for funding.

Although the federal government was generally inactive as an issuer of securities during the decade prior to the War of 1812, it did play a critical role in the reverse process, returning $40 million in principal to investors. Some payments went to citizens and some to bondholders living overseas.[5] A portion of that capital was reinvested in American business enterprises whose shares traded on local exchanges in the largest northern port cities—especially financial institutions such as banks and a few insurance companies. In 1810, before the dissolution of the First BUS, the capital invested in banks in Philadelphia, New York, Boston, and Baltimore totaled $22 million; by 1815 that figure had climbed to $35 million.

Most institutions were tightly held, and the volume of securities traded was undoubtedly small by later standards. Nonetheless, a core of securities brokers in the major cities typically maintained lists of buy and sell prices for bank shares in their localities. Beyond the main money centers, the aggregate sum invested in bank stocks was even larger—$80 million by 1815. Trading in bank stocks outside the emerging money centers was presumably more sporadic, with brokerage functions performed mostly by nonspecialized firms that normally stressed mercantile activities but periodically acted as financial intermediaries.

Securities markets for stock issues were mostly regional. For example, few New Englanders invested in institutions in New York, Philadelphia, and Baltimore—and vice versa. Brokers quoted only the prices of local enterprises. Given the thinness of markets, the American economy was devoid of prominent merchant banking houses or any specialized firms that engaged in underwriting new securities offerings or in related investment banking activities. Brokers handled the sales of outstanding securities in secondary markets, but underwriters capable of taking an exposed financial position in an issue of new securities that ran into the millions of dollars were nonexistent. American agents of European bankers occasionally bought shares for their foreign clients, but none had the facilities for underwriting American issues. Despite the Federalists' best efforts to nurture a domestic capital market, the climate was vastly different in Washington, Boston, New York, or Philadelphia than in Amsterdam or London, where numerous firms stood ready to assist European governments in placing their debt issues by drawing on their lists of eager investors at home and abroad.

The task facing the Treasury Department in 1812 was more formidable than in 1799 or in 1803 because prospective investors had no means of judging the likely volume of fresh borrowings associated with a wide-scale war of unknown length on land and sea against Great Britain, a nation possessing enormous military power. The initial amount sought from lenders was only $11 million, no more than the amount borrowed in 1803; but that figure was only a beginning. The total seemed likely to multiply several-fold before the conflict was settled one way or another, and there was always the chance of unfavorable results—geographically and financially. The open-ended character of the potential drain on the economy shrank the pool of potential investors.

Moreover, as in the past, the Treasury Department attempted to manage its bond sale without the assistance of private underwriters. If one thrust of Jeffersonian ideology had been to prevent the emergence of a network of securities dealers capable of underwriting skyrocketing increases in the national debt, then the events surrounding the War of 1812 indicate that they had succeeded gloriously. The federal government's initial effort to place its new debt with interested investors was typically an in-house effort—and thus decidedly amateurish at its core. The Treasury Department simply announced the subscription date for its bonds and waited patiently for investors to respond. But not enough money came forward to float the entire $11 million issue at a 6 percent yield to investors.

The Treasury began accepting subscriptions starting in May, but only $6.2 million of the initial offering was taken—$4.2 million by banks for their long-term loan portfolios and a mere $2.0 million by individuals. Meanwhile, requests for military expenditures kept pouring in. Under different circumstances, Gallatin might have given greater consideration to the possibility of paying more than 6 percent interest or perhaps offering to sell bonds at discount prices in an effort to attract more investors, but those two options were rejected by Madison and his closest advisers. The president insisted on borrowing at relatively inexpensive rates or pursuing other alternatives.

When the terms offered to long-term investors were insufficiently remunerative to float the issue, Madison instructed Gallatin to ask Congress for permission to pursue an option that had not surfaced at the federal level since 1780: the issuance of some form of inconvertible fiat paper to meet the pressing demands of military suppliers. In this case the secretary was not anticipating the emission of a huge volume of non-interest-bearing paper money with no redemption dates—nothing to compare with the disreputable Continental currency of the revolutionary era. Instead, Gallatin proposed short-term debt instruments fairly similar to the one- and two-year treasury notes issued by the colony of Massachusetts starting in 1751. The exact plan called for the issuance of negotiable treasury bills that were legal tender in public, but not private, transactions with maturity dates of one year or less and carrying an interest rate of 5.4 percent, a shade below the yields on long-term U.S. bonds.

In June 1812 Congress authorized $5 million in treasury bills to cover the shortfall from the unsuccessful bond sale. During the war the government issued a total of $36.7 million in treasury bills, although no more than $17.6 million were outstanding on any given date. Most were issued in denominations of $20, $100, and $1,000. There were exceptions, however. In 1815 the Treasury issued about $2.75 million in treasury bills in small denominations ($3, $5, $10) bearing no interest. Those small bills, little different from the Continental currency of the 1770s, immediately entered the money stock, thereby helping to fuel inflationary expectations and push prices higher. Small bills constituted less than 4 percent of the Treasury's total indebtedness, however, and their overall impact was fairly modest. Unlike Continental currency, the purchasing power of the small bills held up fairly well since holders had the option of converting them at face value into long-term government bonds paying 7 percent interest.

Meanwhile, Gallatin tried again in early 1813 to float another debt issue. In light of the unsuccessful loan of 1812, military indecisiveness, and the opposition of many wealthy New Englanders to the war, the prospects were not encouraging. Congress authorized up to $16 million, and it allowed the Treasury to pay a commission of 0.0025 to private agents who solicited bond sales if outside help was deemed necessary. That provision opened the door to more aggressive marketing. In response to its appeal for funds—the traditionally passive system of merely announcing a subscription date—the Treasury received applications for only about one-third of the sum required through the end of March. That left $10 million unsold. Gallatin then invited interested parties to submit proposals indicating the terms under which they would be willing to purchase the remainder of the issue, with everything on the table for discussion including higher interest rates, discount purchase prices, call privileges, and other features.

During the first week of April 1813, Gallatin engaged in negotiations with representatives of a syndicate of private underwriters and investors. The three principals were Stephen Girard in Philadelphia, John Jacob Astor in New York, and David Parish, the agent of an international banking house who had resided in Philadelphia since 1806. The son of the senior partner in Parish and Company, a firm headquartered in Hamburg, Germany, David Parish was the chief initiator and organizer of the American syndicate.[6] He was presumably familiar with the techniques of forming syndicates and underwriting large issues of government securities, and he transferred those skills to the American capital market. Girard likewise had European origins; born in France in 1750, he had been a resident of Philadelphia since 1776 and had accumulated a mercantile fortune. Diversifying his interests into commercial banking, Girard purchased the headquarters office of the First BUS in 1812 and took over many of its former accounts. Like Parish, Astor was another German-born immigrant who arrived in New York in 1784. Astor had a variety of business interests, but most of his fortune arose from the fur trade and investments in Manhattan real estate.

Gallatin traveled from Washington to Philadelphia in early April to work out the details with Parish and Girard. The syndicate agreed to assume responsibility for marketing the remaining $10.1 million of 6 percent bonds at a discounted price of $88, which produced a current yield to investors of 6.8 percent.[7] Girard and Parish ended up taking $3.1 million each and Astor assumed responsibility for $1.5 million—a total of $7.7 million. To complete the transaction, the principals recruited several independent firms—at least seven and possibly up to twelve—in New York and Philadelphia (and perhaps one or two in Baltimore) to act as junior members of the syndicate. Altogether the junior participants sold about $2.4 million in bonds to various customers.[8]

Boston was not represented on the syndicate list since the war was extremely unpopular in New England, and the prospects for bond sales seemed dim. Nor did the syndicate organizers look for assistance from Charleston and other cities south of Baltimore—a telling omission that was indicative of the immaturity of organized capital markets in the southern states. From the start, Parish had planned to generate sufficient funding in just three money centers: $5.8 million in Philadelphia, $3 million in New York, and $1.2 million in Baltimore.

Broadly speaking, the whole arrangement had most of the elements characteristic of loan contracts routinely negotiated in London and Amsterdam between European governments and various firms involved in underwriting securities offerings. The American syndicate took the government bonds on a "best efforts" basis, meaning that they pledged to do their utmost to place the bonds with bona fide investors at the stated price as rapidly as possible; but they were not unconditionally committed to guaranteeing the transfer of the entire $10 million to the Treasury irrespective of how investors responded. The syndicate organizers had made a serious effort to test the capital market before agreeing to offer investment banking services, however. Thus, they were reasonably certain $10 million would be forthcoming. Nonetheless, the trio of Parish, Astor, and Girard made no irrevocable guarantees and bore no substantial financial risks either individually or severally. Once the transaction was finalized, another aspect of American uniqueness had vanished; the U.S. Treasury had broken with precedent and cooperated on a commission basis with private banking firms capable of raising funds speedily and efficiently.[9]

This precedent-setting transaction benefited all participants. The principal organizers—Girard, Parish, and Astor—assumed responsibility for marketing $7.7 million in government bonds to investors on terms deemed acceptable, and they earned $11,510 in commission fees for their services.[10] Seven other firms received another $6,130 in commissions, a modest 0.0025 of face value, for handling $2.4 million in bond subscriptions, all of which were completed within the month. Treasury Secretary Gallatin had reason for satisfaction as well. With the cooperation of private underwriters, he was able to avoid the embarrassment of a second unsuccessful or unduly prolonged fund-raising campaign. Moreover, the cost of marketing the bonds totaled $17,600—a mere fraction of 1 percent (0.0017 to be exact) of the face value of the bonds, which were unsubscribed when the syndicate entered the picture.

The U.S. government thus experienced its first involvement with financiers performing essentially investment banking functions in April 1813. Fortunately, the venture was reasonably successful. The favorable negotiations with private parties helped to put to rest many of the fears Republicans had expressed since the 1780s about the alleged dangers of allowing the Treasury to come under the influence of loan contractors and securities dealers. The American financiers, by the farthest stretch of the imagination, bore no responsibility either for initiating the war or for attempting to prolong it with the aim of expanding the size of the national debt. Girard was a professed Republican and supporter of President Madison. On the contrary, members of the syndicate of 1813 were considered favorably as patriots who had come to the rescue of the Treasury during trying times.

The association between government and underwriters was a singular event, however, in the context of financing the War of 1812. Despite the success of the 1813 public offering, the participation of underwriters was not repeated. During the next two years the Treasury stuck to the former practice of managing the distribution of new securities without the assistance of outside financiers. Parish, Girard, and Astor made a second attempt to function as loan contractors in connection with the congressional authorization for a $25 million loan in the spring of 1814, but negotiations with the Treasury broke down. Other wealthy men, who had little investment banking experience, were reluctant to step forward. Parish pondered on several occasions the possibility of using his connections in Hamburg to market U.S. government securities in Europe, but the idea never held much promise because the overseas demand for American securities seemed too uncertain in light of the European preoccupation with Napoleon and the consequences of his ambitions.

Gallatin left the post of treasury secretary in May 1813 soon after the conclusion of negotiations with the syndicate. He was succeeded, in turn, by Secretary of the Navy William Jones (later president of the Second BUS), who served as acting treasury secretary through February 1814, by George Campbell through October 1814, and then by Alexander Dallas. Jones managed to sell $8.5 million in

6 percent bonds at $88 in August 1813—the same terms established by the syndicate three months earlier. Thereafter, treasury secretaries had difficulty raising sufficient funds in the capital market to cover military expenditures on equally favorable terms. They resorted to a mix of short-term treasury notes plus occasional sales of long-term bonds to keep the government afloat.

In early 1814 Congress authorized a second bond issue for $25 million, but Secretary Campbell, worried about the difficulties he would likely encounter if he attempted to raise such a large sum in a single public offering, decided on an incremental approach. He sought bids on an initial $10 million loan at 6 percent in May. Applications for $11.9 million at a range of prices poured in, which demonstrated that the Treasury had substantial drawing power even without the assistance of loan contractors. Campbell agreed to sell $9.2 million at a subscription price of $88, which produced a current yield of 6.8 percent to investors, and summarily rejected applications for the additional $2.7 million submitted at lower prices. In selling the $9.2 million, the Treasury agreed that, if any of the remaining authorized bond issue was sold later at a price below $88, then current subscribers would be entitled retroactively to the same consideration—in other words, some form of rebate either in the form of cash or additional securities. The general success of this public offering was primarily the result of a single subscription for $5 million—more than half the issue—from Jacob Barker, a wealthy New York merchant. In this leveraged transaction, Barker had arranged to borrow much of the purchase price from several commercial banks in major cities along the Atlantic Coast by using the newly acquired bonds as collateral.[11]

Secretary Campbell tried to raise another $6 million in August 1814, but with the British threatening to invade the nation's capital, the timing was inopportune. Investors submitted subscription applications for only $2.8 million, and more than four-fifths were at prices yielding 7.5 percent or greater. Campbell accepted subscriptions for $2.5 million at $80, but the transaction netted only $1.3 million because the Treasury was required to adjust the accounts of Barker and others who had subscribed in May. The adjustment was necessary to reflect their negotiated right to any reduced issue price—now $8 lower. In light of the failure of the August offering, about $3 million in government securities were reportedly sent to Europe for sale—consigned to persons unnamed, but plausibly to Parish and Company in Hamburg or other firms named by David

Parish. Secretary Dallas claimed in February 1815 that no sales had occurred in overseas markets, however; so the conclusion that foreign investors played no role in financing the new American war debt seems reasonably safe.

The military campaign on American soil suffered setbacks in the late summer of 1814, exemplified by the British burning of public buildings in Washington and threats to Baltimore. The deteriorating military outlook was reflected in the market value of outstanding U.S. government securities. Government bonds paying 6 percent interest traded at from $75 to $85, which produced yields ranging from 7 to 8 percent.

Soon after accepting Madison's invitation to become treasury secretary in October after Campbell had resigned, Dallas solicited bids on a supplemental loan of $3 million. He focused his attention on commercial banks rather than individuals and placed the loan at the nominal price of $80 in November—the same figure his predecessor had settled for in August. The proceeds realized were actually far less than the nominal figure, however, since payment was largely in the form of bank notes from institutions that had temporarily suspended convertibility into specie. Their bank notes passed at discounts averaging 15 percent of face value, which meant that the net price realized by the Treasury was little more than $65 in *real* terms, which produced a current yield of more than 9 percent to investors.[12] The acceptance of those financial conditions was the low point in the Treasury's wartime funding operations. The status of the nation's credit had not been so questionable in more than a quarter century—not since the prevailing financial disarray on the eve of the constitutional convention of 1787. But the gloom of 1814 was short-lived.

Following the announcement of the signing of the Treaty of Ghent and news of General Jackson's victory in New Orleans early in 1815, the market for government securities began to revive. Prices rose and the yields on outstanding issues had fallen from 9 percent to 7 percent by the spring of 1815. Dallas—paralleling the thinking of Oliver Wolcott, the treasury secretary under President John Adams—decided to halt the issuance of securities at heavy discounts merely to preserve the nominal $60 annual interest payment on every $1,000 bond sold. Instead, he proposed to boost the nominal interest rate closer to existing yields on government bonds already outstanding.

Secretary Dallas sought subscriptions for an issue of $12 mil-

lion at 7 percent interest in March 1815, and adamantly refused
to consider all bids of less than $95, a price that yielded 7.4 per-
cent to investors. Dallas had to face the consequences of his rigid
pricing policies, however, namely an undersubscribed issue. Only
$9.3 million in new securities were sold that year at $95. The Treasury accepted payments in unconvertible bank notes that passed at
discounts as much as 10 percent below face value, so the real cost
of borrowing may have risen above 8 percent. The $2.7 million
shortfall in sales was not seriously missed as events unfolded. With
the rebound in foreign trade after the war, customs duties started
to climb in mid-1815 and jumped to $36 million in 1816—a sum
slightly greater than the total amount collected in the four previous
years. The budget surplus in 1816 exceeded $17 million, and most
of the excess revenue went to retire maturing treasury notes.[13] By
1817 current yields on government bonds had fallen to 6.5 percent
or less—the level at which they had held most of the time from 1790
to 1810.

Although the federal government failed to raise all the funds it
wanted from 1812 to 1815 at interest rates within the range of 6 to
8 percent, given the extenuating circumstances—namely the liquidation of the First BUS—the record of the Treasury Department
was fairly respectable. Its performance far outdistanced the legacy
of its predecessor department during the War for Independence.
One critical difference was that Congress did not need to rely on
state legislatures to share the responsibility of raising troops and
financing the war effort in 1812. The nation had made substantial progress in terms of strengthening its financial markets during
the last quarter century, and the federal government was able to
draw upon commercial banks and individuals for direct financial
assistance.

No market for long-term securities, stocks or bonds, had existed
prior to 1790, but by the 1810s the capital market was functioning
sufficiently well that Congress was able to avoid the option of resorting to the wholesale issuance of fiat monies to generate purchasing
power. Of the $80 million added to the national debt during the
war years, about $60 million, or 75 percent, arose as a result of the
direct sale of government securities to American investors—both to
individuals and to financial services firms such as commercial banks
and insurance companies.[14] By comparison, less than 15 percent of
the cost of the War for Independence had been financed by the
floatation of debt issues, and approximately half of that total had

come from French and Dutch sources rather than domestic investors. The average interest rate paid to attract investors for the five major bond floatations combined was 7.1 percent—again a reasonably respectable rate given the absence of a national bank to provide bridge loans between issue dates. If the interest rate of 5.4 percent associated with short-term treasury notes is included in the calculations, the cost of all the money borrowed by the federal government to fight the War of 1812 averaged about 6.8 percent. All things considered, Alexander Hamilton himself would have been hard pressed to have performed much better than the four treasury secretaries—Gallatin, Jones (acting), Campbell, and Dallas—who held office from 1812 to 1816.

The treasury notes emitted during the war were only distant relatives of the Continental currency issued in the 1770s. In truth, the notes were closer in lineage to the two-year interest-bearing bills that the colony of Massachusetts had begun issuing in the early 1750s. The vast majority of U.S. Treasury notes were printed in denominations of twenty dollars and above and carried an interest component of 5.4 percent. Some circulated as a supplement to the money stock but most holders presumably retained them as short-term investments—as had happened in Massachusetts in colonial times. All issues were refinanced promptly on their maturity dates; moreover, within three years of the end of the war, every short-term treasury note had either been retired with payment in specie or converted into long-term bonds paying 7 percent interest. Not a penny of the cost of the War of 1812 was financed through the partial repudiation of a depreciated fiat issue.

Treasury notes may not have always changed hands at uniform prices during the war years, but all were redeemed at face value. In that respect, both Hamiltonians and Jeffersonians had reason to stand proud.[15] Hamiltonians could do so because every wartime obligation of the federal government proved a reliable store of value if held to maturity, and Jeffersonians were pleased as well because the public debt associated with the issuance of treasury notes was quickly retired. The federal government's aggregate debt obligation dropped more than 15 percent from 1815 to 1818, and then held fairly steady at about $90 million throughout the remaining years of President James Monroe's two terms.

Despite occasional setbacks, the Treasury was generally successful in its wartime borrowing for two key underlying reasons. First, federal debt even at its high point in 1815 was only eighteen dollars per capita for the free population—one-quarter below the comparable figure for 1790. Second, and probably more crucial in the minds of lenders, the nation had never missed an interest payment since 1790, and it had retired nearly one half the outstanding principal over an eight-year period starting in 1803. Investors in U.S. debt instruments knew that the likelihood of repayment in specie dollars was very high, and they ultimately responded positively.

Most of the slowness in filling subscription lists was not because of a dearth of potential investors but arose instead because the Madison administration sought to float its bonds at a fraction of a percent below prevailing yields on government bonds in secondary markets. The government was determined to borrow money at extremely favorable rates irrespective of market conditions. The strong attachment to a maximum allowable rate of 6 percent interest on government bonds, with 8 percent the absolute outside limit, caused the government to muddle through several years of fiscal uncertainty.

That rigidity was more important in explaining the tribulations at the Treasury Department during the war years than the absence of a national bank. To view the situation from a different perspective, if the Treasury Department had conducted auctions of its debt obligations without preconditions and had agreed in advance to accept whatever interest rates emerged by following the same procedures that its modern counterpart routinely employs in capital markets today, then most of the difficulties Gallatin, Jones, Campbell, and Dallas encountered in selling the $80 million in U.S. securities would have likely never arisen. By trying to save their fellow American taxpayers relatively modest sums in interest payments during the next decade or so, the four treasury secretaries only made life unnecessarily difficult for themselves and other influential decision makers in the Madison administration. With the exception of August 1814 when the British captured Washington and burned the capitol building, in all likelihood the Treasury could have raised all the money it required throughout the war if the Madison administration had been more flexible in the management of its interest rate and bond pricing policies.

The wartime emergency also adversely affected the operations of commercial banks in the mid-Atlantic and southern states. For the first time since the creation of a system of privatized banks, a large number of financial institutions faced the prospect of resisting customer runs on their specie reserves, and directors voted to suspend payment temporarily—meaning that they refused to convert bank notes into specie on demand. The suspensions violated the pledge of continuous convertibility into hard money that was usually included in bank charters. The pledge was an expression of the good intentions of bank organizers, not a firm guarantee. Every chartered institution issued bank notes against fractional reserves, which meant that if all the holders of bank notes demanded specie simultaneously, conversion was physically impossible. In an unabated run on bank reserves, only persons who stood near the front of the line at tellers' windows could hope to walk away with specie. Prior to federal deposit insurance in the 1930s, banks often suspended payments in an effort to survive a serious financial crisis. The general suspension in 1814 was the first of many similar episodes in American banking throughout the nineteenth and early twentieth centuries.

Military setbacks in the summer of 1814 produced a panic atmosphere and predictions that requests for conversion might escalate across much of the nation. To forestall that possibility, directors in bank after bank voted to suspend payment in order to hold on to the specie reserves still in their vaults. Even the directors of banks with strong loan portfolios suspended because of the fear that some unfounded rumor might spread throughout the local community and lead to an unwarranted drain of their reserves. Thus, they took defensive steps to protect the institution. The strategy was to suspend payment temporarily and then reinstitute conversion privileges after the war had ended and the financial crisis had safely passed. Directors were unsure about how long the interruption would last—whether weeks, several months, or perhaps even years—but they were determined to wait it out. They were likewise unsure about exactly how the restoration of specie payments would be managed—whether that goal would be accomplished piecemeal or whether some private or public agency to promote interbank cooperation would arise to establish uniform procedures and a common reconversion date.

Commercial banks in the United States in the early national era normally maintained more than adequate specie reserves against their current liabilities, which included both outstanding bank notes and deposits. Directors learned that reserves of 15 to 25 percent were usually sufficient to meet occasional requests for the conversion of currency or deposits into specie. Since the emergence of chartered institutions in the 1780s, banks had had little difficulty maintaining convertibility, even during trade embargoes and periodic business downturns. Given the lack of comprehensive documentation for the period, it is impossible to claim that no bank had ever suspended payment, even momentarily, prior to 1814; but except for the failed banks controlled by the fraudulent Andrew Dexter, suspension was certainly rare. More to the point in this discussion, no general suspension of payments had ever occurred in the United States; never had virtually all banks in a given area decided to disallow conversion for a sustained, indeterminate period of time.

The general suspension of 1814 was triggered by an extraordinary event: the successful invasion of Washington by British troops in August. Citizens suddenly feared the possible loss of the war and a prolonged economic crisis. The public had done business with banks for years without suffering losses from the depreciation of paper currency, but under the changed circumstances, most individuals decided to protect themselves and play it safe. Specie was virtually certain to retain its value irrespective of what happened on the political or economic fronts, but the status of paper money was less certain. Holders of bank notes no longer believed they were absolute substitutes for hard money. Therefore, substantial numbers of note holders descended on banks in the mid-Atlantic and upper south states and demanded conversion. By early fall two-thirds of the nation's banks holding 80 percent of aggregate bank capital suspended payment.

The exception was New England. The British invasion was sufficiently distant that note holders never panicked, and banks in the region offered conversion privileges throughout the period. No statistical evidence indicates that New England banks held higher reserves prior to 1814 and thus were more fortified to ward off the demands for conversion.[16] The difference was that citizens behaved more calmly. The holders of bank notes retained their confidence in the future of the economy and the strength of chartered institutions, and bank directors returned the favor by deciding to conduct business as usual. Meanwhile, the arrival of news about the signing of a peace treaty in early 1815 ended any talk about the necessity of suspending payment in the New England states. Its regional banks had weathered the storm.

Banks elsewhere that were under siege from note holders, or thought they soon might be under siege, had two tactical choices. Directors could either continue to pay out specie in an effort to satisfy anxious customers and possibly defuse the panic, or they could, in a more defensive stance, suspend payment. Acting independently, they chose the latter because the former plan risked the possibility of thoroughly depleting their reserves and thereby making resumption at a later date much more difficult. From a theoretical and practical standpoint, bank directors made the prudent choice. Although some note holders were angered, the business community adjusted rather quickly to altered circumstances.

None of the banks that suspended payments actually closed its doors and halted operations. Instead, the banks remained open for business and continued to offer most of the same financial services previously available—everything except conversion. Bankers made new loans as in the past by issuing currency—now nonconvertible— to borrowers and, in turn, accepted their own currency at face value in repayments of outstanding loans. Meanwhile, bank notes traded hands at fluctuating exchange rates. The situation was analogous to conditions in colonial times when legislative fiat issues circulated in tandem with specie at floating rates.

Once banks had suspended payment, directors were in a favorable position to expand their loan volume since the key restraint on currency issuance had been removed. Yet most bank directors exercised a fair degree of caution. Their behavior can be judged by indirect means, with reference to price changes in the American economy during the war years. In response to accelerating domestic demand and the sharp decrease in the supply of imported goods, wholesale prices for basic commodities climbed by one-quarter in 1813 and then another one-fifth in 1814—an overall rise of 55 percent. Following the treaty signing in late 1814, however, and the resumption of active foreign trade, prices began to retreat, falling nearly 15 percent in 1815 and nearly 20 percent in 1816. When the Treasury forced the resumption of specie payments in 1817, wholesale prices dropped another 5 percent. By the end of the year, prices had reached the same level prevailing in 1810.[17]

Despite the complaints of some disgruntled holders of bank notes, most citizens understood the rationale for the suspension of specie payments and accepted the inconvenience. The public realized the banks' protection of remaining reserves was strictly a temporary measure—a policy likely to be reversed in the not too distant future when conditions had improved. The best gauge of public sentiment was the discount rate at which nonconvertible bank notes passed in routine transactions. The notes did not fall precipitously in value vis-à-vis coin, foreign bills of exchange, and other monetary instruments denominated in specie. The discount rates at which bank notes circulated varied by locale and the perceived strength of the issuing bank, but contemporary reports indicate that paper money passed at 90 to 95 percent of face value in New York, 85 percent in Philadelphia, and as much as 75 to 80 percent in Baltimore and Charleston.[18] The holders of bank notes believed that issuers would, in fact, offer conversion privileges again someday, and public confidence in the viability of the banking system prevented bank notes from spiraling downward in value.

Few banks actually failed during and immediately after the war since the quality of their loan portfolios held up sufficiently well—meaning that the vast majority of borrowers repaid their loans. The favorable outcome merits emphasis because it contrasts so starkly with the sorry performance of the banking system during the next quarter century—starting with the Panic of 1819 and culminating with the aftermath of the Panic of 1837. In the later period, many banks that had suspended conversion privileges eventually declared bankruptcy when the quality of their loan portfolios irreversibly deteriorated either as a result of mismanagement or misfortune. In those cases, a resumption of specie payments never occurred and holders of the currency of a failed bank received nothing, or only a pittance, in liquidation proceedings.

Many writers in the 1820s and 1830s misleadingly used the terms *suspension* and *failure* almost interchangeably, implying that suspension meant failure, which confused not only contemporaries but many subsequent historians. From 1818 to 1840 numerous banks suspended payment as a precautionary measure during troubled times, not because they were in immediate danger of collapse. Some banks that suspended payment in the nineteenth and early twentieth centuries ultimately failed, but most eventually got back on their feet and allowed bank note holders to convert freely to specie. Revival was the scenario generally followed in the period from 1814 to 1817.

Most banks that suspended payment in 1814 were in technical violation of their charter terms. Charters were ad hoc legislative documents and varied from bank to bank even within the same state, yet most agreements specified that any bank that failed to satisfy its debts—meaning the conversion of bank notes and deposits into coin—was subject to the forfeiture of its charter privileges. That provision was aimed at an errant bank in an isolated case, however. The forfeiture rule had little practical application during a universal suspension of payments. No state government wanted to declare a wholesale revocation of all bank charters and order the liquidation of existing institutions since the result would have been to make a difficult situation worse for everyone. Long-standing opponents of privatized banking, of institutions that failed to hold 100 percent reserves, and banks that issued small notes (often defined as below twenty dollars) used this opportunity to gloat about the accuracy of their predictions of imminent financial disaster. The we-told-you-so contingent roared loudly, but it made little headway in terms of altering the institutional structure of the American financial system. Few, if any, commercial banks were asked to forfeit their charters because of the suspension of specie payments in 1814.

Following the general suspension of payments by banks, the federal government fell into line and waived its insistence on the collection of customs and other taxes in specie. The Treasury also willingly accepted bank notes in payment for new issues of securities—a procedure that proved a boon to investors who paid in discounted currencies since the principal was later retired in specie-equivalent funds. By way of comparison, investors who had bought congressional bonds in the late 1770s subsequently had their securities holdings adjusted downward to take into account the depreciated value of the currencies used as a medium of exchange. In the earlier situation, congressional fiat paper had fallen to 50 or 25 percent of specie values—and later plunged to fractions approaching zero. In 1814 through 1816, however, bank notes in the major urban areas did not depreciate by much more than 15 percent at their low point. Investors purchasing government securities with bank notes in 1815 received a small bonus when their principal was returned years later, but their gain was nothing extraordinary.

In the spring of 1816 the federal government was instrumental in coaxing the suspended banks to resume specie payments. The Treasury announced that beginning in February 1817 it would again require the use of specie in the collection of customs, tax revenues, and all other transactions involving the federal government. That gave bankers in the mid-Atlantic and southern states more than nine months to accumulate reserves and prepare for the restoration of conversion privileges. The newly chartered Second BUS assisted the state banks in making the transition back to convertibility, and the shift occurred smoothly on the designated date.

In addition to the innovative use of an investment banking syndicate to distribute government bonds and the general suspension of specie payments by two-thirds of the nation's commercial banks, the War of 1812 era is notable in financial annals for a third reason. The final act in this unfolding historical drama, so to speak, was the chartering of the Second Bank of the United States—an event viewed perhaps more accurately as the belated rechartering of the First BUS. Secretary Gallatin had warned congressional critics of the first national bank in 1809 and again in 1811 that, if recharter failed, a national bank would be sorely missed in the event of a major war or some other unanticipated crisis. Virtually everything Gallatin outlined as an unfortunate possibility came true. The federal government encountered difficulty in floating bonds at interest rates and prices that administration officials found acceptable during the war. Without a national bank to provide convenient bridge loans, the administration had resorted to the issuance of treasury notes to pay suppliers. By 1815 most members of Congress, except a few diehards, were convinced that the task would have been easier if a national bank had existed to aid the Treasury in financing the war. Southerners and westerners, including foremost John C. Calhoun of South Carolina, confessed the mistaken judgments of 1811 and vowed to provide a huge congressional majority for a revived national bank.

As a result of the altered circumstances, the ghost of Hamilton returned to roam congressional halls in 1816, after a brief four-year absence; and the ideals of the nation's first treasury secretary were widely accepted in Washington circles for the next dozen years or so. But in 1828 a change in the political winds blew into the office of president a deadly opponent—Andrew Jackson—who had been infected early in his political career by Republican biases against private institutions and large concentrations of financial power. For reviews of the outcome of the confrontation between Jackson and Nicholas Biddle over the continuance of the national bank, in the seesaw battle between Hamiltonian and Jeffersonian ideals dating back to the early 1790s, readers must consult other sources dealing with later historical periods.[19] Meanwhile, in the aftermath of the War of 1812, Hamilton's plan for organizing the nation's banking system around a single institution with huge capital resources enjoyed the fleeting warmth of Indian summer.

The first effort to test congressional reaction to the possible reestablishment of a federally chartered national bank came early in 1814. A few interested citizens lobbied for reconsideration of the issue. But Representative John Eppes, son-in-law of Thomas Jefferson and chair of the Ways and Means Committee, derailed that initiative. Eppes used his political clout to dismiss the proposal out of hand on constitutional grounds. The political outlook changed after Alexander Dallas accepted President Madison's invitation to assume the duties of treasury secretary in October 1814. Dallas was determined to play an active role in pressing for a national bank. A good friend and close associate of many bankers and financiers—among them the trio of Girard, Parish, and Astor—the secretary corresponded and talked with persons committed to overcoming the reservations of powerful committee chairs in Congress. Dallas also received the green light from Madison to move forward, although the president reserved the right to scrutinize carefully any charter bill that emerged from the legislative process. Dallas and Madison were in agreement that any new national bank formed in 1815 should be required to meet its obligation to assist the government in dealing with the current financial crisis.

Within weeks, Dallas presented a bank plan to Congress for consideration. The new bank was modeled on the predecessor institution with a few modifications. The secretary recommended a capital five times larger: $50 million, with private ownership of 60 percent of the outstanding shares and government ownership set at 40 percent. Dallas proposed that the government appoint public representatives to the board of directors and name as well the president of the institution. The most significant deviation from the original charter terms was the requirement that any newly chartered bank immediately loan the government from $20 to $30 million in bank notes to help in financing the current deficit. Since the administration had proposed that the bank start with only $6 million in specie reserves, Secretary Dallas and President Madison clearly intended that the Second BUS begin operations by issuing millions of dollars in inconvertible bank notes. The state-chartered banks had already suspended payment, the administration reasoned, and it saw no reason why the federal bank should not open its doors on the same footing.

Congress was amenable to approving the establishment of a national bank, but members were unwilling to countenance the issuance of inconvertible bank notes or to approve an amendment requiring directors to offer loans to the Treasury or any other loan applicant. Stripped of those controversial provisions, a bill reestablishing a national bank passed both House and Senate by wide margins in January 1815. Angered by congressional deletions, Madison vetoed the measure. Since the bank was under no obligation to assist the government in its current predicament or in future crises, Madison argued that such an institution would make a marginal contribution to the public welfare at best and that was too little to merit his consent.

Nearly a year passed before Congress and President Madison made another concerted effort to create a second national bank. The war had ended months ago; military expenditures were dwindling; and customs revenues were generating substantial income for government coffers. The budget was shifting rapidly from a deficit position to a healthy surplus, and the Treasury no longer needed short- or intermediate-term financing. The administration dropped its insistence on privileged status for the government at the bank's discount window, and it agreed that all bank notes should be immediately convertible into specie. The legislation passed through Congress in the first quarter of 1816, and Madison signed the bill on April 10.

For longtime survivors in public office, politics can be a curious enterprise that follows winding routes to radically different destinations. The truth of that axiom was vividly illustrated when President James Madison affixed his signature to a bill reestablishing a national bank. A quarter century before, he had led the fight to block the creation of the First BUS on the grounds of its alleged unconstitutionality. In 1811 he remained neutral in the recharter fight and, largely because of his passivity, one key fixture in the Hamiltonian program was dismantled after a tie-breaking no vote in the Senate by his own vice-president. Despite his reluctance to become involved in the legislative deliberations, Madison had moved far down the road from outright opposition to neutrality between 1791 and 1811. That trend continued during the war years; by 1816 he had become a mild advocate of a renewed national bank. Madison never fully embraced the concept; but as a pragmatic leader, he appreciated how the First BUS had served the public interest during the lifetime of its charter and acknowledged the validity of the arguments for its rejuvenation. On that issue he finally allowed his Republican attachment to decentralized financial power to lapse and acceded to the Hamiltonian vision of a financially strong and secure nation, crowned with one truly gigantic commercial bank in a position of unchallenged leadership.

The Second BUS was almost an exact replica of its predecessor.

The main office in Philadelphia and its branches were designated as depositories and payment agents for the Treasury. The main difference was that the invested capital was three and a half times larger: $35 million instead of $10 million. Since the size of the U.S. economy was approximately two and a half times greater in 1816 than in 1792, a substantial increase in capital resources was warranted if organizers expected the institution to once again assume a dominant position in the nation's financial markets. Measured on a per capita basis, the Second BUS was only 40 percent larger than the First BUS. Congressional leaders anticipated continued population growth during the next two decades, which meant that the relative position of the bank in the overall economy was likely to decline gradually as the years passed.

Despite the controversy that had swirled around the national bank since the early 1790s, very few of the original charter terms were altered. Congress had a golden opportunity to demonstrate foresight through the reform of certain rules and regulations that might have precluded the reemergence of objections repeatedly voiced against the national bank prior to 1812. Some had complained about its monopoly status, arguing that the granting of exclusive privileges ran counter to republican values and equal access to market opportunities. When a handful of privatized commercial banks initially went into operation in the 1780s and 1790s, acknowledged experts, among them Hamilton and Morris, had occasionally expressed fears that competitive banking was potentially destabilizing. But the experience of the previous fifteen years had shown conclusively that numerous commercial banks could compete and prosper in local and regional markets. Thus, the success of the Second BUS was not dependent, by any stretch of the imagination, on the retention of monopoly status. The likelihood that Congress would create another competitive institution with a large capital as well as the authority to establish a network of interstate branches during the next twenty years was infinitesimal. No major, or even minor, political figure had visions of multiple bank charters at the federal level. The monopoly provision easily could have been dropped, and in retrospect should have been foregone.

The ownership of stock in the national bank by foreign investors was another lightning rod that should have been eliminated in 1816. Over the years foreigners had invested heavily in the stock of the First BUS. The institution paid a steady and predictable dividend, and it provided a higher return relative to the risk involved than many Europeans could earn on investments in their home markets. Soon after the turn of the century, if not before, foreigners owned more than half of the outstanding stock; by 1810 their share had increased to about three-quarters. Opponents of the national bank in 1811 hammered away at the large number of foreign stockholders because dividend payments went overseas. Defenders argued that the initial inflow of foreign capital to purchase bank stock aided the American economy, and they dismissed the accusations of critics as irrelevant and immaterial.

The critics may have been misguided in their analysis, but they had marshaled sufficient votes in the political arena to defeat a bill to recharter the national bank in 1811. Sponsors of the bank's reincarnation in 1816 could have protected the bank more effectively from future political attack if they had the foresight to enact an outright ban on stock ownership by foreign nationals. A ban on foreign participation would have defused another potentially divisive issue that might arise again in a subsequent recharter debate. Americans had sufficient capital resources to finance the Second BUS without any assistance from overseas. But the issue was passed over and never seriously considered by members of the Madison administration or congressional leadership.

In the nationalist fervor following the war, Congress hoped to return as quickly as possible to normalcy. Legislators wanted to recreate the status quo before the war. Almost everyone now agreed that the First BUS had served the nation well, so no adjustments seemed necessary. Former opponents of the bank had been silenced. In retrospect, the failure to alter the two charter terms most vulnerable to political attack, neither of which was vital to the institution's success, was a misfortunate oversight. Because those weak spots were not eliminated, they left a door wide open for opponents to reorganize and mount a second frontal assault on the Hamiltonian plan for a national bank at the center of the American financial system. As it happened, President Andrew Jackson and his allies cited both issues—foreign ownership and monopoly powers— in the successful campaign to deny recharter to the Second BUS in the 1830s.

Conclusion: Continuities and Innovations

T HE COLONIAL, Confederation, and early national periods combined constitute a momentous era for the institutional development of the American financial services sector. The era was marked by organizational, rather than technological, innovations. For most of the seventeenth century, the economy functioned with a financial system consisting exclusively of coins, no organized banks, and an imperceptible capital market. But beginning in 1690, the economies of North America witnessed a series of innovative financial measures—measures that deviated in certain respects from practices in England and other parts of the British Empire. By 1755, for example, all thirteen colonial legislatures had become involved in the issuance of various forms of fiat currencies, a monetary device that had been disavowed in England in the third quarter of the seventeenth century. Nine colonies persisted in their emission through the 1770s. However, in compliance with restrictive parliamentary legislation, the New England colonies reverted to a system based solely on coinage in 1751. After midcentury those four legislatures were instrumental in nurturing an emerging capital market in the New England region. Their treasuries routinely financed periodic budget deficits through the public sale of transferable notes with one- to five-year maturities to local investors.

More innovative policies were implemented in the United States after the signing of the Declaration of Independence. Fiat currency played a significant role in mobilizing resources for the military effort. Congress and the several states relied on huge emissions of paper money—which in most instances depreciated steadily and

349

thus served as an indirect form of taxation—to finance approximately two-thirds of the cost of the War for Independence. The
remaining one-third of military expenditures was financed through
debt obligations, with roughly three-quarters raised at home and
one-quarter overseas in France and Holland. The individual states
extinguished from one-third to one-half of their debts in the 1780s;
but the federal government made no progress whatsoever, even suspending interest payments on all its obligations, except those held
in Holland. In 1790 the entire federal debt and the unretired state
debts, plus accrued interest, formed the core of an enlarged capital
market that arose in connection with Treasury Secretary Hamilton's
consolidated funding program. The plan was hugely successful, and
less than two years after the federal government began functioning under the Constitution, the new nation possessed an expanding
capital market that supported the securities issues of governmental
bodies and soon thereafter numerous private enterprises—including banks, insurance companies, turnpikes, and bridges. The improvement in the nation's credit standing between 1785 and 1795
was nothing less than spectacular.

Meanwhile, privately owned commercial banks issuing convertible bank notes were established in Philadelphia, Boston, and New
York in the 1780s. Their immediate success increased public confidence in the possible public benefits accruing from the adoption of
a broader system of chartered banks. A political maneuver at the
national level was critical in the privatization movement as well. To
make certain that the golden opportunity to revolutionize the financial system would not be lost, opponents of fiat paper inserted a
clause in the Constitution that disallowed any future currency emissions by state legislatures. Then, to advance their reform agenda,
advocates of privatization induced Congress to create the First Bank
of the United States with an enormous capital of $10 million and
the power to engage in interstate branching. The federal government retained ownership of one-fifth of the shares in the new institution but management was left strictly in the hands of private
stockholders. Congress established no other financial institutions,
but the states were active in chartering competing banks. By 1815
more than two hundred state-chartered commercial banks issued
convertible bank notes and maintained deposits. With only a few
isolated exceptions, the banks were conservatively managed, and
their bank notes proved valuable as a medium of exchange and a
reliable store of value.

Two-thirds of the nation's chartered banks suspended payment during the War of 1812, but the inconvenience to holders of bank notes who sought conversion into specie proved only a temporary interruption in most cases. Few American banks actually failed because of heavy loan losses during the war years, and they resumed full service to customers in 1817. Thus, the still experimental system of privatized chartered banks weathered its first serious storm without sustaining any irreparable damage or attracting a host of anti-bank critics. The detractors came out of the woodwork a few years later in the aftermaths of the financial panics of 1819 and 1837 when many commercial banks actually failed and produced losses for irate currency holders and depositors.

In this period of political and financial innovation, the political leadership soon split over an issue related to privatization. Leaders debated whether the nation should work toward the creation of a centralized financial system modeled on British and Dutch precedents or whether, in contrast, the republic should establish a more decentralized system that allowed the direct participation of thousands of propertied citizens residing in hundreds of communities from Maine to Georgia. Attitudes about the exercise of financial power generally coincided with ideas about the proper distribution of political power. The battle over the locus of financial power was simply another round in the perennial contest between center and periphery that Jack Greene has identified as ongoing in British North America throughout the eighteenth century.[1] Most Federalists leaned toward centralization as the best means of avoiding the possibility of anarchy and disunion, and they supported Hamilton's contention that maintaining the national debt at near its existing level—then about $80 million—would serve to strengthen the loyalty of wealth holders to the federal government.

In the opposite camp, Republicans inspired by Jeffersonian ideals were fearful of the potentially corrupting influence of concentrated financial power on the body politic. They abhorred the prospect of a perpetual national debt and the financial institutions typically associated with its maintenance—meaning a domineering national bank, a bevy of ingratiating loan contractors, and untold numbers of irresponsible speculators in public securities. Any sustenance provided to those alleged parasites undermined the nation's virtue. Given the constitutional ban on legislative loan offices at the state level, Republicans favored a more decentralized commercial banking system with hundreds of small- to medium-sized enterprises under the management of local citizens. That theme of local ownership of financial institutions has remained, incidentally, one of the strongest and most unshakable shared beliefs of American citizens throughout the nineteenth and twentieth centuries even in the face of periodic instability—often instability on a massive scale. Jeffersonians encouraged directors of the First BUS to establish several geographically dispersed branch offices. Thus, despite the objections of a few diehards such as John Taylor, most Republicans were prepared to endorse the policy of allowing private initiative in the financial sector. Following the lead of Thomas Paine, they soon acknowledged the legitimacy of Adam Smith's arguments in favor of the creation of financial institutions issuing bank notes convertible into specie.

Treasury Secretary Hamilton was alert to Jeffersonian complaints about the dangers of a close linkage between a large national bank and an expanding federal debt, as existed in eighteenth-century Great Britain. Therefore, to forestall objections Hamilton included a reassuring provision in the charter terms. The charter forbade the First BUS from acquiring additional public securities for its loan portfolio beyond the amounts initially contributed by subscribers to the bank's stock. That meant that the national bank would hold no more than $6 million in public securities at the high point, or less than 10 percent of the total federal debt outstanding in 1790. Bank directors were granted the authority to sell government bonds, but they were denied the option of later replenishing the depleted portfolio with similar assets. In modern parlance, directors could engage in open market operations in one direction only, and no repurchase agreements were permitted. The inclusion of that charter provision went far in calming Republican fears about the possibility of excessive financial centralization arising from a cozy relationship developing between the U.S. Treasury and bank management. Under those tight restrictions, the national bank was effectively eliminated as an engine for inflating the size of the federal debt in future decades. On that score Jeffersonians were reasonably satisfied, although nothing prevented the bank from making short- to intermediate-term loans to the Treasury that could later be refunded, and thereby perpetuated, through the issuance of long-term securities in the capital market.

During President Washington's two terms in office, the Hamiltonian vision was in the ascendancy. The Treasury raised just enough money to pay the scheduled interest on the national debt, which drove up security prices and lowered yields to 6 percent or less. At the same time there were insufficient funds to make meaningful reductions in the outstanding principal. Meanwhile, the First BUS got off to a flying start. Everything was in place and progressing as Hamilton had hoped by 1792. U.S. government securities and the common stock of the First BUS quickly caught the attention of wealthy Europeans who willingly paid handsome prices to make portfolio investments in American securities. Although neither Philadelphia, Boston, nor New York emerged as a financial center with an international reputation, the movement toward achieving parity with the financial services sectors in England and Holland at some future date had been launched and progress was clearly evident.

Beginning in 1795 with the appointment of Oliver Wolcott to the position of treasury secretary and then accelerating after Republican victories in the election of 1800, Hamiltonian principles suffered steady erosion. Wolcott succeeded in reducing the Treasury's dependency on the First BUS for intermediate-term financing by refunding several million dollars in bank debt with an issue of new securities. Soon thereafter, persistent budget surpluses gave Republican administrations the wherewithal to pursue policies designed to foster greater financial decentralization. Presidents Jefferson and Madison together retired more than half of the outstanding federal debt. With the loss of its best customer at the loan desk, the First BUS shifted the focus of lending activities to mercantile accounts at its branch offices along the Atlantic Coast. Failing to gain enough votes for recharter in 1811 in an extremely close vote that divided Republicans, the national bank went into liquidation. With its departure, one pillar supporting the Hamilton structure had crumbled, and the national debt was being steadily eaten away. True-blue Jeffersonians rejoiced at the repudiation of Hamiltonian policies and the continued diffusion of financial power, but the celebration abruptly ended when a second round of warfare with Great Britain revealed the naivete of their understanding of complex financial affairs at the national level.

The Jeffersonian smugness was shattered by events associated with the effort to finance the War of 1812. Without a national bank to extend more-or-less obligatory loans to the government in a crisis situation, the Madison administration was hard pressed to raise the funds to cover huge budget deficits on favorable terms—meaning at interest rates of 6 percent or less. To cover about one-fifth of the cost of the war, Congress authorized the issuance of so-called treasury notes to military suppliers. The instruments were different from the congressional fiat currency emitted during the War for Independence since they bore an interest rate of 5.25 percent and were promptly retired or renewed on their annual maturity dates. Nonetheless, the necessity of resorting to such unorthodox fiscal measures was politically embarrassing. It just proved that Federalist critics as well as numerous Republicans such as Treasury Secretary Albert Gallatin had been right all along in pleading for the continuance of the First BUS on the grounds of practicality and expediency.

The Treasury also raised money through the floatation of more than $60 million in long-term bonds in the domestic capital market. That sum covered about two-thirds of the cost of the war, a vastly superior performance compared to the low percentage of military expenditures financed by the sale of securities to hesitant investors during the War for Independence.

The presence of a national bank to provide convenient bridge loans would have undoubtedly given the Treasury more flexibility in raising long-term funds in the capital market and might have saved the government a modest amount in future interest expenses. As it stood, the net interest rate paid on new issues of securities was 7.1 percent, a very respectable wartime performance irrespective of occasional setbacks in attracting investors. The domestic capital market proved remarkably vibrant under the circumstances. But the favorable response had a distinctly regional flavor since most of the investors resided in the mid-Atlantic section, with Philadelphia and New York City strongly represented.

The Treasury handled most of the transactions without the aid of third parties, but in 1813 it broke with precedent and signed a loan contract with a syndicate of underwriters that marketed $10 million in bonds for a very modest commission. For decades Republicans had expressed contempt for the allegedly parasitic loan contractors that provided similar investment banking services for bloated European governments, thus the deviation from past principles marked a significant turning point in American financial history. The experience of dealing with an underwriting syndicate proved harmless to American liberties, and the favorable outcome paved the way for more mutually beneficial interaction between government agencies and independent financial services firms during subsequent wartime crises. In the postwar nationalistic euphoria, much of Hamilton's original plan for bolstering the performance and reputation of the American financial sector was resuscitated and reinstituted. Foremost was the chartering of the Second BUS— really the belated rechartering of the First BUS since the new institution was virtually the spitting image of its predecessor except for the expansion of 3.5 times in its capital base to $35 million.

One of the striking characteristics of the increasing sophistication of the American financial services sector in the late eighteenth and early nineteenth centuries was its evenhanded development: parallel movements were noticeable in several distinct financial markets. The refinements were mutually reinforcing, thus creating a favorable climate for further advances—in short, a snowball effect. An increasing number of intermediaries arose to quicken financial markets. Beginning in the last decade of the eighteenth century and then strengthening in the years after 1800, the U.S. financial system became a genuinely comprehensive, integrated network. The expanded financial system offered citizens a widening range of new services.

In harmony with trends elsewhere in the financial services sector, innovation was a byword in the insurance, foreign exchange, and securities markets. Whereas commercial banking and public debt financing were often controversial political issues after independence, advances in ancillary financial markets went forward quietly and largely unchallenged—underlining the pronounced privatization thrust in the financial sector after 1790. Political figures rarely divided along partisan lines over the expansion of ancillary services. With few exceptions ambitious entrepreneurs in the financial sphere received solid backing from shifting coalitions of Federalists and Republicans, and they generally had a free hand to respond to the growing demands of market forces.

The insurance sector in Britain and its North American colonies was boldly experimental in the seventeenth and eighteenth centuries. By the early nineteenth century, the insurance field demonstrated a surprising degree of institutional maturation. Insurance companies that concentrated on marine and fire coverage received numerous charters from state legislatures after 1790—at least thirty firms by 1815 with a combined capital totaling in the millions of dollars. Indeed, a strong case can be made for commercial banks and insurance companies as the two most advanced sectors of the

U.S. economy in the early national period. They were the largest scale enterprises in terms of capitalization, with thousands of shareholders.

Lottery organizers made progress as well. A common method of raising funds for private and public purposes in the colonial era, lotteries maintained their popularity in the early national period. Public debates over the morality of gambling with reference to lottery tickets were subdued. Initially local, some lottery organizers expanded their horizons after the turn of the century and sought buyers in regional and even national markets. Lottery ticket brokers, a new vocation, sprang up in almost every locality with one thousand or more residents. A few of the larger brokerage firms headquartered in the major cities bought tickets from lottery organizers at wholesale and then recruited out-of-town agents to distribute them at retail prices to the general public on a commission basis.

Another financial sector that experienced marked institutional improvement in the early national period was the foreign exchange market. In the colonial era few, if any, broker specialists functioned even in the largest port cities. After 1800 the services available to importers, who typically purchased foreign bills of exchange to settle overseas debts, and exporters, who sold bills to reimburse themselves for the cost of shipments, were enhanced because of the more vigorous activities of broker intermediaries.

Securities brokers made an impact on financial markets starting in the 1780s and accelerating after Hamilton's funding program became a reality early in the next decade. During the colonial years, securities brokers were unknown since neither provincial governments nor organized companies issued long-term debt or equities. From 1790 forward government bonds, federal at first but later including state and municipal issues, and the common stocks of commercial banks and insurance companies formed the core of the trading market. Imitating the practices of securities traders in Amsterdam and London, brokers in New York moved rapidly to create an active market with formal rules and regulations. Some were mandated by state governments—for example, no public auctions—and others were agreed to voluntarily by most of the leading brokerage houses. Futures and options contracts of all varieties, although legally unenforceable in the courts, were commonly issued and traded from 1792 through 1815 and beyond.

A few of the most innovative firms in New York, the one headed by Nathan Prime in particular, advanced to the position of broker-dealers. Prime kept a modest inventory of the most regularly traded securities and made a market for them by offering to buy or sell continuously at published bid and ask prices. Hamilton's ultimate goal of duplicating in New York the capital market atmosphere that had evolved in London during the eighteenth century got off to an encouraging start in the quarter century after ratification of the Constitution and presaged the more positive developments that accompanied the railroad boom of the mid-nineteenth century.

The preceding overview of some of the major events in American financial history through 1815 suggests some of the major themes and arguments developed at greater length in the core of this study. One strong undercurrent was the contest between the advocates of institutional experimentation and those forces more comfortable with accepted theories and traditional practices. With reference to components of the money stock, colonial Americans inherited the conventional wisdom that ruled, virtually unchallenged, in the mother country. The prevailing system assumed the primacy of hard money—silver and gold. By the eighteenth century, the British money stock consisted of two elements. Coins produced at the government mint formed the monetary base; the coinage was supplemented by paper monies issued by private firms, which were supported by reserves and were continuously convertible into hard money upon demand. Any deviation from that dual system and the institutional structure supporting its maintenance was dangerous in the eyes of British overseers of colonial affairs.

Members of Parliament's Board of Trade believed that the adoption of alternative monetary systems by colonial legislatures was ill-advised because their implementation was almost certain to leave local economies vulnerable to the consequences of financial instability. In the North American context, however, several legislative initiatives in the monetary field disregarded the dire warnings of the cautious and paternalistic members of the board. Several colonial experiments contradicted the expectations of skeptics and proved enormously successful in meeting the monetary needs of local citizens, including most social classes and occupational groupings, for decades.

Within the field of monetary and banking history, as distinguished from developments in capital markets and other related financial services, the colonial era was one of the most innovative periods in American history. Denied the convenience of a subsidiary mint to produce English coins for the local population, colonial legislatures experimented with the issuance of fiat currency to supplement the inflows of foreign coins, which were mostly of Spanish origin.

All thirteen colonies eventually emitted similar monies, and nine persisted right up to independence despite British efforts to discourage the practice. Twelve colonial legislatures, all except Virginia, also created loan offices that issued unconvertible currencies to private borrowers who offered mortgages against real estate as security. In contemporary Europe every effort to supplement the money stock with tax anticipation bills or to introduce either public or private currency backed by private mortgages rather than specie reserves had ended in disaster. Thus, the more positive performance of fiat currencies in the British North American colonies was precedent setting.

Indeed, throughout the period from 1690 to 1815, monetary stability was the rule in most regions. This conclusion runs at odds with most previous depictions of the status of American finance through the confederation period. The discrepancy between fact and fancy occurred because historians past and present devoted too much attention to the most dramatic episodes of genuine financial dislocation and neglected to grant similar coverage to more ordinary times. Except for irreversible currency depreciation in North and South Carolina from 1710 to 1740, in New England during the 1730s and 1740s, and when the nation was at war from 1777 to 1781, the American economy was blessed with reasonable monetary stability. During the quarter century before independence, every colony experienced financial tranquillity, and a bold acknowledgment of that fact reemphasizes why Parliament's passage of the Currency Act of 1764 was such an ill-considered, unnecessary, and counterproductive piece of imperial legislation. Some provinces such as Pennsylvania, New York, New Jersey, and Maryland consistently maintained stable currency systems for decades even though they routinely included fiat monies in their money stocks.

After Continental currency—Congress' massive addition to the money stock—had fallen in value to near zero and ceased to circulate, monetary conditions settled down and stayed on a fairly even keel for the rest of the confederation period. Treasurer Robert Morris put the federal government on a strictly specie standard in 1782 where it remained for the next three decades. Six states had likewise adopted a specie standard by the signing of the peace treaty in 1783. On the other hand, seven state legislatures refused to abandon a system that had served their citizens so well for so long, and they continued to emit new issues of fiat currency—both the tax anticipation and mortgage-secured varieties. The postwar issues were modest. They did not exceed in value the stock of coins circulating in the local economy, and therefore Gresham's Law regarding the hoarding of specie did not take effect. In some states those monies dropped sharply in value within months of issuance because of widespread fears about a repetition of the downward wartime spiral. By the end of the decade, however, public confidence in the backing mechanisms—taxes and private mortgage payments—was generally restored. The rate of depreciation slowed and eventually halted. By 1788 most of the currency issues had staged a rebound, and the paper circulated at fairly close to face value.

In those seven states, the role of the legislature in shaping the composition of the local money stock was recreated in conformity with the principles of the successful colonial model. That government role was sustained until a majority attending the federal constitutional convention in 1787 voted to adopt a provision that prevented the direct intervention of state governments in monetary affairs. None of the states already involved in currency issuance reversed course voluntarily in the 1780s and moved toward an exclusively specie standard—only the ratification of the Constitution accomplished that result. The constitutional ban must stand as one of the supreme ironies of the postwar period since nine colonial legislatures had battled Parliament tooth and nail from 1764 to 1773 and even threatened rebellion over the very same issue—namely, their right to interject fiat currencies at will into the stock of money.

The confederation period witnessed another bold experiment that affected the monetary system: the chartering of the first privatized commercial banks in the western hemisphere. Privately owned banks issuing convertible currencies were not a novel concept since they had operated in Great Britain for decades. What was different in the new nation was the proliferation of chartered banking enterprises with the authority to pool the capital resources of hundreds of stockholders. In Great Britain, Parliament had granted similar charter powers to only a handful of banks. As a result the British commercial banking system had oligopolistic origins, while its American counterpart was decentralized and atomistic. Even the First BUS, a national institution with large capital resources, created a system of locally managed branch offices.

American chartered banks were reasonably well capitalized and prudently managed. They issued bank notes convertible into coin upon demand. Only three or four small banks, all linked to the same fraudulent individual, failed prior to 1815. With the success of privatized banks, the American economy enjoyed another quarter century of uninterrupted monetary stability. The placid atmosphere was disrupted for nearly three years because of the pressures and uncertainties associated with the War of 1812. The banks outside of New England suspended specie payments. Nonetheless, the bank notes of institutions in areas where suspension was in effect generally retained from 85 to 90 percent of their stated values. The American public had confidence that once the wartime crisis had passed those banks would recognize their liabilities at full value and reinstitute the conversion privilege. And that confidence was well placed, because in the spring of 1817 chartered commercial banks resumed payment. Few banks actually failed because of the economic dislocations associated with the war.

An overview of monetary and banking developments from the early eighteenth century through 1815 reveals a contradictory pattern. Initially, American legislatures deviated significantly from the guidelines recommended by imperial officials in London. A political contest between locally elected colonial governments and members of the supervisory Board of Trade was recurring in some provinces. Once independence had been achieved, however, American monetary policies moved quickly in the direction of conformity with British principles.

As colonies, American legislatures often challenged traditional notions of financial responsibility. More than half the colonies routinely kept in circulation fiat monies that not only served as a convenient medium of exchange but a reliable store of value as well. The 1780s witnessed a mix of the old and the new. Some states reissued fiat currency, while others refrained. Pennsylvania and New York experimented with the simultaneous circulation of fiat currency and bank notes; and despite fears of potential incompatibility, the monetary systems of both states functioned satisfactorily.

In the effort to establish a more lasting union, the political leadership opted for the more traditional, more conservative option: fiat currency was prohibited after ratification of the Constitution. Hamiltonians and Jeffersonians expressed fundamental agreement about the shift in economic strategy. Federalists hoped to duplicate the British system as much as possible; thus, they automatically favored privatization. Once the rival Republicans realized that the states could exercise control over the chartering of private banks within their borders and generate public revenues from the process, they embraced the circulation of coins and bank notes as a superior system. Tainted by the disreputable performance of congressional continentals, the public's fond memories of the positive role of fiat monies in the colonial era faded very quickly. As a consequence of the American reversal, British and U.S. attitudes about the proper organizing principles for an effective monetary system were very much in unison by the 1790s.

The emergence of a system of privatized, chartered commercial banks proceeded with little controversy in the early national era because opportunities for participation by interested investors, particularly persons of modest wealth, expanded as time passed rather than narrowed. The number of charters proliferated, and the number of persons owning stock had multiplied enormously by 1815. Bank directors were citizens with a wide range of political allegiances; in the 1780s and 1790s nationalists and Federalists were the prime investors in the earliest banks, but Republicans played catch-up after 1800. In terms of their ownership patterns, banks became much more democratic institutions than many Jeffersonians had originally feared. Financial institutions served primarily the needs of merchants and governments, but farmers and artisans were also able to gain access to limited services in many locales. Banks were certainly not committed to egalitarian principles, but neither were they overly aristocratic in their organization and operations. State legislatures no longer had the privilege of issuing fiat currency, but the division of powers under the federal political system provided the breeding ground for a fragmented, atomized banking structure.

In Europe, by way of comparison, banking was typically a vastly more elitist enterprise. During the nineteenth century, the most powerful European banks, through growth and merger, moved to consolidate control over their national financial markets. Commercial banking across the Atlantic Ocean became increasingly oligopolistic. A similar scenario of banking consolidation occurred in neighboring Canada as well. But the path of institutional centralization was not followed in the United States because that arrangement conflicted with long-standing American attitudes about the propriety of denying citizens with moderate wealth the opportunity for widespread entrepreneurial participation in the commercial banking sector.

As the nineteenth century progressed, federal and state legislatures discovered that efforts to limit the size and growth of industrial and transportation firms through their power to specify charter terms was a futile exercise, but they were enormously successful at achieving those ends in the field of commercial banking. Granting high priority to the maximization of opportunities for local participation in ownership and management was a choice dictated by the persistence of a rather unique American obsession. In other, more class-bound societies, circumstances that might have permitted widespread entrepreneurial activity simply never emerged. Elsewhere, the issue was largely moot, and its consideration in recounting historical developments within other nations would probably contribute little to an understanding of the evolution of their financial sectors. In the American context, however, the entrepreneurial factor, with all its idiosyncrasies, holds powerful explanatory powers.

A second major topic deserving more focused analysis was the early development of an indigenous American capital market. Its origins lay in the workings of the local economy, but over the decades capital markets became more regional and finally national in scope. Political disputes about the merits of creating a deeper and broader capital market—in particular market institutions highly responsive to the fiscal requirements of the federal government—were very near the heart of the ideological split between Hamiltonians and Jeffersonians. Hamilton aimed at creating a vibrant American capital market in the British and Dutch tradition. At its center, he envisioned a perpetual national debt—not necessarily an escalating debt that reflected the fiscal policies of the European great powers but nonetheless something sufficiently sizable to place a firm grip on the loyalty of wealthy citizens who participated in political life. U.S. public securities would act as market leaders; their high credit rating at home and abroad would translate into relatively low interest rates, perhaps as low as the 3 to 4 percent associated with British public securities.

The treasury secretary made enormous headway toward that goal in the early 1790s, but antagonistic Republican majorities frustrated those policies after the turn of the century. They dismantled the First BUS and cut the national debt in half. The events surrounding the financing of the War of 1812 led to an unexpected and uncharacteristic rejuvenation of Hamiltonian principles. The war produced a nationalistic euphoria and a reconciliation of the two opposing camps that lasted for another decade or so—until the election of President Andrew Jackson in 1828. Thereafter, Hamilton's grand strategy again came under unrelenting attack.

In the absence of banks and other organized financial institutions in colonial times, persons seeking financing for long-term investments in assets such as land, farm improvements, and bonded workers usually turned to local elites. Kinship and community ties were often instrumental in bringing together borrower and lender. Loans were arranged in an informal person-to-person atmosphere with few intermediaries. Savers willing to loan their money at interest sought security in several ways. Formal notes co-signed by friends and relatives were one mechanism for securing loans. Mortgages also provided fairly reliable security since the value of improved properties in settled areas held steady or rose throughout the period. (The same could not be said about unimproved speculative land on the frontier—witness the bankruptcy of Robert Morris.) In arranging sales of real properties, sellers were typically called upon to assist the buyer in financing the transaction over a three- to five-year period. The so-called creative financing associated with real estate deals in the 1970s and 1980s was, in truth, nothing new under the sun. In urban areas, wealthy persons seeking a fairly safe return on invested funds often funneled their money into the rental housing market. But as far as we know, few Americans invested heavily in British consols and other overseas securities.

One sign of the growth and maturation of capital markets was the increased involvement of third parties, or financial intermediaries. The first institutions to become heavily committed to providing long-term financing to citizens were the colonial legislatures. Starting with South Carolina in 1712, every colony except Virginia established legislative loan offices. In harmony with egalitarian principles, colonial governments placed modest limits on how much a given individual could borrow, a policy that guaranteed broad access to the pool of authorized funds. Virtually any voter with some equity in real property, whether in land or houses, with the latter classification included to satisfy artisans, was eligible to receive financing for up to twelve years at relatively low interest rates, typically 6 to 8 percent. Recipients could use the funds for any purpose without advance approval, but most borrowers presumably invested in boosting their productive capacity.

In administering their loan offices, the legislatures exhibited an unusual degree of farsightedness in stipulating that borrowers amortize their loans regularly. Balloon loans, with the entire principal coming due on a distant maturity date, were typically not written by the loan offices. That point merits emphasis because the greater degree of safety and stability associated with amortization was all too frequently ignored in the nineteenth century. Not until the implementation of New Deal reforms of the 1930s—after a pause of more than 150 years—was the amortized mortgage loan extending over a period of ten years or longer rediscovered and commonly adopted in the U.S. economy. The reinvention of prudent devices and policies previously abandoned has occurred frequently in American financial history.

European intellectuals often theorized about the potential benefits of so-called land banks as a stimulus for economic growth, and many writers authored pamphlets and treatises recommending their establishment. Yet, Americans were the first to demonstrate their viability over the long haul. Members of the Board of Trade were invariably dubious about their operations because the loan offices issued inconvertible currency. Despite the reservations of skeptics, the vast majority of the monies issued by the loan offices were ultimately redeemed at face value. Meanwhile, the loans aided in developing the productive capacities of local economies. The activities of the public agencies proved a boon to taxpayers as well since interest revenues were frequently substantial relative to the size of provincial budgets. In the middle colonies, interest revenues generated by the mortgage assets of loan offices covered all legislative expenditures for several years, and sometimes even decades.

The next important phase in the movement toward a more visible capital market arose in connection with the shift in New England away from fiat currency toward the adoption of an exclusively specie standard. Parliament had dictated that monetary realignment in the Currency Act of 1751. The four colonies affected were prevented from issuing non-interest–bearing tax anticipation bills or any form of fiat currency through loan offices. At the same time they were granted the power to finance budget deficits through the sale of treasury notes with two-year maturities in peacetime, and five-year notes when at war.

After midcentury the New England colonies successfully tapped into local capital markets to finance periodic fiscal deficits. The public securities earned high ratings from lenders since they regularly paid the interest due, usually at the legal limit of 6 percent or thereabouts, and legislatures promptly retired in specie, or re-financed, all maturing notes. The borrowing activities of legislatures reinforced economic trends already under way. Estate records indicate that, by the mid-eighteenth century, members of the upper class exhibited an increasing willingness to hold notes, private mortgages, and other financial assets as a proportion of total wealth. The legislative involvement widened, thickened, and deepened financial markets. On the eve of independence, New England possessed a functioning regional market for public securities with intermediate-term maturities that was unmatched elsewhere in North America.

When the War for Independence erupted in the mid-1770s, Congress set up loan offices in every colony in an effort to borrow directly from citizens some of the funds needed to prosecute the war. That initiative was the first step toward the creation of a capital market genuinely national in scope. In the absence of a tradition of public financing outside of New England, the results were modest at best. From 5 to 7 percent of the overall cost of the war was raised through the sale of U.S. securities in the domestic market. My best estimate is that the thirteen states raised between 5 and 10 percent of the funds to cover their military expenditures through the sale of their respective securities to local investors. Congressional bond sales revealed a distinctly regional character; most transactions occurred in four northern states—Massachusetts, Connecticut, Pennsylvania, and New York. The southern states combined produced a small volume of subscriptions to federal debt issues. That weak response was understandable since southerners in general, including great planters, were unaccustomed to investing in financial assets.

During the 1780s the movement toward a stronger capital market suffered a serious setback at the national level. Congress failed to generate sufficient revenue to meet the interest payments on its outstanding obligations, which jumped several million dollars after soldiers and officers were paid in debt certificates when the army disbanded. With the suspension of interest payments in specie, the market value of U.S. securities fell to one-quarter, or less, of par. Some interest was later paid with so-called indents, another variety of fiat currency, but the symbolic gesture of good faith had little positive effect on financial markets.

The individual states performed much better in terms of meeting their debt obligations. Imbued with a sense of urgency, several state legislatures applied enhanced revenues from stiff new taxes, plus the monies raised from the sale of the confiscated properties of loyalists, to make a significant dent in their public debts in the second half of the decade. One justification for the reissuance of fiat currency in seven states was the opportunity to resume interest payments to holders of public securities. Some of that money went not only to owners of state obligations but also to residents in possession of federal debt certificates. While the market for the securities of a temporarily bankrupt federal government stagnated in the 1780s, most states were holding their own financially; and some legislatures made genuine progress in retiring a portion of the outstanding principal.

The main reason Massachusetts and South Carolina became embroiled in divisive controversies over escalating taxes was their mindless determination to accomplish too much too soon in regard to debt settlement. Retiring the entire principal in four years was the announced policy in Massachusetts, and the sustained effort to collect the required taxes despite widespread public protest triggered Shays' Rebellion. In South Carolina wiser heads assumed control of the state legislature at the first sign of trouble and defused the potential for escalating violence.

Events in Massachusetts were particularly noteworthy, however, since until the disturbances of the late 1780s, the state had been in the forefront of developments in the financial sector, having created an active market for its own treasury notes after midcentury. Perhaps overconfidence in its ability to meet the sternest financial test, a belief engendered by its enviable record from 1750 through the 1770s, was the root cause of the state's predicament in the 1780s. The supreme irony was that, in retrospect, stringent tax policies were totally unnecessary because the release of the final report of the congressional settlement committee in 1793 revealed that Massachusetts (and South Carolina) had contributed more than its share on a per capita basis to the common military effort and that compensation due from the debtor states would be sufficient to cover most of the state's overhanging war debts.

With business leaders in Boston diverted by the effects of Shays' Rebellion, ambitious financiers in Philadelphia and New York seized leadership in the capital market. In particular, they arranged with southern agents to purchase a huge share of the outstanding public securities of the southern states after the announcement of Hamilton's proposal that the U.S. Treasury would assume up to $21 million of the states' obligations. Northerners already owned most of the original federal debt, thus their acquisition of southern debts concentrated even further the geographical ownership pattern for public securities.

The birth of a sizable American capital market coincided with the implementation of Hamilton's funding program in 1790. The states' assumption of federal obligations, which in the mid-1780s had threatened to dilute one of the nationalists' key arguments in favor of a more centralized and powerful federal government, was quickly reversed. The gradualist position with respect to debt retirement won out, and its implementation was carried out at the national level. Under Hamilton's leadership, Federalists advocated the gradual, indeterminate approach; and Jeffersonians generally concurred given the nation's precarious situation—politically and economically. Congress set taxes at modest levels—just enough revenue to cover current interest with nothing left for principal reduction.

Hamilton calculated that the government's firm pledge to maintain regular interest payments alone would be sufficient to drive up bond prices and lower yields to 6 percent or less. It would make little difference to investors that the bonds had no fixed maturity dates. And the treasury secretary's intuition proved absolutely correct. Once the Treasury had begun to issue new public securities, the credit standing of the federal government functioning under its new Constitution soared. News about the establishment of a sinking fund boosted investor confidence. The U.S. credit rating overseas rose almost as fast as at home, and foreign investors, especially the British, purchased millions of dollars worth of government bonds from American holders on secondary markets. The huge success of the subscription offer to raise $10 million in stock for the First BUS one year later provided further convincing evidence of the emergence of a more extensive capital market.

Most of the improvements in the financial services market occurred in the northern states in the early national period. The preponderance of investments in commercial banks was in institutions north of the nation's capital. Philadelphia, New York, and Boston emerged as the main investment centers. A small number of private financial firms organized securities exchanges with strict admission requirements and uniform trading rules. Neither federal nor state governments established regulatory controls over those voluntary associations of brokers and dealers. Private controls were apparently effective since contemporary newspapers reported no sensational stories about major scandals linked to dishonest securities dealers prior to 1815. The number of persons possessing stocks and bonds was a fraction of the general population, and most owners presumably qualified as knowledgeable and sophisticated investors.

Adding to their initial holdings of government bonds and stock in the First BUS, investors increased their investments in the equities of numerous state-chartered commercial banks plus a few insurance companies. In 1795 U.S. public debt issues, which had arisen in the domestic economy (not foreign) and totaled around $45 million at current prices ($60 million face value), dominated the market in terms of their aggregate market value. Following the implementation of Jefferson's debt reduction program and the organization of more than one hundred state banks by 1810, aggregate stock values surpassed debt obligations in the portfolios of U.S. investors. By that date the total value of publicly traded American stocks and bonds was approximately $150 million—which translates into a growth rate of about 8 percent annually over a fifteen-year period, an increase of more than twice the rate of population growth.

Thus, despite initial political and ideological resistance, Hamilton's ambitious plan for deepening and broadening the capital market was proceeding on schedule, but with a Jeffersonian twist. The shift to equity investments in a host of geographically dispersed private enterprises—mainly banks and other financial services firms— was more in harmony with Republican principles of economic and political decentralization and the avoidance of the burden of long-term public debt.

The funding of the War of 1812 primarily through massive borrowing created greater balance between public debt and private equities in the American capital market. Outstanding U.S. bonds rose from $45 million in 1812 to $95 million in 1818, with perhaps one-quarter of the latter figure held overseas. The sum invested in the equities of commercial banks, state institutions plus the Second BUS, climbed to nearly $200 million. Add in collateral investments in insurance and turnpike companies, and the overall American capital market had risen to something in the neighborhood of $300 million in the postwar era, with the federal debt component accounting for less than one-fourth of the total.

Another clear sign of the maturation of the domestic capital market was the relative success of the Treasury Department in floating several bond issues during the war years. Unlike the previous War for Independence, the War of 1812 was financed mainly with a mixture of short- and long-term debt rather than concurrent taxation. If the government had been more willing to compromise on the payment of slightly higher interest rates, rather than trying to hold closely to a 6 to 7 percent return to investors, the whole process likely would have gone forward smoothly without the hitches and delays actually encountered.

An institutional breakthrough occurred in 1813 when the Treasury agreed to pay a syndicate of underwriters, or loan contractors, a small commission for the speedy placement of $10 million in undersubscribed bonds. Based on their limited understanding of investment banking activities in London and Amsterdam, Jeffersonians had warned voters for years about the susceptibility of governments to the allegedly corruptive influences of stockjobbers and speculators. Thus, the absence of anything remotely suggesting sinister motives or activities on the part of syndicate members helped to put Republican minds at ease about the dangers possibly arising from fruitful negotiations between elected governments and persons performing investment banking functions.

The rise of the financial services sector in the first quarter century after Washington's election in 1788 was the result of a thoroughly incestuous relationship between commercial banking and capital markets. The two sectors supported and reinforced each other's mutual development. Government bonds supplied 60 percent of the capital sources initially invested in the First BUS. Soon thereafter, directors of the national bank loaned the Treasury several million dollars to cover budget deficits and maintain the interest payments on U.S. securities that supported their market value. It was not unusual for American wealth holders to arrange to borrow funds from a newly organized bank for the purpose of financing their subscription to its forthcoming stock. The rules against conflict of interest and self-dealing commonly applied in our modern economy were less stringent in this earlier era.

Investments in financial assets had been exceedingly uncommon in the colonial era, except for short-term paper in New England; but that tradition ended abruptly with independence. The capital market expanded more rapidly than the size of the general economy. The securities issued and traded were rarely in manufacturing or transportation enterprises but concentrated instead in banks and insurance companies. The expansion of financial markets occurred, therefore, very nearly within the confines of a closed circle, with only the marginal participation of other sectors of the economy. Manufacturing was conspicuously missing from the organization of local capital markets; few firms were incorporated and fewer still, if any, had their shares regularly traded on local exchanges. Moreover, to demonstrate even further their remoteness from the institutional framework of the financial services sector, most manufacturers received only a fraction of their financing through bank loans since directors typically avoided granting accommodations to such nontraditional customers. The limited availability of outside financing for manufacturers differed only slightly from colonial times. It must be noted in this context, however, that some bank charters granted to applicants residing in the largest port cities dictated the allocation of a certain portion of the institution's loanable funds to persons identified as artisans. But that exception does not invalidate the general proposition that manufacturers remained largely isolated from the effects of improvements in financial services through 1815.

Although manufacturing missed out, the transportation sector was able to participate modestly in the expansion of local and regional capital markets. Turnpike and bridge companies, like commercial banks, were chartered corporate enterprises granted the privilege of raising capital through the sale of securities, overwhelmingly equities, to the general public. Turnpike construction began in Pennsylvania in the mid-1790s, but it was heaviest in the New England states and New York. By 1815 approximately $10 million had been invested in the stocks of turnpike and bridge companies, and those shares occasionally changed hands; but transactions typically occurred after direct negotiations between buyer and seller rather than from the intervention of brokers or other financial intermediaries. Aggregate investment in the shares of transportation firms was no more than 5 percent of the sum invested in financial institutions, however.

In the United States, the segment of the economy that made the earliest contribution to the creation of an infrastructure conducive to institutional change and economic advancement was the financial services sector. For subsequent eras, economic historians have pointed to textile manufacturing, canal building, railroad construction, and steel mills as key stimulants to economic advancement. But not enough credit has been given to the groundwork laid by banks and securities exchanges in the early national era. Building upon the base established in 1815, the number of chartered commercial banks grew from several hundred to more than fifteen hundred by the end of the antebellum era. What emerged was a decentralized commercial banking system with a strong local orientation just as Jeffersonians had advocated from the outset. The foundations laid down in the capital market were drawn upon later as well to finance the huge American investment in canals and railroads after the proven success of the Erie Canal. Although New York continued to lag London as an investment banking center, the international reputation of U.S. securities, both public and private, reached new heights in the second half of the nineteenth century.

Appendix:

Stockholders' Liability

If viewed strictly from a de jure standpoint, the historical evidence regarding whether stockholders in the late eighteenth and early nineteenth centuries had limited or unlimited personal liability for a firm's potential losses is inconclusive. When the charter terms approved by governmental bodies failed to address the issue of stockholder liability, contemporary Americans often expressed uncertainty about the extent of legal responsibility.[1] In practice, meanwhile, it appears that few creditors of failed U.S. banks—consisting mainly of the innocent holders of outstanding bank notes plus a bank's depositors—ever succeeded in recovering even a portion of their losses by proceeding against the personal assets of stockholders.[2] Until the depression following the War of 1812, the legal point was largely moot because there was only one incident of failure during the first three decades of chartered commercial banking. The Farmers Exchange Bank of Glocester, Rhode Island, failed in 1809 because of the grossly fraudulent activities of its principal owner and president, Andrew Dexter.

Based on the precedent of common law in the eighteenth century, incorporation in Great Britain typically did not alleviate stockholders of their responsibilities to creditors in the event of business failure. Only Parliament could charter corporations, and it did so infrequently for business enterprises after the fiasco of the South Sea Company in the 1720s. Stockholders in corporations held the same legal status as multiple participants in the partnership form of business organization. The law recognized no difference between business and personal assets in bankruptcy proceedings involving all types of business enterprises.

The legal question had never arisen in connection with the banking sector, however, because British law, in the aftermath of the South Sea Bubble, had restricted the issuance of paper currency to the Bank of England and to unchartered partnerships with six or fewer partners. Members of British firms that issued currency never doubted their unlimited personal responsibility to creditors. Possibly because of the preemptive competition from the colonial legislatures, no private American firm is known to have issued paper money in substantial quantities for any extended period prior to independence, although no laws appear to have prevented proprietorships and small partnerships from entering the market.

When the founders of the Bank of North America submitted charter applications to Congress and simultaneously to the legislatures of the
several states in 1781, the question of stockholder responsibility for the
excessive debts of the corporation beyond its own assets was not a subject
covered in the charter provisions. Since the question of liability was left
unaddressed, stockholders were presumably unsure about their status.[3] A
few years later, in the debates in the Pennsylvania legislature in late 1786
and early 1787 over a new state charter for the BNA, the issue was aired in
local newspapers. William Findley, a critic of the bank, asserted that limited
liability was unwarranted because it would give stockholders the "power to
ruin their neighbors and benefit themselves without risque."[4] But Robert
Morris in a rebuttal argued that since bank shares often changed hands,
determining which group of stockholders might be personally liable would
likely prove impractical. "I am a stockholder today, but not so tomorrow;
and how is the party to prove that I had any share or interest during the
term of his transactions?"[5] Legislators were unable to resolve the issue, and
following precedent, they avoided any definitive statement about liability
in the charter terms of 1787.

The extent of stockholder liability arose in the organizational history
of the Bank of New York, which opened for business in 1784. The bank
began as a variant of the joint-stock form of organization—defined here as
an enterprise with numerous owners who subscribed to stock certificates
with a stated par value but a firm which held no corporate charter from
any governmental body. The bylaws written by Alexander Hamilton stated
that "no subscriber or stockholder should be answerable for the debts of
the bank beyond the amount of his stock." But some skeptics doubted that
the bylaw would hold up in the event of a suit. Five years later in a petition
to the state legislature, a group of owners formally requested the privilege
of corporate status. The petition stated that the bank was contemplating
an expansion of its capital but that potential investors had been deterred
because of the fear that stockholders would be personally responsible for
all the bank's engagements.

The charter granted by the New York legislature in 1791 contained a
provision that represented a compromise position between the extremes of
narrowly limited liability and completely unlimited personal responsibility.
The focus of the liability clause was in conformity with the charter terms,
which stated that the total debts of the bank, its currency issue and deposits,
should never exceed three times the capital stock. In case of failure, stockholders were liable for up to three times their stock investment; but the
bank's directors, who were invariably stockholders as well, were held personally and unconditionally liable for all "excess" debts if they had voted in
favor of exceeding the charter limitation. Directors absent when the vote
was taken or voting in the negative were absolved from personal responsibility for debts arising from deviations from charter terms, although they

were still liable along with other stockholders for three times the value of their investment.[6] The federal charter for the First Bank of the United States in February 1791 had a similar provision regarding directors.[7]

In two precedent-setting cases in Massachusetts in 1819, the courts ruled that, in situations where the charter terms did not specify the extent of owner liability, stockholders were not liable beyond the amount of their investment. After the Hallowell and Augusta Bank closed its doors and liquidated, two creditors filed separate suits against one of the principal stockholders. Chief Justice Isaac Parker, who drafted the court's opinion covering both suits, wrote that under American common law, which he referred to casually as an expression of "public opinion," stockholder liability was restricted. He pointed to several bank charters recently approved by the state legislature that made stockholders explicitly liable for losses beyond the original capital investment and thus reasoned that earlier charters that were silent on the subject had not intended expanded responsibility.

In another critical case decided in the Maine circuit court district in 1824, Justice Joseph Story was even more adamant about the absence of expanded owner obligations. Story wrote, "The individual stockholders are not liable for the debts of the bank in their private capacities. The charter relieves them of personal responsibility, and substitutes the capital stock in its stead." Legal historian Merrick Dodd has argued that, with the issuance of this opinion, Story was instrumental in introducing the trustee concept to American law as it relates to incorporated enterprises. The directors were acting in a fiduciary capacity toward a group of passive stockholders who had, from a certain perspective, entrusted them with the sound management of their capital under the terms of the corporate charter.[8]

American courts were fairly consistent in upholding one aspect of stockholder liability, however. Stockholders were responsible for the full value of their pledged subscriptions; partial sums paid in to capital accounts were not considered the limit of their investment obligation nor a restriction on liability. During the period of financial distress surrounding the War of 1812, when virtually every commercial bank temporarily suspended the right of noteholders and depositors to convert their claims into specie coins, a few creditors sued the deficient subscribers of certain banks, asking the courts to require payment in full—in specie, of course—of the subscribers' obligation to the chartered corporation. Before those suits could be finally adjudicated, however, the banks had resumed convertibility.[9]

As these examples make clear, the American common law evolved in an entirely different direction from the English tradition regarding the liability of stockholders in corporate enterprises. In the absence of explicit charter provisions specifying responsibility, the courts generally ruled that stockholders were not personally liable beyond the amounts invested or subscribed. In instances where liability was assigned to passive investors, it was normally limited to a specific amount, often a multiple such as two or three times the par value of the shares registered in an owner's name. Meanwhile, the bank directors were identified as a small subset of stockholders with a special responsibility to follow faithfully the terms of the charter and to prevent thereby the implementation of risky lending policies that might lead to excessive losses. In most bank charters the directors' liability was more open-ended and sometimes even unlimited, a status that corresponded more closely with British precedent.

Meanwhile, the attitude of American courts, which looked with favor on the limited liability status of investors in chartered commercial banks and other incorporated enterprises, served to encourage savers who possessed neither the time nor ability for active management to invest their funds in bank equities. Having escaped the restrictions of parliamentary legislation regarding the legality of firms with more than six partners to engage in the issuance of currency, and having received some degree of limited personal liability for corporate debts from state legislatures and the courts, the door was opened wider for savers to place their monies at risk in the equities of banking enterprises. Merchants, planters, and other investors were eager to invest in commercial banks once they had reasonable assurances that their personal liability for the losses incurred by the corporation was not without limit, but an obligation that had clear and specific parameters. Moreover, the belief in restricted stockholder liability arose very early in the nation's history; its presence coincided closely with the creation of publicly chartered commercial banks in the last two decades of the eighteenth century, and that general outlook was confirmed by court rulings in the decade following the signing of the Treaty of Ghent in 1815.

Notes

Chapter 1

1. Governors and colonial assemblies established several unauthorized mints in the seventeenth century, which produced coins for periods ranging from a mere few months to three decades. The mint in Massachusetts began operations in 1652 and produced coins in denominations of three penny, six penny, and one shilling—with a smaller two-penny coin added a decade later. When the King's Commissioners discovered the existence of the illegal Massachusetts mint on a tour of New England in the years after the Restoration, they ordered the suspension of its operations in a directive dated May 1665. However, whether due to indifference, oversight, or—most likely—the outright defiance of English authority, the mint continued to function as late as 1682. Half a century later, in the 1720s, the owner of an English mint received permission from the crown to manufacture a special series of coins exclusively for export to the colonies. But the scheme failed, largely because the variously denominated coins contained only about 50 percent of the metallic weight of their English counterparts and the colonists simply refused to accept them as a store of value and a medium of exchange. Spanish coins in circulation in the colonies, by way of comparison, were officially overrated by only about one-third, a far cry from the nearly 100 percent overvaluation proposed by the English mint operator. For more information on early American mints and coins, see pertinent chapters on the colonial period in Bowers, *History of U.S. Coinage*, and in the Newman and Doty, eds., *Studies on Money in Early America*.

2. According to Myers, *Financial History*, 5, the separate charters granted to Virginia and Maryland permitted local mints, but the two colonies never established them.

3. For a broad discussion of the ideas of seventeenth-century English leaders related to money and the coinage, see the chapter titled "A Crisis over Money," in Appleby, *Economic Thought*, 199–241. She cites flaws in Locke's arguments. Contrary to his assertion regarding the immutability of monetary principles, silver coins had been circulating at face value, or near face value, among the English population for decades in the seventeenth century even though prevailing market prices for their metallic content was about 50 percent of their nominal monetary value. As Appleby points

out, there were numerous instances in England (and we could add other countries) when coins passed routinely at values much higher than dictated simply by the market price of their metallic component. However, Locke was by no means the first individual in the history of economic thought to repudiate the lessons of daily experience or to contradict irrefutable evidence passing right under his nose.

4. For data on the monetary stock, see Horsefield, *Monetary Experiments*, 14.

5. Feavearyear, *Pound Sterling*, 172.

6. Bullion, *Great and Necessary Measure*, 164. About six thousand red-coats were stationed in North America from 1765 to the early 1770s, suggesting that, on average, soldiers and officers received about £16.5 in cash payments annually. Most of the remuneration for foot soldiers and sailors actually came in the form of food, clothing, and lodging, which were paid for with bills of exchange issued against the British Treasury—not with coin. Alden, *South in Revolution*, 51.

7. McCusker and Menard, *Economy of British America*, 338. In the early 1770s the British government allowed Virginia to place an order for about 950,000 half-pennies, stamped "Virginia," with the Royal Mint in London.

8. Newman, "American Circulation of Halfpence," 134. As a result of reading more about the circulation of Spanish and English coins with relatively low denominations in the colonies, I have been led to question the hypothesis raised by John Hanson in "Small Notes" (1980). He suggested that one of the prime motives for the persistent use of paper money might have been a strong desire to introduce monies into the economy that would make easier the negotiation of small transactions. The fact that colonial paper was issued in a wide range of denominations, including some as low as one penny, may indeed have contributed to its popularity; but I would, at present, discount that factor as a very significant reason for the enactment of the currency laws. Hanson cited as prime evidence a publication, signed by seventy-five Philadelphia merchants in 1742, offering prices for various types of specie, "which presumably reveals the denominations of the most common coins circulating in the colony." The lowest value listed was 7 shillings, 6 pence—admittedly an astoundingly high amount. But Hanson's presumption may be incorrect: merchants may have simply chosen not to deal in smaller coins because of the limited potential for profit in exchange and arbitrage. Whatever the explanation, I believe it highly likely that Spanish coins in denominations of eight reales and less were reasonably commonplace in Philadelphia and other coastal areas in the eighteenth century.

9. Flynn, "New Perspective," analyzes how the demand for money affected the size of national stocks of money. McCallum, "Money and Prices," estimates that the per capita stock of money in sterling values, specie and paper combined, varied from region to region: £.70 in New England, £1.75 in the southern colonies, and £2.0 in the middle colonies.

10. McCusker and Menard, *Economy of British America,* 338, likewise assert that the money stock was adequate.

11. See Michener, "Shortages of Money," for the most vigorous exposition of this general line of argument. Michener believes temporary shortages were genuine enough in the eighteenth century, and that contemporaries were correct when they asserted in pamphlets and petitions that such shortages had caused depressions. Depressed business conditions in foreign markets, however, often caused outflows of money in the colonies. In addition to shortages of money, the episodes of depressed economic activity were typically characterized by high interest rates, frequent bankruptcies, unemployment, and widespread resort to the use of shopnotes (private paper issued by merchants), book credit, and barter. When the money supply began to increase, often in response to a rebound in the export sector, economic conditions in the local economy improved and complaints about money shortages declined.

Chapter 2

1. The Chinese were apparently the first society to experiment extensively with fiat currency, but its use ceased in the fifteenth century. Yang, *Money and Credit in China.* The Wexelbank in Stockholm, Sweden, began issuing convertible bank notes in the 1660s. McCusker, *Money and Exchange,* 119.

2. The best brief surveys of banking in England and Scotland have been written by Rondo Cameron in a collection of essays that he also edited titled *Banking in Early Stages of Industrialization.*

3. For estimates of the amounts in default, see Feavearyear, *Pound Sterling,* 111–16, and Horsefield, "Stop Revisited."

4. The best analysis of the Law scandal is Neal and Schubert, "First Rational Bubbles." For an amusing, brief account of the debacle, see Galbraith, *Money,* 27–34.

5. Joslin, "London Private Bankers," 169; Presnell, *Growth of Country Banking,* 2–14.

6. In 1732, for example, a group of 170 persons in Connecticut received a charter from the provincial legislature permitting the establishment of the New London Society for Trade and Commerce. It soon began issuing notes against mortgages totaling more than £15,000. Governor Talcott suspended operations the next year on the grounds that the enterprise had exceeded the terms of its charter. The best account is Stark, "New London Society," but Bushman, *From Puritan to Yankee,* also provides coverage.

7. Perkins, "Conflicting Views on Fiat Currency." The article discusses in much more detail colonial efforts to form private banks.

8. Lester, "Currency Issues," and Schweitzer, *Custom and Contract.*

9. Pennsylvania allowed tenants without real property to use the loan

proceeds as part of the down payment for the acquisition of land that they were currently farming.

10. Massachusetts, Rhode Island, and South Carolina were the exceptions. Currency issued by the loan office depreciated heavily because hundreds of borrowers simultaneously defaulted on mortgage debts, and the legislature failed to authorize the seizure and sale of the properties pledged as collateral. As this manuscript was being written in the late 1980s, debate raged in academic circles about the extent to which tangible backing was a factor in maintaining currency values vis-à-vis specie and foreign bills of exchange not only over the long run but also on a monthly and yearly basis as well. Bruce Smith has argued that collateral was at all times extremely important in preventing depreciation. Smith, "American Colonial Monetary Regimes" and "Some Colonial Evidence." Ron Michener disputes that hypothesis. Instead, he offers an explanation of currency values and commodity prices based on the quantity theory of money. He believes that currency maintained purchasing power mainly because of the existence of de facto fixed exchange rates enforced loosely, but effectively, by wealthy mercantile firms. In colonies with fixed rates, Michener argues that when paper money was introduced into the economy, offsetting specie exports prevented the overall size of the money stock from expanding. Later, when paper was retired, specie flowed back into the colony to replenish the stock of money. As a result of the alternating inflows and outflows of specie, prices rose and fell within a fairly narrow band. The exceptions were in New England and South Carolina, where the volume of currency placed into circulation in the decades before midcentury greatly exceeded the original size of specie stocks. Michener, "Shortages of Money" and "Fixed Exchange Rates." Elmus Wicker has challenged Michener's thesis because of the absence of solid data on the actual size of aggregate money stocks in the colonial era. Wicker to author, private correspondence, October 1986.

11. Benjamin Franklin recommended in the mid-1760s, during the controversy over the Stamp Act, that Parliament establish a land office of its own throughout the colonies. By issuing paper money against mortgaged land, Parliament would provide a uniform monetary system for all thirteen colonies and simultaneously generate sufficient revenues to assume the burden of paying the salaries of the royal governors and make a sizable contribution toward imperial defense expenditures in North America. Franklin's proposed solution had the virtue of linking together the two most divisive issues in colonial-imperial relations: money and taxes. In retrospect, the idea had substantial merit. Its adoption certainly would have been a better choice than the tax policy that parliamentary leaders ultimately selected, namely, their ill-fated decision to attempt to raise revenues through stamp taxes and duties on certain colonial imports.

12. In 1755 Virginia enacted legislation to allow courts to settle all suits involving sterling debts in either local coinage or paper currency at "just" rates of exchange, meaning the market rate prevailing on the date of the

court judgment rather than the colony's official rate of exchange—a fixed rate based on the legal value of its proclamation money. Ernst, *Money and Politics*, 54. English creditors would have preferred, however, the granting of judgments at the market rate prevailing when a debt initially became past due or, alternatively, on the date when the lawsuit was first entered on the court's docket. Some cases were not settled for years; and during the interim between the date of filing and the court's final ruling, the market value of a colony's currency was subject to further depreciation.

13. Richard Lester argued a positive impact from the issuance of fiat currency in a pioneering article published in 1938 titled "Currency Issues to Overcome Depressions in Pennsylvania, 1723 and 1729." In *Custom and Contract*, Mary Schweitzer reinforces that general position. She claims that when government currency replaced commodity money, transaction costs were lowered thus stimulating economic activity. According to her calculations, per capita income rose steadily in Pennsylvania from 1723 to the 1750s.

14. Main, *Society and Economy*, 82. McCusker and Menard point out that probate figures in general may be misleadingly low, however, since money was among the items most likely to be distributed outside of routine probate proceedings, either as gifts made in anticipation of death or by the secretive actions of close relatives—*Economy of British America*, 338, n. 14.

15. Webster, *Political Essays*, 142. Alexander Hamilton's estimate of £6.75 million sterling, offered in a letter to Robert Morris in April 1781, was until recently granted a fair amount of accuracy by financial historians. But Michener, "Fixed Exchange Rates," 277–80, has questioned its validity. He argues that Hamilton's estimate is much too high—on the order of 200 to 300 percent.

16. Jones, *Wealth of a Nation*, table 5.1, p. 128. More recently, McCallum, "Money and Prices," has produced estimates of cash holdings per capita in local money and in British sterling for several colonies over a series of years.

17. The colonial economy was advancing at an annual rate of 3.5 percent versus only 0.5 percent for Great Britain from 1650 to 1775, according to the comparative data in McCusker and Menard, *Economy of British America*, 57.

Chapter 3

1. Book credit was common not only to merchants but to farmers, artisans, and other occupational groups as well. Some scholars have argued that the sums recorded in account books should be included as a legitimate component of the money supply—West, "Money in Colonial Economy." But that reasoning is wrongheaded from several perspectives. As a practical matter, a credit balance listed by one person's name was rarely transferred through offsetting bookkeeping entries to settle an outstanding

debt owed by a third party. *Rarely* is the key work here, because advocates of the "book credit as money" position can point to instances when such transactions did, in fact, occur; but in my mind those instances are the exceptions that prove the general rule. Unlike coin and currency, book credit was not universally transferable nor was it officially recognized as legal tender in the settlement of private debts and the payment of public taxes. On the other hand, those account balances, positive and negative, were crucial components of the credit system. In the absence of banks to extend commercial loans to firms and then later in our own era to finance consumer purchases through credit cards, the provision of credit services in the colonies can be viewed as a system functioning in a much more atomized manner than holds true today. But the basic idea of allowing persons, firms, or governments the privilege of delaying payment—whether made at a subsequent date in form of monetary units, in kind, or in services rendered—is a concept no less applicable in the seventeenth century than in the twentieth.

2. Shammas, "How Self-Sufficient?" She estimates per capita expenditures of £3.5 on imports across provincial borders in the 1760s.

3. Rothenberg, "Market and Massachusetts' Farmers," reveals just how frequently farmers arranged overland transportation for their output to markets in locations fifteen to one hundred miles away.

4. Bellesiles, "Community Strategies," examines in detail the thousands of transactions that William Heywood of Charleston, New Hampshire, recorded in his four-hundred-page account book in the second half of the eighteenth century.

5. Jones, *Wealth of a Nation*, table 5.1, p. 128. In *Society and Economy*, Main was able to generate data for receivables but not for accounts payable in Connecticut. By the late colonial era, he found that receivables accounted for about one-fifth of personal wealth (p. 36). His Connecticut data are generally compatible with Jones' figures for the entire region; her numbers show financial claims, good and doubtful, accounting for 19.3 percent of personal net worth in New England.

6. Shepherd and Williamson, "Coastal Trade," calculated between £600,000 and £700,000 in coastal trade among the colonies, with New England accounting for 45 percent of the imports (p. 87). Since the middle colonies sent substantial amounts of wheat to New England after 1750, it seems likely that Philadelphia grain merchants regularly granted fair amounts of credit to wholesalers in Boston and other ports in the region.

7. Price, *Capital and Credit*, table 2, p. 8.

8. Jones, *Wealth of a Nation*, table 5.3, p. 130.

9. Main, *Society and Economy*, found that accounts receivable climbed from about one-eighth of personal wealth during most of the colonial period in Connecticut to 20 percent toward the end. Jones' data revealed that rural residents in Pennsylvania, New Jersey, and Delaware held almost

twice as many financial assets (£61) as liabilities (£33). Rothenberg, "Markets, Values, and Capitalism," argued that farmers in New England became net suppliers of capital, not borrowers, in the decades immediately after independence.

10. The figures in Jones' study represent the aggregate debts outstanding in a specific year—1774. The numbers include a substantial amount of double counting, however, because one seller's initial decision to extend credit could lead to several derivative transactions within the Anglo-American mercantile network. Suppose, for example, a British merchant granted credit to an American importer who then sold goods to a third merchant in a nearby town and he, in turn, repeated the procedure with a fourth participant—perhaps a storekeeper or the ultimate consumer. The aggregate volume of debt linked to an initial £100 transaction at the top of the chain of credit might generate £500 or more in accounts receivable over a period of twelve to eighteen months. To calculate the *net* investment in mercantile working capital, all the overlapping receivables associated with the sale of a given item of merchandise must be subtracted from the aggregate debts subsequently generated. Unfortunately, there are no estimates of exactly how much overlapping occurred. It is possible, however, to arrive at a minimum figure for net colonial indebtedness. The number to start with is the sum that British creditors had invested in the American market to finance their trading activity. Exclusive of markups for profits, Price put the number at £4 million in the early 1770s. Aubrey Land, in "Economic Behavior," asserted that debts among Virginians themselves exceeded by far all the amounts owed to British creditors, but Jones' data on patterns of southern wealth holding cast doubts about the validity of that assertion. My guess is that much of the domestic lending in the southern market represented a recycling of British credit. Why, after all, would indigenous merchants find it profitable to commit their own funds heavily to working capital if the British were already extending generous lines of credit at very low interest rates? It seems likely that Virginians would take advantage of a favorable situation and allow their suppliers to provide most of the financing for the trade sector. In the northern colonies, where British creditors maintained fewer accounts, American merchants were required to tie up much more of their own capital in financing inventories and receivables. In addition to working capital requirements, we must add the credit applied to finance real estate, building projects, the purchase of bonded workers, and other types of business improvements. Making a guess about the magnitude of net domestic capital invested in the provision of credit services is a risky venture, but I believe £9 million to £12 million embraces its probable parameters in the early 1770s.

11. Breen, *Tobacco Culture*. British firms operating stores in the southern colonies made an effort to call in overdue balances in 1772, and a flock of lawsuits was filed to force payment. Many lawsuits were eventu-

ally settled, however, by converting the sums owed on open account to signed notes at interest. Price, private correspondence with author, December 1987.

12. Price, *Capital and Credit*. Sources of the missing 45 percent are unknown.

13. In *Custom and Contract*, Schweitzer reveals another unique method of raising a down payment that was among the options available to most young people. Like many penniless prospective immigrants, domestic youths could sign indenture contracts specifying the provision of labor services over a period of months or years in return for maintenance and the payment of substantial freedom dues. That mechanism was perhaps a drastic means of creating forced savings, but it was an effective device for some individuals who either lacked self-discipline or simply had no viable alternative.

14. In *Custom and Contract*, Schweitzer found that some Pennsylvania tenants were able to obtain funds from the government loan office to assist in financing the acquisition of an occupied farm from the current landlord.

15. In "Consumer Credit," an article written in the 1940s, Plummer cited cash loans granted by one Philadelphia merchant in amounts ranging from one shilling to more than one hundred pounds.

Chapter 4

1. Some fiat issues did contain an interest component. In instances where interest compounded over the years, some holders decided to retain the bills as an investment vehicle rather than use them as a medium of exchange. Monetary historians still differ about whether the two-year interest-bearing paper issued in New England after 1751 merits inclusion in the money supply or should be counted instead as a debt instrument. I favor the latter choice. We may need to employ someday the modern device of M^1 and M^2 to estimate the size of alternative money stocks in colonial New England.

2. I believe that previous explanations of the law of the land relating to the powers of the state legislatures to issue currency under the Constitution are lacking in certain respects. Most historical accounts state flatly that the national government was granted exclusive authority over all monies, thus precluding the states from augmenting the monetary stock on their own initiative. Section 8 gives Congress exclusive power to "coin money, regulate the value thereof, and of foreign coin." That authority corresponds to the power that Parliament had exercised over the monetary system throughout the British Empire during the seventeenth and eighteenth centuries. Parliament had complete control over the coinage, which meant the estab-

lishment and operation of any mint authorized to manufacture metallic coins. But Parliament did not claim exclusivity within the realm of paper monies, which were routinely issued by private banks in England and Scotland. It failed to set rigid rules regarding the emission of fiat currency in the colonies, in large part because few public officials in Britain were willing to recognize nonmetallic forms of money as wholly legitimate. Meanwhile, Section 10 prohibited the states from coining money, emitting bills of credit, and "making anything but gold and silver coin a tender in payment of debts." The language here is imprecise since it fails to make clear whether the legal tender prohibition extended to public payments as well as to private debt obligations. The assemblies had repeatedly battled Parliament in the 1760s and 1770s over the legal tender issue, and a compromise was finally reached in 1773. The negotiated settlement denied legal tender status for paper in private debts, which covered the accounts of British creditors, but paper money was recognized as a legitimate form of payment in all public transactions. My reading of the documentary evidence and the detailed discussion in Hurst's learned treatise on the legal history of U.S. money suggests that the states and localities were prohibited from *monetizing* their public debts through the issuance of tax anticipation bills, but I see no legal obstacle preventing them from issuing such monies through the other mechanisms relied upon in colonial times. For example, the issuance of currency by a government loan office, a system operational in twelve of the original thirteen colonies, was not presumably outlawed by the wording of the Constitution. Another acceptable procedure would have been the method adopted by Maryland in the 1730s, when the assembly issued an equal amount of currency to every taxable person in the colony, plus extra sums to owners of taxable slaves; those monies represented neither a public debt nor private loan. Moreover, depending on one's interpretation of the wording in Section 10, the states might have been able to declare such paper monies an unrefusable form of payment at their own respective loan offices, and perhaps for all state and local obligations, including taxes. More support for this hypothesis about the leeway in the Constitution relates to subsequent institutional developments in the financial sector; in the early nineteenth century, some states established publicly owned banks that issued paper money in the course of making loans. If state-owned banks had the right to issue currency in the course of transacting business with private citizens, I see no reason why the states could not have accomplished the same result more directly without creating a chartered corporation. One major difference between the colonial loan offices and state-chartered banks was that the latter had the enhanced power to accept deposits. The ability to perform the deposit function may have been the factor that tipped the scales in favor of chartered banks over public loan offices in the new nation. James Willard Hurst, *A Legal History of Money in the United States, 1774–1970* (Lincoln: University of Nebraska Press, 1973), 3–27, 176–85.

Chapter 5

1. Ferguson, *Power of Purse*, 333–34, n22. A report prepared for the House of Representatives in 1790 put the cost at $135 million, but that calculation was made before the final settlement of state accounts in 1793; see Myers, *Financial History of U.S.*, 50–51.

2. The total cost of the Civil War consumed about 20 percent of the nation's aggregate output from 1861 to 1865, but the relative costs borne by geographical sections varied substantially. The war diverted about 15 percent of northern output but consumed approximately one-third of southern production. The differential helps to explain why southern incomes fell so far behind the national average in the postbellum era.

3. Foreign coins, mainly Spanish, remained in circulation well into the nineteenth century and many were granted legal tender status. Coins, both U.S. and foreign, accounted for about one-third of the monies in circulation in 1810 and about 20 percent of the aggregate money stock (coins, bank notes, and deposits).

4. Wicker, pointing to Brock's massive study of colonial finance, has disputed Smith's claim that a substantial volume of Massachusetts notes circulated as currency and therefore merit inclusion in estimates of the provincial money stock. Wicker, "Colonial Monetary Standards," 872–73. Brock stated that some interest-bearing notes in small denominations, under £6 colonial (£4.6 sterling), were issued as bills of credit to meet military payrolls. But, citing a letter from Governor Francis Bernard in 1764, Brock concluded that most treasury notes were denominated in high values, probably £25 to £100, and represented specie loaned directly to the provincial government by a small group of wealthy investors who held the notes until the assigned maturity dates. Brock, *Currency*, 274. I concur with Brock and Wicker.

5. Ferguson, *Power of Purse*, 29, 43.

6. Alexander Hamilton reported to Congress in 1790 that old tenor emissions had totaled $357 million. Other sources have reported numbers in the range of $250 million, and the exact figure may never be known. Hamilton estimated the currency's purchasing power in specie at $92 million, but I have accepted Ferguson's recalculated figure of $47 million specie for old tenor monies, which reflects the application of a more rapid depreciation schedule. In his biography of Hamilton, Ver Steeg claims the specie value was only $37 million.

7. New emission currency sold at discounts of 80 to 85 percent in Boston as late as 1789, but market prices rose sharply during the next two years; by 1792 the discount was only 15 to 20 percent. Davis, *Essays in Earlier History*, 1, 339–40.

8. The states had a better record in regard to maintaining the purchasing power of their currencies than Congress. Overall, state currencies purchased goods and services valued in specie at about 30 percent of their

nominal values. The comparable figure for the federal government was only 20 to 25 percent, with the lower or higher range dependent on whether we count or disregard the counterfeit issues officially withdrawn. Congressional currency had a good record in 1775 and 1776 and a respectable performance in 1777, but it deteriorated apace in 1778 and 1779.

Chapter 6

1. The first unchartered bank in the new nation was the so-called Pennsylvania Bank, formed in the summer of 1780 by about ninety Philadelphia merchants to supply provisions to the Continental army. The announced capital was £300,000, although it remains doubtful that the sums actually paid in approached even a fraction of that figure. Morris subscribed £10,000. Congress agreed to guarantee the firm's interest-bearing notes, and the Treasury put up as security £15,000 in bills of exchange drawn on U.S. accounts in Europe. The subscribers purchased military supplies with promissory notes having maturity dates running up to six months, and they later received reimbursement from the Treasury. The Pennsylvania Bank did not maintain deposits, hold specie reserves, or make direct loans to borrowers. Since the firm never functioned as a formal commercial bank, the title was an unfortunate misnomer. Nonetheless, it formed the loose organizational nucleus for the Bank of North America since many subscribers decided to transfer their investment into the chartered institution. The firm wound up its affairs in 1784. Soon thereafter, a group of Philadelphia merchants proposed the establishment of a chartered commercial bank tentatively titled the Bank of Pennsylvania (simply a reversal in word order) to compete locally with the Bank of North America. Their plans were thwarted in the mid-1780s as one outcome of a huge political controversy, but a revived Bank of Pennsylvania opened under a state charter in 1793.

2. When the Bank of New York was in the process of formation in 1784, there was some discussion about converting it into a branch of the Bank of North America; but New York investors decided that they did not wish to see their local institution come under the administrative control of outsiders, especially rival Philadelphians.

3. Morris to Benjamin Harrison, 15 January 1782; quoted in Ferguson, *Power of Purse*, 135.

4. Only diehards like John Taylor of Caroline continued to rail against bank notes and the alleged evils of privatized commercial banking through the first decade of the nineteenth century. Taylor's warnings fell mostly on deaf ears, because until the War of 1812 and its aftermath, banks almost universally maintained convertibility. Johnson, *Foundations of Economic Freedom*, 113. When some banks failed in the 1820s and repudiated their outstanding paper, however, the more extreme hard money rhetoric was reinvigorated,

and it had a profound effect on Andrew Jackson's attitudes toward banks and bank notes throughout his two terms in office.

5. Lamoreaux, "Banks, Kinship," 659. Her study focused on New England, however, and it is possible that liability patterns in the middle Atlantic states differed.

6. The first statement date with numbers on reserves is the end of 1793, when coin and specie holdings were listed at $462,000. Bank note and deposit liabilities were around $1.5 million, implying reserves of 30 percent or so. Most contemporaries simply ignored deposits and calculated reserve positions strictly against outstanding bank notes, however.

7. I am unaware of any data indicating how far and wide BNA notes might have circulated in the 1780s. During the colonial period, it was quite common for Pennsylvania paper to flow across borders into contiguous colonies, where it frequently passed at rates little different from home.

8. Doerflinger, *Spirit of Enterprise*, 303; Molovinsky, "Pennsylvania's Efforts to Finance the War," 206. In discussing the composition of the Pennsylvania money stock in a comparative context, Doerflinger focused strictly on two numbers: the size of outstanding colonial issues versus the volume of bank notes issued by the BNA. He mentioned in passing the paper monies emitted by the state legislature, but he failed to make any estimates of their magnitude or their contribution to the aggregate money stock in the 1780s. Molovinsky reported that the Pennsylvania issue of 1780 had depreciated by almost 90 percent a year later, but appendix table 4 in Bezanson's monograph on Philadelphia prices indicates that, after falling precipitously from April to July, the issue rebounded sharply in the second half of 1781. By February 1782, the paper traded at only a 20 percent discount from specie, and the exchange rate remained at about that level until its retirement in 1785. Bezanson, *Prices and Inflation*, 345.

9. Doerflinger, *Spirit of Enterprise*, 308.

10. A name similar to the Bank of Pennsylvania's had been affixed to an earlier enterprise organized by a group of local merchants under the leadership of Robert Morris in 1780. Despite the title, it never functioned as a commercial bank but rather as a purchasing agent for the Treasury during the last year or so of the war. The prior firm had wound up most of its affairs by 1784. For more details, see footnote no. 1 on the Pennsylvania Bank.

11. Hamilton to Gouverneur Morris, 4 April 1784, in J. Hamilton, ed., *Papers of Alexander Hamilton*, 1, 418; Morris to Jefferson, 8 April 1784, in Sparks, ed., *Diplomatic Correspondence*, 12, 485. Letters cited in Schwartz, "Beginnings of Competitive Banking," 419–20.

12. Lewis, *Bank of North America*, 67.

13. Quoted in Hammond, *Banks and Politics*, 59.

14. The Bank of New York operated as an unchartered bank from 1784 to 1791, when the goal of obtaining statute limitations on the liability of stockholders led the directors to apply to the state legislature for a cor-

porate charter. For more information about the Bank of New York and the evolution of limited liability for stockholders, see the Appendix.

Chapter 7

1. The entire national debt was not paid off until the mid-1830s, but it rose sharply as a result of the Louisiana Purchase in 1803 and escalating military expenditures linked to the War of 1812. I calculated a payoff year of 1817 for all debts linked to the War for Independence by applying every annual federal surplus from 1790 forward against the initial indebtedness of $70 million.

2. Soltow, *Distribution of Wealth*, 142–44. Loyalist claims totaled about 10 percent of the nation's estimated total wealth in 1774.

3. Becker made the perceptive argument that the South Carolina legislature's actions prevented rebellion in "Combustibles in Every State," a conference paper presentation several years ago and, unfortunately, still unpublished.

4. The percentage of outstanding principal that was paid off in states pursuing a vigorous policy of debt redemption was undoubtedly much higher. That assertion seems reasonable since some of the $18 million absorbed in 1790 represented accrued interest linked to the debts of laggard states. Treasury officials had estimated that $21 million in state securities would prove eligible for the swap program.

5. After the temporary withdrawal of its corporate status by the Pennsylvania legislature, the Bank of North America also operated as an unchartered joint-stock company for several months in late 1785 and early 1786. The Bank of New York finally received a state charter in 1791.

6. The majority of the federal debt held in New York consisted of settlement certificates issued to military personnel for back wages at the end of the war plus a variety of federal debt obligations originally issued to citizens of other states, mostly in the South. The debt obligations had been acquired subsequently for speculative purposes by a few firms in New York City that were active in the secondary market.

7. New Jersey minted three thousand copper token coins valued at one-fifteenth of a shilling, or about 80 percent of an English penny, for the convenience of citizens in negotiating small transactions.

8. In the colonial era, when amortization schedules called for uniform principal reductions starting in the second year—versus starting in the eighth year under the existing program—loan office officials had reissued monies associated with the repayment of principal to other eligible borrowers. In this instance, monies paid to cover the interest due on public loans in the late 1780s and early 1790s were not burned but instead reissued by the state treasury to meet routine public debts as had been the practice before independence.

9. In one of those bizarre political moves involving financial affairs for which Rhode Island was notorious, the individuals who had earlier agreed to participate in the debt settlement program in 1787, and who had received only about twenty cents on the dollar, later tried to convince the federal government to grant them full compensation as well. In June 1791 the state legislature resurrected all war debts and repealed every law relating to their previous liquidation through the issuance of fiat currency. After boasting that all its debts were completely retired in 1788, Rhode Island was now arguing the exact opposite, namely that all its old debts remained outstanding. The U.S. Treasury rejected that contention, however, and refused to cooperate in any program that might have compensated some persons twice for the same claim. Historian Irwin Polishook's brief account of the controversy over the retirement of Rhode Island's wartime debts in the period from 1790 to 1830 is unclear about the exact outcome. He suggests, however, that the state may have made additional payments to individuals who had reluctantly but voluntarily participated in the debt-for-currency swap in 1787. Polishook, *Rhode Island,* 240.

10. I estimated the mean depreciation ratio of 200:1 as follows: the $15 million of old currency retired prior to 1790 was divided by the $70,000 worth of new emission monies specifically allocated for the currency swap program in 1783.

11. The plan for sending funds to the federal government was convoluted. The state paid newly printed currency to local farmers to purchase tobacco; it expected to sell the crop to an overseas buyer for specie and remit the proceeds to Philadelphia. The market price for tobacco apparently fell during the interim, however, and the operation realized losses rather than the anticipated profits. Morrill, *Practice and Politics,* 198.

12. Bronson, "Connecticut Currency," 123.

13. The announced exchange rate was 40:1, but the states had the privilege of reissuing so-called new tenor bills at an effective exchange rate of 20:1.

Chapter 8

1. Analyzing the origins of Shays' Rebellion has been a historical perennial since its occurrence in 1787. We can sample here only a few of the most recent and prominent interpretations. In "Shays'," Pole argued for a political rather than an economic interpretation, pitting the western counties, which were underrepresented in the legislature—in part because of the high cost of travel and lodgings—against rivals along the eastern seaboard over a whole host of political issues, including the balance of sectional power in state government. Szatmary's monograph *Shays',* published in 1980, suggested that the roots of the insurrection can be traced to the clash between traditional, agrarian values versus the encroachments of a

more commercial, market-oriented society. In *Politics without Parties*, Hall carefully described the legislative debates over tax and debt policy in the 1780s. Taylor's earlier study, *Western Massachusetts*, emphasized commercial indebtedness more than taxation, whereas the McDonalds, *Requiem*, focus on high tax rates more than private debts. In "Political Economy of Shays'," an unpublished manuscript loaned to the author, Ernst reviews the monetary and fiscal history of Massachusetts during the entire eighteenth century and ends with an assessment of factors contributing to the rebellion. The only study that attempts to analyze tax policies in a comparative framework is Becker's "Combustibles in Every State," a paper delivered at a national conference in 1982 that remains unpublished to date.

2. Feer, "Shays' Rebellion," disputes the contention that the rebellion weighed heavily on the minds of the delegates attending the constitutional convention in Philadelphia.

3. Bates, "State Finances," 42–52; Norton, "Paper Currency," 63.

4. Bates, "State Finances," appendix 3, p. 159.

5. Ferguson, *Power of Purse*, 254. Massachusetts appraised its fiat currency and treasury notes at their value *when issued* rather than the full extent of their depreciation. For example, treasury notes issued in 1778 were rated at 4:1 vis-à-vis specie, the prevailing market on the issue date, rather than the 40:1 exchange rate that was current for those issues in 1781.

6. Hall, *Politics without Parties*, 203, n. 28, from Governor Bowdoin's speech to the legislature in June 1786.

7. Jensen, *New Nation*, and Bjork, "Weaning of American Economy."

8. The only modern parallel to Massachusetts' fiscal policy was the disastrous policy (by Keynesian standards) implemented by Romanian dictator Nicolae Ceausescu in the early 1980s to pay off the nation's substantial foreign debt in less than a decade. The goal was accomplished but at an extremely heavy cost to the economy and the people. Living standards reportedly declined on the order of 50 percent in Romania during the 1980s because the nation ran huge surpluses in its foreign trade account. After the final payment was made in 1989, Ceausescu's government was able to boast that the nation was free from the dictates of foreign creditors and that avaricious capitalists would no longer be earning interest income from the labor of struggling Romanian citizens. He found little political or economic support anywhere for his bizarre fiscal policies, either in capitalist or socialist camps. However, if Ceausescu had been able to travel back two hundred years to the United States, he might have been able to elicit endorsements from members of the urgency faction in confederation Massachusetts—and possibly from Jeffersonians southward who likewise wanted to rid their governments of all debt obligations as rapidly as possible. Ceausescu was arrested and shot by a firing squad during the political uprisings in eastern Europe in December 1989.

9. Bates, "State Finances."

10. McDonalds, *Requiem*, 32.

11. Bullock, *Historical Sketch*, 1–22, endorsed the fifteen-year redemption period as practical and reasonable, arguing that retirement over that time frame would have caused taxpayers little economic hardship.

Chapter 9

1. Much of the debt issued to southerners—for example, to soldiers returning from the war—was subsequently sold to northern investors. Particularly active were several mercantile firms in Philadelphia and New York City that diversified into the financial services sector. Federal debt certificates traded at low prices from 1782 to 1788 because Congress had suspended payment of interest. Certificates acquired on the secondary market from out-of-state residents were generally ineligible for the various swap programs at the state level.

Chapter 10

1. The best Hamilton biographies are by Forrest McDonald and John Miller cited in the bibliography. An excellent introductory sampler of the reactions of contemporary political rivals plus the interpretations of later historians remains the Cantor edition, *Hamilton,* in the Great Lives Observed series. A representative collection of contemporary views about debt funding and the national bank, as well as other economic issues in the 1790s, is found in Johnson, *Foundations of Economic Freedom.* For an outstanding explanation of Hamilton's financial program, see Swanson, *Origins of Fiscal Policies.* The author grants the treasury secretary too much credit for originality and stresses too strongly the influence of European financial theorists for my tastes—still it remains an indispensable book.

2. Schubert, "International Integration of Financial Markets," 300.

3. Dickson, *Financial Revolution,* 487.

4. See Neal, "First Rational Bubble"; Brewer, *Sinews of Power;* Patterson and Reiffen, "Effect of Bubble Act."

5. Jones, *Wealth of Nation,* tables 5.2, 5.5, 5.7, 5.10.

6. Congress also received a subsidy of $1.6 million from the French government, plus a subsidy of $180,000 and loans of $175,000 from the Spanish.

7. Norton, "Paper Currency," chart of treasury notes, 49; the newspaper quotation is from fn. 11, p. 48.

8. The Jeffersonians tended to identify strongly with France, and the immature character of the Paris capital market relative to London and Amsterdam may have elicited more votes of approval in some quarters. Yet, it is difficult to conceive of Americans, whatever their political leanings,

condoning the sale of venal offices as was common in France under the old regime.

9. Economic historians long ago disavowed the assertion that the two nationally chartered banks in 1792 and 1816 were genuine central banks, in large part because the banks failed to act as lenders of last resort in financial crises. Yet, in my view, continued use of that term along with the qualifier "quasi" or "embryonic" is justified since the national banks did seek to control the activities of the smaller state banks through the regular redemption of their outstanding bank notes and, under Biddle in the 1820s, the Second BUS occasionally took limited responsibility for the short-term performance of the overall economy. Biddle, for example, occasionally intervened in the foreign exchange market to dampen seasonal fluctuations. Contrary to the later assertions of President Andrew Jackson, both national banks also gave the nation an exceedingly safe paper currency—similar to what the Bank of England had accomplished overseas.

10. Jefferson to Washington, 9 September 1792. I found the quotation in Swanson and Trout, "Alexander Hamilton's Hidden Sinking Fund," and they reported the source as Paul L. Ford's *The Writings of Thomas Jefferson* (10 vols. New York, 1892–99), vol. 6, 105.

11. Brewer, *Sinews of Power*. The author explains: "Perhaps the single most frequently made complaint about the expansion of the eighteenth-century fiscal-military state was that it had created a 'financial interest,' a consortium of bankers, 'monied men,' investors, speculators and stockjobbers who lived parasitically off the state's need to borrow money to fund its wars. According to their critics, financiers were responsible for a multitude of sins. They were commonly viewed as part of a whig plot to tie the public to the new regime of 1688 and as the true power behind ministry and monarch" (p. 206).

12. McDonald, *Hamilton*, 168. See *Hamilton Papers*, 6:81–84, 111.

13. Hamilton's fear of a crash redemption program was justified because during Jefferson's eight years in office, the government ran an aggregate surplus of $41 million. Because of legal limitations on the recall and retirement of U.S. securities, Secretary of the Treasury Albert Gallatin was unable to use all the financial resources at his disposal to retire even larger chunks of the federal debt. Some of the surplus monies went to pay for the Louisiana Purchase in 1803. Even so, when Jefferson left office, the debt was down to $57 million and steadily sinking. On a per capita basis, the debt burden had fallen from more than $25 in 1790 to less than $10 by 1810.

14. The government could also borrow up to $2 million annually at interest rates not exceeding 5 percent to purchase securities with coupon rates of 6 percent. Such refunding did not reduce the overall indebtedness but did allow the Treasury the opportunity to refund a portion of the debt at slightly lower interest rates.

15. Swanson in *Origins of Fiscal Policies* provides an outstanding summary of the arguments offered by advocates of sinking funds.

16. In his 1790 report, Hamilton proposed that creditors be given the option of swapping their old debts for other types of financial devices as an alternative to new federal securities. Among the ideas advanced was one proposal, which Congress failed to approve, that would have allowed holders to accept so-called tontines—interest-bearing insurance policies of sorts in which persons were grouped into various age categories and survivors received shares of the interest previously allotted to the deceased. Those who lived the longest began with returns of only 4 to 5 percent but ended up with many multiples of that amount in their last years. The plan was innovated by Lorenzo Tonti in France in the 1650s and used thereafter at times by both the French and English governments. A key advantage, in this context, was that the government was never obligated to pay back the principal outstanding to any of the participants. When the last survivor of a given group of subscribers died, the whole obligation was canceled. Three joint authors—Jennings, Swanson, Trout—in "Hamilton's Tontine Proposal" argued that Hamilton's advocacy of a tontine scheme for the United States proves that the treasury secretary was serious about the elimination of the national debt. But I remain doubtful. Certainly, he did not press the issue with Congress in 1790. Perhaps Hamilton realized that the success of tontines might diminish the prospects for his plan to create a thriving capital market based on marketable securities.

17. Smith, "Of Public Debts," quote in vol. 5, chap. 3.

18. Risjord and DenBoer, "Evolution of Parties," 204. Ferguson, *Power of Purse*, 298, called Madison's statements in 1790 a sharp reversal of position. Madison had publicly opposed the concept of discrimination in 1783, and he never raised the issue in November 1789 when Hamilton explicitly asked for comments and criticisms of an advance draft of the message delivered to Congress in January 1790. Madison explained his actions by claiming that he was suddenly overcome with sympathy for the original holders because of reports of rampant speculation, but Ferguson labeled that justification "dubious" since speculation had been continuous for the last seven years. Banning, "Hamiltonian Madison," adds that Madison wanted a wider dispersion of benefits, believing Hamilton's plan inappropriate for a republican government.

19. Hamilton was initially keen on retaining New York as the capital city in 1789, but he failed to generate much support from his own congressional delegation, which favored Philadelphia or another location in Pennsylvania. With New York City out of the running, Hamilton was more open to compromise on the site of a permanent capital city.

20. Treasury documents do list the names of persons who registered for the receipt of indents linked to securities initially issued in states different from the owner's residence. Of the domestic principal of $27 million, 10 percent was registered by December 1787, 17 percent by March 1789,

and 34 percent by June 1791. Those numbers suggest that the volume of interstate trading in federal securities rose dramatically after the new government was successfully organized and congressional debates about the debt had begun. Ferguson, *Power of Purse*, 255–57.

21. In one verified transaction in 1793, the 3 percent bonds sold for $65, which translates into a current yield of 4.6 percent. The deferred-interest 6 percents sold on the same date for $70. Assuming they rose steadily to par in 1800 when interest payments were scheduled to begin, their rate of appreciation would have produced a return of about 6 percent. How high bond prices actually rose (or possibly fell) was dependent on prevailing yields seven years hence, thus there was an element of uncertainty regarding future interest rate trends. That factor was reflected in the prices of this series of U.S. securities during the 1790s. The interest-deferred securities had some of the properties of today's so-called stripped treasury bonds. Collins, "Continental Bonds."

22. Ferguson, *Power of Purse*, 252.

23. Yields of 8 to 12 percent on government obligations were common in France during the eighteenth century, and the same was true for securities issued by many continental governments.

Chapter 11

1. The financial data on the bank are found in Holdsworth, *First Bank*, 48–49.

2. Some members of the Adams administration favored the issuance of discounted securities at a 6 percent coupon rate; priced at 75 or thereabouts, the bonds would have produced an 8 percent current yield to investors. But Wolcott was against the idea of discounted bonds on principle. Bolles, *Financial History*, 198.

3. Blodget reports a Treasury loan of $700,000 on the books of the First BUS in 1805 in his *Economica*, p. 185.

4. Bruchey, "Hamilton and State Banks," discusses the possible absorption of state banks into the BUS network.

5. The main office also issued so-called post notes, payable in specie at some future date, typically thirty days, which were transferable by endorsement. (Post notes are similar in concept to post-dated checks in the modern era.) The demand bank notes issued by the main office were instantaneously convertible at all branches; those issued by one branch office were normally convertible at the other six branches, but not typically at the Philadelphia office. Wettereau, "First Bank," 282.

6. The Second BUS under the administration of President William Jones initially allowed interbranch convertibility, and that liberal policy contributed to the bank's difficulties in 1818 and 1819.

7. The official records and accounts of the First BUS have not sur-

vived; the supposition is that all the official records perished in the great
Treasury fire of March 1833. Scattered and incomplete information for
the 1790s was discovered at the Cincinnati Historical Society in the papers
of Oliver Wolcott, who succeeded Hamilton as treasury secretary in 1795.
For more information about archival sources on the bank, see Wettereau,
"New Light."

8. Redlich, "Origins of Created Deposits," claims little deposit creation through bank lending occurred much before the 1820s and 1830s, but
other evidence suggests that the practice was fairly common in the 1790s.

9. The data on stock prices comes from Holdsworth, *First Bank*, 136.
After 1810, market prices dropped to slightly below par in anticipation of
the bank's imminent liquidation.

10. Johnson, *Foundations of Economic Freedom*, emphasized in 1973 that
despite differences over congressional charter powers and the discrimination between original and final holders of public securities, Hamiltonians
and Jeffersonians shared similar views on a whole host of economic topics,
including the duty of government to create an atmosphere that permitted
citizens every opportunity to become property holders and thereby useful
members of society.

11. Curiously, in my view, the opponents of the charter did not concentrate on the exclusiveness issue in the debates of 1791. The proposed
"monopoly" status of the First BUS would, on the face of it, seem to have
been vulnerable to attacks from persons drawn to the liberal, antimonopoly
ideology espoused by Adam Smith. Anti-federalists were opposed to any
and all congressional charters whether multiple or singular. The monopoly
issue did not play a prominent role in the defeat of the recharter bill in
1811, but acted as a lightning rod in the 1832 confrontation over the Second BUS, and unnecessarily because exclusivity was not a prerequisite for
the success of either bank. I addressed that topic in an article published
in 1989 on the Second Bank, but most of the arguments advanced would
apply equally well to its predecessor; see Perkins, "Lost Opportunities for
Compromise."

12. In 1832 President Andrew Jackson cited the high percentage of
foreign ownership as among the many reasons for denying recharter to the
Second BUS, and he gave the issue a new twist. Since so many shares had
fallen into nonvoting status, Jackson alleged that Americans owning only a
minority of the aggregate shares but a majority of the voting shares were
in a position to exert excessive control over the elections of members of the
board of directors, which was grossly unfair because it placed too much
voting power in too few hands. Privately, he complained that most U.S.
stockholders were his political opponents—probably true—who purposely
voted against candidates for the board who Jackson hoped to see elected—
almost certainly a grossly exaggerated accusation. Whatever the real truth
about the partisan activities of American stockholders, the failure to place

limits on foreign ownership was politically dangerous both in 1791 and 1816; see Perkins, "Lost Opportunities for Compromise."

13. The government received 8 percent dividends on its investment in bank stock so the net expense was only $320,000, or only 4 percent—the same interest due on the aggregate funded debt through 1800. Once the Treasury started borrowing from the bank to cover budget deficits in the 1790s, it paid the standard 6 percent rate and the net expense to tax-payers rose. After Hamilton departed, the Treasury Department began selling its shares in the bank, and the revenue from dividends that had offset some of the interest expenses was correspondingly reduced.

14. A second means of estimating the additional loan volume is to cal-culate the interest revenues necessary to pay dividends of 8 percent on the par value of capital stock. Following the custom of the era, bank directors voted to retain few earnings to strengthen the capital base. Minus expenses, which were probably low since directors received no compensation, and minus the small number of salaried officers, often only the branch's cashier plus a few clerks, the bank needed on the order of $1 million in gross reve-nues. Subtracting the fixed inflow of $480,000 from the U.S. government, the additional revenues required could have been generated by loans out-standing of $8.7 million. If true, the portfolio of earning assets would have exceeded capital by only two-thirds in the first year of operations.

15. Wettereau, "Branches of First Bank," 93.

16. Both speeches are reprinted in Krooss, ed., *Documentary History,* 386–400.

Chapter 12

1. Gallatin, "Report on the Bank of the United States," 3 March 1809. Reprinted in Ferguson, ed., *Selected Writings of Gallatin,* 265.

2. The story of Andrew Dexter's elaborate scheme to print volumes of bank notes without adequate specie reserves and to keep several banks afloat in Massachusetts and Rhode Island for months by shipping currency to distant points is colorfully told in Hammond, *Banks and Politics,* 172–76. The record suggests that Dexter may have been the first American to negotiate an early version of an LBO—the leveraged buyout that be-came so popular in financial circles in the 1970s and 1980s. According to Hammond, Dexter was able to buy the Glocester Bank in 1808 "with the bank's own assets" in a creative transaction that simultaneously made him the "bank's chief debtor."

3. Goldin and Lewis, "Role of Exports." The authors estimated that per capita income fell at an annual rate of 0.34 percent from 1774 to 1792 and then rose at 1.1 percent from 1793 to 1805. During the entire three decades, incomes climbed overall only 7 percent, an average of only

0.25 percent annually. Estimates of comparable growth rates in the colonial period range from 0.3 percent to 0.5 percent. Those numbers suggest that the revolutionary generation experienced one of the slowest periods of income growth since European colonization in the seventeenth century.

4. For a list of the banks in operation in 1800, see Klebaner, "American Banks, 1781–1801," 530–33.

5. Naomi Lamoreaux in "Banks, Kinship" characterized early New England banks as institutions created primarily to serve the aspirations of their creators and owners rather than the financial requirements of the wider community. Banks in the region provided a safe currency for the general public but offered little else in terms of credit facilities and other financial services. My guess is that her generalization would be less valid in other parts of the nation in the early national period, where banks typically had larger capitalizations and broader ownership patterns. In the larger cities many merchants who agreed to serve on boards of directors, a task often viewed as public service to the community, owned just a few shares. As a result, the names listed in the loan portfolios of early banks were likely more diverse than twenty-five years later in most communities.

6. The data on New England banks come from Fenstermaker, Filer, and Herren, "Money Statistics"; the authors' long-term goal is to chase down comparable information on early banks in other states as well.

7. For a discussion of financial services in the four major port cities, see Krooss, "Financial Institutions," 111.

8. Risjord, *Chesapeake Politics*, 473–76.

9. Quoted in Reubens, "Burr, Hamilton," 114.

10. Hunter, "Manhattan Company," 137–42.

11. Sylla, Legler, and Wallis, "Banks and State Finance," 401.

12. Hammond, *Banks and Politics*, 187–88.

13. According to Sylla, "Forgotten Men of Money," a substantial number of private bankers performed a variety of financial services from independence through the Civil War. Most of the firms he cites were doing business between 1830 and 1860. Presumably, private bankers were conducting business in the early national period as well. Only four states had passed laws restricting currency issues by unchartered firms as late as 1809, and enforcement was lax in many areas. Sylla suggests that many private bankers decided to apply for charter status when restraining orders went into effect in their states. The proposition seems plausible since the number of applications for chartered commercial banks rose sharply after 1810; eight states passed restraining acts from 1810 to 1818. Nonetheless, private banks were generally on the periphery; few had a major impact on the size of the money supply, with the exception of the Girard Bank in Philadelphia.

14. The Girard Bank's founding comes near the end of the period under review, and therefore it receives less attention than might have otherwise been the case. In his *Finance and Enterprise*, Donald Adams noted that Girard required loan customers to maintain compensating deposit balances

with the bank even though he paid no interest. Girard may have been an innovator in that respect. The effect of compensating balances was to increase the real interest rate on borrowed funds. For example, with the requirement of compensating balances of 20 percent, the real interest expense on a loan with the nominal rate of 6 percent jumps to 7.5 percent. Through the 1960s many American commercial banks demanded compensating demand deposits, on which no interest could be legally paid, from business customers—at least that was still the rule when I worked briefly for the Chase Manhattan Bank in 1963–64. Since that date, deregulation has dramatically altered the relationship between borrowers and lenders.

Chapter 13

1. One of the oldest surviving English policies, dated 1547, covered the *Santa Maria* on a voyage from Cadiz, Spain, to London. As a result of a lawsuit, details ended up in the records of the Admiralty Court. Raynes, *British Insurance*, 29.

2. Brewer, *Sinews of Power*, 194.

3. Shepherd and Walton, *Shipping, Maritime Trade*, 76.

4. Stock quotations for shares of London Assurance and Royal Exchange Assurance appeared in Boston newspapers as early as 1721. Royal Exchange Assurance stock was quoted at 30 and London Assurance at 22 to 25 in the *News-Letter* of 17 April 1721; the quotations were based on a London news source dated 8 October 1720. Hardy, *Early Insurance*, 27.

5. Gillingham, *Marine Insurance*, 102.

6. Hardy, *Early Insurance Offices*, 25–26, 32.

7. White, *Beekman Papers*, 17, 32, 38, 73.

8. Gillingham, *Marine Insurance*, 31–33. From April to December 1762, Kidd & Bradford covered risks totaling £670,000. The firm collected premiums of £71,000 (an average rate of 10.5 percent) and paid out losses of £21,000—yielding a profit of £50,000.

9. Shepherd and Walton, *Shipping, Maritime Trade*, 76.

10. For information on the earliest firms in Connecticut, see Woodward, *Insurance in Connecticut*, 1–14.

11. Ruwell, "Transformation of Marine Insurance Companies," 45.

12. Zelizer, *Morals and Markets*, 2.

Chapter 14

1. Ezell, *Fortune's Merry Wheel*, 49.

2. The federal government had no need for investment banking services in the early 1790s since its massive issue of bonds arose from the conversion of debt certificates already outstanding. Commercial banks and

insurance companies sought investors primarily in local markets and relied on newspaper announcements, handbills, and word of mouth to market their shares to investors. The evidence suggests that they were remarkably successful, with millions of dollars placed in private hands at low distribution costs.

3. Neal, *Rise of Financial Capitalism,* plus a series of complementary articles cited in the bibliography.

4. A similar debate arose in New York financial circles after the 1987 stock market crash with reference to the role of computer-driven program trading by leading U.S. brokerage firms. A government investigation subsequently concluded that program trading was not a significant destabilizing force in securities markets. Some brokerage firms that had suspended the practice in the wake of the crash decided to resume program trading after the release of the government report.

5. Ferguson, *Power of the Purse,* 251, 258.

6. Earlier historical accounts had suggested that brokers and auctioneers were at odds over the scheduling of daily auctions, but Werner and Smith, *Wall Street,* 12–19, show that cooperation rather than conflict was the rule.

7. The Pennsylvania legislature considered a similar bill to forbid futures contracts in April 1792, but it was tabled and never came to a vote. Werner and Smith, *Wall Street,* 101. The restrictive New York law was repealed in 1858.

8. Werner and Smith, *Wall Street,* 25.

9. Werner and Smith, *Wall Street,* 51.

10. Werner and Smith, *Wall Street,* 175. The volume of dealer trading was 2,894 shares, with Prime accounting for 2,465, or 85 percent.

11. McCusker, *Money and Exchange.* Bills on second- and third-class acceptors, often new firms with little credit history, traded at lower rates unless endorsed by persons in the colonies with impeccable credentials. Organized credit rating systems such as those later formulated by credit and mercantile agencies did not exist in this era; estimates of credit worthiness were often imprecise and subject to the whims of rumor. Longevity in meeting debts at certain levels was probably the most reliable indicator of credit worthiness, but that system was always subject to breakdowns when the tide turned against established merchants or a general business contraction caught them overextended.

12. Cole, "Evolution of Foreign-Exchange Market," 398, cites a letter of credit issued in 1800 by a merchant in Beverly, Massachusetts, as an early example of the performance of that financial service. I know of no earlier instance of issuance by an American guarantor.

Chapter 15

1. See Drew McCoy's entry on political economy in Peterson, ed., *Thomas Jefferson*, 101–18.

2. Price quotations starting from 1799 are in Martin, *Boston Stock Market*, 127.

3. Most of the $5 million went to refinance loans on the books of the First BUS, as discussed in chapter 11. If Wolcott had decided to hold out for a nominal interest rate of 6 percent, investors would have advanced no more than 75 percent of par value—the price adjustment necessary to convert 6 percent interest into an 8 percent yield for bond purchasers.

4. The contemporary statistician Samuel Blodget, *Economica*, 198, estimated that in 1803 foreigners owned $43 million of the U.S. federal debt, or slightly more than half of the bonds outstanding. English investors held $25 million and Dutch investors $15 million. English and Dutch investors combined held another $14 million in the stocks of various American commercial banks.

5. The government retired some securities outright and bought others in the open market for accumulation in the sinking fund. In either event, monies were returned to individuals for investment in other assets.

6. An outstanding account of the activities of the underwriting syndicate is found in an article in *Pennsylvania History*, a somewhat unusual source for business and economic history; see the bibliographic citation under Adams, "Beginnings of Investment Banking." Information about Parish is scattered and not always reliable. His Scottish grandfather established a firm based in Hamburg in the mid-eighteenth century. The family enterprise was actively engaged in the performance of financial services for European governments and wealthy investors in northern Europe. David Parish was born in 1778 and sometime in his twenties opened a branch office of Parish & Co. in Antwerp. In "Parish and War of 1812," Hitsman recounts the voyage to the United States in connection with a large shipment of gold in 1806 and discusses the involvement in land speculation and iron production in upstate New York. Parish was also involved in negotiations with his friend Treasury Secretary Dallas about chartering the Second BUS in 1814 and 1815. In *Rise of Merchant Banking*, Chapman identified him as a resident of Hamburg in 1818. According to Walters in "American Career," Parish left the United States never to return in July 1816, later joined Fries & Co. in Vienna until its failure in 1825, and the next year, despondent about his insurmountable debts, committed suicide.

7. Adams, *Finance and Enterprise*, 29–44, and "Beginnings of Investment Banking," 110. All subscribers to the $16 million loan received the same terms, including those who had subscribed before the April deal was struck between Gallatin and the syndicate.

8. Adams, "Beginnings of Investment Banking," table 2. The junior

members of the syndicate in Philadelphia specifically identified in government documents as earning sales commissions were Biddle & Wharton, William Overman, William J. Bell, Joseph Taggart, George Simpson, and Louis Clapier. Government records are less complete for New York. However, the associates of Astor likely included former treasury secretary Oliver Wolcott, Herman Le Roy, George Griswald, David Ogden, George Newbold, and the firm of Minturn & Champlin. How many bonds junior members of the syndicate in New York sold to their respective clients is impossible to state with precision because government documents show Astor receiving a lump sum payment of $3,750 for all commissions earned on transactions in the New York market. The bond purchases by Baltimore investors may have been handled primarily, or perhaps even exclusively, by Philadelphia firms.

9. For a detailed analysis of bond sales in the Philadelphia market by subscription sizes, see the statistical tables in Adams, "Beginning of Investment Banking."

10. Except for Girard and Parish, all the underwriters, including Astor and his associates in New York, earned the authorized commission of 0.0025 on their sales volume. For reasons not fully understood, Girard and Parish agreed to market their share of the securities for half that rate—only 0.00125. In subsequent eras, the principal underwriters and syndicate organizers typically earned higher fees than their subcontractors for the services performed, not less. So why the reduced fees in this instance? One hypothesis is that the lower rate arose because of a negotiated tie-in with Girard's commercial banking activities since Girard Bank was named as a major depository for government funds.

11. Barker's memoirs, *Incidents in Life*, written forty years after the fact, are the main source for the events surrounding the loan of March 1814 and thus may not be absolutely reliable. His account is imprecise about how much of the $5 million represented funds already in his possession versus how much he anticipated buying on margin by using his newly acquired securities as the collateral for bank loans. He mentioned arrangements to borrow funds from commercial banks located in six cities: Boston, Salem, New York, Philadelphia, Baltimore, and Charleston. During the next several months, Barker and other subscribers encountered obstacles in meeting the schedule of deferred payments because the Treasury refused to release securities against partial payments; it insisted that the entire subscription balance be paid before the distribution of any securities. That requirement made it difficult for purchasers to collateralize their escalating bank loans. Later, rumors circulated that Barker was dumping securities on the market in order to raise money in violation of his agreement with the Treasury—allegations that he took great pains to deny in his memoirs. Barker also tried to pressure Campbell to transfer government deposit accounts to those banks that were committed to financing his huge purchase order—and thereby indirectly financing the government. But Campbell

balked, explaining that if he granted Barker's requests, he would, in effect, be penalizing those banks that had assisted the government in floating the loan of 1813. Campbell presumably had foremost in mind the Girard Bank in Philadelphia and Wolcott's Bank of America in New York.

12. Subscribers to the May and August offerings of $16 million combined later claimed that they too were entitled to adjustments in their purchase prices to bring their net cost down to $65 as well. Secretary Dallas resisted their demands, but four decades later, in 1855, Congress agreed to settle the claim. Bolles, *Financial History*, 231–32.

13. Congress reimposed excise and direct taxes during the war, but the administration was reluctant to reach too deeply into the pockets of citizens because of the fear of stirring up more antiwar sentiment and antagonizing even further New Englanders, who were vocally opposed to the trade restrictions linked to the war. Tax revenues from 1812 through 1815 covered only 15 percent of the cost of the war. Customs duties remained the key source of revenue for the federal government during and after the war.

14. Studenski and Krooss, *Financial History*, are normally very reliable as a source for facts and figures, but their statement on page 76 of the second edition about bonds being sold for bank notes worth a mere 65 percent of face value is grossly exaggerated. Only the bond issues in late 1814 and 1815 were sold for bank notes passing at discounts—about $12 million, or just one-fifth of total bond sales. The authors were probably taken in by the flamboyant rhetoric of the nineteenth-century financial historian Albert Bolles, a card-carrying gold bug, who repeated and endorsed the accusations of contemporaries who criticized the suspension of payments in 1814. To support their accusation that the Treasury received only $28 million in specie value from roughly $60 million in bond sales, critics included in their calculations the discounts allowed investors on 6 percent bonds to bring yields up to prevailing market rates. The discounts had absolutely nothing to do with currency depreciation. My recalculation of the loss in purchasing power from the acceptance of discounted bank notes is vastly lower—in the neighborhood of 3 percent for the aggregate long-term debt, a figure far less than reported in many otherwise fairly reliable secondary sources.

15. Former president Thomas Jefferson suggested at one point late in the war to his old friend Gallatin that Congress should consider the revival of policies dating from the 1770s and issue from $200 to $300 million of fiat currency to finance the war effort if the fighting continued. Fortunately, such irresponsible advice was casually ignored. Secretary of State Monroe expressed an interest in Jefferson's proposal but President Madison was not impressed. Apparently Jefferson had a limited understanding of how much American financial markets had matured during the last three decades, including the eight years of his own administration. Bolles, *Financial History*, 237–38.

16. Smith and Cole, *Fluctuations*, 28, claim that American banks sus-

pended payment in part because of the drain of silver to Canada, but their evidence for that allegation is unstated. They argue too that New England banks accumulated specie in 1812 and 1813 because the federal government bought a large volume of goods in the region with bank notes issued by institutions in the mid-Atlantic and southern states. New Englanders thereupon demanded conversion into specie and built up their reserves at the expense of others. Documentation of those interregional specie flows is still unavailable as far as I know.

17. Price data from Warren and Pearson, *Wholesale Prices,* table 29, p. 73. Although the subject is far beyond the scope of this study, a cursory glance at the price data raises questions about the linkage between the events surrounding the war and the subsequent Panic of 1819. Perhaps the postwar recession, in fact, had little connection with wartime disruptions. The resumption of specie payments by all commercial banks in early 1817 had restored price levels to their prewar levels by the end of the year. The additional price decline of 20 percent from 1817 to 1820 dropped levels way below those prevailing from the date that the series begins in 1798 and continues through 1811, the last prewar year.

18. The estimates of discount rates are found in Hammond, *Banks and Politics,* 228.

19. Literally hundreds of publications touch on the recharter battle over the Second BUS. Readers interested in my singular contribution to the scholarly literature should consult "Lost Opportunities for Compromise."

Conclusion

1. Greene, *Peripheries and Center.*

Appendix

1. Handlin, "Origins of Corporations," 1–23.

2. Hammond, *Banks and Politics,* 179.

3. Davis, *Essays in History of Corporation,* 45.

4. Findley, *Pennsylvania Herald and General Advertiser,* 30 Dec. 1786. I thank Hans Eicholz for calling the debate in Philadelphia over a new state charter for the BNA to my attention.

5. Morris, ibid., 3 January 1787.

6. Domett, *Bank of New York,* 8; Livermore, "Unlimited Liability," 683.

7. Holdsworth, *First Bank,* 126.

8. Dodd, *Business Corporations,* 90–91. The three case citations are: *Vose v. Grant,* 15 Mass. 505 (1819); *Spear v. Grant,* 16 Mass. 9 (1819); and *Wood v. Dummer,* 3 Mason 308, 30 Fed. Cas. 435, no. 17, 944 (C.C.D. Me.

1824). In a related case filed in 1819, which did not involve a bank, a New York court interpreted the state's general incorporation law of 1811 to mean that stockholders assumed liability for the face value of their shares plus an equal amount—in other words, double liability. See the discussion of *Penniman v. Bridge*, 8 Cowan 392, 395 (1926) in Seavoy, *Origins of Corporation*, 72.

9. Hammond, *Banks and Politics*, 179.

Bibliography

General References

American State Papers: Finance. 5 vols. Washington, D.C.: Gales & Seaton, 1832.

Appleby, Joyce. *Economic Thought and Ideology in Seventeenth-Century England.* Princeton: Princeton University Press, 1978.

Barbour, Violet. *Capitalism in Amsterdam in the Seventeenth Century.* Baltimore: Johns Hopkins University Press, 1950.

Bellesiles, Michael A. "Community Strategies for Dealing with Poverty: The New England Frontier, 1760–1820." Unpublished manuscript, University of California, Irvine, 1986.

Bisschop, W. R. *The Rise of the London Money Market, 1640–1826.* London: Frank Cass, 1910.

Bordo, Michael. "Explorations in Monetary History: A Survey of the Literature." *Explorations in Economic History.* 23 (1986): 339–415.

Brewer, John. *The Sinews of Power: War, Money, and the English State, 1688–1783.* New York: Knopf, 1989.

Bruchey, Stuart. *Enterprise: The Dynamic Economy of a Free People.* Cambridge: Harvard University Press, 1990.

Brugger, Robert. *Maryland: A Middle Temperament, 1634–1980.* Baltimore: Johns Hopkins University Press, 1989.

Bullock, Charles J. *Essays on the Monetary History of the United States.* New York: Macmillan, 1900.

———. *Historical Sketch of Finances and Financial Policy of Massachusetts, 1780–1905.* New York: Macmillan, 1907.

Cameron, Rondo, et al. *Banking in the Early Stages of Industrialization: A Study in Comparative Economic History.* New York: Oxford University Press, 1967.

Chapman, Stanley. *The Rise of Merchant Banking.* London: George Allen & Unwin, 1984.

Clapham, John. *The Bank of England: A History.* 2 vols. Cambridge: Cambridge University Press, 1944.

Daniell, Jere. *Experiment in Republicanism: New Hampshire Politics and the American Revolution, 1741–1794.* Cambridge: Harvard University Press, 1970.

Dickson, P. G. M. *The Financial Revolution in England: A Study in the Development of Public Credit, 1688–1756.* London: St. Martin's, 1967.

Dowling, S. W. *The Exchanges of London.* London: Butterworth & Co., 1929.

Feavearyear, Albert. *The Pound Sterling: A History of English Money.* Oxford: Clarendon Press, 1963. (This book is the second edition, with revisions by E. Victor Morgan, of Feavearyear's 1931 classic under the same title.)

Foulke, Roy. *The Sinews of American Commerce.* New York: Dun & Bradstreet, 1941.

Galbraith, John Kenneth. *Money: Whence It Came, Where It Went.* Boston: Houghton Mifflin, 1975.

Kindleberger, Charles P. *A Financial History of Western Europe.* London: George Allen & Unwin, 1984.

Krooss, Herman, ed. *Documentary History of Banking and Currency in the United States.* 4 vols. New York: McGraw-Hill, 1969.

Krooss, Herman, and Martin Blyn. *A History of Financial Intermediaries.* New York: Random House, 1971.

Krooss, Herman, and Paul Studenski. *See* Studenski, Paul, and Herman Krooss.

Lamplugh, George. *Politics on the Periphery: Factions and Parties in Georgia, 1763–1806.* Newark: University of Delaware Press, 1986.

McDonald, Forrest, and Ellen McDonald. *Requiem: Variations on Eighteenth-Century Themes.* Lawrence: University of Kansas Press, 1988.

Myers, Margaret. *A Financial History of the United States.* New York: Columbia University Press, 1970.

———. *The New York Money Market: Origins and Development.* New York: Columbia University Press, 1931.

Neal, Larry. *The Rise of Financial Capitalism: International Capital Markets in the Age of Reason.* New York: Cambridge University Press, 1990.

———. "The Rise of a Financial Press: London and Amsterdam, 1681–1810." *Business History Review* 62 (1988): 163–78.

———. "How the South Sea Bubble Was Blown Up and Burst." Chap. 5 in *Financial Panics in Historical Perspective,* edited by Eugene White. New York: Dow-Jones-Irwin, 1990.

———. "The Integration and Efficiency of the London and Amsterdam Stock Markets in the Eighteenth Century." *Journal of Economic History* 47 (1987): 97–115.

Neal, Larry, and Eric Schubert. "The First Rational Bubbles: A New Look at the Mississippi and South Sea Schemes." Working paper no. 1188, University of Illinois, September 1985.

North, Douglass, and Lance Davis. *Institutional Change and American Economic Growth.* Cambridge: Cambridge University Press, 1971.

Nussbaum, Arthur. *A History of the Dollar.* New York: Columbia University Press, 1957.

Patterson, Margaret, and David Reiffen. "The Effect of the Bubble Act on the Market for Joint Stock Shares." *Journal of Economic History* 50 (1990): 163–71.

Porter, Glenn, ed. *Encyclopedia of American Economic History*. 3 vols. New York: Scribner's, 1980.

Pressnell, Leslie S. *Country Banking in the Industrial Revolution*. Oxford, England: Clarendon Press, 1956.

Richards, R. D. *The Early History of Banking in England*. London: P. S. King & Son, 1929.

———. "Early English Banking Schemes." *Journal of Economic and Business History* 1 (1928–29): 36–76.

Robinson, Maurice. *A History of Taxation in New Hampshire*. New York: Macmillan, 1903.

Rothenberg, Winifred. "The Market and Massachusetts' Farmers, 1750–1855." *Journal of Economic History* 41 (1981): 283–315.

———. "Markets, Values, and Capitalism: A Discourse on Method." *Journal of Economic History* 44 (1984): 174–78.

———. "The Emergence of a Capital Market in Rural Massachusetts, 1730–1838." *Journal of Economic History* 45 (1985): 781–808.

Schubert, Eric. "Innovation, Debts, and Bubbles: International Integration of Financial Markets in Western Europe, 1688–1720." *Journal of Economic History* 48 (1988): 299–306.

———. "Arbitrage in the Foreign Exchange Markets of London and Amsterdam during the Eighteenth Century." *Explorations in Economic History* 26 (1989): 1–20.

Schweikart, Larry, ed. *Encyclopedia of American Business History: Banking and Finance to 1913*. New York: Facts on File, 1990.

Smith, Adam. *Wealth of Nations*. London, 1776.

Sparks, Earl. *History and Theory of Agricultural Credit in the United States*. New York: Thomas Crowell, 1932.

Studenski, Paul, and Herman Krooss. *A Financial History of the United States*. 2d ed. New York: McGraw-Hill, 1963.

Warren, G. F., and F. A. Pearson. *Wholesale Prices for 213 Years, 1720 to 1932*. Ithaca: Cornell University Press, 1932.

White, Eugene. "Inflationary Finance in the Eighteenth Century: A Comparative Study of Colonial America, Spain, and France." Unpublished article manuscript.

———. *Financial Panics in Historical Perspective*. New York: Dow-Jones-Irwin, 1990.

White, Philip, ed. *The Beekman Mercantile Papers, 1746–1799*. 3 vols. New York: New York Historical Society, 1956.

Wilkins, Mira. *The History of Foreign Investment in the United States to 1914*. Cambridge: Harvard University Press, 1989.

Yang, Lien-sheng. *Money and Credit in China: A Short History*. Cambridge: Harvard University Press, 1952.

Colonial Period

Billias, George. "The Massachusetts Land Bankers of 1740." *University of Maine Studies*, 2d ser. (1959): 1–53.

Bowers, Q. David. *The History of United States Coinage*. Los Angeles: Bowers & Ruddy Galleries in cooperation with Johns Hopkins University Press, 1979.

Breen, Timothy H. *Tobacco Culture: The Mentality of the Great Tidewater Planters on the Eve of the Revolution*. Princeton: Princeton University Press, 1985.

Brock, Leslie V. *The Currency of the American Colonies, 1700–1764: A Study in Colonial Finance and Imperial Relations*. New York: Arno Press, 1975. (Ph.D. dissertation, 1941)

———. Manuscript draft for unfinished book on currency in colonial America. Charlottesville: University of Virginia. Microfilm.

Bullion, John R. *A Great and Necessary Measure: George Grenville and the Genesis of the Stamp Act, 1763–1765*. Columbia: University of Missouri Press, 1982.

Bushman, Richard. *From Puritan to Yankee: Character and the Social Order in Connecticut, 1690–1765*. Cambridge: Harvard University Press, 1967.

Clowse, Converse. *Economic Beginnings of Colonial South Carolina, 1670–1730*. Columbia: University of South Carolina Press, 1971.

Countryman, Edward. "The Uses of Capital in Revolutionary America: The Case of the New York Loyalist Merchants." *William and Mary Quarterly* 69 (1992): 3–28.

Crouse, Maurice. *The Public Treasury of Colonial South Carolina*. Columbia: University of South Carolina Press, 1977.

Davis, Andrew McFarland. "Currency and Banking in the Providence of Massachusetts-Bay." *Publications of the American Economic Association*, 3rd ser., vol. 1, no. 4 (1900): 1–443, and continued in vol. 2, no. 2 (1901): 1–332.

Doherty, Kerry W., and Dennis O. Flynn. "Money as a Microeconomic Topic: The Case of Sixteenth-Century Price Inflation." Unpublished manuscript, 1984.

Ernst, Joseph A. "Genesis of the Currency Act of 1764: Virginia Paper Money and the Protection of British Investments." *William and Mary Quarterly*, 3rd ser., 22 (1965): 33–74.

———. *Money and Politics in America, 1755–1775*. Chapel Hill: University of North Carolina Press, 1973.

Ferguson, E. James. "Currency Finance: An Interpretation of Colonial Monetary Practices." *William and Mary Quarterly*, 3rd ser., 10 (1953): 153–80.

Flynn, Dennis. "A New Perspective on the Spanish Price Revolution: The Monetary Approach to the Balance of Payments." *Explorations in Economic History* (1978): 388–406.

Greene, Jack P. *Peripheries and Center: Constitutional Development in the Extended Polities of the British Empire and the United States.* Athens: University of Georgia Press, 1986.

———. *Pursuits of Happiness: The Social Development of Early Modern British Colonies and the Formation of American Culture.* Chapel Hill: University of North Carolina Press, 1988.

Greene, Jack P., and Richard Jellison. "The Currency Act of 1764 in Imperial-Colonial Relations, 1764–1776." *William and Mary Quarterly* 18 (1961): 485–518.

Gwyn, Julian. "British Government Spending and the North American Colonies, 1740–1775." In *The British Atlantic Empire before the American Revolution,* edited by Peter Marshall and Glyn Marshall. London: Frank Cass, 1980.

———. "Financial Revolution in Massachusetts: Public Credit and Taxation, 1692–1774." *Social History* 17 (1984): 59–77.

Hamer, Philip, et al., eds. *The Papers of Henry Laurens.* 11 vols. Columbia: University of South Carolina Press, 1968–1988.

Hanson, John R. "Money in the Colonial American Economy." *Economic Inquiry* 17 (1979): 281–86.

———. "Small Notes in the American Colonies." *Explorations in Economic History* 17 (1980): 411–20.

Horsefield, J. Keith. *British Monetary Experiments, 1650–1710.* London: G. Bell and Sons, 1960.

———. "The 'Stop of the Exchequer' Revisited." *Economic History Review* 35 (1982): 51–28.

Jones, Alice Hanson. *Wealth of a Nation To Be: The American Colonies on the Eve of the Revolution.* New York: Columbia University Press, 1980.

Joslin, D. M. "London Private Bankers, 1720–1785." *Economic History Review* 7 (1954): 167–86.

Land, Aubrey. "Economic Behavior in a Planting Society: The Eighteenth-Century Chesapeake." *Journal of Southern History* 33 (1967): 469–85.

Lester, Richard. "Currency Issues to Overcome Depressions in Pennsylvania, 1723 to 1729." *Journal of Political Economy* 46 (1938): 324–75.

Main, Jackson Turner. *Society and Economy in Colonial Connecticut.* Princeton: Princeton University Press, 1985.

McCallum, Bennett. "Money and Prices in Colonial America: A New Test of Competing Theories." *Journal of Political Economy* 100 (1992): 143–61.

McCusker, John J. *Money and Exchange in Europe and America, 1600–1775: A Handbook.* Chapel Hill: University of North Carolina Press, 1978.

———. "Colonial Paper Money." In *Studies on Money in Early America,* edited by Eric P. Newman and Richard Doty, 94–104. New York: American Numismatic Society, 1976.

McCusker, John J., and Russell R. Menard. *The Economy of British America, 1607–1789.* Chapel Hill: University of North Carolina Press, 1985.

Michener, Ron. "Shortages of Money in Colonial New England: An Explanation." Unpublished manuscript, 1983.

———. "Fixed Exchange Rates and the Quantity Theory in Colonial America." In *Empirical Studies of Velocity, Real Exchange Rates, Unemployment and Productivity*, edited by K. Brunner and A. H. Meltzer, 233–307. Amsterdam: North-Holland, 1987.

———. "Backing Theories and the Currencies of Eighteenth-Century America: A Comment." *Journal of Economic History* 48 (1988): 682–92.

Nettels, Curtis P. *The Money Supply of the American Colonies before 1720.* Madison: University of Wisconsin Press, 1934.

Newman, Eric P. *The Early Paper Money of America.* Racine, Wisconsin: Whitman Publishing, 1967.

———. "American Circulation of English and Bungtown Halfpence." In *Studies on Money in Early America*, edited by Eric P. Newman and Richard G. Doty, 134–72. New York: American Numismatic Society, 1976.

Pares, Richard. *War and Trade in the West Indies, 1739–1763.* Oxford: Clarendon Press, 1936.

Perkins, Edwin J. *The Economy of Colonial America.* 2d ed. New York: Columbia University Press, 1988.

———. "Conflicting Views on Fiat Currency: Britain and its North American Colonies in the Eighteenth Century." *Business History* 33 (1991): 8–30.

Plummer, Wilbur. "Consumer Credit in Colonial Philadelphia." *Pennsylvania Magazine of History and Biography* 66 (1942): 385–409.

Price, Jacob M. *Capital and Credit in British Overseas Trade: The View from the Chesapeake, 1700–1776.* Cambridge: Harvard University Press, 1980.

Purvis, Thomas L. *Proprietors, Patronage, and Paper Money: Legislative Politics in New Jersey, 1703–1776.* New Brunswick: Rutgers University Press, 1986.

Raesly, Ellis. *Portrait of New Netherland.* New York: Columbia University Press, 1945.

Rawle, Francis. *Ways and Means for the Inhabitants of Delaware to Become Rich.* Philadelphia, 1724. Privately reprinted, Philadelphia, 1878.

Schweitzer, Mary. *Custom and Contract: Household, Government, and the Economy in Colonial Pennsylvania.* New York: Columbia University Press, 1987.

Shammas, Carole. "How Self-Sufficient was Early America?" *Journal of Interdisciplinary History* 13 (1982): 247–72.

———. "Consumer Behavior in Colonial America." *Social Science History* 6 (1982): 67–86.

Shepherd, James F., and Gary Walton. *Shipping, Maritime Trade, and the Economic Development of Colonial North America.* Cambridge: Cambridge University Press, 1972.

Shepherd, James F., and Samuel Williamson. "The Coastal Trade of the

British American Colonies, 1768–1772." *Journal of Economic History* 32 (1972): 783–810.

Sheridan, Richard. "The British Credit Crisis of 1772 and the American Colonies." *Journal of Economic History* 20 (1960): 161–86.

Smith, Bruce. "American Colonial Monetary Regimes: The Failure of the Quantity Theory and Some Evidence in Favor of an Alternate View." *Canadian Journal of Economics* 18 (1985): 531–65.

———. "Some Colonial Evidence on Two Theories of Money: Maryland and the Carolinas." *Journal of Political Economy* 93 (1985): 1178–1211.

———. "The Relationship between Money and Prices: Some Historical Evidence Reconsidered." *Quarterly Review: Federal Reserve of Minneapolis* 12 (1988): 18–32.

Solomon, Raphael E. "Foreign Specie Coins in the American Colonies." In *Studies on Money in Early America,* edited by Eric P. Newman and Richard G. Doty, 25–42. New York: American Numismatic Society, 1976.

Stark, Bruce. "The New London Society and Connecticut Politics, 1732–1740." *Connecticut History* (1984): 1–21.

Thayer, Theodore. "The Land Bank System in the American Colonies." *Journal of Economic History* 13 (1953): 145–59.

Weiss, Roger W. "The Issue of Paper Money in the American Colonies, 1720–1774." *Journal of Economic History* 30 (1970): 770–84.

West, Robert Craig. "Money in the Colonial American Economy." *Economic Inquiry* 16 (1978): 1–15.

Wicker, Elmus. "Colonial Monetary Standards Contrasted: Evidence from the Seven Years' War." *Journal of Economic History* 45 (1985): 869–84.

Confederation Period

Alden, John R. *The South in the Revolution, 1763–1789.* Baton Rouge: Louisiana State University Press, 1957.

Armentrout, Mary Travers. "A Political Study of Virginia Finance." Ph.D. diss., University of Virginia, 1934.

Bates, Whitney. "The State Finances of Massachusetts, 1780–1789." Master's thesis, University of Wisconsin, 1948.

———. "Northern Speculators and Southern State Debts: 1790." *William and Mary Quarterly,* 3rd ser., 19 (1962): 30–48.

Becker, Robert. "Salus Populi Suprema Lex: Public Peace and South Carolina Debtor Relief Laws, 1763–1788." *South Carolina Historical Magazine* (1979): 65–75.

———. *Revolution, Reform, and the Politics of American Taxation, 1763–1783.* Baton Rouge: Louisiana State University Press, 1980.

———. "'Combustibles in Every State': A Frame of Reference for Shays' Rebellion." Paper presented at the annual meeting of the Organization of American Historians, Philadelphia, 1982.

Behrens, Kathryn. *Paper Money in Maryland, 1727–1789.* Baltimore: Johns Hopkins University Press, 1923.

Bezanson, Anne. *Prices and Inflation during the American Revolution: Pennsylvania, 1770–1790.* Philadelphia: University of Pennsylvania Press, 1951.

Bjork, Gordon. "The Weaning of the American Economy: Independence, Market Changes, and Economic Development." *Journal of Economic History* 24 (1964): 541–60.

Bond, Beverly. *State Government in Maryland, 1771–1781.* Baltimore: Johns Hopkins University Press, 1905.

Bowdoin, James. "Speech to General Court," 2 June 1786. In *Massachusetts Acts and Laws* 4: 910–13.

Bronson, Henry. "An Historical Account of Connecticut Currency, Continental Money, and the Finances of the Revolution." Vol. 1, part 2 of *Papers of New Haven Colonial Historical Society* (1865): 1–192. An outstanding older source.

Buel, Richard, Jr. *Dear Liberty: Connecticut's Mobilization for the Revolutionary War.* Middletown: Wesleyan University Press, 1980.

Bullock, Charles J. *The Finances of the United States from 1775 to 1789.* Madison: University of Wisconsin Press, 1895.

Coleman, Kenneth. *The American Revolution in Georgia, 1763–1789.* Athens: University of Georgia Press, 1958.

Collier, Christopher. *Roger Sherman's Connecticut: Yankee Politics and the American Revolution.* Middletown: Wesleyan University Press, 1971.

———. "Continental Bonds in Connecticut on the Eve of the Funding Measure." *William and Mary Quarterly,* 3rd ser., 22 (1965): 646–51.

Doerflinger, Thomas. *A Vigorous Spirit of Enterprise: Merchants and Economic Development in Revolutionary Philadelphia.* Chapel Hill: University of North Carolina Press, 1986.

East, R. A. *Business Enterprise in the American Revolutionary Era.* New York: Columbia University Press, 1938.

———. "Massachusetts Conservatives in the Critical Period." In *The Era of the American Revolution,* edited by Richard Morris, 349–91. New York: Columbia University Press, 1939.

Ernst, Joseph A. "The Political Economy of Shays' Rebellion in Long Perspective: The Merchants and the Money Question." Unpublished manuscript, 1986.

Feer, Robert. "Shays' Rebellion and the Constitution: A Study in Causation." *New England Quarterly* 42 (1969): 388–410.

Ferguson, E. James. "State Assumption of Federal Debt during the Confederation." *Journal of American History* 36 (1951): 403–24.

———. *The Power of the Purse: A History of American Public Finance, 1776–1790.* Chapel Hill: University of North Carolina Press, 1961.

———. "The Nationalists of 1781–1783 and the Economic Interpretation of the Constitution." *Journal of American History* 55 (1969): 241–61, and reprinted in Lance Banning, *After the Constitution: Party Conflict in the New Republic*. Belmont, Calif.: Wadsworth Publishing, 1989.

Foner, Eric. *Tom Paine and Revolutionary America*. New York: Oxford University Press, 1976.

Hall, Van Beck. *Politics without Parties: Massachusetts, 1780–1791*. Pittsburgh: University of Pittsburgh Press, 1972.

Handlin, Oscar and Mary Handlin. "Revolutionary Economic Policy in Massachusetts." *William and Mary Quarterly*, 3rd ser., 4 (1947): 3–26.

Harlow, Ralph. "Economic Conditions in Massachusetts during and after the Revolution." *Colonial Society of Massachusetts Publications* (1920): 163–91.

———. "Aspects of Revolutionary Finance, 1775–1783." *American Historical Review* 35 (1929–30): 46–68.

Higgins, W. Robert. "A Financial History of the American Revolution in South Carolina." Ph.D. diss., Duke University, 1969.

Hoffman, Ronald. *A Spirit of Dissension: Economics, Politics, and Revolution in Maryland*. Baltimore: Johns Hopkins University Press, 1973.

James, Cyril. "The Bank of North America and the Financial History of Philadelphia." *Pennsylvania Magazine of History and Biography* (1940), 56–87.

Jensen, Merrill. *The New Nation: A History of the United States during the Confederation, 1781–1789*. New York: Vintage, 1950.

Kaminski, John Paul. "Paper Politics: The Northern State Loan Offices during the Confederation, 1783–1790." Ph.D. diss., University of Wisconsin, 1972.

Low, Augustus. "Virginia in the Critical Period." Ph.D. diss., University of Iowa, 1941.

Main, Jackson Turner. *The Sovereign States, 1775–1783*. New York: Franklin Watts, 1973.

———. "The American States in the Revolutionary Era." In *Sovereign States in an Age of Uncertainty*, edited by Ronald Hoffman and Peter Albert, 1–30. Charlottesville: University Press of Virginia, 1981.

McCormick, Richard. *Experiment in Independence: New Jersey in the Critical Period, 1781–1789*. New Brunswick: Rutgers University Press, 1950.

McDonald, Forrest. *We the People: The Economic Origins of the Constitution*. Chicago: University of Chicago Press, 1958.

———. *Novus Ordo Seclorum: The Intellectual Origins of the Constitution*. Lawrence: University of Kansas Press, 1985.

Molovinsky, Lemuel. "Pennsylvania's Legislative Efforts to Finance the War for Independence: A Study of the Continuity of Colonial Finance, 1775–1783." Ph.D. diss., Temple University, 1975.

Morrill, James R. *The Practice and Politics of Fiat Finance: North Carolina in the Confederation, 1783–1789*. Chapel Hill: University of North Carolina Press, 1969.

Morris, Richard. *The Forging of the Union, 1781–1789*. New York: Harper & Row, 1987.

Nevins, Allan. *The American States during and after the Revolution, 1775–1789*. New York: Macmillan, 1927. An older book that stands up surprisingly well half a century later.

Nordholt, Jan Willem Schultze. *The Dutch Republic and American Independence*. Translated by Herbert Rowen. Chapel Hill: University of North Carolina Press, 1982.

Norton, William. "Paper Currency in Massachusetts during the Revolution." *New England Quarterly* 7 (1934): 43–69.

Papenfuse, Edward C. "The Legislative Response to a Costly War: Fiscal Policy and Factional Politics in Maryland, 1777–1789." In *Sovereign States in an Age of Uncertainty*, edited by Ronald Hoffman and Peter Albert, 134–56. Published for the U.S. Capitol Historical Society. Charlottesville: University Press of Virginia, 1981.

Pole, J. R. "Shays' Rebellion: A Political Interpretation." In *The Reinterpretation of the American Revolution*, edited by Jack P. Greene, 416–34. New York: Harper & Row, 1968.

Polishook, Irwin. *Rhode Island and the Union, 1774–1795*. Evanston: Northwestern University Press, 1969.

Rakove, Jack. *The Beginnings of National Politics: An Interpretative History of the Continental Congress*. New York: Knopf, 1979.

Ratchford, Benjamin U. *American State Debts*. Durham: Duke University Press, 1941.

Rich, Myra L. "The Experimental Years: Virginia, 1781–89." Ph.D. diss., Yale University, 1966.

Riley, James C. "Foreign Credit and Fiscal Stability: Dutch Investment in the United States, 1781–1794." *Journal of American History* 64 (1978): 654–78.

Robinson, Edward Forbes. "Continental Treasury Administration, 1775–1781: A Study in the Financial History of the American Revolution." Ph.D. diss., University of Wisconsin, 1969.

Schweitzer, Mary. "State-Issued Currency and the Ratification of the U.S. Constitution." *Journal of Economic History* 49 (1989): 311–22.

Selby, John. *The Revolution in Virginia, 1775–1783*. Williamsburg: Colonial Williamsburg Foundation, 1988.

Singer, Charles. *South Carolina in the Confederation*. Philadelphia: University of Pennsylvania Press, 1941.

Sumner, William Graham. *The Financier and the Finances of the American Revolution*. New York: Dodd, Mead & Co., 1891.

Szatmary, David. *Shays' Rebellion: The Making of an Agrarian Insurrection*. Amherst: University of Massachusetts Press, 1980.

Taylor, Robert. *Western Massachusetts in the Revolution*. Providence: Brown University Press, 1954.

Upton, Richard. *Revolutionary New Hampshire*. Hanover: Dartmouth College Publications, 1936.

Ver Steeg, Clarence. *Robert Morris, Revolutionary Financier*. Philadelphia: University of Pennsylvania Press, 1954.

Wilson, Janet. "The Bank of North America and Pennsylvania Politics, 1781–1787." *Pennsylvania Magazine of History and Biography* (1942): 3–28.

Confederation and Early National Periods

Banning, Lance. "The Hamiltonian Madison." *Virginia Magazine of History and Biography* 92 (1984): 3–28.

Bruchey, Stuart. *Robert Oliver: Merchant of Baltimore, 1783–1819*. Baltimore: Johns Hopkins University Press, 1956.

Cantor, Milton, ed. *Hamilton*. Great Lives Observed series. Englewood Cliffs, N.J.: Prentice-Hall, 1971.

Cornell, Saul. "Aristocracy Assailed: The Ideology of Backcountry Anti-Federalism." *Journal of American History* 76 (1990): 1148–72.

Crowl, Philip. *Maryland during and after the Revolution: A Political and Economic Study*. Baltimore: Johns Hopkins University Press, 1943.

Forsythe, Dall. *Taxation and Political Change in the New Nation, 1781–1833*. New York: Columbia University Press, 1977.

Gras, N. S. B. *The Massachusetts First National Bank of Boston, 1784–1934*. Cambridge: Harvard University Press, 1937.

Hamilton, Alexander. *Papers of Alexander Hamilton*, edited by Harold Synett. 27 Vols. New York: Columbia University Press, 1961–87.

Handlin, Oscar, and Mary Handlin. "Origins of the American Business Corporation." *Journal of Economic History* 5 (1945): 1–23.

Hendrickson, Robert A. *The Rise and Fall of Alexander Hamilton*. New York: Van Nostrand Reinhold, 1981.

Hurst, James Willard. *The Legitimacy of the Business Corporation in the Law of the United States, 1780–1970*. Charlottesville: University Press of Virginia, 1970.

———. *A Legal History of Money in the United States, 1774–1970*. Lincoln: University of Nebraska Press, 1973.

Kennedy, Roger. *Orders from France: The Americans and the French in a Revolutionary World, 1780–1820*. New York: Knopf, 1989.

Konkle, Burton Alva. *Thomas Willing and the First American Financial System*. Philadelphia: University of Pennsylvania Press, 1937.

Lewis, Lawrence. *A History of the Bank of North America*. Philadelphia: Lippincott, 1882.

Matson, Cathy. "Public Vices, Private Benefit: William Duer and His Circle, 1776–1792." In *New York and the Rise of American Capitalism*, edited by William Pencak and Conrad Wright, 72–123. New York: New York Historical Society, 1989.

McDonald, Forrest. *Alexander Hamilton: A Biography.* New York: Norton, 1979.

McMaster, John B. *The Life and Times of Stephen Girard: Mariner and Merchant.* Philadelphia: Lippincott & Co., 1918.

Miller, John C. *Alexander Hamilton and the Growth of the New Nation.* New York: Harper & Row, 1959.

Purcell, Richard. *Connecticut in Transition, 1775–1818.* Washington, D.C., and London: American Historical Association and Oxford University Press, 1918.

Risjord, Norman. *Chesapeake Politics, 1781–1800.* New York: Columbia University Press, 1978.

Risjord, Norman, and Gordon Denboer. "The Evolution of Political Parties in Virginia, 1782–1800." *Journal of American History* 60 (1974): 961–84, and reprinted in *After the Constitution: Party Conflict in the New Republic,* edited by Lance Banning. Belmont, Calif.: Wadsworth Publishing, 1989.

Schwartz, Anna J. "The Beginnings of Competitive Banking in Philadelphia, 1782–1809." *Journal of Political Economy* 55 (1947): 417–31.

Seavoy, Ronald. *The Origins of the American Business Corporation, 1784–1855.* Westport, Conn.: Greenwood Press, 1982.

Shalhope, Robert. *John Taylor of Caroline.* Columbia: University of South Carolina Press, 1980.

Swanson, Donald. *The Origins of Hamilton's Fiscal Policies.* Gainesville: University of Florida Press, 1963.

Sylla, Richard. "Small-Business Banking in the United States, 1780–1920." In *Small Business in American Life,* edited by Stuart Bruchey. New York: Columbia University Press, 1980.

———. "Early American Banking: The Significance of the Corporate Form." *Business and Economic History* 14 (1985): 105–23.

Early National Period

Adams, Donald, Jr. *Finance and Enterprise in Early America: A Study of Stephen Girard's Bank, 1812–1831.* Philadelphia: University of Pennsylvania Press, 1978.

———. "The Beginning of Investment Banking in the United States." *Pennsylvania History* 45 (1978): 99–116.

Appleby, Joyce. "What is Still American in the Political Philosophy of Thomas Jefferson?" *William and Mary Quarterly,* 3rd ser., 39 (1982): 287–309.

———. "Commercial Farming and the 'Agrarian Myth' in the Early Republic." *Journal of American History* 68 (1982): 833–49.

———. *Capitalism and a New Social Order.* New York: New York University Press, 1984.

———. "Republicanism in the History and Historiography of the United States." *American Quarterly* 58 (1985): 461–73.

———. "Republicanism in Old and New Contexts." *William and Mary Quarterly*, 3rd ser., 43 (1986): 20–34.

———. "Capitalism and Democracy in Revolutionary America." Paper presented at colloquium, February 1990, Department of History, University of California, Los Angeles.

Bainbridge, John. *Biography of an Idea: The Story of Mutual Fire and Casualty Insurance.* Garden City, N.Y.: Doubleday, 1952.

Barbour, Violet. "Marine Risks and Insurance in the Seventeenth Century." *Journal of Economic and Business History* 1 (1928–29): 561–96.

Banning, Lance. "Jeffersonian Ideology Revisited: Liberal and Classical Ideas in the New American Republic." *William and Mary Quarterly*, 3rd ser., 43 (1986): 1–19.

———, ed. *After the Constitution: Party Conflict in the New Republic.* Belmont, Calif.: Wadsworth, 1989.

Barker, Jacob. *Incidents in the Life of Jacob Barker.* New York: privately printed, 1855.

Baughman, James. "Early American Checks: Forms and Functions." *Business History Review* 41 (1967): 421–35.

Blodget, Samuel. *Economica: A Statistical Manual for the United States of America.* Washington, D.C.: privately printed, 1806. Reprint. New York: Augustus Kelley Publishers, 1964.

Bolles, Albert. *The Financial History of the United States from 1789 to 1860.* 3 vols. 4th ed. New York: D. Appleton, 1894. Reprint. New York: Augustus Kelley Publishers, 1969.

Brown, Kenneth. "Stephen Girard, Promoter of the Second Bank of the United States." *Journal of Economic History* 2 (1942): 125–48. (This older article has serious flaws and omissions.)

Bruchey, Stuart. "Alexander Hamilton and the State Banks, 1789 to 1795." *William and Mary Quarterly*, 3rd ser., 27 (1970): 347–78.

Callendar, Guy. "The Early Transportation and Banking Enterprises of the States in Relation to the Growth of Corporations." *Quarterly Journal of Economics* 17 (1902): 111–62.

Calomiris, Charles. "The Motives of U.S. Debt-Management Policy, 1790–1880: Efficient Discrimination and Time Consistency." *Research in Economic History* 13 (1991): 67–105.

Catterall, Ralph. *Second Bank of the United States.* Chicago: University of Chicago Press, 1903.

Clendenin, William. "Brief Outline History of Life Insurance." In *The Bible of Life Insurance*, edited by Elizur Wright, 5–64. Chicago: American Conservation Co., 1932.

Clough, Shephard. *A Century of American Life Insurance: A History of the Mutual Life Insurance Company of New York, 1843–1943.* New York: Columbia University Press, 1946.

Cochran, Thomas. *Frontiers of Change: Early Industrialism in America.* New York: Oxford University Press, 1981.

Cole, Arthur H. "Evolution of the Foreign-Exchange Market of the United States." *Journal of Economic and Business History* 1 (1928–29): 384–421.

Cooke, Jacob. *Tench Cox and the Early Republic.* Chapel Hill: University of North Carolina Press, 1978.

Cope, S. R. *Walter Boyd: A Merchant Banker in the Age of Napoleon.* London: Alan Sutton Publishing, 1983.

Davis, Joseph. *Essays in the Earlier History of the American Corporation.* Cambridge: Harvard University Press, 1917.

Davis, Lance, and J. R. T. Hughes. "A Dollar-Sterling Exchange, 1803–1895." *Economic History Review* 13 (1960): 52–78.

Dewey, Davis. *State Banking before the Civil War.* Washington: Government Printing Office, 1910.

Dickson, P. G. M. *The Sun Insurance Office, 1710–1960.* London: Oxford University Press, 1960.

Dodd, E. Merrick. *American Business Corporations until 1860.* Cambridge: Harvard University Press, 1954.

Domett, Henry. *A History of the Bank of New York, 1784–1884.* New York: G. P. Putnam's Sons, 1884.

Ellis, Richard. *The Union at Risk: Jacksonian Democracy, States' Rights, and the Nullification Crisis.* New York: Oxford University Press, 1987.

Episodes of History in the Stories of the United States and the Insurance Company of North America, 1792–1917. No author named. Privately printed, 1916.

Ezell, John S. *Fortune's Merry Wheel: The Lottery in America.* Cambridge: Harvard University Press, 1960.

Fenstermaker, J. Van. *The Development of American Commercial Banking, 1782–1837.* Kent, Ohio: Kent State University Press, 1965.

———. "The Statistics of American Commercial Banking, 1782–1818." *Journal of Economic History* 25 (1965): 400–413.

———. "A Comparison of the Development of Local Capital Markets in Boston, New York, Philadelphia, and Baltimore, 1800–1860." Paper delivered at Economic History Association meeting, San Francisco, 1987.

Fenstermaker, J. Van, John E. Filer, and Robert S. Herren. "Money Statistics of New England, 1785–1837." *Journal of Economic History* 44 (1984): 441–53.

Ferguson, E. James, ed. *Selected Writings of Albert Gallatin.* Indianapolis: Bobbs-Merrill, 1967.

Gallatin, Albert. *See* Ferguson entry.

Gillingham, Harrold. *Marine Insurance in Philadelphia, 1721–1800.* Philadelphia: privately printed, 1933.

Goldin, Claudia, and Frank Lewis. "The Role of Exports in American Economic Growth during the Napoleonic Wars, 1793–1807." *Explorations in Economic History* 17 (1980): 6–25.

Gouge, William. *A Short History of Paper Money and Banking in the United States*. Philadelphia: T. W. Ustick, 1833. Reprint. New York: Augustus Kelley Publishers, 1968.

Greeley, Horace, et al. *The Great Industries of the United States: Being an Historical Summary of the Origin, Growth, and Perfection of the Chief Industrial Arts of This Country*. Hartford, Conn.: Burr & Hyde, 1872.

Hammond, Bray. *Banks and Politics in America From the Revolution to the Civil War*. Princeton: Princeton University Press, 1957.

———. "Long and Short Term Credit in Early American Banking." *Quarterly Journal of Economics* 49 (1934–35): 79–103.

Hardy, Edward. *Early Insurance Offices in Massachusetts, from 1724 to 1801*. Published for Insurance Library Association, Boston, in *Reports of 1888–1900*. Boston: Frank Wood, 1901.

Hawthorne, Daniel. *The Hartford of Hartford: An Insurance Company's Part in a Century and a Half of American History*. New York: Random House, 1960.

Hedges, Joseph. *Commercial Banking and the Stock Market before 1863*. Baltimore: Johns Hopkins University Press, 1938.

Hickey, Donald. *The War of 1812: A Forgotten Conflict*. Urbana: University of Illinois Press, 1989.

A History of the Insurance Company of North America of Philadelphia. No named author. Philadelphia: Press of Review Publishing and Printing Co., 1885.

Hitsman, J. Mackay. "David Parish and the War of 1812." *Military Affairs* (1962–63): 171–77. (Now retitled *Journal of Military History*)

Holdsworth, John Thomas. *The First Bank of the United States*. Washington: Government Printing Office, 1910.

Huebner, Solomon. "The Development and Present Status of Marine Insurance in the United States." *Annals of American Academy of Political and Social Science* (1905): 421–52.

Hunter, Gregory. "The Development of Bankers: Career Patterns and Corporate Form at the Manhattan Company, 1799–1842." *Business and Economic History* 14 (1985): 59–77.

———. "The Manhattan Company: Managing a Multi-unit Corporation in New York, 1799–1842." In *New York and the Rise of American Capitalism: Economic Development and the Social and Political History of an American State, 1780–1870*, edited by William Pencak and Conrad Wright, 124–46. New York: New York Historical Society, 1989.

James, Marquis. *Biography of a Business, 1792–1942: Insurance Company of North America*. Indianapolis: Bobbs-Merrill, 1942.

Jennings, Robert, Donald Swanson, and Andrew Trout. "Alexander Hamilton's Tontine Proposal." *William and Mary Quarterly*, 3rd ser., 45 (1988): 107–15.

John, A. H. "The London Company and the Marine Assurance Market of the Eighteenth Century." *Economica* 25 (1958): 126–41.

Johnson, E. A. J. *The Foundations of American Economic Freedom: Government and Enterprise in the Age of Washington*. Minneapolis: University of Minnesota Press, 1973.

Klebaner, Benjamin. "State-Chartered American Commercial Banks, 1781–1801." *Business History Review* 53 (1979): 529–38.

———. *American Commercial Banking: A History*. Boston: Twayne Publishing, 1990.

Klein, Daniel. "The Voluntary Provision of Public Goods? The Turnpike Companies of Early America." *Economic Inquiry* 28 (1990): 788–812.

Klubes, Benjamin B. "The First Federal Congress and the First National Bank: A Case Study in Congressional Interpretation." *Journal of the Early Republic* 10 (1990): 19–41.

Krooss, Herman. "Financial Institutions." In *The Growth of the Seaport Cities, 1790–1825*, edited by David Gilchrist, 104–38. Charlottesville: University Press of Virginia, 1967.

Lamoreaux, Naomi. "Banks, Kinship and Economic Development: The New England Case." *Journal of Economic History* 46 (1986): 647–68.

Lesene, J. Mauldin. *The Bank of the State of South Carolina*. Columbia: University of South Carolina Press, 1970.

Livermore, Shaw. "Unlimited Liability in Early American Corporations." *Journal of Political Economy* 43 (1935): 674–87.

Lunt, Dudley. *The Farmers Bank: An Historical Account of the President, Directors, and Company of the Farmers Bank of the State of Delaware, 1807–1957*. Privately printed, 1957.

Martin, Joseph. *Boston Stock Market*. Boston: privately printed, 1886.

McCoy, Drew. *The Elusive Republic: Political Economy in Jeffersonian America*. Chapel Hill: University of North Carolina Press, 1980.

———. "Political Economy." In *Thomas Jefferson: A Reference Biography*, edited by Merrill Peterson. New York: Scribner's, 1986.

McDonald, Forrest. *The Presidency of George Washington*. New York: W. W. Norton, 1974.

Morgan, H. Wayne. "The Origins and Establishment of the First Bank of the United States." *Business History Review* 30 (1956): 472–92.

Myers, Charles. "Retirement of the First Federal Debt: A Test of Vincent Ostrom's Theory of 'Democratic Administration'." Ph.D. diss. University of California, Davis, 1993.

Nelson, John R. *Liberty and Property: Political Economy and Policy Making in the New Nation, 1789–1812*. Baltimore: Johns Hopkins Press, 1987.

North, Douglass. *The Economic Growth of the United States, 1790–1860*. New York: W. W. Norton, 1966.

O'Donnell, Terence. *History of Life Insurance in Its Formative Years*. Chicago: American Conservation Co., 1936.

Officer, Lawrence. "Dollar-Sterling Mint Parity and Exchange Rates, 1791–1834." *Journal of Economic History* 43 (1983): 570–616.

Oviatt, F. C. "Historical Study of Fire Insurance in the United States." *Annals of American Academy of Political and Social Science* (1905): 335–58.

Perkins, Edwin J. "Lost Opportunities in the Bank War: A Reassessment of Jackson's Veto Message." *Business History Review* 61 (1987): 531–50.

Raynes, Harold E. *A History of British Insurance.* 2d ed. London: Pitman, 1964.

Redlich, Fritz. *The Molding of American Banking: Men and Ideas.* 2d ed. New York: Johnson Reprint Co., 1968. Originally published in two separate volumes in 1947 and 1951.

———. "On the Origin of Created Deposits in the Commonwealth of Massachusetts." *Business History Review* 43 (1969): 204–8.

Reisman, Janet. "Money, Credit, and Federalist Political Economy." In *Beyond Confederation: Origins of the Constitution and American National Identity,* edited by Richard Beeman et al., 128–61. Chapel Hill: University of North Carolina Press, 1987.

———. "Republican Revisions: Political Economy in New York after the Panic of 1819." In *New York and the Rise of American Capitalism: Economic Development and the Social and Political History of an American State, 1780–1870,* edited by William Pencak and Conrad Wright, 1–44. New York: New York Historical Society, 1989.

Reubens, Beatrice. "State Financing of Private Enterprise in Early New York." Ph.D. diss. Columbia University, 1960.

———, "Burr, Hamilton, and the Manhattan Company." *Political Science Quarterly,* pt. 1 (1957): 578–607; pt. 2 (1958): 100–125.

Risjord, Norman. *The Old Republicans: Southern Conservatism in the Age of Jefferson.* New York: Columbia University Press, 1965.

Ruwell, Mary. *Eighteenth-Century Capitalism: The Transformation of American Marine Insurance Companies.* New York: Garland, 1993.

Seavoy, Ronald. "The Constitutionalization of Laissez-Faire Business Policy in the United States." *Essays in Economic and Business History* (1991): 35–50.

Smith, Walter B. *Economic Aspects of the Second Bank of the United States.* Cambridge: Harvard University Press, 1953.

Smith, Walter B., and Arthur Cole. *Fluctuations in American Business, 1790–1860.* Cambridge: Harvard University Press, 1935.

Soltow, Lee. *Distribution of Wealth and Income in the United States in 1798.* Pittsburgh: University of Pittsburgh Press, 1989.

Starnes, George. *Sixty Years of Branch Banking in Virginia.* New York: Macmillan, 1931.

Stover, John. "Canals and Turnpikes: America's Early-Nineteenth-Century Transportation Network." In *An Emerging Independent Economy, 1815–1875,* edited by Joseph Frese and Jacob Judd, 60–98. Tarrytown, N.Y.: Sleepy Hollow Press, 1980.

Straus, Ralph. *Lloyd's: The Gentlemen at the Coffee-House.* New York: Carrick & Evans, 1938.

Supple, Barry. *The Royal Exchange Assurance: A History of British Insurance, 1720–1970.* Cambridge: Cambridge University Press, 1970.

Swanson, Donald. "The Second Bank of the United States and The Attempted Bank Bail Out During the War of 1812." *Durell Journal of Money and Banking* (1992): 31–39.

Swanson, Donald, Robert Jennings, and Andrew Trout. "Alexander Hamilton's Tontine Proposal." *William and Mary Quarterly,* 3rd ser., 45 (1988): 107–15.

Swanson, Donald, and Andrew Trout. "Alexander Hamilton's Hidden Sinking Fund." *William and Mary Quarterly,* 3rd ser., 49 (1992): 102–10.

———. "Alexander Hamilton, 'the Celebrated Mr. Neckar,' and Public Credit." *William and Mary Quarterly,* 3rd ser., 47 (1990): 422–30.

Sylla, Richard. "Forgotten Men of Money: Private Bankers in Early U.S. History." *Journal of Economic History* 36 (1976): 173–88.

Sylla, Richard, John Legler, and John Wallis. "Banks and State Public Finance in the New Republic: The United States, 1790–1850." *Journal of Economic History* 47 (1987): 391–404.

Timberlake, Richard. *The Origins of Central Banking in the United States.* Cambridge: Harvard University Press, 1978.

Trebilcock, Clive. *Phoenix Assurance and the Development of British Insurance, 1782–1870.* Cambridge: Cambridge University Press, 1985.

Trenerry, C. F. *The Origin and Early History of Insurance.* London: P. S. King & Son, 1926.

Trescott, Paul. "Federal-State Financial Relations, 1790–1860." *Journal of Economic History* 15 (1955): 227–45.

———. *Financing American Enterprise: The Story of Commercial Banking.* New York: Harper & Row, 1963.

Trout, Andrew. *See* Donald Swanson.

Walters, Raymond. *Alexander James Dallas: Lawyer, Politician, Financier.* Philadelphia: University of Pennsylvania Press, 1943.

Walters, Raymond, and Philip G. Walters. "The American Career of David Parish." *Journal of Economic History* 3 (1944): 149–66.

Webster, Noah. "Sketch of the History and Present State of Banks and Insurance Companies in the United States." In *Miscellaneous Papers.* Vol. 4, 1–48. New York, 1802. Reprint. New York: Burt Franklin, 1967.

Weiss, Harry B., and Grace M. Weiss. *The Early Lotteries of New Jersey.* Trenton, N.J.: Past Times Press, 1966.

Wettereau, James O. "The Branches of the First Bank of the United States." *Journal of Economic History* 2 (1942): 66–100.

———. "New Light on the First Bank of the United States. *Pennsylvania Magazine of History and Biography* 61 (1937): 263–85.

————. *Statistical Records of the First Bank of the United States.* New York: Garland Publishing, 1985.

Wildes, Harry Emerson. *Lonely Midas: The Story of Stephen Girard.* New York: Farrar & Rinehart, 1943.

Zelizer, Viviana A. Rotman. *Morals and Markets: The Development of Life Insurance in the United States.* New York: Columbia University Press, 1979.

Index

427

McCallum, Bennett, 378, 381
McCoy, Drew, 401
McCusker, John, 320, 378–79, 381, 400
McDonald, Ellen, 181, 391
McDonald, Forrest, 180–82, 216, 221, 391–93
Menard, Russell, 378–79, 381
Merchant banking, 32, 319–23
Mexico, 13, 23, 81
Michener, Ron, 379, 380, 381
Miller, John, 392
Mint ratio, 14, 16, 18–19
Mints, 13–28, 51, 81, 86, 247, 357, 377
Molovinsky, Lemuel, 388
Money stock, 3, 13–55, 76–82, 86, 134, 143, 146, 150, 256, 271–72, 357, 379–80, 398; size of, 55, 129, 247, 378, 388
Monied elite, 7, 9, 178, 212, 265, 270, 278
Monopoly power, 273–75
Monroe, James, 337, 403
Morgan, Wayne, 250
Morrill, James, 390
Morris, Robert, 99, 106–16, 126, 128–30, 133–35, 145–46, 148, 161, 196, 200, 207–10, 225, 230, 233, 241, 243, 251, 267, 289, 313, 347, 358, 363, 374, 381, 388, 404
Morris notes, 115–16, 176
Mortality tables, 302–3
Mortgage loans, 3–4, 41, 44–46, 56, 67–70, 73, 77, 125–26, 131–33, 143, 148, 151, 153, 162, 165, 168, 178, 188, 206, 237, 270, 358–59, 363; by insurance companies, 299
Mutual Assurance Company, 299
Mutual companies, 292–99

National debt, 86, 95, 99–105, 109–10, 138–39, 196, 199–234, 239, 245–46, 261, 263–64, 270, 313, 327–48, 354, 365, 389, 393, 403
Neal, Larry, 202, 310, 379, 392, 400
Nelson, John, 265
New England, 4, 26, 30, 43, 48–51, 53, 57, 60, 78, 81, 89–92, 95, 102, 180, 204, 206, 271–72, 307, 330, 340, 349, 358, 364, 369–70, 388

New Hampshire, 48, 93, 166, 171–72, 191, 205, 279–80, 307
New Jersey, 42, 46, 49, 61, 71, 78, 89, 92–93, 99, 143–44, 147, 152–54, 164, 188, 191, 195, 209–10, 307–8, 313, 358, 382, 389
New Orleans, La., 242, 263, 324
Newport, R.I., 289
New tenor monies, 97–98, 107, 171–72, 386, 390
New York, 5, 7, 24–25, 44, 46, 49, 78, 89, 92–93, 99, 114, 133, 143, 149–52, 159, 164–65, 185, 191–92, 195, 209, 216, 271, 275, 303, 307–8, 312, 358, 360, 365–66, 370, 374, 389, 400
New York City, 40, 42, 53, 102, 121, 149–51, 165, 187, 201, 211, 224, 226, 230, 235, 242–43, 246, 249, 255, 263, 271, 273, 276, 287–89, 305, 309–10, 313–17, 320–21, 328–29, 331–32, 342, 350, 353–54, 367, 371, 389, 392, 394
Norfolk, Va., 242
North Carolina, 4, 43, 78, 93, 100, 138, 143, 145, 157, 164, 191–93, 195, 216, 230, 307, 358

Officer, Lawrence, 321
Options trading, 309–12, 314–15, 356

Paine, Thomas, 119–20, 269, 352
Panic of 1819, 277, 281, 342, 351, 404
Parish, David, 331–33, 345, 401
Parker, Isaac, 375
Parliament, 6, 13, 19–20, 22–28, 30, 36, 39, 48, 50–51, 62, 80–81, 88–95, 103, 112, 116, 150, 154, 160, 188, 202, 204, 207–8, 211–12, 220, 236, 257, 280, 293–94, 296, 306, 308, 357–59, 364, 373, 380, 384–85
Pennsylvania, 5, 46, 49, 53, 61, 71, 78, 89, 92, 94, 99, 102, 106–7, 114, 119, 128–29, 132, 143, 145–49, 151–52, 164–65, 169, 177, 187, 191, 195, 207, 209, 216, 229, 251, 271, 277, 279, 303, 358, 360, 365, 370, 374, 379–80, 382, 384, 388, 394
Pennsylvania Bank, 387

Historical Perspectives on Business Enterprise Series
Mansel G. Blackford and K. Austin Kerr, Editors

The scope of the series includes scholarly interest in the history of the firm, the history of government-business relations, and the relationships between business and culture, both in the United States and abroad, as well as in comparative perspective.

REGULATED ENTERPRISE:
Natural Gas Pipelines and Northeastern Markets, 1938–1954
Christopher James Castaneda

MANAGING INDUSTRIAL DECLINE:
The British Coal Industry between the Wars
Michael Dintenfass

HENRY E. HUNTINGTON AND THE CREATION OF SOUTHERN CALIFORNIA
William B. Friedricks

MAKING IRON AND STEEL:
Independent Mills in Pittsburgh, 1820–1920
John N. Ingham

EAGLE-PICHER INDUSTRIES:
Strategies for Survival in the Industrial Marketplace, 1840–1980
Douglas Knerr

WOLF CREEK STATION:
Kansas Gas & Electric Company in the Nuclear Era
Craig Miner

A MENTAL REVOLUTION:
Scientific Management since Taylor
Edited by Daniel Nelson